Getting Started
WITH ELECTRONIC COMMERCE

Getting Started
WITH ELECTRONIC COMMERCE

Floyd Fuller

Appalachian State University

THE DRYDEN PRESS

A DIVISION OF HARCOURT COLLEGE PUBLISHERS

Fort Worth   Philadelphia   San Diego   New York   Orlando   Austin   San Antonio
Toronto   Montreal   London   Sydney   Tokyo

VICE PRESIDENT, PUBLISHER	*Mike Roche*
EXECUTIVE EDITOR	*Christina A. Martin*
DEVELOPMENTAL EDITOR	*Larry Crowder*
PROJECT EDITOR	*Charles J. Dierker*
ART DIRECTOR	*Scott Baker*
SR. PRODUCTION MANAGER	*Serena Barnett*

ISBN: 0-03-022257-5
Library of Congress Catalog Card Number: 99–067304

Address for Domestic Orders
The Dryden Press, 6277 Sea Harbor Drive, Orlando, FL 32887-6777
800-782-4479

Address for International Orders
International Customer Service
The Dryden Press, 6277 Sea Harbor Drive, Orlando, FL 32887-6777
407-345-3800
(fax) 407-345-4060
(e-mail) hbintl@harcourtbrace.com

Address for Editorial Correspondence
The Dryden Press, 301 Commerce Street, Suite 3700, Fort Worth, TX 76102

Web Site Address
http://www.harcourtcollege.com

Printed in the United States of America
9 0 1 2 3 4 5 6 7 8   751   10 9 8 7 6 5 4 3 2 1

The Dryden Press
Harcourt College Publishers

Millions of people are blessed with wonderful sisters, but probably none more than I have been. Throughout my life, my three sisters have brought great joy and happiness not only to me, but also to everyone in my family. Their love, devotion, and support have been a constant source of encouragement that has motivated me to pursue and complete several projects, including this work. As a token of my love, appreciation, and respect, I am honored to dedicate this book to my three sisters …

Agnes Blalock, Doris Marsh, and Nell Adams

The Dryden Press Series in Computer Technologies

Adams
First Steps Series
   Word 2000
   Word 97
   Excel 2000
   Excel 97
   Access 2000
   Access 97
   Powerpoint 2000
   Powerpoint 97
   Outlook 2000
   Windows 98

Coorough
Getting Started with Multimedia

Fenrich
Practical Guidelines for Creating Instructional Multimedia Applications

Fuller/Manning
Getting Started with the Internet

Fuller
Getting Started with E-Commerce

Gordon and Gordon
Information Systems: A Management Approach
Second Edition

Gray, King, McLean, and Watson
Management of Information Systems
Second Edition

Harris
Systems Analysis and Design for the Small Enterprise
Second Edition

Larsen/Marold
Using Microsoft Works 4.0 for Windows 95: An Introduction to Computing

Laudon and Laudon
Information Systems and the Internet: A Problem-Solving Approach

Licker
Management Information Systems: A Strategic Leadership Approach

Lorents and Morgan
Database Systems: Concepts, Management, and Applications

Martin
Discovering Microsoft Office 2000
Discovering Microsoft Office 97

Martin/Parker
PC Concepts
Second Edition

Mason
Using Microsoft Excel 97 in Business

McKeown
Information Technology and the Networked Economy

Millspaugh
Object-Oriented Programming with C++

Morley
Getting Started with Computers
Second Edition

Morley
Getting Started: Web Page Design with Microsoft FrontPage 2000
Getting Started: Web Page Design with Microsoft FrontPage 98
Getting Started: Web Page Design with Microsoft FrontPage 97

Parker
Understanding Computers: Today and Tomorrow
2000 Edition

Spear
Introduction to Computer Programming in Visual Basic 6.0

Martin and Parker
Mastering Today's Software Series

Texts available in any combination of the following:
   Windows 98
   Windows NT Workstation 4
   Windows 95
   Windows 3.1
   Disk Operating System 6.0 (DOS 6.0)
   Disk Operating System 5.0 (DOS 5.0)
   Microsoft Office 2000
   Microsoft Office 97 Professional Edition
   Microsoft Office for Windows 95 Professional Edition
   Word 2000
   Word 97
   Word 7.0 for Windows 95
   Word 6.0 for Windows
   Corel WordPerfect 7.0 for Windows 95
   WordPerfect 6.1 for Windows
   WordPerfect 6.0 for Windows
   WordPerfect 5.1
   Excel 2000
   Excel 97
   Excel 7.0 for Windows 95
   Excel 5.0 for Windows
   Lotus 1-2-3 97
   Lotus 1-2-3 for Windows (5.0)
   Lotus 1-2-3 for Windows (4.01)
   Lotus 1-2-3 (2.4)
   Lotus 1-2-3 (2.2/2.3)
   Quattro Pro 4.0
   Quattro Pro 6.0 for Windows
   Access 2000
   Access 97
   Access 7.0 for Windows 95
   Access 2.0 for Windows
   Paradox 5.0 for Windows
   Paradox 4.0
   dBASE 5 for Windows
   dBASE IV (1.5/2.0)
   dBASE III PLUS
   PowerPoint 2000
   PowerPoint 97
   PowerPoint 7.0 for Windows 95
   Outlook 2000
   A Beginner's Guide to QBASIC
   A Beginner's Guide to BASIC

Netscape Navigator 4.0
Internet Explorer 2000
Internet Explorer 4.0

The Dryden Online Series in Information Technology
  Computers Online
  Learning Office 2000

Learning Office 97
Learning Windows 98
Introduction to the Internet
Introduction to Multimedia
Introduction to Visual Basic 6.0
Systems Analysis and Design

PREFACE

It is unlikely that any other field is more dynamic, exciting, and influential than the computer field. Probably everyone would agree that modern computer technologies have a significant impact on how we live, learn, play, and work. During recent years, the Internet and World Wide Web have become an important part of life for millions of people in our society and throughout the world.

Within just a few years after the introduction of the Internet and Web, individuals, businesses, and governments would discover and create technologies that would allow their use for commercial purposes. Today thousands of individuals, companies, organizations, and governmental units use the Internet and Web for an impressive variety of commercial applications—a technological phenomenon called electronic commerce, or similar descriptions such as electronic business or Internet business. Simply defined, electronic commerce refers to the use of the Internet and Web to sell, distribute, market, and purchase products and services electronically.

The development, implementation, and growth in electronic commerce applications are increasing at a phenomenal rate. Thousands of businesses that initially scoffed at this new technology have quickly embraced electronic commerce technologies as a fast, relatively inexpensive, and efficient strategy for establishing new markets, increasing sales, marketing products and services, and many other business activities.

Colleges and universities now recognize the importance of electronic commerce in their curricula. Many academic programs devote a portion of courses such as management, marketing, retailing, and distribution to the coverage of various electronic commerce topics. Numerous other schools now offer a separate course devoted exclusively to a study of this exciting field.

Despite the popularity and explosive increase in electronic commerce, few textbooks address the total needs of students. *Getting Started with Electronic Commerce* will help students develop an extensive understanding of this important field in both their personal and professional lives.

The goal of *Getting Started with Electronic Commerce* is to immerse students in this exciting and dynamic field and to identify the applications and opportunities available to anyone. The primary objectives of this book are to increase student awareness, stimulate interests, broaden abilities, develop resourcefulness, and enhance student self-confidence in harnessing this cutting-edge technology.

Three overall themes converge in *Getting Started with Electronic Commerce:*

1. Computer technologies are now advanced so that users can have almost immediate access to information and opportunities that were unavailable until recent years.

2. Advances in computer technologies are occurring at a phenomenal pace, and in recent years have brought about new commercial opportunities for businesses, organizations, and governmental units to upgrade and streamline routine day-to-day business activities.

3. Electronic commerce technologies provide opportunities for any individual or business to establish a presence on the Internet and Web and to become actively engaged in electronic commerce applications.

The text is organized broadly into four parts. The first part introduces students to basic communications and network concepts and to the Internet, World Wide Web, and electronic commerce. The second part explains how individuals, businesses, and governments use electronic commerce technologies in routine day-to-day activities and transactions. The third part identifies and explains opportunities and issues involving electronic commerce. The fourth part includes two appendixes that explain the process of getting started with, and using, the Internet and the purpose, importance, and use of browsers and search engines.

Key Features

Chapter Outlines and Objectives

Each chapter begins with an outline and a set of learning objectives to guide students as they read and learn the material.

Feature Boxes

Each chapter contains special feature boxes that highlight Internet, Web, and electronic commerce topics of interest. Typically, feature boxes such as *E-Commerce Technology, E-Commerce Leaders,* and *E-Commerce International* appear throughout the book.

End-of-Chapter Review Material

Each chapter concludes with a summary and a list of key terms. Students can also use an accompanying series of matching and review questions to review the chapter's concepts and to reinforce learning.

Individual and Group Activities

Carefully selected individual and group activities at the end of each chapter are designed to help students explore and experience Internet, Web, and electronic commerce applications. Students are encouraged to visit sites on the Web and to discuss electronic commerce applications and opportunities with classmates and others. They are also urged to be creative and find Web opportunities and applications that are related to work, school, life, and leisure.

Appendixes

The end of the book contains two appendixes. Appendix A explains the process of getting started with the Internet. Appendix B presents an explanation of Web browsers and search engines. Both are intended to provide additional student insights into the world of cyberspace.

Supplements

Web Site

Useful instructor resources are available for downloading from the Web site at http://www.harcourtcollege.com/infosys/fullerec. At this site, instructors can download the book's Instructor's Manual and Test Bank. The Test Bank contains a variety of questions for each chapter. Types of questions include multiple-choice, true-false, completion, matching, and short-answer. Each question is identified with its type and degree of difficulty.

Acknowledgments

The author extends his gratitude to the many professionals who worked diligently to make this book successful. Reviewers prove the wisdom of the old adage, "More heads are better than one." Our reviewers added fresh insights and a real-world perspective to this project. Their interest, valuable comments, and overall support of this project have made writing this book an enjoyable experience. To each of the following reviewers, a mere "thank you" hardly seems appropriate for their valued contributions: Steve Balough, Arizona State University; Dan Conway, University of Florida; Robin Desman, Tulane University; Mary Jones, Mississippi State University; Stephen Shackelford, University of Kentucky Lexington Community College.

The author thoroughly enjoyed writing this book. The professionals at Harcourt College Publishers have been outstanding in their contributions and support. A special thanks is due to the following: Christina A. Martin, executive editor; Larry Crowder, developmental editor; Scott Baker, art director; Linda Blundell, permissions editor; Charlie Dierker, project editor; and Darryl King, production manager.

A Final Thought

The author and the publisher welcome your suggestions and recommendations. We are committed to serving the needs of students and faculty. Like the Internet itself, the writing and publishing process is evolutionary and participatory. We encourage you to join us in bringing you the best educational resources in this field. Toward that end, we welcome your comments, ideas, suggestions, and criticisms. Each will be considered carefully as the next edition of this book is being prepared. Address your correspondence to:

Floyd Fuller
c/o Computer Technologies Editor
Harcourt College Publishers
301 Commerce Street, Suite 3700
Fort Worth, TX 76102

CONTENTS

CHAPTER ONE

Introduction and Overview

AFTER COMPLETING THIS CHAPTER, YOU WILL

1. Identify and explain the main purpose of various communications hardware devices, communications media, and protocols.
2. Distinguish between the Internet and World Wide Web.

3. Define the term "electronic commerce" and give examples of electronic commerce applications in our global economy.
4. Explain briefly the nature of a transaction processing system and its value to a business enterprise.
5. Give examples of business-to-customer electronic commerce applications.
6. Give examples of business-to-business electronic commerce applications.
7. Explain the nature of electronic data interchange (EDI) and why the technology is important for routine business activities.
8. Give examples of government-to-society electronic commerce applications.
9. Explain the importance of establishing one's presence in electronic commerce.
10. Identify several relevant legal issues, concerns, and problems.
11. Identify some present and emerging trends in electronic commerce.
12. Identify some related career opportunities.

Introduction

During the past two decades, enormous progress has been made in the computing field. Today, the Internet and World Wide Web are providing users with a variety of online opportunities. From the comfort of one's own home, office, or school, a user can electronically travel the world to find and retrieve almost any kind of information.

The Internet and the Web allow individuals, businesses, organizations, and governmental units to engage in numerous kinds of electronic commerce activities. Anyone can create a Web site and, as a result, thousands of sites are now available to visitors.

The Internet, the Web, and electronic commerce technologies are undergoing rapid changes and improvements. As we enter the next millennium, electronic commerce will become increasingly important. These technologies will likely alter the ways in which we live our lives, learn, perform our work, and conduct our business activities.

Communications and Networks

Data communications, or simply **communications,** refers to the transmission (sending or receiving) of data and information between two or more computers over communications media such as telephone lines. Communications makes it possible to transmit text, voice, data, sound, and video among computers.

A computer **network** consists of two or more computers connected by means of communications media (Figure 1.1). A network may consist of several computers, terminals, and other devices that allow users to access programs, data, and information.

Many networks are based on a **client/server model.** With this model, a person uses a personal computer (called the client) to send requests to another computer (called the server) that relays the information back to the client.

FIGURE 1.1

Illustration of a Network

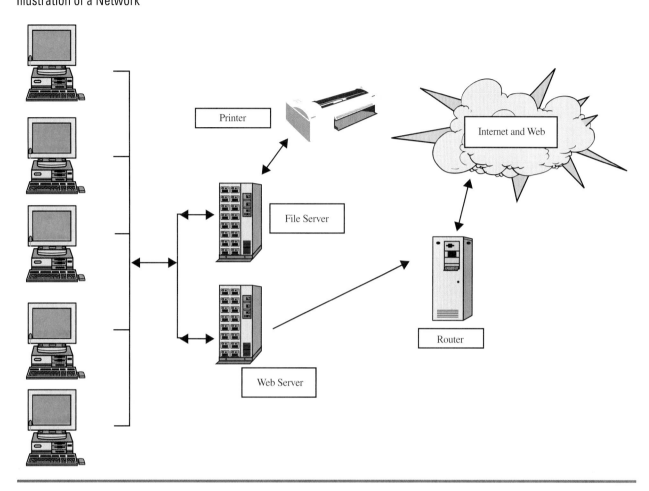

Communications Equipment and Software

Cables connect computers located close to each other. Computers dispersed over wide distances often require a variety of special equipment.

A **modem** is an electronic device that enables a computer to send and receive data over telephone lines by converting the data into a format that can then be carried along a standard telephone line. A modem at the receiver's computer automatically converts the data back into computer format.

A **network interface card (NIC)** is an electronic circuit card installed in one of the computer's expansion slots. The card contains circuits that coordinate the sending and receiving of transmissions.

A **server** is software installed on a computer network that allows users to share files, applications software, and hardware devices. A large network may use more than one server.

A **router** is an electronic device that directs the flow of blocks of information, called **packets,** between networks and across the Internet. Routers use a routing table (a kind of road map) to send data from router to router and a set of rules that helps a packet get closer to its destination with each step along the pathway.

Communications often travel over long distances and must travel through networks that may be similar and networks that may be dissimilar. In these cases, gateways and bridges are needed. A **gateway** consists of hardware and software that allow communication between *dissimilar* networks. A **bridge** consists of hardware and software that allow two *similar* networks to communicate.

For information to be transmitted between computers using telephone lines and a modem, communications software is required. **Communications software** allows you to connect your computer to another computer on which programs and data are stored and to access the stored programs and data.

Communications software often contains a number of useful features. Most packages allow you to send and receive files to and from other computers, access computers around the world, send and receive electronic mail messages, send and receive faxes, and access the Internet and online services.

Communications Media

A **communications medium** is a physical linkage that allows a computer in one location to be connected to a computer in another location for the purpose of transmitting and receiving data and information. Because communications occur worldwide, a combination of communications media may be used. Types of media include telephone lines (twisted pairs cable), coaxial cable, microwaves, satellites, and fiber-optic cable.

Communications Protocols

A **protocol** is a set of rules and procedures for exchanging information between computers. Protocols determine the formats for how computers communicate with each other and how errors are detected. Over the years, numerous protocols have been developed.

Communications in Action

Computer technology has revolutionized the way we communicate. Examples of modern electronic communications include voice mail, electronic mail, electronic bulletin boards, videoconferencing, faxes, and telecommuting.

A **voice mail** system is a computer's version of an answering machine service.

Electronic mail, or **e-mail,** is a fast and inexpensive way of sending, receiving, storing, and forwarding messages electronically. An **electronic bulletin board system (BBS)** is a computer system that maintains an electronic list of messages. Anyone with access to the bulletin board can post messages, read existing messages, or delete messages. **Videoconferencing** is the use of computers and television cameras to transmit video images and the sound of the participants to a remote location that has compatible equipment (Figure 1.2). A facsimile machine, commonly called a **fax machine,** makes it possible to transmit documents and drawings over telephone lines from one location to another in a manner that is faster and often cheaper than sending the document via an overnight shipping service or through the mail.

Computer Networks

A computer network may be small or large, simple or complex, and may cover a small geographical area, such as a single building, or a large geographical area, such as the entire United States and beyond.

Local area networks (LANs) are private communications networks that serve the needs of companies typically located in the same department or building. LANs typically use a special type of computer, called a **file server,** that allows other computers to share its resources. Local area networks are often classified by

FIGURE 1.2
Video Conferencing

Video conferencing equipment allows users at different locations to transmit and receive video and audio signals over communications media.

their physical configurations, called **topologies.** Three basic physical network topologies are **star, bus,** and **ring.** Software used with a special type of ring network, called a **token ring network,** uses an electronic signal, called a token, for sending and receiving data across the network.

Network Security

Organizations go to great lengths to ensure network security and the security of their programs and information. Access to a network may be restricted to users that are issued specific usernames and passwords. A **username** is a name (or word) used to gain access to a computer system. A **password** is a secret series of characters that enable a user to access a computer, file, or program. On a network each user must enter his or her username and/or password before the computer will respond.

The Internet, the Web, and Electronic Commerce

The development of the Internet and World Wide Web has proven to be among the most important, useful, and amazing developments in the history of computing. The use of both services is rapidly becoming commonplace in our modern global society.

The **Internet** (or **Net**) is a global network of computer networks. It is the largest and best-known network in the world.

The **World Wide Web** (also called the **Web, WWW,** or **W3**) is a global system of linked computer networks that allows users to jump from place to place on the Web. The Web is a retrieval system based on technologies that organize information into Web pages. Not all sites on the Internet are available to everyone. Available sites are called **Web sites.**

Information at available Web sites is in the form of Web pages. A **Web page** is a hypermedia file stored at a particular Web site. A **hypermedia file** is a file containing any combination of text, graphics, sound, and video. Web pages may also contain hyperlinks to other Web sites and to other Web pages. A **hyperlink** (or

E-Commerce Leaders

Tim Berners-Lee

Many people regard Timothy Berners-Lee as the "Father of the World Wide Web." His discoveries have provided computer users around the world with online opportunities unimagined until recently.

Berners-Lee graduated with honors in 1976 from the Queen's College at Oxford University, England. Following his graduation, he spent the next few years working at companies that engaged in various technological projects.

He spent six months working as an independent consultant software engineer at CERN, the European Particle Physics Laboratory in Geneva, Switzerland. There he wrote for his own use his first program for storing information, including using random associations. The program formed the conceptual basis for the future development of the World Wide Web.

In 1989 he proposed a global hypertext project, to be known as the World Wide Web. The project was designed to allow people to work together by combining their knowledge in a web of hypertext documents. He wrote the first World Wide Web server and the first client, a hypertext browser/editor. This work was started in October 1990, and the World Wide Web program was first made available within CERN in December and on the Internet at large in the summer of 1991.

Through 1991 and 1993, Berners-Lee continued working on the design of the Web, coordinating feedback from users across the Internet. His initial specifications of URLs, HTTP, and HTML were refined and discussed in larger circles as the Web technology spread.

In 1994, Berners-Lee joined the Laboratory for Computer Science (LCS) at the Massachusetts Institute of Technology (MIT) as director of the W3 Consortium that coordinates W3 development worldwide. The consortium's goal is to realize the full potential of the Web, ensuring its stability through rapid evolution and revolutionary transformations of its uses.

Berners-Lee has earned numerous honors and awards. In 1995 he received the Kilby Foundation's Young Innovator of the Year Award and was corecipient of the ACM Software Systems Award. He has honorary degrees from the Parsons School of Design, New York (D.F.A., 1996), and Southampton University (D.Sc., 1996), and he is a distinguished fellow of the British Computer Society.

simply **link**) is in the form of boldfaced text, underlined text, or an icon that, when clicked on using a mouse, takes you to another Web site or Web page.

To access and move about (usually called **browsing** or **surfing**) the Web, you must have a navigational program, called a browser, installed on your computer or network. A **browser** is a software tool (program) that makes it easy for you to find and display Web pages. The two most popular browsers are **Netscape Navigator** and **Internet Explorer.** After activating either browser, the user issues a request to visit a specific Web site or page by entering the site's address, called the **URL** (short for Uniform Resource Locator).

When you first access a specific Web site, the first page you will see is that site's **home page.**

The Web uses a language, called **HyperText Markup Language (HTML),** which allows a user to view Web pages. The language is designed to allow Web page developers to create Web pages in which the appearance of the pages is determined by the developer. Web browsers have the ability to display Web pages in HTML format. A newer Web language called **eXtensible Markup Language,** or **XML,** is gaining in popularity.

E-Commerce Technology

XML—Web Language of the Future

A new Web language, called eXtensible Markup Language (XML) is gaining widespread acceptance among Web users and site developers around the world. XML is essentially a subset of IBM's SGML (Standard Generalized Markup Language) markup language and bridges the gap between SGML and the somewhat limited capabilities of HTML (HyperText Markup Language). XML, in its earliest form, was developed in 1996 when the World Wide Web Consortium (W3C) commissioned a group of markup language experts, organized and led by Sun Microsystems' Jon Bosak, to deal with the limitations of HTML. At present, W3C is attempting to develop an acceptable standardized XML version.

This Internet phenomenon of the moment may someday power the second generation of the World Wide Web. The latest browsers understand XML, students are signing up for classes to learn it, and new companies are being formed to take advantage of it.

Two significant Web problems are that the Web is becoming slower with increasing usage and it's often difficult to find the one piece of information needed when performing an online search. XML is designed to be a potential solution to these two problems.

Currently, the most popular Web language is HyperText Markup Language (HTML). HTML is easy to learn and use, but it has difficulty doing some of the things users want done. A main limitation is in the use of tags. HTML tags are used to indicate that a paragraph follows or to identify a headline. However, HTML tags cannot mark text that says, for example, "The price of the item is" on an electronic commerce Web site.

XML is designed to solve this problem by specifying what the information is rather than what the information looks like. XML uses tags or markers just as HTML does, but whereas HTML marks the text to say, "This is in italics," XML marks the text to say, "The price of the item is." Newer browsers are XML enabled, which means that the browser can sort and manipulate this data right at the desktop.

XML will likely replace HTML and may also replace EDI (Electronic Data Interchange), as XML and EDI perform similar functions and transferring information via the Internet is relatively inexpensive. Meanwhile the two will be used in tandem. The new language offers several advantages. For example, if the user asked a travel site for flight times between San Francisco and Chicago, the browser could receive not only the schedule but also a small program that could select the flights by cost, time of day, or even seat selection. The browser could do the work that previously had to be done by the server.

XML can streamline electronic commerce applications. Businesses that use the Web need to be able to specify, "This is an order number" or "This is a part number." Each part of a business document needs to be identified.

Many groups have begun developing their own applications for XML. In medical applications, for example, there is an urgent need for a single, easy-to-use language capable of saying on the Web "This patient's X-ray is negative" or "This patient's white blood count is low" so that many machines can communicate quickly. New companies are forming to take advantage of XML. Erutech, a Seattle startup, will offer XML-based services for the health insurance industry.

The future for XML is bright. Business, medicine, and education represent three fields likely to embrace this new Web language. Continuing refinements and improvements will ensure its adoption as the Web language of the future.

Source: *The Charlotte* (North Carolina) *Observer,* July 1, 1999, section D, pp. 3–4.

Internet and Web Applications and Uses

The Internet and the Web provide users with access to information sources, databases, libraries, multimedia, and much more. They provide an efficient and inexpensive way for individuals and small companies to market products and services and to conduct other business activities. They offer features and applications including electronic mail, information searches and retrieval, entertainment, and home shopping.

An **electronic mail system** allows a user to send and receive messages electronically through, and between, networks from one computer to another computer. A **search engine** allows a user to search for, locate, and retrieve, information on the World Wide Web. A special type of software, called a **chat program,** allows users to communicate with others. Many people join groups, called **chat groups** or **chat rooms,** to discuss topics of mutual interest.

Electronic Commerce

Electronic commerce is a modern business methodology in which information, products, services, and payments are exchanged via computer networks within a global society. This definition implies that information, products, and services can be produced and marketed by a company or individual and sold to customers anywhere in the world. It also implies that this methodology can be used to reduce costs, improve the quality of products and services, speed up the delivery of products and services, and improve overall business performance.

Transaction Processing Systems (TPSs)

Electronic commerce applications require that transactions be processed online. A **transaction processing system (TPS)** is an information system that uses standard procedures to collect and process the day-to-day routine transactions that routinely flow through an organization.

Thousands of TPSs are currently in operation in a wide variety of organizations. One example is a system that captures routine sales transactions (Figure 1.3). Another is an order-entry system. When an order is received, a trained order-entry clerk follows standard procedures to enter and process the order.

TPSs are used in many other industries as well, including banking, commercial loan processing, stock and bond management, transportation, health care, legal practices, manufacturing, retail operations, and utilities. TPSs are used for accounts receivable, accounts payable, inventory control, invoicing, order processing, payroll, purchasing, shipping and receiving, and general ledger applications. Without a transaction processing system, it would be much more difficult to conduct business transactions over the Internet.

Business-to-Customer Applications

Using the Internet, retailers can sell goods and services to customers and, in return, receive payments. Businesses can conduct normal business activities with other businesses including suppliers, and governments can provide services quickly and efficiently. Manufacturers use it to communicate with suppliers and to recruit employees. Retailers can find new markets for their products. Mail-order businesses can purchase inventories and contact shippers.

FIGURE 1.3
Transaction Processing Systems

Transaction processing systems (TPSs), like the one shown here, allow routine day-to-day transactions to be processed quickly and efficiently.

Electronic Commerce Structures

Online shopping, also called **electronic shopping** or **e-shopping,** is using a computer and Internet access to locate, examine, purchase, sell, and pay for products over the Internet. As more consumers, called **electronic shoppers** or **e-shoppers,** flock to the Internet, electronic commerce between businesses and consumers will continue to expand.

Businesses, organizations, and individuals alike use the Internet to sell products and services. The home page for many retailers serves as a virtual storefront, similar to the storefront of a physical building located on a city street. A **virtual storefront** is a computerized storefront (entryway) through which potential customers can enter to view, and possibly purchase, a company's products and services.

Some companies offer their products and services via electronic shopping malls. An **electronic shopping mall** is an online mall with many electronic stores offering a variety of products and services, such as computers, clothing, and sporting goods. For many online shoppers, these malls represent a new and exciting way to shop.

An **online catalog** is a computerized version of a printed catalog. For retailers and customers alike, catalogs provide a convenient way to shop. Many retailers have already placed catalogs on the Web.

Specialized software, called **intelligent agents,** aids shoppers seeking bargain prices or additional product information. These programs aid shoppers in searching the Web for the lowest priced products.

Online Payments

Payments for goods and services purchased online can be made in various ways, including credit accounts, credit cards, traditional payments, or by providing a personal identification number (PIN). Some companies are developing technologies that allow for small purchases, although most of these efforts have met with limited success.

Consumer Online Shopping

Millions of consumers regularly shop the Internet for products ranging from gifts and toys to cars and even homes. Many of the products available in stores are also available for purchase over the Internet. Almost any product can now be purchased online. Figure 1.4 shows a partial list of product categories, along with Web sites where each can be purchased.

Other Online Applications

Although online shopping is perhaps the most enticing electronic commerce activity, many other online applications and opportunities are available. Businesses and organizations are flocking to the Internet to provide a variety of useful and unique products and services, including online information and news, education, banking, investing, and auctions. Several colleges and universities, including the University of Maryland University College (Figure 1.5), are now offering courses and degree programs online.

FIGURE 1.4

Product Categories and Web Sites

CATEGORY	COMPANY	WEB SITE
Automobiles	Autobytel	http://www.autobytel.com
	Autoweb	http://www.autoweb.com
	CarPoint	http://www.carpoint.com
Books, tapes, movies, CDs	Amazon.com	http://www.amazon.com
	Reel	http://www.reel.com
	Borders	http://www.borders.com
	Barnes and Noble	http://www.barnesandnoble.com
	CDNow	http://www.cdnow.com
	Music Boulevard	http://www.musicboulevard.com
Clothing	L.L. Bean	http://www.llbean.com
	The Gap	http://www.thegap.com
	Lands' End	http://www.landsend.com
Computers	Dell Computer	http://www.dell.com
	IBM	http://www.ibm.com
	Gateway	http://www.gateway.com
Gifts	Cybershop	http://www.cybershop.com
	Never Forget	http://www.neverforget.com
Sports and fitness	Foot Locker	http://www.footlocker.com
Toys and games	Toys "R" Us	http://www.toysrus.com
	eToys	http://www.etoys.com

FIGURE 1.5

University of Maryland University College Web Page

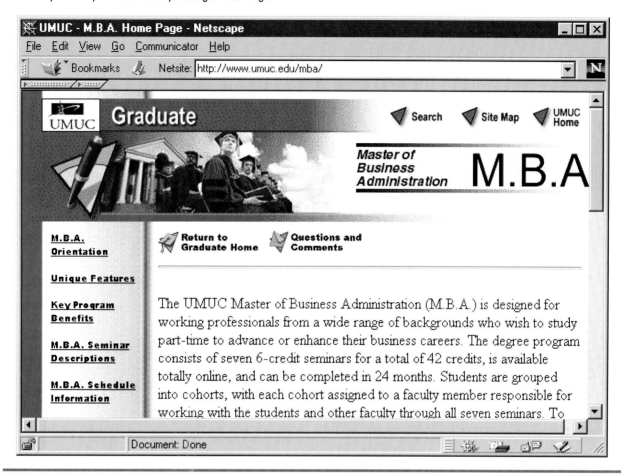

Business-to-Business Applications

Electronic commerce is playing an ever-increasing role in business-to-business applications. Continuing developments and improvements in electronic commerce technologies provide new opportunities for businesses and organizations to improve efficiency, service, and quality, and to increase productivity and profitability.

Value Chains

Today's company managers are more aware of the interdependence of business activities, functions, and operations, which can be managed more effectively by means of information systems. This awareness is known as the concept of value chain.

The concept of **value chains** is one in which a business firm is viewed as a series of basic, or chain, activities, each of which adds value to the firm's products or services. For example, a retailer adds value to products by making the products available to customers in a timely manner and a manufacturer adds value to its products during each phase of the manufacturing process.

Electronic commerce technologies allow manufacturing firms to streamline their manufacturing processes by employing and linking (integrating) automated manufacturing systems using computer and communications technologies. The purpose of these integrated systems is to make the information produced by one system immediately available for use by other systems. This allows companies to respond more quickly to customers, suppliers, employees, and others needing information.

Electronic Data Interchange (EDI)

The electronic exchange of business documents and forms can be accomplished by means of a telecommunications technology called electronic data interchange (EDI). **Electronic data interchange (EDI)** is the direct computer-to-computer capability to transfer business forms and documents from one computer to another. Some companies use EDI for routine transactions, including billing and purchase orders. In situations involving repeat business, such as a manufacturing company ordering materials from suppliers, EDI offers several advantages. Transaction costs are reduced. The time required for transmitting forms and documents is reduced, the volume of paper flow is reduced, and data entry errors can be minimized. Some companies have developed EDI applications that allow orders from customers to be automatically created, processed, and shipped without human intervention.

Financial EDI

Some businesses use a form of EDI technology called financial EDI to transmit payments electronically. **Financial EDI** technology provides for the electronic transmission of payments and associated remittance information between a payer and a payee and their respective banks. It allows businesses to replace the labor-intensive activities of producing, mailing, and collecting checks through the banking system with the automated and electronic transmission and processing of instructions for payment. Delays in processing checks are eliminated because both the payer and payee's bank accounts can be accessed and updated the same day.

Health care providers, including hospitals, doctor's offices, ambulance services, and others, use financial EDI technologies to bill private insurance companies and government agencies, such as Medicare. Some insurance companies and government agencies use EDI technologies to remit payments for services to patients.

Government-to-Society Applications

Federal, state, and local governments are among the strongest supporters and users of electronic commerce technologies. Leadership provided by the federal government has allowed Internet, Web, and electronic commerce technologies to flourish throughout the world. Governments at all levels—federal, state, and local—are using these technologies to serve the public interests in ways similar to those used by businesses to serve customers.

Several federal, state, and local governments are actively involved in electronic commerce applications. An important activity of every government is procurement. **Procurement** refers to the act of acquiring, or obtaining, products and services. To function effectively, every government must have the necessary resources, including products, services, and employees. Authorized companies visiting some of these sites can offer contract bids by filling out electronic bid forms and sending them to the appropriate department or agency.

FIGURE 1.6

State of New Mexico Home Page

The Federal Government and Electronic Commerce

Most federal departments, agencies, and commissions have established and maintain Web sites. Each site is designed to serve the interests and needs of visitors.

An important purpose of federal Web sites is to provide information and assistance to the public. By providing information and assistance, the government is providing a service just as businesses provide services to customers. In this sense, **service** may be defined as the provision of information and assistance to the public.

State Governments and Electronic Commerce

State governments maintain Web sites designed to inform and assist users. Several states are actively engaged in electronic commerce activities and promote electronic commerce as an efficient and cost-effective way to conduct business (Figure 1.6).

State Web sites provide various forms of information and assistance. Home pages typically contain links that enable users to locate various kinds of information, including useful business information and information about various governmental activities, legislation, employment opportunities, and links to pages containing electronic commerce information, forms, and applications. At some sites, a visitor can access and retrieve tax documents and forms, employee retirement application forms, and employee insurance forms. Companies authorized to conduct business with the state can download bid forms that can be completed and transmitted electronically to the appropriate department or agency.

Local Governments and Electronic Commerce

Some local governments use the Internet and electronic commerce technologies to conduct business activities. Federal and state authorities are assisting local governments by providing financial and other resources to assist local governments in the development, implementation, and operation of electronic commerce technologies. Some federal and state agencies provide funds in the form of grants to local governments wanting to establish electronic commerce capability and to use this capability to improve public services and to streamline business activities.

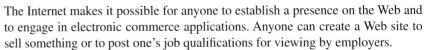

Establishing Your Presence in Electronic Commerce

The Internet makes it possible for anyone to establish a presence on the Web and to engage in electronic commerce applications. Anyone can create a Web site to sell something or to post one's job qualifications for viewing by employers.

Web pages are often stored together on a network device called a **Web server.** For example, a retailer might store multiple catalog pages together on the company's Web server. Individuals, called **Web authors,** produce Web pages. **Web publishing** refers to the placing of Web pages on a Web server. A **Webmaster** is a trained individual responsible for managing a Web site.

Web Page Design

Creating a Web site requires skill and careful planning. When creating a Web site, you should determine your objective, identify and know your audience, consider the possibilities, plan and design your site, and create the pages.

As a Web site developer, you have a number of options for creating Web pages. You can employ a Web professional to create your pages based on your plan and design. If you are skilled in the use of a Web programming language, such as HTML, VRML, or XML, you can use the language to create the pages. The other option is to use a software program, such as Microsoft's FrontPage, that simplifies Web page creation.

HTML is the language in which most Web pages are written. **Virtual Reality Modeling Language (VRML)** is a Web language that allows a user to create three-dimensional objects and environments, called *VRML worlds.* More and more companies and organizations are embracing VRML because of its effectiveness. However, XML is also increasing in popularity and becoming the preferred language of many Web authors.

Designing Your Site for Success

Every Web site developer wants the site to be successful (Figure 1.7). To be successful, you need to be mindful of a few key factors. First, keep in mind the purpose of your site and its potential visitors. Second, the content must be accurate and up to date. Third, your site's structure should be kept simple. Finally, choose colors that are appealing to visitors.

FIGURE 1.7

A Successful Commercial Web Site

Visitors to your Web site will quickly notice the components of your Web pages. Multimedia components can render your pages more effective. The term **multimedia** refers to a combination of sound, images, and graphics, in addition to text. Pages should contain a combination of text and other multimedia elements that render the site more informative and attractive.

Text consists of words, phrases, and paragraphs. Text is the most common Web page component. Text provides information being sought by viewers. The text you use should be understandable, interesting, and informative.

Clip art consists of stored figures, cartoons, and images that can be inserted into Web pages. Used effectively, clip art images can contribute significantly to the value of a Web page.

Digitized pictures are sometimes used to enhance Web pages. A **digitized picture** is a picture (photograph) taken with a digital camera (Figure 1.8). A **digital camera** captures a picture (photograph) and stores it in digital format on a medium such as a disk. Once captured and stored, a digitized picture can be inserted onto a Web page.

Scanned pictures and images can be added to Web pages. A **scanner** is a device that scans and captures all or part of a printed page, photograph, or image in a format that can be interpreted by a computer. The scanned material is stored on a disk in digital form. Once stored, the material can be inserted onto a Web page.

FIGURE 1.8

A Digital Camera

Sound is multimedia in the form of words, music, or special sound effects, such as those made by an automobile engine or a waterfall. Using special equipment and software, sounds can be captured and stored on a disk or CD-ROM. Commercially produced sound can be purchased. Used effectively, sounds can be impressive and can add to your site.

Publishing and Promoting Your Web Site

If you want people to visit your site, view your work, or perhaps buy your product, you need to let them know about your site. You need to register your site and, to attract viewers, promote it.

You can attract visitors to your site by getting other people and organizations to include a link on their pages to your site. This makes it easy for people reading other pages to jump quickly to your site.

Web banners are an effective way to promote Web sites. A **banner** is a rectangular graphic displayed in marquee fashion on a Web page. A banner can be any size. Banners provide some of the most prominent exposure possible on the Web. An interested user can quickly connect to another site by clicking on a banner.

Several companies set aside areas on their Web pages where you can advertise your pages. The Internet Link Exchange is a company that helps you to advertise your Web site.

After creating a Web site and publishing your pages, you need to maintain your site. Information on your pages must be kept interesting, accurate, and current. Failure to properly maintain your site can be disastrous because it will ensure that first-time visitors will not return. Visitors are more likely return to properly maintained sites.

Issues, Concerns, and Problems

Issues, concerns, and problems often accompany the introduction of new technologies. The more complex the technology, the more controversial the issues seem to be. Today we face a new set of issues regarding the Internet, the Web, and electronic commerce.

Control of the Internet and the Web is a controversial issue. Should there be control over the Internet and the Web and, if so, should control rest with the government, businesses, or individuals? Should the Internet and the Web be left alone? Perhaps a workable solution to the issue of control would be to educate users to act responsibly so that the Internet will remain available to everyone.

Users have a responsibility to exercise courtesy and sound judgment in their communications and dealings with others. The word **ethics** refers to personal standards involving one's behavior. Basic ethical standards dictate that we abide by commonly accepted ethical standards in our relationships with others.

Rules for acceptable behavior on the Internet are called **netiquette** (an abbreviation for "Net etiquette"). An important point to remember when using the Internet is that each of us is expected to be ethical and to practice proper netiquette any time we use the Internet and the Web.

Legal Issues, Concerns, and Problems

The Internet and the Web have given rise to several legal issues, concerns, and problems. Over time, some will be resolved, others will remain, and still others are likely to emerge.

The nature of the Internet lends itself to the potential for fraud, and fraud is increasing on the Internet. Fraud victims are being subjected to a variety of scams and cons. The best way for an Internet user to protect against fraud is to use extreme caution when asked for money, credit card numbers, or personal information.

A **spam** is an unwanted, unsolicited e-mail advertising message. A spam can be sent to many people at the same time, thereby creating a problem for many Internet users (Figure 1.9).

A **scam** is the deliberate attempt to cheat or defraud the public by false or misleading claims. The Internet is a vehicle of choice for many scammers who prey on unsuspecting and vulnerable individuals.

There is considerable concern over pornographic and obscene materials available on the Internet. This problem is now being extended to electronic commerce as some sellers are now offering graphic pornographic pictures and images for sale over the Internet.

Most people agree that pornographic and obscene materials should not be made available to children. Congress is being pressured to increase penalties for those who put child pornography on the Internet.

There is considerable concern about attempts by some state governments to levy taxes on Internet users. Suggestions and recommendations include levying sales taxes on products and services purchased over the Internet and taxing a user each time he or she accesses the Internet. States argue that these new tax revenues would enable them to improve education, build new roads, and improve and expand government services. Opponents argue that such taxes are unconstitutional and would create many problems. Companies doing business on the Internet argue that taxing the sales of products and services would reduce sales and therefore slow the development and growth of electronic commerce while still in its infancy. Users argue that most states typically do not levy taxes on the sale of products and services across state boundaries.

A major concern is the potential for virus attacks. A **virus** is a program that can disrupt or destroy the normal operations of a computer. Fortunately, **antivirus programs** are available that can detect the presence of most viruses and eradicate them. However, these programs may not be able to detect and eradicate all viruses, particularly newer ones. A new and different virus must be known before an antivirus program can be written that can detect and eradicate it.

FIGURE 1.9
A Spam E-Mail Advertising Message

Eudora version 1.4.4.

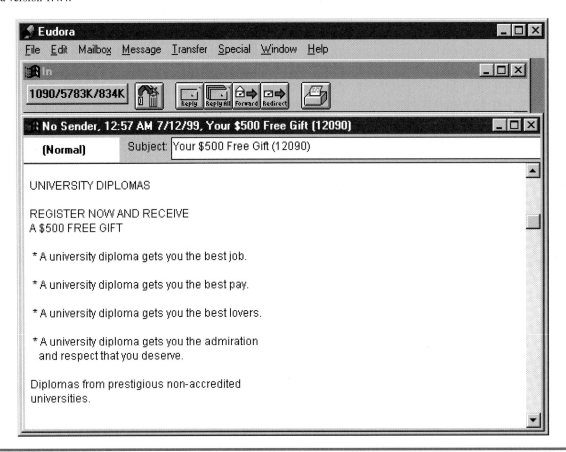

An issue currently being debated is the severity of penalties for distributing a virus over the Internet. Some people feel that harsh penalties should be imposed; others favor milder penalties.

Security

Security is a major concern of businesses, organizations, and agencies, many of which have invested millions of dollars to develop programs, files, and data.

Many companies have networks connected to the Internet, and almost all take extra precautions when any of their computers are connected to the Internet. One precaution is to build firewalls around their systems. On the Internet, a **firewall** is hardware or a form of software that restricts information that passes between a private network and the Internet. Other measures often taken to ensure security include requiring user IDs and/or passwords to gain access.

Information theft is a serious problem in our society. Thieves use the Internet to steal all kinds of information ranging from corporate secrets to credit card numbers. Thieves can use the Internet to illegally obtain credit card numbers; they then make purchases charged to the card owners.

The Internet offers exciting challenges for some computer enthusiasts, who devote tireless hours to searching for unique ways of doing things on the Internet.

In recent years, two groups of users have gained widespread attention and caused concern.

One group has been labeled **computer crackers.** These are people who try to gain unauthorized access to computer systems to alter, damage, or steal information by guessing user IDs and passwords. The other group consists of **computer hackers.** These are individuals who generally have expert knowledge about many computer systems and may test their skills by breaking into computer systems. Although computer hackers do not cause damage or steal information, they may view information stored in computer systems.

On the Internet, **espionage** refers to the act of spying. There are many well-documented cases in which unauthorized persons used the Internet to gain access to government and private computer systems to view confidential information.

Sabotage refers to the willful destruction of property. On the Internet, saboteurs try to gain entry into computer systems to destroy information. The work of saboteurs can be devastating. Because of the potential seriousness of acts of sabotage, penalties for these offenses are often severe.

Social Issues, Concerns, and Problems

Some issues, concerns, and problems are social rather than legal because they affect society at large. Nevertheless, the issues, concerns, and problems are controversial and important because of their potential impact on users.

Companies and other organizations have used mailing lists for many years to send notices, announcements, and advertisements to those whose names and addresses are on the lists. A **mailing list** is a list of entries (often individuals) in which each entry consists of a name or title, mailing address, telephone number, and other information. The use of mailing lists by Internet online service companies and service providers has become a controversial issue. The central issue concerns ownership of, and the right to use, personal information supplied by subscribers. Once a subscriber provides personal information to an online service or Internet provider, who has legal ownership of the information?

Internet (online) gambling is rampant, and an estimated 300 gambling sites are currently available. Some studies have predicted that, if left alone, revenues from Internet gambling will increase from $650 million in 1998 to $3.1 billion in 2001. This controversial issue has captured the attention of both parents and government officials because Internet gambling involves children as well as adults. Gambling opponents argue that because casino gambling operations are illegal when conducted over telephone lines across state boundaries, they shouldn't be legal over the Internet. Further, they argue that children can access gambling sites and participate in gambling activities without being aware of the potential consequences.

Other people can intercept and read messages sent across the Internet. This is especially true for electronic mail (e-mail) messages and other information such as that supplied when ordering products and services. A major issue regarding electronic mail and online purchases is centered on the issue of **privacy.** The issue is whether an employer has a right to intercept and read employee e-mail messages. Some employers argue they have a legal right to read employee e-mail because the company or organization owns the e-mail resources, such as the computers and software. They further argue that employees are being paid for the time they spend when using e-mail on company time. Employees argue they have a right to privacy and that an e-mail message should be considered the private property of the individual.

There is growing concern about online games depicting violence. Many of these games are available to young people, and some believe playing them may influence violent behavior. Incidents at some schools have focused greater public attention on violent online games.

Over time, new issues, concerns, and problems will likely emerge. As they do, everyone has a responsibility to react objectively and responsibly.

Present and Emerging Trends and the Future

The Internet, the Web, and electronic commerce are exciting and useful technologies. In each area, we can identify some present and emerging trends.

Present and Emerging Trends

A **trend** is a movement or progression in a general direction. We often hear this word in everyday conversation to describe a pattern of change, such as warmer weather or higher food prices. In the computing field, we often experience changing trends. Trends affecting computer hardware and software also affect the Internet, the World Wide Web, and electronic commerce because all are interrelated.

A **standard** is a format, language, or protocol that has been approved by a recognized standards organization or is accepted as a de facto standard by the industry. A **de facto standard** is a format, language, or protocol that has become a standard not because it has been approved by a standards organization but because it is widely used and recognized by the industry as being standard.

In the future, the trend will continue away from de facto standards and toward the establishment and acceptance of standards approved by recognized and accepted standards organizations. This trend will streamline electronic commerce applications and open the way for development of new Internet and electronic commerce technologies, including transmissions protocols that will promote future growth and development in these dynamic areas.

Older computers are viewed as dinosaurs and most are now housed in museums. Ever since computers began appearing in the late 1940s and early 1950s, the trends have been toward the development and manufacture of computers that are smaller, faster, more powerful, more versatile, and that have expanded capabilities and storage capacities.

Another hardware trend is toward improvements in computer components and peripheral devices, including monitors, modems, printers, and graphics and sound cards. Higher resolution monitors, faster modems, high-resolution printers, and improved graphics and sound cards are being introduced almost daily.

The trend is toward software that allows users to be more productive and toward integrated **software suites,** which contain useful programs that function smoothly together so that data can be moved from one application to another. As more and more users take advantage of opportunities available with the Internet, the Web, and electronic commerce, improvements are being made to browsers and search engines, and new browsers and search engines are introduced periodically. Businesses are pressuring communications companies and hardware and software developers to design and produce equipment and software to facilitate electronic commerce applications.

A trend continues toward the development of devices that facilitate Internet and Web usage. Several manufacturers have introduced devices that, when connected to a standard TV set, allows users to access the Internet and Web through their TV screens. Several companies now offer Internet and Web appliances and new and improved devices are being developed—a trend that will likely continue as more users are eager to have Internet access.

Connectivity refers to the ability of a program or device to link with other programs and devices. The trend is toward greater connectivity.

Thousands of businesses, organizations, and government agencies are engaged in electronic commerce and others are becoming involved each day. All are actively recruiting trained and experienced computer professionals in an effort to be competitive. The demand for skilled technical personnel has skyrocketed during recent months. Companies are actively recruiting Web developers, network managers, Webmasters, communications specialists, and other employees to fill vacancies in technical areas. A major trend now exists in which students and others are becoming educated and trained in specialized areas that will unlock the door for future employment opportunities. The demand for well-trained specialists will likely outpace the supply during the foreseeable future.

Improvements in production technologies will allow manufacturers to produce internal storage chips and boards containing greater storage capacities. Internal storage costs will continue to decline making computers less expensive.

New and improved auxiliary storage devices and media will appear. Hard disk capacities may reach 100 gigabytes within a few years. Floppy disk capacities will also increase. New auxiliary storage devices and media will emerge.

Improvements will be made to browsers and search engines, both of which will become faster and offer more features. As new upgrades are introduced, we can anticipate improved interfaces, faster access, and greater versatility.

Improvements will occur in Web page design programs, such as Microsoft's FrontPage, and new programs will be introduced. Learning to use these programs will become easier for first-time users, and the programs will offer an even greater number of design tools and features.

The most notable improvements will occur in electronic commerce products. The market for these products is expanding rapidly, and many producers are taking advantage of the opportunities they foresee.

The Future

Some of the most impressive and useful advances will occur in the area of voice and data communications. Data transmission bandwidths will be expanded.

Companies that produce devices for data communications are improving existing devices and developing new ones with wider bandwidths. Each week thousands of new Internet users are going online, and hundreds of additional companies, organizations, and agencies are establishing their presence on the Internet. To meet this continually increasing demand for access and usage, communications companies are developing new technologies that provide faster access and accommodate user needs.

Manufacturers of communications devices, such as modems, are also improving their products and developing new ones. To remain competitive, companies are researching new and improved technologies that can provide faster data transmission.

Data communications channels, devices, media, and technologies will continue to be improved. Today, cellular devices and technologies are common. The future holds promise for the rapid development of better data communications technologies.

We can look forward to significant improvements in Internet technologies. New and improved processors are making Internet access and usage faster and more convenient. Internet and Web servers are becoming faster and more dependable. Communication channel bandwidths are being broadened to accommodate more data and provide faster transmission.

The Internet is growing and changing at an extraordinary pace. New portable Internet appliances will provide access to the Internet from remote locations.

Electronic mail messages now must be typed before they can be sent to friends and colleagues. Eventually, video e-mail will become available. A **video e-mail** system will allow a user to record a video and send it over the Internet.

Web portals, including such well-known portals as Yahoo!, Lycos, America Online, and Netscape, will aggressively compete for advertising sales and revenues. Yahoo! began as a search engine, but has evolved into a leading Web portal (Figure 1.10). Similar to a large doorway to a shopping mall, a **Web portal** is a doorway to information available on the Web and to various Web sites.

In the near future, technological improvements will be made in electronic payment systems. Smart cards will become more widely accepted and their use will increase as improvements are made in smart card technologies, which is the subject of much present-day research. Future computers may even come with components, such as embedded slots, that will facilitate online purchases by allowing smart cards to be used for making online payments.

We can expect other forms of electronic payment systems to appear. Manufacturers and online merchants alike are eager to develop new systems that will simplify online payments for purchases of products and services.

FIGURE 1.10

Yahoo! Web Portal

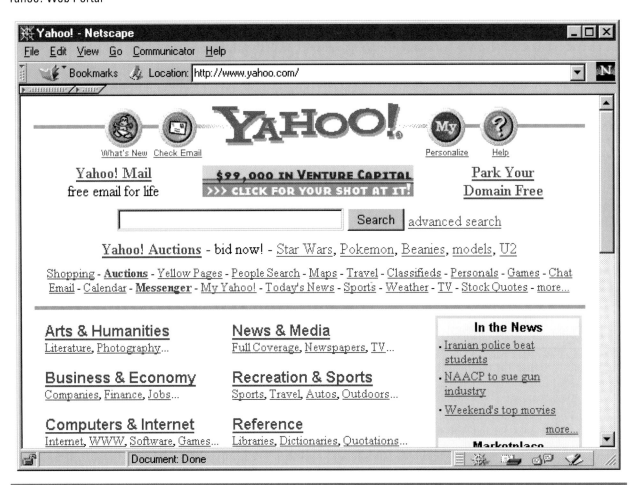

Career Opportunities

The Internet, the Web, and electronic commerce have opened up new and interesting career opportunities, several of which can command selective employment options and high salaries.

One of the fastest-growing and most interesting career opportunities today is that of Web page designer. Many businesses and organizations are recruiting individuals who can design attractive and informative Web pages that contain information and graphics on topics such as company products and services, college and university programs, and organizational services. Many businesses and organizations employ their own Web page designers who create such pages and update existing ones as needed.

The responsibility for data communications systems falls to data **communications specialists,** who are responsible for developing, implementing, and maintaining the communications networks and the communications software that control the flow of data among devices in the network. The rapid growth and expansion of the Internet and the Web have created a high demand for data communications specialists.

A relatively new career opportunity is that of Internet service representative, sometimes referred to as an ISR. An **Internet service representative** answers telephone and electronic inquiries from customers who encounter problems while installing communications or related software on their computer or who experience difficulties when trying to access the Internet.

Even now, high demand exists for trained individuals who can design, install, and operate electronic conferencing systems. A **videoconferencing specialist** is a trained and skilled individual who can design, install, and operate video conferencing systems that are needed by businesses, organizations, and others. Video conferencing systems consist of audio-visual equipment, including cameras and electronic presentation devices, that when connected via computers allow participants to immediately communicate orally and visually.

Other career opportunities are likely to emerge. As we move forward into the next century, many changes will occur in electronic commerce. Even experienced professionals cannot foresee all of the changes. Those that do occur will have a significant impact on our lives.

The ability to transmit and receive information electronically by means of communications and network technologies makes the Internet, the Web, and electronic commerce possible. These important technologies are the central topics of the next chapter.

SUMMARY

During recent years numerous advances have been made in the computing field. Today, the Internet and the World Wide Web are providing users with many online opportunities. The Internet and the Web allow individuals, businesses, organizations, and governmental units to engage in various kinds of electronic commerce activities. Anyone can create a Web site and, as a result, thousands of sites are now available to visitors.

Data communications and network technologies often require a variety of hardware devices, software, and communications media. Hardware devices include modems, network interface cards, servers, routers, gateways, bridges, and other devices.

Communications software allows users to connect their computers to other computers on which programs and data are stored and to access the programs and data. It also allows users to send and receive files to and from other computers, access other computers around the world, send and receive electronic mail messages, send and receive faxes, and access the Internet and online services.

Communications media allow information transmissions among computers and networks. Types of media include telephone lines, coaxial cables, microwaves, satellites, and fiber-optic cables.

Communications protocols provide the rules and procedures for exchanging information between computers. Protocols determine the formats for how computers communicate with each other. Communications applications include voice mail, electronic mail, electronic bulletin boards, videoconferencing, faxes, and telecommuting.

The development of the Internet and the World Wide Web are among the most important, useful, and amazing developments in the history of computing. The Internet (or Net) is a global network of computer networks. It is the largest and best-known network in the world. The World Wide Web (WWW) is a global system of linked computer networks that allows users to jump from place to place on the Web. Electronic commerce is a modern business methodology in which information, products, services, and payments are exchanged via computer networks within a global society. This definition implies that information, products, and services can be produced, marketed, and sold to customers anywhere in the world. It also implies that this methodology can be used to reduce costs, improve the quality of products and services, speed up the delivery of products and services, and improve overall business performance.

Electronic commerce applications require that transactions be processed online. Transaction processing systems (TPSs) are used to collect and process routine transactions. TPSs are used for processing accounts receivable, accounts payable, inventory control, invoicing, order processing, payroll, purchasing, shipping and receiving, and general ledger applications. Without these systems, it would be much more difficult to conduct business transactions over the Internet.

Electronic commerce technologies have made possible business-to-customers applications, business-to-business applications, and government-to-society applications. These kinds of applications benefit everyone—businesses, individuals, and government. Businesses can sell goods and services to customers and, in return, receive payments. Businesses can conduct normal business activities with other businesses including suppliers, and governments can provide services quickly and efficiently.

Electronic commerce technologies are playing an increasing role in business-to-customer applications by allowing businesses to market and sell a variety of products and services over the Internet. Using electronic payment systems, customers can make online purchases and transmit payments electronically.

Electronic commerce is playing an ever-increasing role in business-to-business applications. Continuing developments and improvements in electronic commerce technologies provide new opportunities for businesses and other organizations to improve efficiency, service and quality, to increase productivity and profitability, and to strengthen and improve value chains.

Federal, state, and local governments are among the strongest supporters and users of electronic commerce technologies. Leadership provided by the federal government has allowed Internet, Web, and electronic commerce technologies to flourish throughout the world. Governments at all levels—federal, state, and local—are using these technologies to serve the public interests in ways similar to those used by businesses to serve customers.

Procurement is an important government application using electronic commerce technology. Government must have the necessary resources, including products, services, and employees. Authorized companies visit some government sites and offer contract bids by filling out electronic bid forms and sending them to the appropriate department or agency.

The Internet and the Web make it possible for anyone to establish a presence on the Web and to engage in electronic commerce applications. Anyone can create a Web site to sell something, to post job qualifications for viewing by employers, or for various other purposes.

Issues, concerns, and problems often accompany the introduction of new technologies. The more complex the technology, the more controversial the issues seem to be. Today we face a new set of issues regarding the Internet, the Web, and electronic commerce. Among the many issues, concerns, and problems are control of the Internet, Internet fraud, unwanted spams, illegal scams, pornography and obscenity, viruses, privacy, and mailing lists.

Security is a major concern of businesses, organizations, and agencies, many of which have invested millions of dollars to develop programs, files, and data. Many companies have networks connected to the Internet, and almost all take extra precautions when their computers are connected to the Internet.

The Internet, the Web, and electronic commerce are exciting and useful technologies. In each area, we can identify some present and emerging trends. Important trends include universally approved and accepted standards, faster and more powerful computers, greater connectivity, improved peripheral devices, and broader bandwidths.

The Internet, the Web, and electronic commerce have opened up new and interesting career opportunities, several of which can command selective employment options and high salaries. Today, there is a high demand for employees skilled in the use of various Internet, Web, and electronic commerce technologies.

KEY TERMS

antivirus program (17)
banner (16)
bridge (4)
browser (6)
browsing (surfing) (6)
bus (5)
chat group (chat room) (8)
chat program (8)
client/server model (2)
clip art (15)
communications medium (4)
communications software (4)
communications specialist (23)
computer cracker (19)
computer hacker (19)
connectivity (21)
data communications (communications) (2)
de facto standard (20)

digital camera (15)
digitized picture (15)
electronic bulletin board system (BBS) (4)
electronic commerce (8)
electronic data interchange (EDI) (12)
electronic mail (e-mail) (4)
electronic mail system (8)
electronic shopper (e-shopper) (9)
electronic shopping mall (9)
espionage (19)
ethics (17)
eXtensible Markup Language (XML) (6)
fax machine (4)

file server (4)
financial EDI (12)
firewall (18)
gateway (3)
home page (6)
hyperlink (link) (5)
hypermedia file (5)
HyperText Markup Language (HTML) (6)
information theft (18)
intelligent shopping agent (9)
Internet (Net) (5)
Internet Explorer (6)
Internet service representative (ISR) (23)
local area network (LAN) (4)
mailing list (19)
modem (3)
multimedia (15)

netiquette (17)
Netscape Navigator (6)
network (2)
network interface card
  (NIC) (3)
online catalog (9)
online shopping
  (electronic shopping
  or e-shopping) (9)
packet (3)
password (5)
privacy (19)
procurement (12)
protocol (4)
ring (5)
router (3)
sabotage (19)
scam (17)
scanner (15)

search engine (8)
server (3)
service (13)
software suite (20)
sound (16)
spam (17)
standards (20)
star (5)
text (15)
token ring network (5)
topology (5)
transaction processing
  system (TPS) (8)
trend (20)
Uniform Resource
  Locator (URL) (6)
username (5)
value chains (11)
video e-mail (22)

videoconferencing (4)
videoconferencing
  specialist (23)
Virtual Reality
  Modeling Language
  (VRML) (14)
virtual storefront (9)
virus (17)
voice mail (4)
Web author (14)
Web page (5)
Web portal (22)
Web publishing (14)
Web server (14)
Web site (5)
Webmaster (14)
World Wide Web (Web,
  WWW, or W3) (5)

END-OF-CHAPTER ACTIVITIES

Matching

Match each term with its description.

a. procurement
b. gateway
c. hypermedia
d. scam

e. client/server
f. electronic data
  interchange (EDI)
g. electronic commerce

h. Webmaster
i. banner
j. data communications

_____ **1.** The transmission of data and information between two or more computers over communications media.

_____ **2.** A trained individual responsible for managing a Web site.

_____ **3.** The act of acquiring, or obtaining, products and services.

_____ **4.** The deliberate attempt to cheat or defraud the public by false or misleading claims.

_____ **5.** The direct computer-to-computer capability for transfer of business forms and documents from one computer to another computer.

_____ **6.** A network model in which a person using a personal computer sends requests to another computer that relays the information back.

_____ **7.** A rectangular graphic displayed in marquee fashion on a Web page.

_____ **8.** A file containing any combination of text, graphics, sound, and video.

_____ **9.** A modern business methodology in which information, products, services, and payments are exchanged via computer networks within a global society.

_____ **10.** Hardware and software that allows communications between dissimilar networks.

Review Questions

1. Data communications is essential for electronic commerce. What is data communications?

2. Give examples of some modern electronic communications that were identified in the chapter.

3. What is a transaction processing system?

4. What are some ways in which online payments can be made for goods and services?

5. What is the meaning of the term *value chain?*

6. What is electronic data interchange (EDI) and what are some of the advantages offered by this technology?

7. What key factors should be kept in mind in order to develop a successful Web site?

8. Identify some legal issues, concerns, and problems that were explained in the chapter.

9. Identify some social issues, concerns, and problems that were explained in the chapter.

10. Distinguish between a *standard* and a *de facto standard.*

Activities

1. Even if you live in a small area with few businesses, there are probably businesses and organizations in your area that have Web sites. If so, visit and carefully examine and critique the site. Prepare a written critique of the site. In your written critique, indicate the features you find informative and impressive. Also identify features you dislike or find to be of little or no value.

2. In the chapter several issues, concerns, and problems were identified and explained, but space limitations prevented every Internet, Web, and electronic commerce issue, problem, or concern from being identified and explained. There are others that are identified in computer magazines, newspapers, and other news media. Using your school library and other sources, identify two or three others issues, concerns, or problems. Prepare a brief written summary of each.

3. Many businesses of all sizes are now using transaction processing systems to process routine transactions, such as sales. Visit one of these businesses in your area and ask a knowledgeable employee to explain how the system works and how it benefits the company. Prepare a written report that includes details about how the system works and specific benefits gained.

4. Find out if your local government has a Web site. If it does, use a computer in your school's computer lab to visit the site. While at the site, prepare a written summary of the kinds of information available including links to other sites and documents, and indicate whether electronic commerce opportunities are available at the site.

5. This is a group activity. Your instructor will arrange class members into groups of four to six students. Each student will visit one business site and one government site. While at these sites, each student will prepare a brief written analysis of the site including the site's physical appearance, content, links, and features for conducting electronic commerce activities. When students have completed this assignment, the brief written analyses will be combined into a single written report and turned in to the instructor. Each report will summarize the business sites and government sites separately.

CHAPTER TWO

Communications and Networks

AFTER COMPLETING THIS CHAPTER, YOU WILL:

1. Define the term *communications* and identify some kinds of data that can be transmitted from one computer to another computer.

2. Identify five special communications devices explained in the chapter and the main purpose of each device.
3. Explain briefly the purpose of communications software.
4. Explain briefly the different types of communications media presented in the chapter.
5. Define the term *protocol* and tell why protocols are needed for communications.
6. Give examples of communications in action.
7. Explain what a local area network is and why an organization may choose to install a local area network instead of using individual unlinked computers.
8. Identify and describe briefly three local area network topologies.
9. Explain the purpose of an intranet and why intranet security is a concern for many organizations.
10. Explain what an extranet is and why an organization may want to make information stored on an extranet available for public use.

Most computer users know that computers have become important communications devices. When connected to other devices and communications technologies, such as telephone equipment, a computer is capable of communicating with other computers anywhere in the world. This capability, referred to as connectivity, allows computer users to quickly and easily access information stored on other computers located throughout the world.

Today, users of personal computers (PCs) can communicate and share information with other computer users. They can use their computers to communicate with large computer databases to retrieve stock market information, weather forecasts, movie schedules at local theaters, and much more. Businesses, government agencies, academic institutions, and other types of organizations use computers for communications purposes. Communications between computers has become an integral part of the daily business operations of airlines, banks, hotels, retail stores, and many other types of businesses.

This chapter provides an overview of communications between computers. It identifies and describes some of the terminology, equipment, and applications pertaining to computers and as communications devices. It also explains how computers can be linked to create networks that allow users to communicate with each other and to share information, hardware, and software. This linkage has dramatically changed the way people, businesses, and organizations communicate and conduct their daily activities and business operations.

What Is Communications?

Communications, also called **data communications,** is a broad term that refers to the transmission (sending or receiving) of data and information between two or more computers over communications media, such as standard telephone lines. The terms *telecommunications* and *teleprocessing* are also used to describe communications. **Telecommunications** refers specifically to the combined use of computers, networks, and communications media that enables information to be

FIGURE 2.1

Electronic (E-Mail) Messaging

Electronic mail (e-mail) is a fast and efficient way to communicate. After typing the recipient's address, a subject, and a message, the message can be sent to the recipient in a few seconds. Computer files can also be attached to the message.

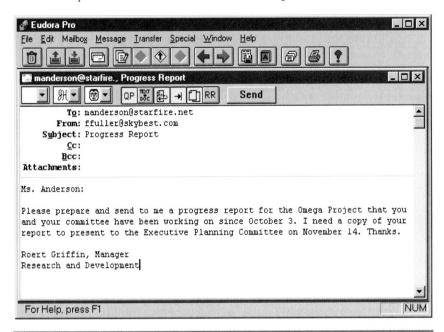

transmitted and received among computers throughout the world. **Teleprocessing** refers to the use of a computer and communications equipment to access stored files on computers in other locations. Because the difference between these terms has become blurred in recent years, we will refer to the process of transmitting information of any type over communications media as simply **communications.**

Instead of mailing a typed letter to a friend, communications allows you to send your message from your computer to your friend's computer within a few seconds (Figure 2.1). Communications also allows you to access and view information stored on thousands of computer systems throughout the world.

Communications makes it possible to transmit text, voice, data, sound, and video among computers. For example, a medical specialist at a large hospital in the United States can use a computer to observe a surgical operation being performed and captured by camera in rural Africa and can immediately provide the operating surgeon with expert advice.

Communications Equipment and Software

Later in this chapter you will learn about computer networks in which two or more computers are linked to allow individual users and groups to communicate with each other and to share information. Because of their complexity, networks often include specialized hardware devices and software programs. In the following sections, several network hardware and software components are identified and explained. The types and quantities of these devices and programs being used can, and frequently does, vary among different types of networks.

Cable Modems Provide Faster Internet and EC Access

Telephone lines are typically used to connect to most Internet service providers and online services. These lines consist of standard cable, fiber-optic cable, or a combination of both. Information flows over these lines. When you want to receive information, such as a document or file, you send a command from your computer to your Internet service provider's (ISP) central computer called a "server," where the services' information is stored. The server obeys your command and sends the requested information back to your computer.

For you to send a command and receive the requested information, you need a modem—an electronic device that connects your computer to the phone line. Your modem allows information to enter your computer at varying rates, depending on its capacity. A telephone modem, like the one you might buy at a computer store, allows information to enter your computer at rates ranging from 2,400 bits of information per second to approximately 56,000 bits of information per second. The invention of the telephone modem helped bring the Internet into reality by allowing data to be sent easily and cheaply anywhere in the world.

Cable modems represent the next advance in transmission technology. A cable modem does the same thing as a telephone modem—but faster and better. Conceptually, a cable modem is similar to a telephone modem, but it is much more sophisticated.

A telephone modem is an electronic card installed inside your computer in your computer's COM (Communications) port with a standard telephone line plugged into the modem. A COM port is a standard, but slow, component of most home computer systems. It is not designed to handle data at high speeds.

Unlike most telephone modems, cable modems are external devices usually housed in metal boxes. Several activity lights on the front of the box indicate when the modem is in use. A cable modem uses a different type of card, called a network interface card (NIC), installed in a standard PCA, ISA, or PCMCIA slot in your computer. A NIC allows for much faster information transmission than does a standard COM port.

Individual cable modem speeds vary, depending on the type and model. Typically, cable modems are capable of speeds ranging from 500 kbps (500,000 bits per second) to 10 mbps (10,000,000 bits per second).

Cable networks are shared resources that are typically available to many users. There's always a possibility that someone might try to access your information during transit. If this happens, the person might be able to intercept, reconstruct, alter, or damage the information, such as e-mail messages or other confidential information.

Some cable modems have encryption and decryption capability. They only encrypt information being sent along the cable network. Information sent across the Internet is not encrypted. Other software is needed to encrypt and decrypt information sent across the Internet.

Cable modems offer other advantages for the user. To contact your provider's server, you don't have to wait for a dialed connection as you do when using a telephone modem and standard telephone lines. Your telephone line isn't tied up.

Cable modems provide easy, fast, and efficient access to your service provider's central computer. Your ISP or online service can provide you with details about cable modems, their availability in your area, and charges for this type of connection.

Communications Equipment

In situations where two or more computers are located close to each other (for example, within a few hundred feet) they can be connected to each other by cables. However, when computers are dispersed over wider distances the transmissions between them weakens and special communications equipment is needed to change or strengthen the transmission so that it can travel farther. These devices include modems, network interface cards, repeaters, and multiplexers.

MODEMS

A **modem** is an electronic device that enables the computer to transmit (send and receive) data over telephone lines. This device automatically converts the digital data into analog form that can then be carried along a standard telephone line. Upon arrival at the receiver's computer, a modem at the receiving computer automatically converts the analog data back into digital form that the computer can understand, as illustrated in Figure 2.2.

Three main types of modems are internal, external, and cellular, and all types perform the same functions. An **internal modem** is contained on a circuit board that is inserted into a slot inside a computer. An **external modem** is a self-contained device, outside the computer, that plugs into a computer in the same way you would plug in a keyboard. Recently, **cellular modems** that do not require wires are finding popularity with laptop and notebook computer users. Cell stations resembling tall, metal telephone poles pick up signals from cellular modems in their vicinity and pass along the communications through regular telephone lines.

An important factor to consider in choosing a modem is the speed at which it can send and receive data. Modem speed is measured as the number of bits (0s and 1s) that can be transmitted per second, called the **baud rate.** Modems can transmit data at rates ranging from 300 to approximately 56,000 bits per second (bps). When a large amount of data are to be transmitted, a faster modem may be preferred.

FIGURE 2.2

How Modems Work

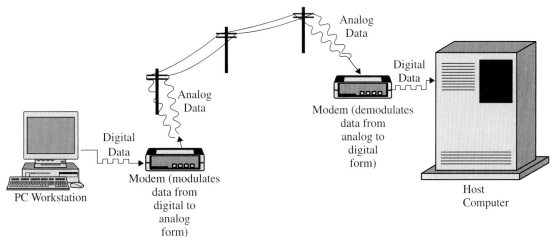

FIGURE 2.3

A Network Interface Card

A network interface card (NIC) installed inside a computer allows the computer to be linked to a local area network by connecting the card to a server by means of a coaxial cable or fiber-optic cable.

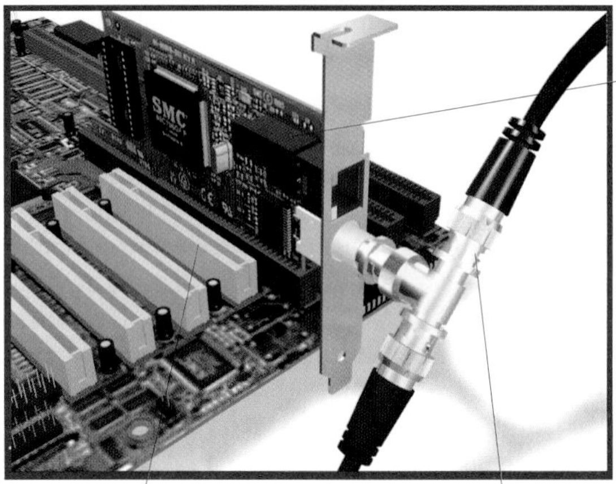

Rear view of workstation, with case removed

Network Interface Card (NIC)

Expansion Slot

T-connector for Coaxial Cable

NETWORK INTERFACE CARDS

A **network interface card (NIC)** is an electronic circuit card installed in one of the computer's internal expansion slots that connects to the cable or wireless technology used to connect computers and other devices to the network (Figure 2.3). The card contains circuits that coordinate the transmission and receipt of transmissions. An example of a network interface card is an Ethernet card.

SERVERS

A **server** is the software installed on a computer network that allows users to share files, applications software, and hardware devices (Figure 2.4). A large network may use more than one server.

ROUTERS

A **router** is an electronic device that directs the flow of information packets between networks and across the Internet. Routers use a routing table (a kind of road map) to send data from router to router, and they follow a set of rules that help a packet get closer to its destination with each step along the pathway. Routers ultimately deliver the packets to the intended network and to a computer that then reassembles the message.

MULTIPLEXERS

A **multiplexer** is a special electronic device that increases the efficiency of a network system by allowing 8, 16, 32, or more low-speed devices, such as PCs, to share simultaneously a single high-speed communications medium, such as a telephone line (Figure 2.5). When used to connect devices with the host computer, the

FIGURE 2.4

A Network Server

A network server typically is a more powerful computer to which other computers, such as PCs, are connected. Although a network server may not be required for a local area network, they are often used for storing programs, files, and databases that can be accessed and used by other computers connected to the network.

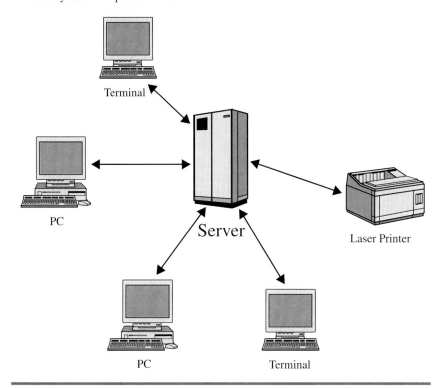

John Chambers

John T. Chambers, president and CEO of Cisco Systems Inc., is a strong believer in the power and future of both highly technical and personal networks.

Following a six-year tenure at IBM and an eight-year tenure at Wang Laboratories, Chambers joined Cisco Systems Inc. as executive vice president in 1991. In 1995 he was promoted to his present position as president and chief executive officer. When Chambers first joined Cisco, the company was a relatively small developer and producer of computer network devices and systems with revenue of $70 million. By late 1998, the company's net worth had increased to more than $100 billion.

Routers are important Cisco products. Routers are electronic devices that direct the flow of information packets between networks and across the Internet. They use a routing table (a kind of road map) to send data from router to router and a set of rules that helps a packet get closer to its destination with each step along the pathway. Routers ultimately deliver the packets to the intended network and ultimately to a computer that reassembles the message.

Chambers was an early visionary who was able to foresee the potential of networks and the Internet. He and Cisco are at the forefront of business and communications technologies. The future of technology, they believe, is about communicating rather than computing power. The electronic devices that people will use to communicate with one another will become as varied and unique, and they will be connected via standardized communications networks. Cisco's technology will reside at all the critical network connections, enabling data to move quickly and efficiently from one place or device to another.

Cisco faces substantial competition in its efforts to create and produce new and powerful devices that will combine text, voice, and video for transmission over networks. Although several companies share this goal, Cisco might well be the dominant player in this area.

To maintain its present leadership position, Chambers and Cisco provide customers with more than just products. The company provides customers with free consulting services, including how to run with the Internet pack, save money, get into new markets, and generally flourish by using the power of networks.

Cisco's business operations are based around the Internet. Eighty percent of Cisco's annual $2 billion in materials purchases are handled via electronic networks, in which computers at either end communicate directly with one another. Cisco itself mainly does only the final assembly of its routers. The company provides its suppliers with detailed orders and descriptions on how to build its components, as well as with computerized scripts for testing those parts. The less time and fewer people Cisco devotes to manufacturing, the better its profit margins.

Cisco also is encouraging its customers to place orders via the World Wide Web. Company executives say Cisco is booking as much as $20 million a day via the Web. The goal is to link Cisco's ordering and production system so tightly that a customer's order triggers component suppliers to ship their parts. That makes products more tailored to customer needs and shrinks inventories. Internally, Cisco now handles all employee expenses and a growing number of customer service and support tasks via Web page applications. Proxy voting for shareholders is a candidate for the Internet.

Profile of Cisco Systems, Inc.

Founded: 1984

Headquarters: San Jose, California

Employees: 14,800 worldwide

CEO and president: John T. Chambers

Web address: www.cisco.com

Sources: Cisco Systems, Hoover's Online, The Router's Line of Work. All contents copyright © 1992–1998 by Cisco Systems, Inc.; Elizabeth Corcoran, "The Cisco Connection: Network Giant Has Seen the Future—And Is Poised to Piece It Together," *The Washington Post*, August 9, 1998. © Copyright 1998 The Washington Post Company

multiplexer accepts data from several devices, combines or *multiplexes* them, and sends them immediately across a single high-speed medium to a second multiplexer that divides or *demultiplexes* the data and then transmits them to the host computer.

Communications often travel over long distances and must travel through networks that may be similar and networks that may be dissimilar. In these cases, special hardware and software technologies, called gateways and bridges, are needed.

GATEWAYS

A **gateway** consists of hardware and software that allows communication between *dissimilar* networks (Figure 2.6). For example, a gateway is needed if paralegal

FIGURE 2.5

A Multiplexer

A multiplexer speeds communications by combining information being transmitted from several low-speed devices, such as PCs, and sending the information concurrently to their destinations. The use of a multiplexer can reduce communications costs when information is sent over long distances.

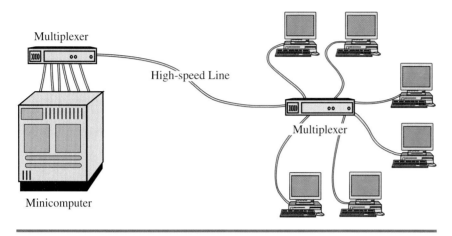

FIGURE 2.6

A Gateway

A gateway consists of hardware and software that provide for the transmission of data between networks that are dissimilar, such as between a ring network and a star network.

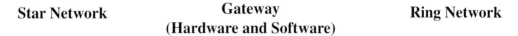

Star Network   **Gateway (Hardware and Software)**   **Ring Network**

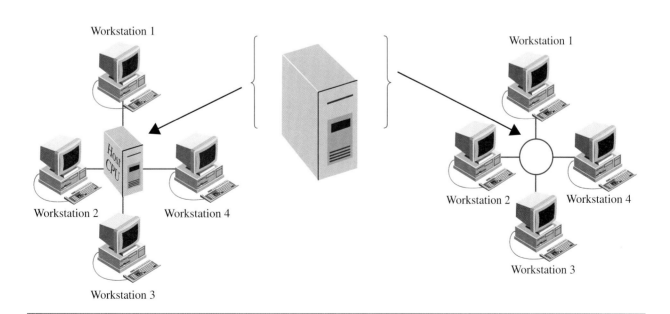

assistants at a law office using a certain kind of network want to retrieve legal information stored on a different type of network.

BRIDGES

A **bridge** consists of hardware and software that allows two *similar* networks to communicate (Figure 2.7). If the paralegal assistants in the previous example want to retrieve legal information stored on the same kind of network the paralegal assistants are using, a bridge connecting the two similar networks allows communications to occur between the networks.

Communications Software

For information to be transmitted between computers using telephone lines and a modem, a special kind of software called **communications software** is required. Communications software allows you to connect your computer to another computer on which programs and data are stored, and to access the stored programs and data. When you buy a new computer with a modem, your computer usually comes with communications software already installed. If not, you can purchase a communications software package from a variety of sources.

FIGURE 2.7

A Bridge

A bridge consists of hardware and software that provide for the transmission of data between networks that are similar, such as between a bus network and another bus network.

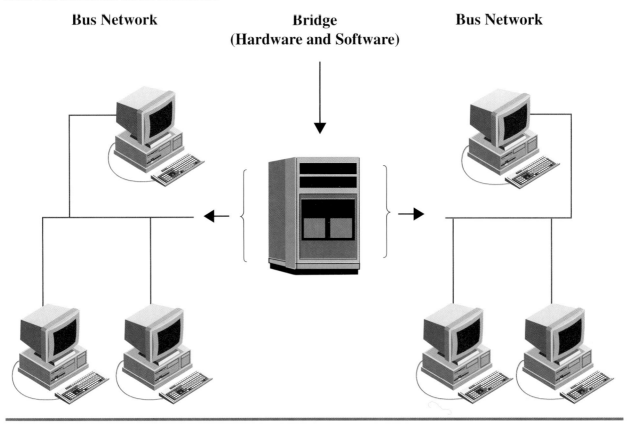

Communications software packages contain a number of useful, but sometimes different, features. Most packages allow you to do the following:

- Send and receive files to and from other computers
- Access other computers around the world
- Send and receive electronic mail messages
- Send and receive faxes
- Access the Internet and online services such as America Online and the Microsoft Network

In addition to those listed, communications software packages often contain other important programs and features. For example, one feature allows you to transmit binary files or ASCII files over a telephone line. A **binary file** is a machine-readable-only file in which data are in the form of only two numbers (0s and 1s). Executable files and numeric files are typically in binary format. An **ASCII file** is a human-readable file in which the data are in the form of human-readable text. For example, a document produced using a word processor contains text and possibly numbers. When the document is saved on a disk, the text is saved along with formatting codes, such as paragraph indents and page breaks. However, the user may choose to save the document as an ASCII file. If so, all text will be saved, but the formatting codes will not be saved.

The more features available with your communications software package, the better. When discussing communications software with a potential supplier, you should inquire about the features available with the communications software package.

Communications Media

A **communications medium** is a physical link that allows a computer in one location to be connected to a computer in another location for the purpose of transmitting and receiving data and information. A variety of communications media are used to move data from one location to another. Telephone lines *(twisted pairs cable)* and *coaxial cable* transmit data through electrical charges or pulses. *Microwaves* and *satellites* send data by way of electromagnetic waves. More recently, *fiber-optic cable* and laser transmission allow data to travel as light pulses, at approximately 186,000 miles per second, or the speed of light. The choice of communications media affects not only the speed of transmissions but the amount of noise (electrical interference) that will exist. For instance, data traveling across fiber-optic cables do not have the electrical interference problems associated with media such as traditional telephone wire.

TWISTED PAIRS CABLE

One of the older communications media consists of insulated wires twisted together to form a cable called **twisted pairs cable** (Figure 2.8). One of the wires in each pair is for sending, the other for receiving. The pairs are often bundled in packs of hundreds or thousands, placed underground, and branched to buildings and individual rooms where they await use in phone jacks. Besides telephone use, twisted pairs are often used to connect computers in networks and transmit data over relatively short distances. This technology is inexpensive but susceptible to noise. To ensure intelligible transmissions, cable lines are refreshed; meaning the signal is strengthened every couple of miles at repeater stations.

FIGURE 2.8
Twisted Pairs Wires

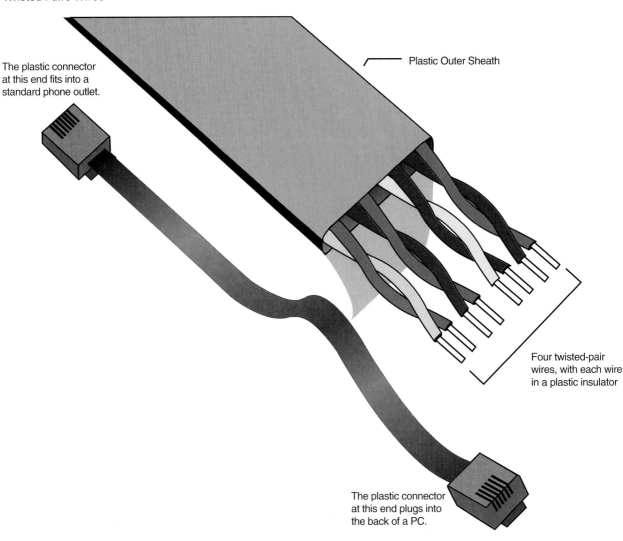

The plastic connector at this end fits into a standard phone outlet.

Plastic Outer Sheath

Four twisted-pair wires, with each wire in a plastic insulator

The plastic connector at this end plugs into the back of a PC.

COAXIAL CABLE

First introduced by the cable television industry to provide clear video transmission, coaxial cable gained popularity for other forms of data transmission due to its speed and lack of noise. **Coaxial cable** is a copper wire surrounded by a thick band of insulation, wire mesh, and rubber or plastic (Figure 2.9). It is more expensive than twisted pairs cable, but it has a higher capacity (100 million bits per second) and can span longer distances than twisted pairs cable before it needs refreshing. Telephone companies use coaxial cable for undersea phone lines as well as for replacing twisted pairs cables underground. It is also popular for connecting computer systems located in the same office building.

MICROWAVE SYSTEMS

A **microwave system** transmits data through the atmosphere in the form of high-frequency signals similar to radio waves. Data are transmitted between

FIGURE 2.9
Coaxial Cable

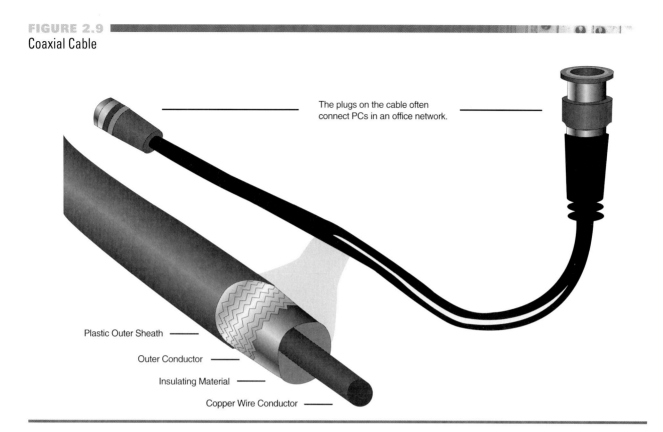

The plugs on the cable often connect PCs in an office network.

Plastic Outer Sheath ———

Outer Conductor ———

Insulating Material ———

Copper Wire Conductor ———

microwave towers, as shown in Figure 2.10. Because the transmitted signals travel in a straight line and do not bend, towers must be in line of sight of one another, meaning there must be no visible obstructions between the sending microwave station and the next microwave station that will receive the transmission.

FIGURE 2.10
Microwave Transmission

A microwave system transmits data through the atmosphere in the form of high-frequency signals similar to radio waves between microwave towers. Because the transmitted signals travel in a straight line and do not bend, towers must be in line of sight of one another. The distance between the towers is dictated by the terrain and the surrounding areas but is rarely more than 30 miles.

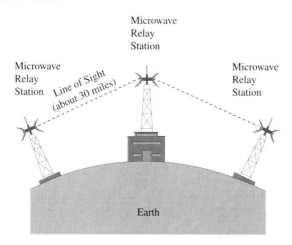

Microwave Relay Station

Microwave Relay Station

Line of Sight (about 30 miles)

Microwave Relay Station

Earth

The distance between the towers is dictated by the terrain in the surrounding areas but is rarely more than 30 miles. At greater distances, noise is picked up because of the moisture in the air and in the earth's surface. Microwave towers are often placed on top of mountains or tall buildings to ensure unobstructed transmission routes. Each microwave tower along the route picks up the signal, amplifies it, and relays the amplified signal to the next tower.

SATELLITE SYSTEMS

Communications satellites are positioned 22,300 miles above the equator and orbit the earth at exactly the same speed as the earth's rotation, making them appear to stay in the same place in the sky when viewed from the ground. This is called a *geosynchronous orbit*. A **satellite** is a solar-powered electronic device that contains a number of small, specialized radios called *transponders* that receive signals from transmission stations on the ground called *earth stations,* amplifies the signals, and transmits them to the appropriate locations (see Figure 2.11). One of the benefits of **satellite systems** is the small number of satellites and repeater stations needed to transmit billions of bits of data per second over long distances. As few as three satellites properly positioned in the sky can provide access to the entire earth's surface.

Satellites only last seven to 10 years in orbit. The cost involved in building a satellite, sending it into orbit, maintaining it, and replacing it can be enormous. This has led to the formation of companies that supply the technology for a fee to those who wish to make use of it but not incur the total cost. Such economies of scale make the technology affordable to a greater number of businesses and organizations. Several satellites are now orbiting the earth to handle domestic and international data, video, and voice communications. For instance, banks use

FIGURE 2.11

Satellite Transmission

Communications satellites are positioned 22,300 miles above the equator and orbit the earth at exactly the same speed as the earth's rotation, making them appear to stay in the same place in the sky when viewed from the ground. A satellite is a solar-powered electronic device that contains a number of small, specialized radios called *transponders*. They receive signals from transmission stations on the ground, called earth stations, amplify the signals, and transmit them to the appropriate locations.

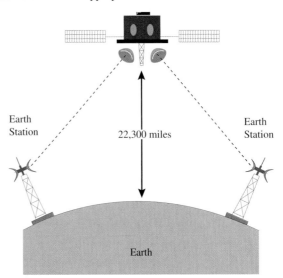

satellites daily to transmit thousands of customer transactions to other banks. A bank in Los Angeles can transfer money from a customer's account at the bank to the customer's account at another bank in Rome, Italy, within a few seconds using satellite transmission.

FIBER-OPTIC CABLE

Fiber-optic cable and lasers represent two technologies that permit the transfer of data with the following benefits:

- High volume
- Speed
- Low error rate
- High security
- Long life

With **fiber-optic cable,** data are converted to light pulses and transmitted by laser through tiny threads of insulated glass or plastic. Each thread, about 1/2000-inch in diameter, is capable of carrying thousands of telephone conversations (see Figure 2.12). Billions of bits of data are transferred per second. Transmission

FIGURE 2.12
Fiber-Optic Cable

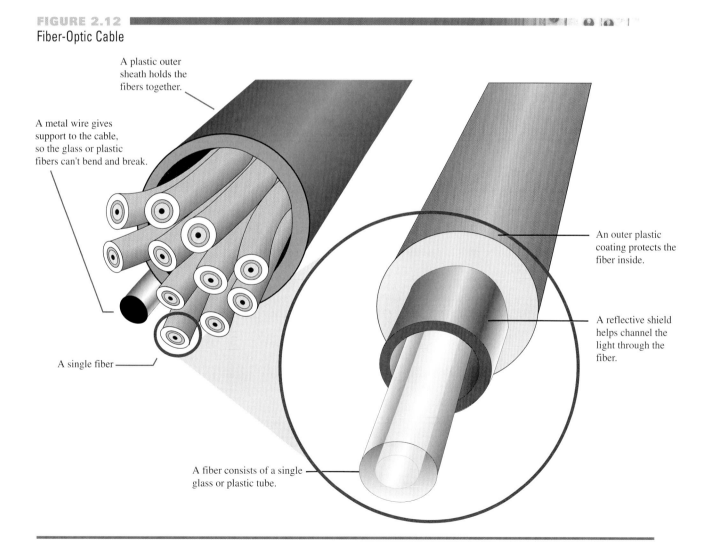

A plastic outer sheath holds the fibers together.

A metal wire gives support to the cable, so the glass or plastic fibers can't bend and break.

A single fiber

A fiber consists of a single glass or plastic tube.

An outer plastic coating protects the fiber inside.

A reflective shield helps channel the light through the fiber.

speed is about 10,000 times faster than that with copper wire. Fiber-optic cable also offers a relatively high degree of safety. It is difficult to tap into a beam of light, and taps are more easily detected. Fiber-optic cable may prove to be more cost-effective than other types of transmission media due to its very long life.

The communications media or channels described here are used throughout the world by individuals, businesses, and organizations. When data are to be sent over long distances, several different media are often used together, as shown in Figure 2.13. Large companies with branch offices throughout the United States, for example, often use combinations of channels to send data between locations. The same holds true for companies with offices in foreign countries.

Characteristics of Data Transmission

Now that you are familiar with the types of media used for communications, it is time to examine the characteristics of the data being transmitted. Following are discussions of the characteristics that govern data transmission.

ANALOG VERSUS DIGITAL TRANSMISSION

There are two distinct forms in which data may exist and can be transmitted: analog and digital. Computers are referred to as digital machines, meaning that data inside a computer are in digital (binary) form (as groups of 0s and 1s) that represent letters of the alphabet, numbers, and special characters. Output from a computer is also in digital form, as groups of 0s and 1s. Thus, **digital data** are data represented as groups of 0s and 1s. For example, the group of numbers "01000001" represents the letter "A" inside the computer. This differs from

FIGURE 2.13

Combined Communications Media

When data are to be sent over long distances, several different media are often used together. Large companies with branch offices throughout the United States, for example, often use combinations of channels to send data between locations. The same holds true for companies with offices in foreign countries.

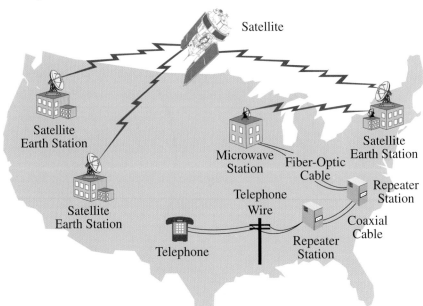

analog data in which the data are represented as patterns of waves. An example is a voice message being transmitted from a caller's telephone to a recipient's telephone along a standard twisted pairs telephone line. Digital and analog formats are illustrated in Figure 2.14.

Information traveling along a standard telephone is normally in analog form. A problem exists when a message in digital form (such as an e-mail message) is transmitted from the sender's computer to the recipient's computer over a standard telephone line. This problem is easily solved by modems.

ISDN

Although traditional communications channels are analog, digital channels are also available that do not require a modem. Some telephone companies now offer customers ISDN service. **ISDN (Integrated Services Digital Network)** is a technology that makes it possible for users to transmit information in digital form along traditional copper-based telephone lines. ISDN is a set of international standards for using software to control the transmission of data, voice, and video simultaneously sent as digital signals over twisted pairs telephone lines. Twisted pairs lines traditionally are used for analog transmissions. ISDN lines are capable of carrying several types of data including voice messages, computer data, graphics, and video along the same channel. Sending data along digital rather than analog lines greatly enhances the speed of communications. Some large companies have begun the development ISDNs that make use of fiber optics for even faster, more secure communications.

Protocols

A **protocol** is a set of rules and procedures for exchanging information between computers. Protocols determine the formats for how computers interact, or communicate, with each other and how errors are detected. Fortunately, a user is not required to perform complex tasks to use protocols. Internet service providers or online services provide the necessary protocols for our use. However, users should be aware of their importance to the Internet and World Wide Web.

FIGURE 2.14
Digital and Analog Data Forms

To send and receive data via a communications medium, such as a standard telephone line, it often must be converted from digital form to analog form and vice versa.

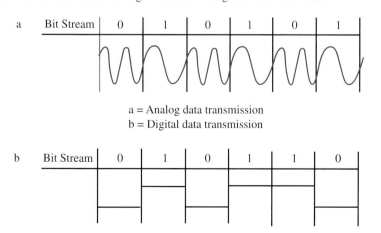

a = Analog data transmission
b = Digital data transmission

FIGURE 2.15

Examples of Communications Protocols

Communications protocols are software programs that define how computers interact, or communicate, with each other and how errors are detected. Fortunately, a user is not required to perform complex tasks to use protocols. Over the years, numerous protocols have been developed. This list shows some of the more commonly used communications protocols.

PROTOCOL NAME	TYPE	DESCRIPTION
ATM	Link	Abbreviation for Asynchronous Transfer Mode. This recently developed protocol allows for the transmission of data, voice, and video.
Ethernet	Link	A widely used protocol for local area networks.
Token Ring	Link	A local area network protocol that allows only one computer at a time to transmit.
AppleTalk	Transport and routing	A protocol that links Apple Macintosh computers.
TCP/IP	Transport and routing	Abbreviation for Transmission Control Protocol/Internet Protocol. This protocol is used with the Internet.
HTTP	Application	Abbreviation for HyperText Transfer Protocol. HTTP is a protocol used by the World Wide Web for transferring pages from the host computer (server) to a user's computer (client). The protocol is typed in lowercase letters as http, followed by a colon, two slashes, the letters www, and a period.
PPP	Link	Abbreviation for Point-to-Point Protocol. This is a protocol that allows a personal computer user with a modem to access the Internet.
FTP	File Transfer	Abbreviation for File Transfer Protocol.

Over the years, numerous protocols have been developed. Efforts are currently underway to simplify protocols by establishing standards that all computer and communications equipment manufacturers will adopt and follow. Based in Geneva, Switzerland, the International Standards Organization has defined a set of communications protocols called the **Open Systems Interconnection (ISO)** model. The United Nations has adopted the ISO model. However, unless and until all manufacturers adopt ISO, a variety of protocols will remain in use. Figure 2.15 shows a sample of communications protocols now being used.

Communications in Action

Computer technology has revolutionized the way we communicate and the way in which much work is done throughout the world. Let's examine a few applications made possible by this new technology.

Voice Mail

How many times have you missed an important telephone call or wasted your time trying to reach someone by telephone? These frustrating experiences can be avoided with the use of **voice mail.** Voice mail systems are the computer version of an answering machine service. They are now popular for business use. Instead of no one answering, or bouncing from one person's telephone to another when the original recipient is unavailable, voice mail allows you to leave a message in a voice mailbox. The spoken message is digitized and stored in bit form. When the receiver retrieves the stored messages, they are reconverted into their analog form so that the messages can be heard.

Electronic Mail

Similar to voice mail is the application of **electronic mail,** or **e-mail.** E-mail is a fast and inexpensive way of sending, receiving, storing, and forwarding messages electronically. E-mail is good for interoffice operations. When someone is on the phone or in a meeting, you can leave the person messages, attach files if necessary, and get on with your business without the aggravation of trying to connect with the individual throughout the day.

By using e-mail, you can send messages to those connected to the system whenever you want, and the recipients can read the messages at their convenience, as shown in Figure 2.16. It is a very efficient means of communication. Everyone connected to the system is given codes that are their addresses. The address is not location specific; messages can be retrieved from remote locations.

FIGURE 2.16

Electronic Mail

Electronic mail, or e-mail, is a fast and efficient way to communicate with others. An e-mail message, can be sent to multiple recipients, and attachments can be added to a message. The recipient of an e-mail message can easily reply and can forward the message to other persons.

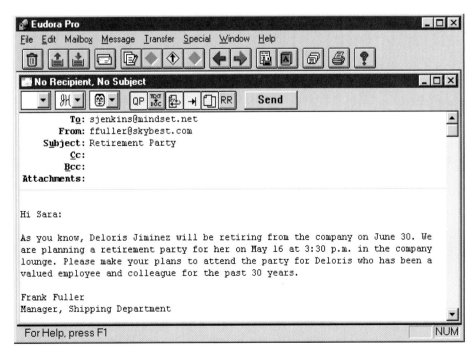

When logged into the system, users are automatically notified when they have mail. This makes it convenient for sales representatives, for instance, who wish to check their messages on a daily basis while they are on the road. Their notebook computers can be connected to their main offices through hotel telephone lines, giving them access to messages that can then be answered and forwarded as appropriate.

Electronic Bulletin Boards

You're already familiar with bulletin boards located in school hallways, dormitories, and student centers. An electronic bulletin board is merely a computerized extension of this bulletin board concept.

An **electronic bulletin board system (BBS)** is a computer system that maintains an electronic list of messages where anyone with access to the bulletin board can post messages, read existing messages, or delete messages. A bulletin board uses data communications systems to link personal computers with messages systems. To use a bulletin board, you need a personal computer, a modem, and the number of a bulletin board service. Just dial the number to see a list of messages and follow the onscreen instructions to post a message or to read one. Bulletin boards represent a cost-effective means for communicating with groups of individuals who have information on topics they wish to share. The Internet is an example of a BBS used by universities and research institutions to facilitate the open exchange of information. The Internet connects hundreds of thousands of computers on networks throughout the world, as you will learn in the next chapter.

Teleconferencing

Teleconferencing allows an "electronic" (instead of face-to-face) meeting to be conducted between people at distant locations. The simplest system is a basic conferencing system, which is a single communications software package installed on a company's mainframe or minicomputer. Each conference participant must have a personal computer with communications software already installed, plus a telephone and a modem. Once connected, all participants may send and receive messages via their computers. Messages can be directed to an individual, a group, or to all participants. The software notifies each participant of an incoming message.

By adding cameras to the teleconferencing system, you have a conferencing system known as **videoconferencing.** A videoconferencing system is shown in Figure 2.17.

Fax Machines

A facsimile machine, commonly referred to as a **fax machine,** makes it possible to transmit documents and drawings over telephone lines from one location to another in a manner that is faster and often cheaper than sending the document overnight or through the mail. Virtually anything that can be written or drawn on paper can be sent to a receiving fax machine. However, fax machines are designed to handle paper that is a specific size; normally sheets of paper that measure 8½ by 11 inches. Some machines use standard plain paper, whereas other machines require a chemically treated, thermal paper.

Each fax machine is given a standard telephone number, called its fax number. To send a document from one fax machine to another, the sender inserts the page(s) into the machine and dials the receiver's fax number. The machine from

FIGURE 2.17
Videoconferencing

which you are sending the fax notifies the receiving machine that the document is being transmitted. The digitized data are transmitted along a telephone line to the receiving machine, where the data are reconstructed into their original form and printed. The machine tells you when your document has arrived at its destination. Fax machines are standard equipment in most modern offices, and PCs can be equipped with add-in boards, called a **fax/modems,** that enable users to send and receive faxes using their computers.

Telecommuting

With rapid advancements in communications technologies, it was only a matter of time before individuals and organizations discovered that some people could perform work for their employer at home, on a part-time or full-time basis. Many employees who work from their homes are involved in data entry operations, such as accessing company files or updating company records. Their work can be accomplished from home using communications systems that allow communication with their organizations' central computers.

When someone works at home and communicates to the office via a computer and modem, it is known as **telecommuting.** This is one of the fastest growing areas in computing today. Between 1987 and 1995, the number of Americans working at home, at least part of the time, increased from 23 million to 51 million and the number continues to rise.

There are advantages and disadvantages associated with telecommuting. Benefits include the following:

- Potential for higher productivity
- Increased job opportunities for persons who are physically impaired and parents with small children
- Reduced travel time and savings on transportation costs
- Reduced office space required

Disadvantages include the following:

■ Lack of face-to-face interactions with fellow workers

■ Inability to obtain technical help quickly if a problem occurs or if questions arise

■ Lack of direct management supervision

Computer Networks

A **network** consists of two or more computers that are connected by means of one or more communications media or channels (Figure 2.18). A network may consist of a collection of computers, terminals, and other equipment that uses communications media to share data, information, hardware, and software. It allows individuals and employees convenient access to programs, data, and other information stored on another computer. It also allows individual users to communicate with each other.

Many networks are based on a **client/server model** for sharing information (Figure 2.19). With this model, one uses a personal computer or terminal (the client) to send information to another computer (the server), which then relays the information back to the client or to another computer (another client). For example, suppose you are a subscriber to the Microsoft Network and send an e-mail message to a friend who is also a Microsoft Network subscriber. The message is sent from your computer (client) to Microsoft's computer (server), which, in turn relays the message to your friend's computer (client). When users subscribe to different services, messages may be routed through more than one server.

A type of network in which data is sent over long distances to computers scattered over a large geographical area is known as a *wide area network*. On a smaller scale, *local area networks* send data among computers located in close proximity to each other, such as in the same building.

FIGURE 2.18

A Network

A network is a computer system that uses communications hardware and software to connect computers. The way in which a network is configured is called the network topology. The computers shown here are linked so that their users can communicate with each other.

FIGURE 2.19
Client-Server Model

Many networks are based on a client-server model for sharing information. With this model, the user employs a personal computer or terminal (the client) to send information to another computer (the server), which then relays the information back to the client or to another computer (another client).

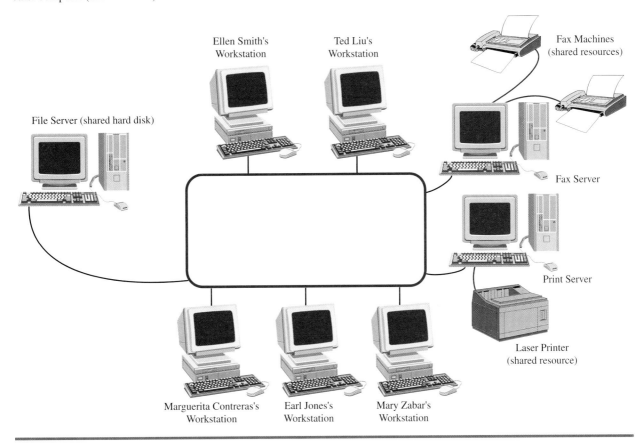

Various types of wide area networks are in use today. In the following sections, we look at some common types. Then we will examine various types of local area networks.

Wide Area Networks

Keep in mind that a **wide area network (WAN)** covers a large geographical area. An example is a long-distance telephone network. Many telephone companies in the United States are linked electronically. They are also electronically linked with other international telephone companies. As communications media and devices continue to improve in speed, capacity, and security, individuals and businesses are discovering more reasons for and benefits in sending and receiving data over long distances through communications media.

METROPOLITAN AREA NETWORKS

Some wide area networks are limited to a smaller geographical area, such as a city or town. In such a case, the network is often referred to as a **metropolitan area network,** or **MAN.**

PUBLIC ACCESS NETWORKS

Networks maintained by telephone companies, called common carriers, such as the Bell network, MCI, US Sprint, and AT&T, are called **public access networks (PANs)** because they provide voice and data communications channels across long distances to anyone who can pay the fee. More recently, companies that own satellite transmission facilities have developed PANs also.

VALUE-ADDED NETWORKS

Companies that use the facilities of common carriers to offer the public additional communications services at a subscription fee are called **value-added networks (VANs).** Services include access to network databases, electronic mail, and information processing. Subscribers need only make a local modem call to access a VAN. Data is then routed between the subscriber's computer, the VAN's local terminal, and a long-distance host computer. Two of the most popular services offered by VANs are information retrieval and electronic data interchange (EDI). Examples of VANs that provide this service include America Online and MCI Mail.

Local Area Networks

Local area networks (LANs) are private communications networks that serve the needs of companies located in the same building with two or more computers or in nearby buildings, such as a college campus. LANs make it convenient to share not only databases but also software and hardware, such as hard disks and printers. LANs typically use a special type of computer, called a **file server,** that allows other computers to share its resources. With a file server and a high-capacity hard disk, called a **disk server,** users can access programs and data just as easily as if they were on their individual hard drives on which the programs and data were stored. Having these items on the disk server frees up space on the hard disks in their individual computer systems for their specific files. Similarly, a **print server** allows multiple users to use the same printer. Sharing resources such as applications programs, expensive hard disk capacity, and high-quality printers over networks saves companies large amounts of money in software and equipment costs.

Network Topologies

Local area networks are often classified by their topologies (physical configurations): star, bus, ring, and token ring. The computers linked in networks are often called **workstations** or *nodes.* **Network topology** refers to the way computers and peripherals are configured to form networks. One way to think of a topology is to examine a map showing roads, rivers, railroads, and other items such as cities and mountains. Looking down at the map, you can view the relationship of various physical locations. A diagram of a network topology is similarly viewed. This allows a viewer to locate each network component. In the following sections, we examine various types of networks, or topologies.

STAR NETWORKS

In a **star network,** multiple computers and peripheral devices are linked to a central, or host, computer in a point-to-point configuration (Figure 2.20). The **host computer** is typically a more powerful minicomputer or mainframe computer. Any communications between the computers must be routed through the host computer. Companies with multiple departments that need centralized access to

FIGURE 2.20

Star Network

In a star network, multiple computers and peripheral devices are linked to a central, or host, computer in a point-to-point configuration. The host computer is typically a more powerful minicomputer or mainframe computer. Any communications between the computers must be routed through the host computer. Companies with multiple departments that need centralized access to databases and files often prefer this topology. One downfall of the star topology is its dependence on the host computer. Because all communications go through the host, the network becomes inoperable if the host fails to function properly.

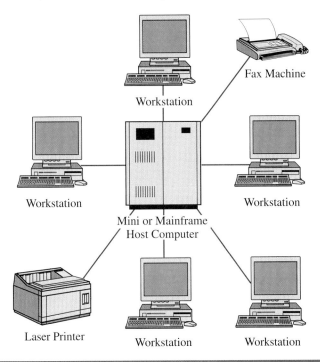

Workstation

Fax Machine

Workstation

Workstation

Mini or Mainframe
Host Computer

Laser Printer

Workstation

Workstation

databases and files often prefer this topology. One downfall of the star topology is its dependence on the host computer. Because all communications go through the host, the network becomes inoperable if the host fails to function properly.

BUS NETWORKS

A **bus network** does not contain a host computer. Instead, all computers are linked by a single line of cable called a **bus,** as shown in Figure 2.21. All communications travel the length of the bus. As they pass, each computer hooked to the network checks to see if it is the assigned destination point. Because there is no host computer, the malfunction of one computer does not affect communications among other computers. Bus topologies commonly use coaxial or fiber-optic cables. The bus network is less expensive than the star network, but it is sometimes less efficient.

RING NETWORKS

In a **ring network,** there is no host computer. Instead, each computer is connected to two other computers in the ring (see Figure 2.22). Communications are then passed in one direction from the source workstation to the destination. If one computer isn't working, the computer is bypassed. One difficulty with ring networks, however, is that if two computers are trying to send communications at the same time, one or both of the messages may become garbled. Ring networks are not used as often as the previous two configurations.

FIGURE 2.21

Bus Network

A bus network does not contain a host computer. Instead, the computers are linked by a single line of cable, called a bus. All communication travels the length of the bus, and each computer hooked to the network checks to see whether it is the assigned destination point. Because there is no host computer, the malfunction of one computer does not affect communications among other computers. Bus topologies commonly use coaxial and fiber-optic cables. The bus network is less expensive than the star network, but it is sometimes less efficient.

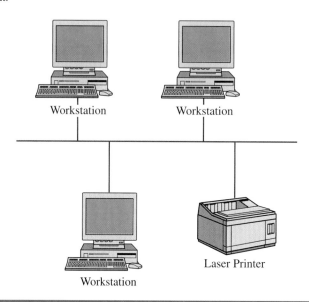

FIGURE 2.22

Ring Network

In a ring network, there is no host computer. Instead, each computer is connected to two other computers in the ring. Communications are then passed in one direction from the source workstation to the destination. If one computer isn't working, the computer is bypassed. One difficulty with ring networks, however, is that if two computers are trying to send communications at the same time, one or both of the messages may be garbled.

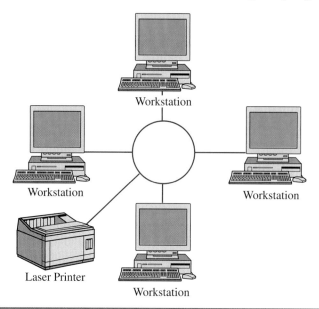

TOKEN RING NETWORKS

To eliminate errors due to two or more communications being sent at the same time, **token ring networks** were developed, in which a pattern of bits, called a **token,** is passed from one computer to another sequentially around the ring. Only when a computer has the token may the computer transmit a communication, as shown in Figure 2.23. The token ring network is more expensive than the others, but it is usually more efficient.

Network Security

Organizations go to great lengths to ensure network security and the security of the programs and information stored on the network. An organization can make certain kinds of information available to some users within the organization while restricting access to other users within the same organization. For example, a business may provide specific access codes only to employees in the accounting department that allows accounting employees to access financial data. Without these codes, other employees cannot access financial data.

Access to a network may also be restricted to users that are issued specific usernames and passwords. A **username** is a name (or word) used to gain access to a computer system. A username may be an abbreviation for the user's full name, such as *rthompson,* for Robert Thompson. A **password** is a secret series of characters that enable a user to access a computer, file, or program. On a network, or other multiuser system, each user must enter his or her password before the computer will respond to commands. This helps to ensure that unauthorized users

FIGURE 2.23

Token Ring Network

To eliminate errors due to two or more communications being sent at the same time, token ring networks were developed in which a pattern of bits, called a token, is passed from one computer to another sequentially around the ring. Only when a computer has the token may the computer transmit a communication.

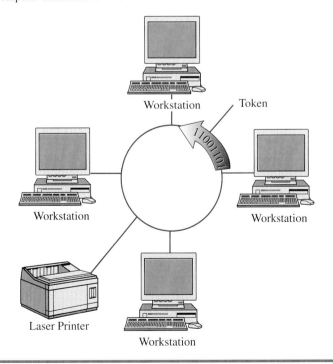

FIGURE 2.24

User Entering a Username and Password

Some computer networks require users to enter usernames and passwords in order to access programs, data, and files stored on the network, thereby assuring that only authorized users will have access.

do not have access to the computer or network (Figure 2.24). Also, access to data files and programs may require a specific password.

Intranets

Many companies, organizations, and government agencies have highly secure networks on which sensitive data (including electronic commerce transactions) are stored. Access to the information is typically restricted only to employees and authorized users.

The prefix *intra* means *within*. Thus, access is restricted to authorized users *within* the agency, company, or organization.

What Is an Intranet?

An **intranet** is a network that is normally restricted to users *within* a company or organization. Intranets typically offer many of the features and services that are available on the Internet (explained in the next chapter). An intranet typically uses the Internet as its transmission medium. Intranet sites are the same as sites on the World Wide Web (also explained in the next chapter), but people on the Internet cannot access information stored on an intranet site.

A main reason for a company or organization's setting up an intranet is to share programs and information among the organization's users, such as managers and employees. Documents for internal use only, including product designs, workplace procedures, and company newsletters, can be placed on an intranet. Transferring files from an intranet is often easier than using floppy disks or CD-ROM disks.

Information transfers over an intranet are relatively fast. This provides for the efficient transfer of video and sound files among intranet users. Product demonstrations and training videos can easily be distributed to anyone connected to the intranet.

Many companies have installed intranets that allow for the transfer of e-mail messages and documents among connected users. This allows users to send and receive e-mail messages with other files, such as a spreadsheet or word processing document, attached to the message.

Many organizations use newsgroups that allow employees to share information about the organization or about a specific project. For example, users working as a team on a specific project can post questions on the intranet so their colleagues working on the same project can view and respond to the questions. Another intranet feature, called *chat groups,* allows users to discuss topics efficiently. Using an intranet feature called *video chat,* a user can hold meetings with users in another office or department.

Any type of computer, such as IBM-compatible and Macintosh, can be connected to an intranet. Also, any type of computer capable of using a special type of software, called a Web browser, can access information available on an intranet Web site. Web sites are explained in the next chapter.

How an Intranet Works

An intranet works the same as a local area network that is *not* connected to other networks outside the organization. Stored information is available to authorized users within the organization and certain kinds of information may be made available only to specific persons, groups, or departments within the organization. For example, access to new product designs may be restricted to employees in the research and design department that have been issued special passwords that allow them to view the data. Figure 2.25 illustrates how a hypothetical intranet works.

Setting Up an Intranet

To set up an intranet, a company's computers are connected to one or more special computers, often referred to as *servers.* A network computer on which programs, data, and other information are stored contains one or more special programs, called a **server,** which allows users to access the stored programs, data, and other information. Technically speaking, a server is a computer program. In a sense, the program listens for a user making a request and responds by performing the requested action (such as downloading a requested program or data to the user's computer.

However, it should be noted that many computer professionals use the term *server* to refer to both the computer and the software that makes it possible for users to access the programs, data, and other information stored on the computer. Throughout the remainder of this book, the term *server* will be used to refer to both the computer *and* the server software.

A **file server** is a computer on which programs, files, and documents are stored. A special type of program allows the stored programs, files, and documents to be shared with computers on the intranet. An intranet may also use a **mail server** on which e-mail messages are stored and routed to their destinations. Other servers, such as a **security server,** may be added to prevent unauthorized access to programs and files stored on the intranet. Other special-purpose hardware devices may also be used, such as routers. A **router** is a specialized electronic device that regulates the flow of information through an intranet. Among other actions, a router chooses the most efficient route for the information to travel.

A company must also install intranet software that, among other things, manages the intranet and provides useful intranet features, such as electronic mail, database management, and security applications. Most intranet software is a collection of various applications contained in one package, called an **intranet suite.**

FIGURE 2.25

An Intranet

In an intranet, access to the organization's stored information is restricted to authorized users. For example, authorized accounting personnel may be allowed to access accounting data but not access marketing data. Access by unauthorized persons is blocked by firewall hardware and software.

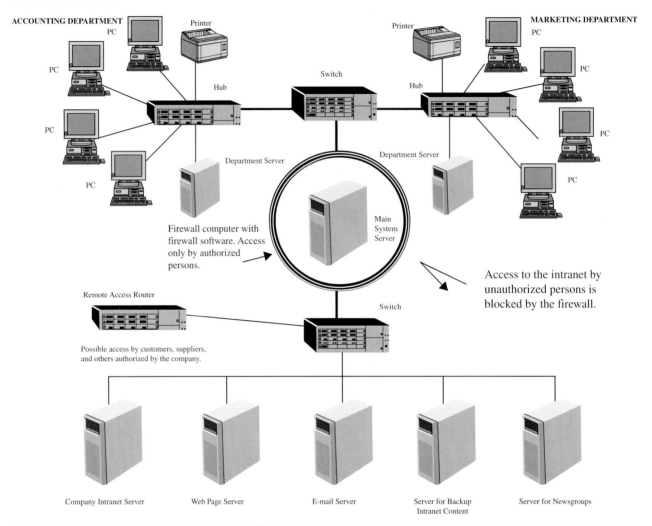

During installation, any combination of applications in a suite can be installed. Examples of popular intranet suites are SuiteSpot from Netscape Communications Corporation, IntranetWare from Novell, and BackOffice from Microsoft Corporation.

Intranet Security

Many organizations that have an intranet are also connected to the Internet. Most use a special computer and software, called a firewall, to maintain security on the intranet to prevent Internet users from accessing information stored on the organization's intranet. A **firewall** is a computer or software that prevents unauthorized individuals from accessing the intranet by preventing a particular address from making requests of a network. Some organizations with intranets restrict employees from accessing certain parts of the Internet, such as chat groups. In such cases, employees are able to view information on an intranet site but unable to view any sites on the World Wide Web. Also, an intranet can be set up so that some intranet applications, such as newsgroups, require a user to enter a user-name and password to view information.

Extranets

Earlier it was noted that intranets are designed mainly for internal use within a company or organization. Variations of intranets, called extranets, have been de-veloped that make certain information and features available to users both inside and outside the company or organization. Thousands of organizations have in-stalled networks on which information is stored that can be shared internally within the organization and also by authorized persons and groups outside the or-ganization. (See Figure 2.26 for one application of an extranet.)

FIGURE 2.26
Electronic Order Form

More and more companies are connecting to the Internet and the World Wide Web to allow customers to order company products elec-tronically. This speeds up the ordering process, resulting in faster deliveries.

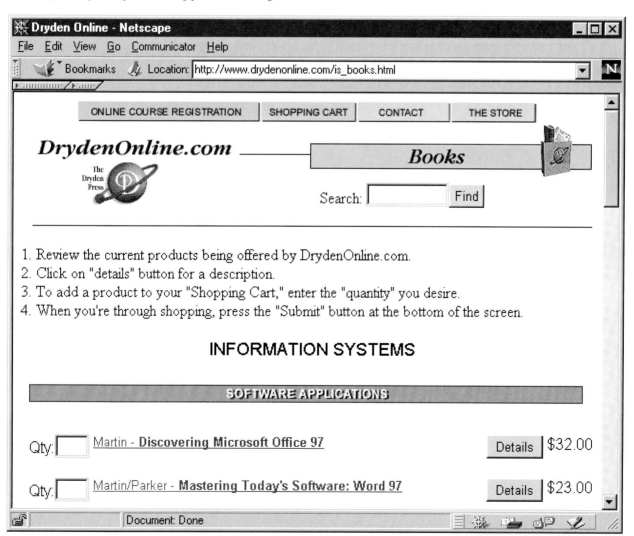

What Is an Extranet?

Simply defined, an **extranet** is a private network set up by a company that allows certain users, such as outside employees and authorized customers and suppliers, to access the company's internal computerized applications and data via the Internet. Some companies restrict access by requiring a user to enter a username and/or password.

Extranet Applications

An extranet can be set up that provides many useful services. If set up properly, mobile workers can connect their notebook computers to a company extranet via a telephone line. Once connected, workers can send and receive e-mail messages. Managers can page mobile workers carrying small pagers. More than 36 million people now use pagers and the number is increasing rapidly. Some newer pagers allow users to exchange e-mail messages with other people having an e-mail connection. Extranets may also allow for the transmission of faxes.

An extranet can be quite useful in human resource development. Many companies are continually recruiting new employees—a sometimes costly activity involving expensive travel, lodging, and other expenses. A company can post announcements of job openings and job application forms, and can provide links for prospective job applicants to other documents containing information about area housing, transportation, medical facilities, schools, and recreation. For employees, insurance claim forms can be posted, as well as forms for filing employee grievances and complaints.

Like intranets, extranets are excellent technologies for doing business. For example, a clothing manufacturer can post an advertisement for bids for raw materials such as fabric, labels, and thread. An accompanying bid form allows potential suppliers to submit a bid to supply these materials quickly and easily.

Extranets are important in supply-chain applications. An extranet can provide for the exchange of information between a company and its suppliers. For example, a company can contact a supplier via an extranet to order materials or inventory items.

Extranets have also proven themselves in the public sector. Government agencies often use extranets to improve social services. Using a computer and a connection, a government employee can check on retirement benefits, sick time, and leave time. Law enforcement personnel can check a person's criminal record. A state trooper can quickly determine whether a particular automobile has been stolen.

The number of potential extranet applications is virtually unlimited. Each day, more applications are being implemented. Many companies and organizations have discovered that their extranets have become an integral part of their daily operations.

Looking Ahead

In this chapter we learned about communications. We learned also that communications allows computers to be linked to form networks in which users of networked computers can communicate and share information. Intranets and extranets were explained, as well as the main purposes of each.

In the next chapter, we will focus attention on the Internet and the World Wide Web. We will learn what the Internet and World Wide Web are and explore ways these two technologies are being used by millions of individuals and organizations around the world.

SUMMARY

Communications, also called data communications, is a broad term that refers to the transmission (sending or receiving) of data and information between two or more computers over communications media, such as standard telephone lines. Other terms that describe communications are telecommunications and teleprocessing. Special communications equipment includes modems, network interface cards, servers, multiplexers, gateways, and bridges. Communications software allows you to connect your computer to another computer, such as a Web server.

A communications medium is a physical link that allows a computer in one location to be connected to a computer in another location for the purpose of transmitting and receiving data and information. Types of communications media include twisted pairs cable, coaxial cables, microwave systems, satellite systems, and fiber-optic cables.

A protocol is a software program containing a set of rules and procedures for exchanging information between computers.

Communications applications include voice mail, electronic mail (e-mail), electronic bulletin board systems (BBS), teleconferencing, videoconferencing, fax machines, and telecommuting.

A network consists of two or more computers that are connected by means of one or more communications media or channels. Many networks are based on a client/server model for sharing information. With this model, one uses a personal computer or terminal (the client) to send information to another computer (the server), which then relays the information back to the client or to another computer (another client).

A wide area network (WAN) covers a large geographical area. Types of wide area networks include metropolitan area networks (MANs), public access networks (PANs), and value-added networks (VANs).

Local area networks (LANs) are often classified by their topologies (physical configurations): star, bus, ring, and token ring. In a star network, multiple computers and peripheral devices are linked to a central, or host, computer in a point-to-point configuration. A bus network does not contain a host computer. Instead, computers are linked by a single line of cable, called a bus. In a ring network, there is no host computer. Instead, each computer is connected to two other computers in the ring. Communications are then passed in one direction from the source workstation to the destination. In a token ring network a pattern of bits, called a token, is passed from one computer to another sequentially around the ring. Only when a computer has the token may the computer transmit a communication.

Organizations often go to great lengths to ensure network security and the security of the programs and information stored on the network by installing special hardware and software, called firewalls, and by requiring users to enter usernames and passwords.

An intranet is a network that is normally restricted to users *within* a company or organization.

An extranet is a private network set up by a company that allows certain users, such as outside employees and authorized customers and suppliers, to access the company's internal computerized applications and data via the Internet.

KEY TERMS

analog data (45)
ASCII file (39)
baud rate (33)
binary file (39)
bridge (38)
bus (53)
bus network (53)
cellular modem (33)
client/server model (50)
coaxial cable (40)
communications (31)
communications
  medium (39)
communications
  software (38)
data communications
  (30)
digital data (44)
disk server (52)
electronic bulletin
  board system (BBS)
  (48)
electronic mail (e-mail)
  (47)
external modem (33)
extranet (60)
fax machine (48)
fax/modem (49)

fiber-optic cable (43)
file server (52)
firewall (58)
gateway (37)
host computer (52)
Integrated Services
  Digital Network
  (ISDN) (45)
internal modem (33)
intranet (56)
intranet suite (57)
local area network
  (LAN) (52)
mail server (57)
metropolitan area
  network (MAN) (51)
microwave system (40)
modem (33)
multiplexer (34)
network (50)
network interface card
  (NIC) (34)
network topology (52)
Open Systems
  Interconnection (ISO,
  International
  Standards
  Organization) (46)

password (55)
print server (52)
protocol (45)
public access network
  (PAN) (52)
ring network (53)
router (34)
satellite (42)
satellite system (42)
security server (57)
server (34)
star network (52)
telecommunications
  (31)
telecommuting (49)
teleconferencing (48)
teleprocessing (31)
token (55)
token ring network (55)
twisted pairs cable (39)
username (55)
value-added network
  (VAN) (52)
videoconferencing (48)
voice mail (47)
wide area network
  (WAN) (51)
workstation (52)

END-OF-CHAPTER ACTIVITIES

Matching

Match each term with its description.

a. star network
b. e-mail
c. local area network
d. firewall

e. communications
f. protocol
g. password
h. extranet

i. gateway
j. network
k. intranet
l. telecommuting

_____ **1.** The combined use of computer systems and communications media for sending and receiving data.

_____ **2.** A set of rules and procedures for exchanging information between computers.

_____ **3.** A fast and inexpensive way of sending, receiving, storing, and forwarding messages electronically.

_____ **4.** Consists of two or more computers that are connected by means of one or more communications media.

_____ **5.** A topology in which multiple computers and peripheral devices, such as printers, are linked to a host computer in a point-to-point configuration.

_____ **6.** A secret series of characters that enables a user to access a computer, file, or program.

_____ **7.** A technology that allows an employee to work at home and communicate with the office via a computer and a modem.

_____ **8.** A private communications network that serves the needs of companies or organizations located in the same building.

_____ **9.** A computer or software that prevents unauthorized individuals from accessing an intranet.

_____ **10.** Hardware and software that allows communication between dissimilar networks.

_____ **11.** A network within a company or organization.

_____ **12.** A private network that allows certain users, such as outside employees and authorized customers and suppliers, to access the company's internal computerized applications and data via the Web.

Review Questions

1. What is the meaning of the term _communications_ as it applies to computing?

2. Explain what a modem is and describe its purpose.

3. Identify several pieces of equipment that may be used to facilitate communications between computers and networks.

4. Identify the types of communications media explained in the chapter.

5. What are protocols? Why are protocols necessary for communications between computers and networks?

6. What is the difference between a wide area network and a local area network?

7. Identify four network topologies.

8. What is the main difference between an intranet and an extranet?

Activities

1. Computers in the computer lab at your school may be linked in a network. Ask your instructor if your lab computers are networked. If so, ask your instructor to explain the type of network your school uses and the type(s) of communications media used to link the computers. Also, ask your instructor which kind(s) of servers are used with the network. After obtaining this information, prepare a written topology drawing showing the devices and how information flows between computers and server(s).

2. Numerous computer magazines contain articles about intranets. Most of the printed magazines are also online and available to you on the Web. Here is a list of some popular magazines that are available online:

MAGAZINE NAME	WEB ADDRESS
PC Magazine	http://www.pcmagazine.com
Infoworld	http://www.infoworld.com
PC Week	http://www.pcweek.com
Datamation	http://www.datamation.com
Computer World	http://www.computerworld.com

For this activity, you can either search through issues of one or more of the magazines in your school's library or visit the magazine's Web site. Find two articles about intranets. After carefully reading the articles, prepare a written summary of each article.

3. Many computer magazines also contain articles about extranets. For this activity, you can either search through issues of one or more of the magazines in your school's library or visit the magazine's Web site. Find two articles about extranets. After carefully reading the articles, prepare a written summary of each article.

4. Several computer companies manufacture and sell servers, including the companies listed here:

COMPANY NAME	WEB SITE ADDRESS
Compaq Computer Corporation	http://www.compaq.com
Dell Computer Corporation	http://www.dell.com
Gateway Computer Corporation	http://www.gw2k.com
IBM Corporation	http://www.ibm.com
NEC	http://www.nec.com
Micron Electronics	http://www.micronpc.com

Visit one of the sites listed and find information about one of the company's servers. Examine the information (called specifications) carefully. Prepare a written list of the server's specifications, including (but not limited to) the server's speed, type of processor(s), and amount of hard disk storage. Be sure to include all of the server's specifications.

5. Your instructor may want to invite someone from the computer technology group on your campus to visit your class to describe how the campus network topology was designed and how it is connected to the Internet. Your class might find it interesting to learn how the current topology evolved from its original topology.

6. This is a team project. Your instructor will divide the class into groups with four or five students on each team. Many computer manufacturers listed in Activity 4 produce and sell network servers. Each team member will visit one of the Internet sites for these companies and view the information about one server available from the company. After reading the information, the team member will prepare a written list of the server's main features. Lists prepared will be assembled into a single report and turned in to the instructor.

CHAPTER THREE

The Internet, the Web, and Electronic Commerce

AFTER COMPLETING THIS CHAPTER, YOU WILL:

1. Explain the nature of the Internet.
2. Briefly explain how the Internet evolved.
3. Briefly explain how information travels across the Internet.
4. Briefly explain the nature of the World Wide Web.
5. Identify four different ways you can connect to the Internet and the Web.
6. Define the terms Web site, Web page, and home page.
7. Explain the purpose of hyperlinks.

8. Briefly explain the nature of browsers and search engines.
9. Identify five applications or purposes for which you might use the Web.
10. Identify and briefly explain three network configurations presented in the chapter.
11. Briefly explain the purpose of transaction processing systems (TPSs).
12. Briefly explain the nature of electronic commerce and give an example of how you might become involved in electronic commerce.

The Internet

By this time, nearly everyone has heard about the Internet and the World Wide Web. The development of the Internet and the World Wide Web has proven to be among the most important, useful, and amazing developments in the history of computing. Both are rapidly becoming commonplace in our modern global society. Each day millions of people use these technologies for a variety of applications and purposes (Figure 3.1).

The Internet affects the way we live, work, learn, play, and communicate. Today, it is shaping our world, our lives, and our future, and it offers us unlimited opportunities. Yet, for some, the Internet still remains a mystery.

What Is the Internet?

The **Internet** (or **Net**) is a global network of computers linked via communications software and media for the purpose of sharing information. In fact, it is the largest and best-known network in the world. Just a few years ago, few people could have imagined such a huge network and the impact it would have on our lives.

All kinds of computers can be connected to the Internet. Your PC, your neighbor's Macintosh, your bank's mainframe system, and NASA's supercomputers can be connected to the Net at the same time (Figure 3.2).

FIGURE 3.1

Using the Internet

FIGURE 3.2
The Internet

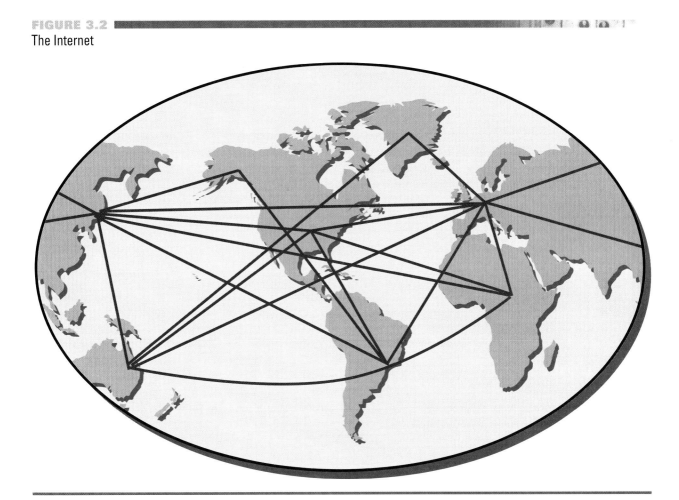

Origin and History of the Internet

Although the Internet and Web are fairly recent phenomena, neither evolved overnight. Their development represents an evolution that will likely continue well into the 21st century and perhaps even beyond.

The Internet was first developed in 1969 as an experimental project. During the Cold War that followed World War II, the U.S. government was concerned that the Soviet Union might be ahead of the United States in the development of defense weaponry. As a result, President Eisenhower authorized the creation of the **Advanced Research Projects Agency (ARPA)** in 1957 to advance the technological defenses of the United States. The agency's name was later changed to **DARPA** (short for **Defense Advanced Research Projects Agency**). One of DARPA's major contributions was the development of the TCP/IP family of protocols that are widely used today. In 1962, Dr. J. C. R. Licklider was put in charge of ARPA's research into how the military could effectively use computer technology. Licklider expressed his ideas about how computers should be used to connect people by means of what he called an "intergalactic network," which became known as **ARPANET** (an abbreviation for **Advanced Research Projects Agency Network**). In 1969 ARPANET was formed to guard defense systems against enemy attack.

A main ARPANET function was to link military scientists working on specialized government projects at four different universities. ARPANET allowed the scientists to communicate with each other and to share data files and research findings via computers. A second function was to create a backup national communications system in case of war or other disaster. The first host computer on the network was at UCLA. Soon afterward, other host computers at Stanford Research Institute (SRI), the University of California at Santa Barbara, and the University of Utah were added. Each location could send and receive data and messages to and from each of the other institutions.

Other college, university, and private sites were later added to ARPANET. By 1971, the ARPANET had grown to 23 host computers connecting universities and government research centers around the country. ARPANET was successfully demonstrated to the public in 1972.

The first international connections to ARPANET occurred in 1973 with the addition of England and Norway. Electronic mail (e-mail) capability was added in 1981. E-mail allowed users to send personal electronic messages to other specified users on the network. Between 1984 and 1989 the number of connected host computers increased from 1,000 to 100,000.

In 1989 a network called NSFNET was developed and implemented by the National Science Foundation. The **NSFNET** was a network that connected various supercomputers located throughout the United States, thereby providing users with enormous computing power. NSFNET soon became the backbone of what we now know as the Internet. During its first few years, private corporations were barred from using NSFNET. NSFNET quickly became the victim of its own success and in 1991 lifted the restriction on commercial use, thereby clearing the way for the Internet, the Web, and the age of electronic commerce.

As more networks became linked, the term *Internet* was coined to represent the interlinking of computer networks around the world. Soon afterward, the two founding networks, ARPANET and NSFNET, became part of the Internet.

In 1991 a team led by Mark McCahill released a program called **Gopher.** Gopher was the first point-and-click way of navigating the files on the Internet. That same year, researcher Tim Berners-Lee at a research institute in Switzerland posted on the World Wide Web the first computer code with the ability to combine words, pictures, and sounds.

A program called **Mosaic,** the first graphics-based Web browser, became available in 1993. Traffic on the Internet quickly increased at an annual growth rate of more than 300,000 percent.

While serving as a member of the U.S. House of Representatives in 1986, Representative Al Gore coined the term **information superhighway,** or **I-Way,** to describe the administration's plan to deregulate communication services and widen the scope of the Internet by opening carriers, such as television cable, to data communication. Later, as vice president, Gore encouraged the development and expansion of the Internet as a vehicle for sharing information worldwide.

The NSFNET reverted back to a research project in 1994, leaving the Internet in commercial hands with the Web comprising the bulk of Internet traffic. A team of programmers at Sun Microsystems release an Internet language, called **Java,** which radically alters the way applications and information can be retrieved, displayed, and used over the Internet.

The Internet celebrated its 25th anniversary in 1994, leaving military strategies that influenced its birth as a mere historical footnote. By this time, approximately 40 million people were connected to the Internet, and more than $1 billion per year had been spent at Internet shopping malls. Internet-related companies, including Netscape Communications Corporation with its Netscape Navigator Web browser, had become the darlings of high-tech investors. The age of the Internet had arrived.

Today, many people telecommute over the Internet, allowing them to choose where to live based on the quality of life rather than their proximity to work.

E-Commerce Technology

VideoGate Technologies Provides Face-to Face Dealing on the Internet

VideoGate Technologies, located in Charlotte, North Carolina, has attracted its first customers for a potentially groundbreaking video call center technology that allows Internet users to see and talk to sales representatives while shopping and banking online. Companies already signed up include Hendrick Automotive Group, Man Travels, TeamVest, Corporate Fleet Services, and Central Piedmont Community College.

Companies will pay $1,000 to $4,000 a month for the call center technology and listings on VideoGate's Web site. VideoGate's Web site (www.videogate.com) will serve as a sort of video call center search engine.

According to Richard D'Agostino, VideoGate's founder and president, "It's going to change electronic commerce." D'Agostino stated that if Internet shoppers have questions about a product, such as an automobile or a mortgage, or an airline schedule, they can get answers instantly "as we've done it for ages and ages—face to face."

Computer users with VideoGate's free software and a high-speed connection now can shop for cars or corporate jets or plan trips by conversing with on-screen customer service operators via the Web. Those operators, in turn, will be able to lead customers through sales presentations or help them fill out online forms—such as loan applications—by remotely controlling customers' computer screens.

Videoconferencing over the Internet has been cumbersome because most consumers now connect to the Internet using telephone modems at speeds between 28.8 and 56 kilobits per second—too slow for full-motion video. However, the arrival of faster modems, such as cable modems or high-speed telephone lines, will make Internet video more practical.

New services will include Time Warner's Road Runner cable modem service, which is expected to be available soon throughout Mecklenburg County, North Carolina. VideoGate's user software soon will be available for download free from Time Warner's Charlotte, North Carolina, Road Runner Web site. Other services may be expected to provide similar services in the near future.

Source: *The Charlotte* (North Carolina) *Observer,* October 27, 1998, pp. 1D and 2D.

Schools use the Internet as a huge electronic library with untold possibilities. Physicians use the Internet to consult with other physicians half a world away. As the next generation of people grows up, accustomed to communicating through a keyboard, life on the Internet will become an increasingly important part of life on Earth (Figure 3.3).

FIGURE 3.3

Internet Time Line

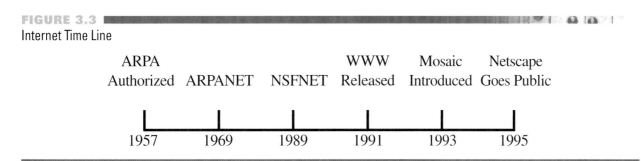

ARPA Authorized	ARPANET	NSFNET	WWW Released	Mosaic Introduced	Netscape Goes Public
1957	1969	1989	1991	1993	1995

How Information Travels across the Internet

If you're like most Internet users, you might wrongfully assume that the transmission of information across the Internet is a simple process. On the contrary, the process is actually quite complex.

To understand how information travels across the Internet, let's assume that you have just completed a research project for your instructor and that your typed report consists of several hundred pages that are due the next day. Assume also that the post office and parcel delivery services no longer accept large packages for overnight delivery. One alternative would be to divide your report into small groups (for example, five pages in each group), insert each group in an envelope, and mail all the envelopes at the same time hoping all will arrive on time. Upon arrival, your instructor would be able to reassemble all the pages. As awkward as this may seem, this scenario illustrates the how the Internet works.

When information is sent across the Internet it is first divided into fixed-length blocks of data, called **packets,** by the **Transmission Control Protocol/Internet Protocol (TCP/IP),** a protocol that governs the flow of data across the Internet by specifying the rules for creating, addressing, and sending packets. This process is known as **packet switching.** The TCP portion divides the message you are sending into packets and then numbers each packet so that the message can be reconstructed at the receiving end. The IP portion sends each packet on its way by specifying the IP addresses of the sending and receiving computers so that routers will be able to route the packets to the appropriate computer. A long file, such as the research report in the previous paragraph, may actually be broken into several hundred packets.

There are two reasons why information is divided into packets. The first is that many messages are flowing across the Internet at the same time. The packets may be routed to take advantage of the best available Internet resources, avoid busy lines, and balance the workload along the Internet. For example, if one part of the Internet (for example, a particular telephone line) is not working properly, the packets can still get through via other routes. The second reason is to assure that the information arrives correctly. Noise or static on a telephone line can be devastating if an entire message, such as a large file, is being transmitted and a small segment (even one or two bytes) is garbled. Sending information in smaller segments (packets) and verifying that the information was received correctly helps ensure the accuracy of the information. If one or two packets are received incorrectly, the entire message does not have to be sent again.

During transmission, packets are sent from your computer to your local network, Internet service provider, or online service. From there, they are sent through many levels of computers, networks, and communications media before reaching their final destination that may be in another city or in another country. A variety of hardware devices process the packets and route them to their appropriate destinations. These devices (explained in Chapter Two) include hubs, bridges, gateways, routers, and repeaters.

Despite its size and complexity, the Internet works extremely well at handling millions of messages every day. Moreover, continuing improvements in hardware and software will render the Internet and Web even more efficient and useful in the days and years ahead.

Different types of computers can connect to the Internet and communicate with each other because they all speak the same kind of "networking language." A main "language" that allows various kinds of computers to be connected to the Internet is TCP/IP. Many other protocols are also used with the Net.

When you're using TCP/IP, your computer is assigned a unique number, known as an **Internet Protocol address** or simply **IP address.** (In a way, an IP address is like a phone number.) An IP address consists of a series of numbers separated into groups by periods. An example is 205.73.39.211, which is the address of a specific computer; no other computer has this same IP address number. It allows you to have your own "identity" on the Net. A computer that is assigned an IP address can "talk to" other computers with IP addresses. On the Net, there are countless computer-to-computer connections like this at any given time.

The World Wide Web (WWW)

During its early years the Internet was difficult to use because it was slow and users were required to enter complex commands because user-friendly graphical user interfaces (GUIs) had not yet been introduced. Thus, Internet use was limited primarily to academic settings. This changed in 1989 when Berners-Lee proposed the idea of a *World Wide Web.* He envisioned the concept of organizing information stored on the Internet into pages called *Web pages.*

The Web gained momentum when Microsoft's graphical user interface (GUI), called Windows 3.0, was introduced. As the use of Windows 3.0 and later versions became widespread, Web browsers designed to work smoothly with Windows's graphical user interface were developed, making Web surfing easy and even fun for users. Within a few years, Berners-Lee's vision had become a reality, the result being the evolution of the World Wide Web. Today, the Web is the most interesting, useful, and fastest growing part of the Internet.

The **World Wide Web** (also called the **Web, WWW,** or **W3**) is a global system of linked computer networks that allows users to jump from one place on the Web to another place on the Web. It is a retrieval system based on technologies that organize information into Web pages.

In the previous chapter, you learned that access to some networks may be restricted to authorized users. For example, some information stored on intranets is restricted to authorized users with passwords. Thus, not all sites on the Internet are available to everyone. Sites that are accessible to anyone are called **Web sites** and are a part of the World Wide Web. Therefore, the Web is smaller than the Internet but is the fastest growing part of the Internet.

The amount and kinds of available information varies among Web sites and is in the form of Web pages. A **Web page,** sometimes called a document, is a hypermedia file stored at a particular Web site. A **hypermedia file** is a file containing any combination of text, graphics, sound, and video. Web pages may also contain one or more hyperlinks to other Web sites and to other pages available at the same site or at a different Web site. A **hyperlink** (or simply **link**) is in the form of bold-faced text, underlined text, or an icon that, when clicked on using a mouse, takes you to another Web site or Web page.

Connecting to the Internet and the Web

Your computer can be connected to the Internet in one of the following ways.

- ■ *Direct connection to the Internet.* The fastest way to access the Internet is with a direct connection. To have a direct connection, your computer must be configured with TCP/IP software and must be connected to a local area network (LAN) that is linked to an Internet host computer. Many colleges, businesses, and other organizations are connected in this way. At many colleges, all a student needs to access the Internet is to enter a valid username and/or password.

■ *Connect via (subscribe to) an online service.* An easy way to connect to the Internet is to subscribe to a commercial online service, such as the Microsoft Network (MSN) or America Online (AOL). For users working from their homes and for those wanting to link their home personal computer to the Internet, this is a popular choice. Online service companies provide an electronic gateway to the Internet that allows subscribers to access many of the Internet's most popular features, including electronic mail. The gateway links a subscriber's computer to the Internet.

■ *Connect via an Internet service provider.* Many companies offer connections to the Internet for a fee. An example might be a local cable TV provider. To sign up, some companies send the customer one or more diskettes or a CD-ROM and a packet of written information explaining the service, rate charges, and installation instructions. After the software is installed, the customer dials into the provider's host computer. Once online, the customer is on the Internet and has access to all the Internet's features.

■ *Connection via long-distance telephone companies.* The federal government has eased regulations of the telecommunications industry. As a result, several companies are entering the competition of providing telecommunications services, and more technologies are emerging. In 1996 AT&T began offering its 80 million residential long-distance customers access to the Internet at an initial cost of $19.95 per month for unlimited access. Sprint and MCI also offer access to customers. Some smaller utilities companies are entering this competitive arena. Internet and World Wide Web service by long-distance telephone companies will make use of standard telephone lines and equipment already in place. Most users having a telephone can obtain access to the Internet and World Wide Web.

The process of connecting a personal computer to the Internet can be accomplished easily. Appendix A contains detailed information about how you can gain access to the Internet. Appendix B explains the nature of browsers and search engines and how they can be used to take full advantages of opportunities available on the Internet and the Web.

Accessing and Using the Web

The emergence of Microsoft's Windows 3.0 (and later versions) with its graphical user interface, along with improved computers and software with advanced graphics capabilities, has stimulated the general public's interest in the Web. These advancements allow you to access the Web by using a mouse to point to and click on an icon on the screen (Figure 3.4). An **icon** is a small picture or symbol on a computer screen that represents an object, a program, or an activity. After gaining access to the Internet, you can click on an icon to activate a program that allows you to move from place to place on the Web.

To access and move about (usually called **browsing** or **surfing**) the Web, you must have a navigational program, called a browser, installed on your computer or network. A **browser** is a software tool (program) that makes it easy for you to find and display Web pages by removing the complexity of having to remember the syntax of commands to find and display the pages. In short, a browser allows you to navigate the Web easily and quickly.

Today, many browsers compete for a share of the browser market. The two most popular browsers are **Netscape Navigator** from Netscape Communications Corporation and **Internet Explorer** from Microsoft Corporation. Either browser can be downloaded for free from the company.

FIGURE 3.4

Windows Desktop with Two Browser Icons

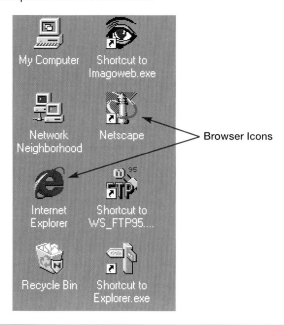

Browser Icons

Most of the early browsers were stand-alone products. Today, many software products have one or more built-in browsers, allowing you to switch back and forth between a browser and other applications.

If you subscribe to an Internet service provider or to a commercial online service company, such as the Microsoft Network or America Online, the company will include at least one browser with the software you receive to install on your computer. Before subscribing to an Internet service provider, you should inquire about the programs and features available with the software.

When surfing the Web, you can view pages consisting of multimedia that often include a combination of text, graphics, video, and sound. When you first access a specific Web site, the first page you will see is that site's home page. A site's **home page** often contains links to other pages at that site or to other Web sites.

The Web uses a language, called **HyperText Markup Language (HTML),** which allows you to view Web pages (Figure 3.5). The language is designed to allow Web page developers to create Web pages in which the appearance, or design, of the pages is determined by the developer. Web browsers have the ability to display Web pages in HTML format. Thus, HTML is designed to allow for presentations from computers to people. A new and improved Web language, called **eXtensible Markup Language,** or **XML,** is gaining in popularity among companies that develop and sell Web browsers. XML describes the content of the information rather than the physical appearance of the information as displayed by a browser. Thus, XML provides for presentations from one computer to another computer. Microsoft Corporation now uses XML in the development of its newer browsers and Netscape plans to use it in its newer browsers.

A Web browser program, such as Microsoft's Internet Explorer or Netscape's Navigator, is easy to learn and use. After activating either browser, you issue a request to visit a specific Web site or page by simply typing an address, called the **URL** (short for **Uniform Resource Locator** and pronounced "earl"), for the site you want to visit and then pressing the Enter key. Within a few seconds, the site's home page will appear on the screen.

Netscape Communications Corporation

Netscape Communications Corporation, located in Mountain View, California, is a leading provider of Internet applications software that supports information exchange and commercial transactions over the Internet. The company was founded in 1994 by Dr. James H. Clark, who earlier founded Silicon Graphics, and by Marc Andreeson, who created the Mosaic browser, which featured a graphical user interface that greatly simplified Internet navigation. The primary mission of Netscape is to be a leading provider of software that links people and information over intranets and the Internet.

In 1994 Netscape developed and refined an innovative way to distribute software when it made the first copies of its Web browser, called Netscape Navigator, available for download over the Internet. Netscape's Internet Web site is now the most heavily trafficked site in the world, serving close to five million users and receiving more than 120 million hits each day. The site provides both information and services, ranging from technical support to the ability to purchase and download numerous Netscape software products. It also provides a showcase of both Netscape technology and the technologies and services offered by Netscape partners and developers. Netscape maintains Web sites in 10 languages, communicating the latest intranet and Internet company news to users and customers worldwide.

The company's Netscape Communicator software is an integrated set of client programs for open mail, groupware, editing, calendaring, Web browsing, and pushing content delivery. Together with Netscape SuiteSpot servers, Netscape Communicator advances the features and capabilities available to users of the Internet and corporate intranets. Communicator software includes a variety of applications including Navigator, a Web browser, which is one of the most popular tools for accessing the World Wide Web and journeying through cyberspace. The company also offers a full line of clients, servers, development tools, and commercial applications to create a complete platform for next-generation, live online applications.

Netscape's electronic commerce software, called CommerceXpert, consists of five products—Netscape ECXpert and DeveloperXpert, Netscape SellerXpert, Netscape BuyerXpert, Netscape PublishingXpert, and Netscape MerchantXpert—for buying, selling, merchandising, and delivering content over the Internet. Based on the same open protocols and scalable security architecture used for communication over the Internet, the CommerceXpert family provides the infrastructure that enables cross-company transactions and the business applications for selling, procuring, and merchandising. In short, CommerceXpert allows companies to automate their procurement processes as well as market, sell, and deliver personalized content and services directly to customers over the Internet.

The Internet—which interconnects thousands of public and private networks worldwide—provides millions of users with access to information from around the globe. This complex web of networks forms the pathway for a global information revolution that will eventually link businesses, public and private agencies, and educational centers with one another and with customers. In addition, businesses are rapidly adopting this technology for their own internal use, building private enterprise networks, or intranets, that serve as a rapid and efficient means of sharing information and providing services within companies, and between companies and their partners and customers. Accessing, navigating, publishing, and sharing information over the Internet and intranets has created a new market opportunity—one that Netscape Communications Corporation was founded to address.

FIGURE 3.5

A Web Page and Corresponding HTML Code

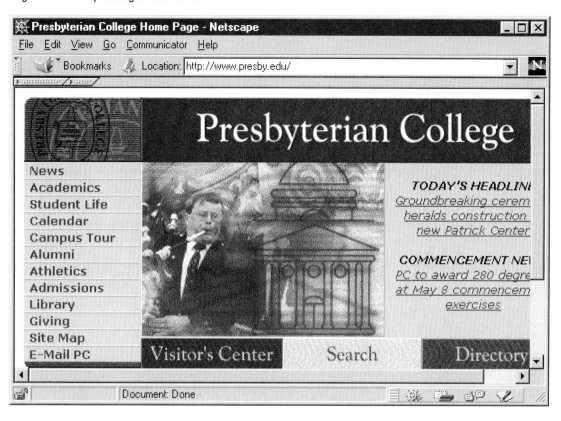

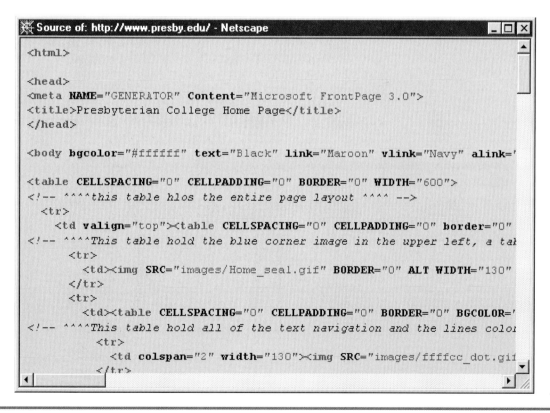

FIGURE 3.6
A Uniform Resource Locator (URL)

Bookmarks   Location: http://www.presby.edu/home.htm

A Web address is somewhat similar to an address placed on the envelope containing a message being mailed to another person. After entering (typing) the correct URL in the specified area of your Web browser's home page, the site's home page will be displayed on your screen, as shown in Figure 3.6.

Most Web pages use a communications protocol called **HTTP,** which stands for **HyperText Transfer Protocol,** for transferring data from the host computer to your computer. Many addresses are typed in lowercase as *http,* and followed by a *colon, two slashes,* the letters *www,* and a *period.* However, not all Web addresses require that the letters *www* be typed as a part of the address. For example, the address for Netscape's home page is *http://home.netscape.com.* There are also other address formats for Web sites.

The first part of the address usually (but not always) consists of the letters *http* followed by a *colon* and *two forward slash characters.* This group of characters identifies the specific protocol to be used (in this case the Hypertext Transfer Protocol, or http). The letters *www* indicate that the site or page you are seeking is located on the World Wide Web.

The second part of the address is the *domain name,* which is the Web address of the computer where the Web page is located. The domain name includes periods and may be followed by a slash. In Figure 3.7, the domain is NASA, which is a government agency.

The third part of the address, which is optional, is the file specification. The *file specification* is the name of a particular file or file folder. At some Web sites a vast amount of information is available for retrieval and viewing. At these sites, information is often arranged and stored in folders, just as you might store information in folders in a file cabinet. If you know the name of the particular file or page you are seeking, or the name of the folder containing the information, accessing the information is easier and faster (Figure 3.8).

After requesting to visit a particular site by typing the site's URL and pressing the Enter key, the request is sent to the Internet where **Internet routers** examine

FIGURE 3.7
Address for the NASA Web Site

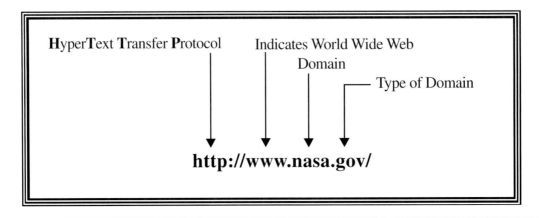

FIGURE 3.8
Address for a Specific Folder

Bookmarks   Go to: www.harcourtcollege.com/infosys/fullerec/student/

the request to determine the specific Web server to which the request is to be sent. The Web server receives the request and uses the "http" communications protocol to determine which page, file, or object is being requested. Upon finding the requested home page, file, or object, the server sends it back to your computer where it is displayed on the computer screen.

Internet and Web Size and Demographics

The Internet is already enormous and is growing rapidly. Because of its size and continuing growth, it is difficult (perhaps even impossible) to determine the size of the Internet. If you research its size, you will find conflicting information on the number of Web sites, the number of users, and so on. Despite the conflicting figures, some estimates of its size and demographics gathered from various sources are listed here. Keep in mind that the Internet is expanding rapidly and the numbers are changing daily.

- The Internet consists of more than 100,000 networks.
- There are more than 10 million host computers on the Internet. (A host computer is defined as a computer with at least one home page.)
- There are between 35 million and 80 million users worldwide.
- There are 3 million computers connected to the Internet.
- More than 21,500 organizations are connected to the Internet.
- Internet users are located in nearly 150 countries.
- There are between 100,000 and 400,000 Web sites on the Internet.
- The average age range of Internet users is 30 to 35.
- The average income range of Internet users is $50,000 to $70,000 per year.

Several research organizations conduct periodic surveys of Internet and Web usage and demographics. Each year, the Georgia Institute of Technology conducts a survey of Internet and Web usage and demographics and compiles and publishes the results. A survey was run from April 10, 1998, through May 15, 1998, in which more than 10,000 Web users participated. Complete survey results can be seen at http://www.gatech.edu/gvu/user_surveys.

Following is a summary of statistics from the Georgia Tech, and other, research surveys:

- The number of U.S. households online continues to increase, and will continue to do so in the years ahead. In recent years, the general demographics of the user population have moved closer to the demographics of the general population.
- The age of the average Web user is 34.1 years. Although 36.4 percent of users in the United States are more than 40 years old, the average age of European users is in the 21- to 30-year-old range. Among all respondents, users in the 21- to 30-year-old range have the most online experience.

- Females represent 38.7 percent of all users. Europe is considerably less gender-balanced with females accounting for only 16.3 percent of users. For the rest of the world (mostly Canada and Australia, but not the United States), females account for 30.5 percent of users. Younger users are more likely to be female. In the age range 11 to 20, an impressive 43.8 percent are female, while in the 50 and over range, 33.9 percent are female. Among first-time users, 51.7 percent are female compared to 48.3 percent male.

- The average educational level of users is declining. However, most users are highly educated with 80.9 percent having at least some college experience and 50.1 percent having obtained at least one college degree. People who have used the Internet for four years or more are likely to have advanced degrees (such as a master's or Ph.D.) than newer users.

- Among all users, 32.7 percent spend an average of 10 to 20 hours using the Web each week, 26.4 percent spend more hours using the Web, and 40.9 percent spend fewer hours using the Web. Those who have used the Web longer tend to spend more hours online than those who have used the Web for a shorter period of time.

- The number of Web users is increasing worldwide. More than one million Mexican users are now online. Nearly one million Russian households are now online and the number is increasing rapidly. At present, European and Asian countries represent the fastest growing segments of the Internet.

- The dominant language on the Internet is English. English is used by 56 percent of users worldwide. However, many other languages are also used by the other 44 percent of users (or 56 million users worldwide). Figure 3.9 shows the most popular non-English languages and the percentage of users using a non-English language.

These figures suggest that the Web's size and range of applications will continue to grow rapidly. Every day more computer users are going online. Some will be content to curiously surf the Web, whereas others will be more interested in online shopping. Educational institutions are going online to offer distance-learning

FIGURE 3.9

Non-English Languages Used on the Internet

A variety of languages are used on the Internet. In addition to English, Spanish and Japanese are widely used languages.

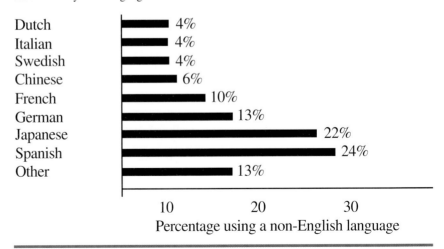

opportunities to students—particularly older students. Businesses appear eager to take advantage of online opportunities to market their products and services. Later chapters of this book focus on how businesses use the Internet and the Web to improve productivity and increase profits.

Internet and Web Applications and Uses

The Internet today is a worldwide computer network, linking individuals, organizations, and countries in a vast blanket of connections. It provides users with access to information sources, databases, libraries, multimedia, and much more. Perhaps equally important, it provides an efficient way for companies and organizations to conduct business operations within the organization, with suppliers and customers, and with others. Also, it provides an efficient and relatively inexpensive way for individuals and small companies to market products and services and to conduct other business activities.

The Internet offers you immediate information search and retrieval capabilities. It also offers global communications at little or no cost. These two features make it a strong competitor for companies and organizations such as the U.S. Postal Service, telephone companies, and FedEx. You control the medium. You determine the content of the message and who receives it. Most correspondence is done so quickly it can be considered almost real time (almost instantly).

Internet use is not limited to private individuals and businesses. Medical expertise in the finest research hospitals is immediately available for consultation by doctors working in remote regions of Africa, India, or South America. Students can correspond with professors at their school and with other individuals throughout the world. Online shopping on the Internet has exploded in recent years and will become even more common in the future.

As you can see, the Internet and the Web offer a variety features, applications, and services. The following sections explain briefly some common ones.

Electronic Mail

An **electronic mail system** allows you to send and receive messages electronically through, and between, networks from one computer to another computer. Each user of the Internet has a unique e-mail address. Many users have multiple e-mail addresses depending on their location and purpose. A person's e-mail address might be found on a Web page, on a business card, in an Internet service provider's directory of users, in a college or university's faculty and student directory, in a newspaper or magazine advertisement, or in a listing of company employees. For example, the Boeing Company's internal mailing list contains more than 150,000 employee e-mail addresses. Figure 3.10 shows an example of a typical e-mail address.

FIGURE 3.10

A Typical E-Mail Address

INDIVIDUAL'S NAME	INDIVIDUAL'S E-MAIL ADDRESS
John Smith	*jsmith@mindscene.com*

Finding Information

A vast storehouse of information awaits you on the Web. Easy-to-use search engines provide you with a way to search for, locate, and view information. A **search engine** is a software program that facilitates queries by allowing you to enter search criteria to locate specific information on the Web. A **query** is a word or phrase entered in a search engine program that specifies the type of information you want to view. In short, a search engine allows you to search for, locate, and retrieve information on the World Wide Web. Unlike a browser, in which an address is entered to access a specific Web site, a search engine allows you to locate specific information and automatically retrieve Web pages by entering search criteria (a query). For example, assume you want to find information about wolves for a report you are writing for a science class. You can use a search engine to retrieve a list of articles on this topic simply by typing your search criteria—*wolves* in this case—into the search box and clicking on the search button. A list of articles will appear on your screen. Then, you can view one of the articles just by clicking on it, as shown in Figure 3.11.

Many excellent search engines are available. Some of the more popular names include Yahoo!, Hotbot, WebCrawler, Excite, Lycos, and AltaVista. Also, some browsers contain a *Search* button. By clicking on the Search button, a list of search engines appears from which you can make a selection.

FIGURE 3.11

List of Articles Resulting from a Query

Some search engines do a better job of searching that do others. AltaVista, for example, searches deeper than most by searching a larger number of databases.

Information Retrieval

Universities, libraries, and government agencies have large databases filled with information available to Web users. By simply logging in, you can research specialized topics, such as geography or genetics. Much of the 1990 federal census data, the world's largest database, is available for public viewing. It contains extensive national and regional information about housing and population demographics for more than 270 million Americans. Students find this area helpful for doing their course research projects (see Figure 3.12).

Accessing Files with File Transfer Protocol (FTP)

You have learned that millions of Web pages are available on the World Wide Web and that these pages can be accessed using search engines. Many more files and programs are available on the Internet that are not part of the World Wide Web. You can access these files and programs using an Internet service called **file transfer protocol,** abbreviated **FTP.**

FTP is a popular use of the Internet that allows you to retrieve files from another computer on the Internet to your computer—a process called **downloading.** You can download many types of files, including text files, files that you can run

FIGURE 3.12

Home Page of the U.S. Census Bureau

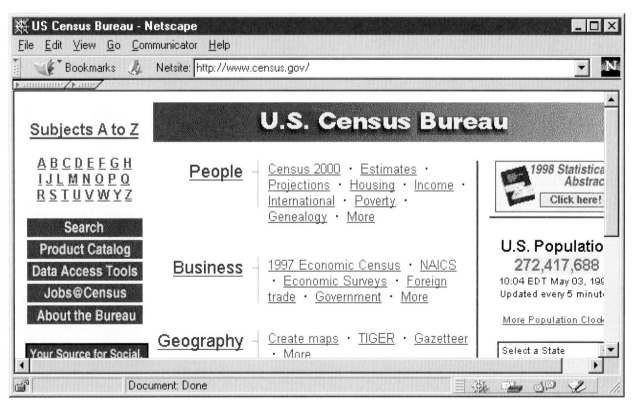

on your computer, graphics files, and audio files. People using FTP download many files daily. FTP can also be used to transfer files from your computer to another computer—a process called **uploading.**

An FTP site is a computer on the Internet where files are stored. Colleges and universities, government agencies, companies, organizations, and individuals maintain FTP sites. Some FTP sites allow for **anonymous access,** which means that you can access files at these sites without entering a user ID or a password. Some anonymous FTP sites allow you to view files without having to enter anything at all. Others allow you to access files by entering the word *anonymous* when prompted to enter your user ID or password.

Some FTP sites are private, allowing only users with account numbers and passwords to access files. To access files at these sites, you must use an authorized user ID and password.

FTP works on a client-server model. To transfer files, you must have FTP client software installed on your computer. A program on the FTP server called an FTP daemon enables you to transfer (upload or download) files.

FTP has a set of commands used to transfer files. To upload or download files, normally you enter an account number (or username) and password. However, if you are using FTP with some software, including Netscape Navigator, you do not have to enter commands. All you need to do is point and click, just as you would to select hyperlinks.

Files and subdirectories at FTP sites are stored in different directories, just as some files stored in your computer are stored in directories. Like files stored on your computer, every file has a filename, followed by a period, and then an extension. You can access a file by typing the full filename, or you can simply click on the filename if you are using a program such as Netscape Navigator. Many FTP sites maintain a directory called **Pub** (short for Public). Files contained in the Pub directory are available for access by the public.

Some FTP files are quite large and are compressed so that they are stored more easily and can travel across the Internet faster. Before a compressed file can be read, it must be decompressed using a decompression program. Therefore, to access and read compressed files you must have a decompression program installed on your computer. A decompression program is sometimes available from sites where you download a file. A popular decompression program for PCs is PKZip. Another easy-to-use program is WinZip.

Files containing a combination of text, graphics, and sound are developed using coding schemes. To view or use these coded files, you have to download them to your computer and then unencode them using special software. A popular encoding scheme is named UUencode. A **UUencode** program contains instructions for both encoding and decoding these large multimedia files.

A File Transfer Protocol called **WS_FTP** is a client application for use in a Windows environment. It was designed to take full advantage of the point-and-click capabilities of the Windows 3.1 or a newer Windows environment. WS_FTP is easy for a beginner to use and offers a full set of functions for an experienced user. Many Internet providers supply subscribers with a WS_FTP program on an installation disk or CD-ROM together with a manual explaining its use for accessing files stored on other computers. WS_FTP enables you to access files from computers around the world.

You can send large files, such as lengthy reports, over the Internet by using FTP. When FTP is used, a file being sent is converted into ASCII format or binary format. FTP programs allow you to select which format you want to use. Upon arrival at its destination, the files can be reformatted into readable form by using a word processor or other program.

Chat Groups (Chat Rooms)

Special software, called **chat programs,** allow individuals to use the Web to communicate with other people having similar interests. Many people join groups, called **chat groups** or **chat rooms,** to discuss topics of mutual interest, such as current events, politics, and the environment. Comments and opinions, often frank and uncensored, can be exchanged freely and anonymously with other group participants.

Entertainment

The Web can be used for playing online games. Many games are stored at various Web sites and can be accessed by users wanting to play a game. Chess, checkers, monopoly, bridge, and a variety of other games are available.

Home Shopping

Thousands of products and services can be purchased via the Web. Each year consumers purchase millions of products and services ranging from airline tickets to automobiles. Computer manufacturers, including Compaq Computer Corporation, IBM, Dell Computer Corporation, and Gateway Computer Corporation, have Web sites that allow customers to purchase computer products direct from the manufacturer. Small companies are beginning to use the Web as an efficient and cost-effective way to market their products and services.

Payments can be made using a credit card. However, many people are reluctant to divulge credit card information for fear that the information provided may be intercepted and used by others. To combat this fear, many sellers use encryption systems to improve information security. **Encryption** simply scrambles or encodes the customer's credit card number at one end of the connection, transmits it in a scrambled format, then unscrambles or decodes it at the receiving end. Wal-Mart, America's largest retailer, has initiated an extensive Internet shopping service. Figure 3.13 shows Wal-Mart's home shopping page.

FIGURE 3.13
Wal-Mart's Home Shopping Page

Our Free Market Economy

The U.S. economic system is truly a historical marvel. Adam Smith, the well-known 18th-century British economist, first described his vision for a free market economy in his two-volume publication titled *An Inquiry into the Nature and Causes of the Wealth of Nations*. Smith suggested that an economic system would thrive if left alone by government. He used the French term *laissez-faire* to refer to a minimum of government influence and interference in the economy. Smith's vision later became the framework for the U.S. economic system, which has become the envy of the entire world.

Despite its complexity, the U.S. economic system still holds to the basic principles of laissez-faire—minimum government interference. The result has been that the U.S. free market system has flourished because individuals and companies are free to pursue their own economic and business interests. Today, the U.S. economy abounds with giant corporations, midsize businesses, and small one-owner shops providing a wealth of products and services available to people throughout the world.

Individuals are free to pursue a variety of meaningful interests. Many choose professional careers in various fields, including law, medicine, research, education, computing, and consulting. Others choose to become business specialists in specific fields such as management, marketing, accounting, finance, and production. Still others prefer to become entrepreneurs by establishing their own companies, agencies, or organizations. Entrepreneurs abound in small companies, such as insurance agencies, real estate agencies, small retail stores, plumbing companies, and barbershops. Entrepreneurial opportunities exist in every town and city and in many business and professional fields.

Business: Lifeblood of Free Market Economies

Business has been called the *lifeblood* of free market economies. History has shown that excessive government involvement and control in the business sector has served only to stagnate economic development and growth. The Soviet economy crumbled during the 1980s as the result of excessive government planning and control of business. Today, the Cuban economy is in crisis. The North Korean economy faces stagnation. The world map is glittered with countries in crisis because of overly burdensome government control.

The American economy is a shining exception. In the United States, federal, state, and local governments encourage and promote private business by enacting legislation assuring competition among competing businesses. Monopoly practices are discouraged. The U.S. Small Business Administration assists new businesses by guaranteeing loans by private lenders to qualified borrowers and by providing new businesses with professional business advice. Each year, millions of U.S. citizens enter the competitive arena in a variety of new business ventures ranging from the formation of large stock-issuing corporations to small individual or family businesses.

Some fail whereas others succeed. Some entrepreneurs, such as Bill Gates of Microsoft Corporation and Andrew Grove of Intel Corporation, pioneered their visions into large corporations that changed the way Americans and others live, work, and conduct their daily activities. Free enterprise makes it possible to pursue one's dreams and visions for a better future.

Today, the Internet and the Web provide a different and challenging way for existing companies, and for prospective entrepreneurs, to pursue their business interests and goals. Thousands of companies, organizations, and new entrepreneurs are now using Internet and Web technologies for a variety of business activities and applications. Large companies use the Internet and the Web for a range of applications including the recruitment of new employees, raw materials acquisitions, and marketing. Thousands of new entrepreneurs now use the Internet and the Web as a vehicle for marketing products and services.

Electronic Commerce

You have learned that the Web represents a worldwide linkage of personal computers, networks, communications media, and specialized hardware and software that allows individuals, companies, organizations, and government agencies to communicate easily, quickly, and effectively. Having learned this, it's easy to understand that it would be only a brief time before users would begin using the Web for a host of business applications. That time has arrived with a virtual explosion of various kinds of commercial applications.

The business world has embarked on a new and exciting technological methodology called by various names—among them, electronic commerce, e-commerce, Internet commerce, I-commerce, Internet business, and I-business. In the discussions that follow, we will use the term *electronic commerce* in referring to this new technological methodology.

Because this methodology has become so extensive and broad based, **electronic commerce** is defined as a modern business methodology in which information, products, services, and payments are exchanged via computer networks within a global society. This definition implies that information, products, and services can be produced and marketed by a company or individual and sold to customers anywhere in the world. Also, it implies that any business or organization can use this methodology internally or externally to reduce costs, to improve the quality of products and services, to speed up the delivery of products and services, and to perform any number of activities to improve business performance.

The foundation on which electronic commerce is built is the information superhighway, or I-Way (explained earlier in this chapter), which provides for the worldwide flow of information, products, and services among individuals, businesses, organizations, and government agencies. The I-Way continues to evolve with new technologies and methodologies emerging almost daily.

In its present form, the I-Way is a convergence of various technologies and methodologies. **Content convergence** refers to the translation of all types of content information into digital form, including text, sound, graphics, movies, music, videos, and business documents and advertisements. An important feature of content convergence is *multimedia* in which text, sound, graphics, animation, and other elements are combined in digital form for transmission (Figure 3.14). **Transmission convergence** refers to the compression and storage of information in digitized form so it can travel efficiently over various types of communications media. **Device convergence** refers to the development and introduction of various computers, televisions, and other devices that facilitate the transfer of information from one location to another location.

Electronic commerce makes it possible for businesses and organizations of any size and type to conduct business operations using these technologies. Many have physical locations where products and services are displayed and sold. Some also advertise and sell their products and services via the Web. A list of these business and organizations would be quite lengthy; however, a few include popular retailers such as L.L. Bean, Lands' End, and CompUSA (Figure 3.15).

FIGURE 3.14
Multimedia Components

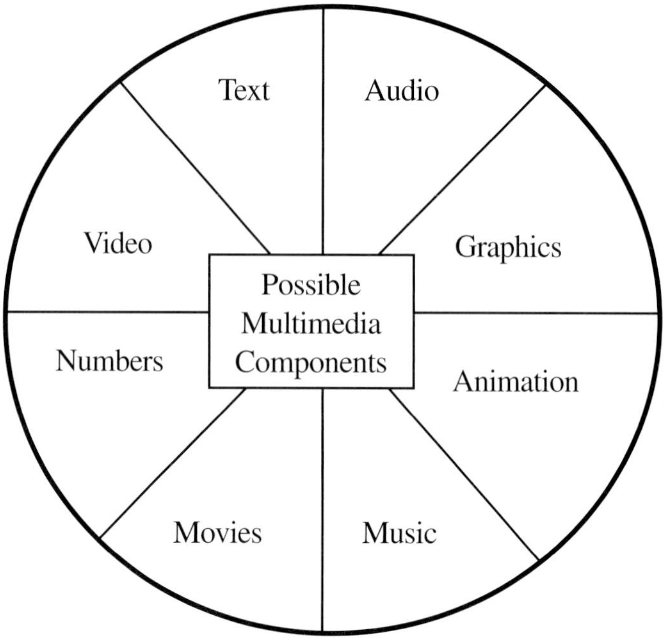

FIGURE 3.15
L.L. Bean Home Shopping Page

FIGURE 3.16

Small Business Access to the Web

The Web provides an opportunity for would-be entrepreneurs to enter the business world with minimal expense. New entrepreneurs with limited financial and other resources can offer their products and services via the Web easily and inexpensively by creating and posting pages on the Web describing their offerings. Many enterprising and imaginative new entrepreneurs have taken advantage of opportunities available via the Web to start new businesses (Figure 3.16). Some have been quite successful, and a few have earned millions of dollars in this way.

Thousands of large businesses have discovered the opportunities available to them on the Web. Most already have networks in place and have linked their networks to the Internet and the Web allowing them to place orders with suppliers for delivery when needed. For example, some manufacturers now use the Web for ordering raw materials for delivery at the precise time they are needed in the manufacturing process. They also use the Web for other applications, including employee recruitment, announcements for competitive bids, and communication among employees, managers, and others (Figure 3.17). Other applications are being discovered and implemented periodically.

Business-type Web applications are not confined to businesses, and similar private organizations. In their operations, government agencies are among the most creative and frequent Web users. The Internal Revenue Service, as well as several states, now allows individuals or families to file tax returns electronically. An individual can check his or her social security record online with the Social Security Administration. Law enforcement officials can quickly check the validity of a motorist's drivers license. Job seekers can view position openings posted on the Web by state and local Employment Security Commissions. The list of applications is lengthy and increasing daily.

FIGURE 3.17

Job Opportunities Posted by a University

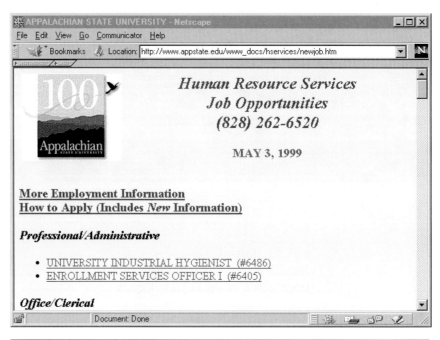

Electronic Commerce System Configurations

Electronic commerce is worldwide in scope and encompasses thousands of networks. The configuration of each network is determined mainly by a company's or organization's goals and what the company or organization is attempting to accomplish. For example, a company wanting only to sell products or service to customers will have one type of network configuration, whereas another company wanting to also use the Internet to obtain raw materials for use in the manufacture of its products may have a different network configuration.

For convenience, networks used for electronic commerce can be categorized into three main configurations, or categories. These categories are described in the following sections. Each category has unique functions and support software.

People-to-People Systems (PPSs)

People-to-people systems (PPSs) directly connect individuals or groups together to collaborate on common problems or to communicate about specific issues (Figure 3.18). Two or more users can share a common application over the network, such as a team project, even if the application is not on one user's computer. The connections, made when needed, allow simultaneous discussions and exist long enough to complete the task. There is substantial flexibility in how the connections are made and who will be involved.

Software support for a PPS ranges from applications such as word processing, spreadsheets, and graphics to shared messages, databases, and videoconferencing. This configuration is much like a conference telephone call, with the added feature that each participant also has powerful computing capabilities available to process, analyze, and share common information.

FIGURE 3.18

People-to-People System

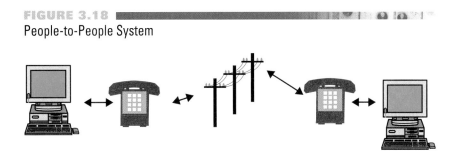

People-to-System-to-People Systems (PSPSs)

People-to-system-to-people systems (PSPSs) are an extension of the people-to-people configuration. In this process, a computer is added to the network to supply support, storage, or coordination for all users (Figure 3.19). The central computer allows participants to connect and work with one another, at the same or at different times. Communications do not have to occur at exactly the same time. The best example of this system type is e-mail: If the recipient is not available when the message is sent, the central computer stores the message until the receiver is ready to accept it. Think of the computer as an answering machine for each participant that inventories all forms of communication between the group members and then delivers the communications on demand, when requested.

Principal applications of PSPSs are electronic mail, calendar and scheduling programs, electronic forms, data collection, work-flow management systems, and electronic catalogs and shopping. Home shopping via the Web is a rapidly growing application of PSPSs today.

FIGURE 3.19

People-to-System-to-People System

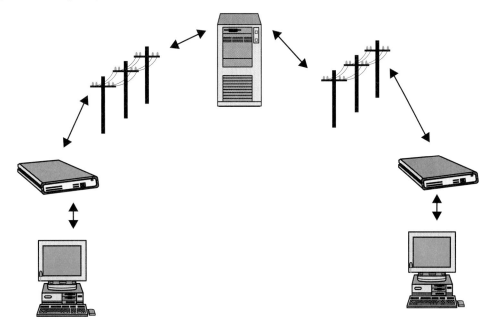

System-to-System System

System-to-System Systems (SSSs)

System-to-system systems (SSSs) directly connect computers in different organizations (Figure 3.20). The systems operate autonomously with little or no direct human involvement. They replace paper-oriented communications processes such as inventory ordering, invoicing, payroll, and shipping. Electronic information flows into the organization, between involved departments needing access to the information, to and from suppliers, and to and from customers.

Principal applications are electronic data interchange (EDI), electronic funds transfer (EFT), and transfers of technical data. **Electronic data interchange (EDI) systems** use computers to automatically transfer inventory, delivery, and billing information between organizations, in which the flow of electronic data replaces the flow of paper documents. **Electronic funds transfers (EFT) systems** enable payments to be made electronically. Banks use these systems to clear the traders' financial accounts. Both systems reduce paper flow and reduce the "float" or delays of money transfers that occur in financial transactions.

Transaction Processing Systems (TPSs)

Many people are familiar with transaction processing systems because they come into contact with them in their work or when they purchase goods and services. A **transaction processing system (TPS)** is an information system that uses standard procedures to collect and process the day-to-day data that routinely flow through an organization. With a transaction processing system, the processing cycle is routine and sequential with little variation. Computerized information systems used for transaction processing have the following characteristics:

- They process routine business transactions quickly and efficiently.
- They are used mostly by nonmanagement employees.
- The people using these systems are required to make few, if any, decisions.
- They are designed to process large amounts of detailed data generated by the daily activities of the business.

TPSs evolved from manual systems that became too labor intensive. TPSs were the first computer applications implemented by many organizations. Early in their history, TPSs were used primarily for **batch processing** applications in which a batch (a collection) of transactions were collected, stored, and processed at one time. For example, in many organizations employee time cards were collected at the end of designated time periods, and all employee paychecks were processed at once (in a "batch"). TPSs also automated the processing of accounts payable. Invoices would be collected over a certain period of time, and then the data from all invoices would be entered into the computer and processed for payment.

Thousands of TPSs are currently in operation in a wide variety of organizations. One example is an airline reservation system. A reservation or travel agent follows a standard set of procedures when requesting information from or entering information into a flight database. For instance, the agent will query the database as to whether there is a seat available on a specific flight and then enter appropriate information when a reservation is made. An agent must enter the purchaser's name, the time and date of departure and arrival, and where the ticket is to be picked up. (Some airlines are now using ticketless travel systems—you simply prepay with a credit card and enter directly from the gate.)

Another example is an order-entry system. When an order is received, a trained order-entry clerk follows standard procedures to enter the order into the system. After an order has been entered, the computer system follows a set of standard procedures to process the order.

TPSs are used in many other industry processes as well, including banking systems, commercial loan processing, stock and bond management, transportation, health care, legal practices, manufacturing, retail operations, and utilities. TPSs are used for accounts receivable, accounts payable, inventory control, invoicing, order processing, payroll, purchasing, shipping and receiving, and general ledger applications. Essentially, most common business functions use TPSs.

Besides providing many organizations with the ability to process routine day-to-day business transactions quickly and efficiently, TPSs can also be set up to collect historical information on sales, customer buying habits, financial information, and so on. These historical databases are valuable sources of input data for the organization's other information systems.

Transaction processing systems are widely used in electronic commerce. Transactions conducted over the Internet typically are recorded and processed immediately. For example, you can visit a specific Web site that shows products or services for sale, make a selection, and enter the required information from a keyboard including a credit card number. The transaction will be entered immediately into the system and the transaction completed (Figure 3.21). Without transaction processing systems, it would be much more difficult, if not impossible, for companies to conduct business transactions over the Internet.

FIGURE 3.21

Transaction Processing System

A customer in Bismarck, North Dakota, uses a credit card to place an order for a new computer. The order data travels across communications channels to the seller in New York, where the company uses its computer system to process the order. The transaction data are then sent to the bank in Dallas that issued the customer's credit card, which uses its computer system to record and process the financial transaction. Following final processing, order data are sent to the company's distribution center in Los Angeles, where final processing is completed. The merchandise is then shipped to the customer.

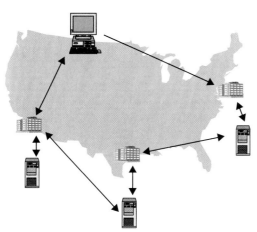

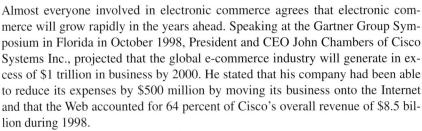

Electronic Commerce Growth and Demographics

Almost everyone involved in electronic commerce agrees that electronic commerce will grow rapidly in the years ahead. Speaking at the Gartner Group Symposium in Florida in October 1998, President and CEO John Chambers of Cisco Systems Inc., projected that the global e-commerce industry will generate in excess of $1 trillion in business by 2000. He stated that his company had been able to reduce its expenses by $500 million by moving its business onto the Internet and that the Web accounted for 64 percent of Cisco's overall revenue of $8.5 billion during 1998.

Although the range of electronic commerce applications is extensive, the sale and purchase of products and services is perhaps the best-known electronic commerce application. Several research organizations now gather and analyze statistical data to determine the extent to which the Web is being used in the sale and purchase of products and services.

In 1997 and again in 1998, Nielson Research Media and CommerceNet, two leading research firms, conducted and published joint electronic commerce research studies that identified electronic commerce growth and demographics. The 1998 report compares data gathered in 1998 with data gathered in 1997. Information contained in this report was based on telephone interviews of nearly 5,000 randomly selected respondents age 16 and older. According to Nielson, the respondents were statistically representative of the overall U.S. and Canadian populations.

The most recent study showed that 78 million people used the World Wide Web during the first six months of 1998. Of this number, 20 million users made purchases via the Web. The following figures are highlights of shopping and purchasing activity from the 1998 study conducted by Nielson Media Research and CommerceNet. Figure 3.22 shows selected Web shopper demographics and an increase in most user categories.

FIGURE 3.22

Current Web Shopper Demographics

- There are now 48 million Web shoppers, an increase of 37 percent from September 1997.

- There are now 20 million Web purchasers, an increase of 100 percent from September 1997.

- Seventy-one percent of Web purchasers are men and 29 percent are women—unchanged from September 1997.

- Women represent 36 percent of all online book buyers and 12 percent of all online computer hardware buyers.

- Among persons age 16–24, the top items purchased on the Web are books, CDs/cassettes/videos, and clothing.

- Among persons 50 years old and older, the top items purchased on the Web are books, software, and computer hardware.

- Consumers under the age of 35 represent 65 percent of all persons buying clothing on the Web and 64 percent of all persons buying CDs/cassettes/videos.

- Consumers 35 years old and older represent 63 percent of all persons buying computer hardware on the Web, 59 percent of all persons buying software, and 58 percent of all persons buying books.

Figure 3.23 identifies popular categories of items purchased via the Web and the increased purchases of items in each category between 1997 and 1998. The most popular category is books, followed in order by computer hardware, computer software, CDs/cassettes/video, travel, and clothing.

Figure 3.24 shows the top categories of purchases via the Web by men. Among male customers, the most popular category of items purchased via the Web was computer hardware, followed in order by books, computer software, CDs/cassettes/videos, travel, and clothing.

Figure 3.25 shows the top categories of purchases via the Web by women. Among female customers, the most popular category of items purchased via the Web was books, followed in order by CDs/cassettes/videos, clothing, computer software, travel, and flowers/cards.

This information illustrates the growth in electronic commerce. From the information in the figures, you can see clearly that electronic commerce is a rapidly

FIGURE 3.23
Items Purchased on the Web, 1998 versus 1997

ITEMS	NUMBER OF 1998 PURCHASES	CHANGE FROM 1997
Books	5.6 million	Increase of 3.3 million
Computer hardware	4.4 million	Increase of 2.4 million
Computer software	4.0 million	Increase of 1.2 million
CDs/cassettes/videos	3.4 million	Increase of 2.0 million
Travel (air, hotel, etc.)	2.8 million	Increase of 1.6 million
Clothing	2.7 million	Increase of 1.8 million

FIGURE 3.24
Top Items Purchased on the Web by Men, 1998 versus 1997

ITEMS	NUMBER OF PURCHASES, 1998	CHANGE FROM 1997
Books	3.6 million	Increase of 2.2 million
Computer hardware	3.9 million	Increase of 2.0 million
Computer software	3.1 million	Increase of 0.8 million
CDs/cassettes/videos	2.3 million	Increase of 1.2 million
Travel (air, hotel, etc.)	2.1 million	Increase of 1.3 million
Clothing	1.6 million	Increase of 1.2 million

FIGURE 3.25
Top Items Purchased on the Web by Women, 1998 versus 1997

ITEMS	NUMBER OF PURCHASES, 1998	CHANGE FROM 1997
Books	2.0 million	Increase of 1.3 million
Flowers/cards	0.7 million	Increase of 0.4 million
Computer software	0.9 million	Increase of 0.4 million
CDs/cassettes/videos	1.1 million	Increase of 0.7 million
Travel (air, hotel, etc.)	0.8 million	Increase of 0.4 million
Clothing	1.1 million	Increase of 0.7 million

growing field. This field is likely to continue its present trend of rapid growth during the foreseeable future. Among experts in this field, there is little doubt about the future of electronic commerce. Electronic commerce will play an important role in business applications and in everyday life well into the next millennium.

Your Role in Electronic Commerce

In this chapter several large and medium-size businesses and organizations engaged in electronic commerce were identified, but electronic commerce applications and practices are not limited to large and medium-size businesses and organizations. A small business or an individual can take advantage of opportunities that are now available to everyone.

Many small businesses and individuals are taking advantage of opportunities to become actively involved in electronic commerce. Some examples include local insurance and real estate agencies, local newspaper publishers, local tourism organizations, self-employed craftspeople, small advertisers, lawyers, and local florists.

The Web can be a marvelous and powerful tool that enables you to advertise and sell products and services of any kind. Thousands of individuals are now using the Web for a virtually unlimited variety of applications. Today, thousands of students are posting their resumes on the Web where they can be viewed by hundreds of prospective employers. Web pages containing pictures and descriptions of family-owned bed-and-breakfast facilities appear regularly. Many artists take advantage of the Web to display images and descriptions of their work.

Opportunities in electronic commerce are available to everyone, including you. The following chapters identify and explain a variety of electronic commerce applications including business-to-customer applications, business-to-business applications, and businesses-to-society applications. Later in this book, you will learn how you can establish your company/organization's or your own individual presence in electronic commerce.

SUMMARY

The Internet (or Net) is a global network of computers linked via communications software and media for the purpose of sharing information. The term *Internet* was coined to represent the interlinking of computer networks around the world.

A program called Gopher was the first point-and-click way of navigating the files on the Internet. A program called Mosaic was the first graphics-based Web browser.

Vice President Al Gore coined the term *information superhighway*, or *I-Way*, in describing and encouraging the development and expansion of the Internet as a vehicle for sharing information worldwide.

Information being sent across the Internet is first divided into fixed-length blocks of data, called packets, by the Transmission Control Protocol/Internet Protocol (TCP/IP), a protocol that governs the flow of data across the Internet by specifying the rules for creating, addressing, and sending packets. This process is known as packet switching. A variety of hardware devices processes the packets and routes them to their appropriate destinations. These devices include hubs, bridges, gateways, routers, and repeaters.

The World Wide Web (also called the Web, WWW, or W3) is a global system of linked computer networks that allows users to jump from one place on the

Web, called a Web site, to another place on the Web. A home page is the first page you see when you go to a particular Web site. A site's home page often contains links to other pages at that site or to other Web sites.

A Web page, sometimes called a document, is a hypermedia file stored at a particular Web site. A hypermedia file is a file containing any combination of text, graphics, sound, and video. Web pages may also contain one or more hyperlinks to other Web sites or other Web pages. A hyperlink (or simply *link)* is in the form of boldfaced text, underlined text, or an icon that, when clicked on using a mouse, takes you to another Web site or Web page.

Your computer can be connected to the Internet in several ways, including a direct connection to the Internet, by subscribing to a commercial online service, by connecting via an Internet service provider, or by connecting via a long-distance telephone company.

A browser is a program that allows you to find and display Web pages. Two popular Internet browsers are Netscape Navigator and Internet Explorer. After activating a browser, you can visit a Web site by entering the site's address, called the Uniform Resource Locator (or URL).

The Web uses a language, called HyperText Markup Language (HTML), that allows you to view Web pages. A new and improved Web language, called eXtensible Markup Language, or XML, is gaining in popularity among companies that develop and sell Web browsers. Most Web pages use the HTTP protocol for transferring data from the host computer to your computer.

The Internet and the Web offer a variety features, applications, and services, including electronic mail, finding information, information retrieval, file transfer, chat groups, entertainment, and home shopping.

A search engine is a software program that facilitates queries by allowing you to enter search criteria to locate information on the Web. A query is a word or phrase entered in a search engine program that specifies the type of information you want to view.

Electronic commerce is a modern business methodology in which information, products, services, and payments are exchanged via computer networks within a global society. Encryption is achieved by using special software that scrambles or encodes the information at one end of the connection, transmits it in a coded format, then decodes (decrypts) it at the receiving end.

The foundation on which electronic commerce is built is the information superhighway, or I-Way. The I-Way is a convergence of various technologies and methodologies. Content convergence refers to the translation of all types of content information into digital form, including text, sound, graphics, movies, music, videos, business documents, and advertisements. Transmission convergence refers to the compression and storage of information in digitized form so it can travel over various types of communications media. Device convergence refers to the development and introduction of various computers, televisions, and other devices that facilitate the transfer of information from one location to another location.

Networks used for electronic commerce can be categorized into three main configurations, or categories. People-to-people systems (PPSs) directly connect individuals or groups together to collaborate on common problems or to communicate about specific issues. With people-to-system-to-people systems (PSPSs), a central computer is added to the network to supply support, storage, or coordination for all users. System-to-system systems (SSSs) directly connect computers in different organizations. The systems operate autonomously with little or no direct human involvement.

EDI systems use computers to automatically transfer inventory, delivery, and billing information between organizations, in which the flow of electronic data replaces the flow of paper documents. EFT systems enable payments to be made electronically. Banks use these systems to clear the traders' financial accounts. Both systems reduce paper flow and reduce the "float" or delays of money transfers that occur in financial transactions.

A transaction processing system (TPS) is an information system that uses standard procedures to collect and process the day-to-day data that routinely flow through an organization. TPSs are essential for processing electronic commerce applications.

KEY TERMS

Advanced Research
  Projects Agency
  Network (ARPANET)
  (67)
Advanced Research
  Projects Agency
  (ARPA) (67)
anonymous access (82)
batch processing (90)
browser (72)
browsing (surfing) (72)
chat groups (chat
  rooms) (83)
chat programs
content convergence
  (85)
Defense Advanced
  Research Projects
  Agency (DARPA)
  (67)
device convergence
  (85)
downloading (81)
electronic commerce
  (85)
electronic data
  interchange (EDI)
  systems (90)
electronic funds
  transfer (EFT)
  systems (90)

electronic mail system
  (79)
encryption (83)
eXtensible Markup
  Language (XML) (73)
file transfer protocol
  (FTP) (81)
Gopher (68)
home page (73)
hyperlink (link) (71)
hypermedia file (71)
HyperText Markup
  Language (HTML)
  (73)
HyperText Transfer
  Protocol (HTTP) (76)
icon (72)
Information
  Superhighway
  (I-Way) (68)
Internet (Net) (66)
Internet Explorer (72)
Internet Protocol
  address (IP address)
  (70)
Java (68)
Mosaic (68)
Netscape Navigator
  (72)
NSFNET (68)
packet (70)

packet switching (70)
people-to-people
  systems (PPSs) (88)
people-to-system-to-
  people systems
  (PSPSs) (89)
Pub (82)
query (80)
search engine (80)
system-to-system
  systems (SSSs) (90)
transaction processing
  system (TPS) (90)
Transmission Control
  Protocol/Internet
  Protocol (TCP/IP)
  (70)
transmission
  convergence (85)
Uniform Resource
  Locator (URL) (73)
uploading (82)
UUencode (82)
Web page (71)
Web site (71)
World Wide Web (Web,
  WWW, or W3) (71)
WS_FTP (83)

END-OF-CHAPTER ACTIVITIES

MATCHING

Match each term with its description.

a. browser   e. hypermedia   i. search engine
b. Internet   f. HTML   j. transaction processing system
c. packet   g. hyperlink   k. World Wide Web
d. Web site   h. Gopher   l. electronic commerce

_____ **1.** A global network of computers linked together via communications software and media for the purpose of sharing information.

_____ **2.** A system that enables transactions to be processed immediately.

_____ **3.** The first point-and-click way of navigating the files on the Internet.

_____ **4.** A fixed-length block of data.

_____ **5.** A file that contains any combination of text, graphics, sound, and video.

_____ **6.** Boldfaced text, underlined text, or an icon that, when clicked on using a mouse, takes you to another Web site or Web page.

_____ **7.** A global system of linked computer networks that allows users to jump from one location to another location.

_____ **8.** A site that is accessible to anyone and is a part of the World Wide Web.

_____ **9.** A software tool (program) that makes it easy for you to find and display Web pages by removing the complexity of having to remember the syntax of commands to find and display the pages.

_____ **10.** A Web language that allows you to view Web pages.

_____ **11.** A software program that facilitates queries by allowing you to enter search criteria to locate information on the Web.

_____ **12.** A modern business methodology in which information, products, services, and payments are exchanged via computer networks within a global society.

Review Questions

1. What is the Internet?
2. What is the World Wide Web? Why might a business or organization want to establish a site on the Web?
3. Briefly explain how information is sent across the Internet.
4. Identify four ways your computer can be connected to the Internet and Web.
5. Briefly explain the nature of electronic commerce.

Activities

1. Information about this textbook, *Getting Started with Electronic Commerce,* is available at the Web site of the publisher, The Dryden Press. The company's

Internet address is http://www.dryden.com. Using this address and the Internet, visit the site and find the information provided about the book you are using.

2. There are thousands of commercial Web sites that provide information about products and services offered for sale by the company. Addresses for these Web sites can be obtained from a variety of sources, including magazines, TV commercials, and newspapers. Visit five sites. While viewing each site, prepare a written list of features you like about the site and a list of features you do not like (or believe could be improved).

3. The Internet and the Web contain valuable information about job and career opportunities. Using the search engine available to you, search for employment opportunities for students in your field of study, such as biology, chemistry, English, human relations, or accounting. Make a list of job opportunities found and whether the company or organization allows individuals to submit an employment application using the Internet.

4. Visit a company or organization in your area that has a computer network. Request that you be allowed to interview computer personnel. If you are given permission and have an opportunity to interview someone with knowledge of the company's network, learn the purposes for which the network is used, including electronic commerce applications. Take detailed notes during your visit. Following your visit, prepare a written report of your findings.

5. This is a team project. Your instructor will divide the class into groups (teams) with four or five students on each team. Many computer magazines contain articles about electronic commerce. The Internet addresses of a few popular magazines are listed here. Each team member will visit one of these sites and find two articles dealing with a topic about electronic commerce. After reading two articles, each team member will prepare a brief written summary of each article. All article summaries will be combined to form a group project, which will be turned in to the instructor.

MAGAZINE NAME	WEB ADDRESS
PC Magazine	http://www.pcmagazine.com
Infoworld	http://www.infoworld.com
PC Week	http://www.pcweek.com
Datamation	http://www.datamation.com
Computer World	http://www.computerworld.com

Business-to-Customer Applications

AFTER COMPLETING THIS CHAPTER, YOU WILL:

1. Explain the nature of online shopping.
2. Explain briefly the difference between worldwide online shopping and local online shopping.
3. Explain briefly the nature of a virtual storefront.
4. Define an online shopping mall and explain how an online mall differs from an online store.
5. Explain the nature of an online catalog and describe briefly how an online catalog can aid an online shopper.
6. Explain the nature of intelligent shopping agents and how they work.
7. Identify some online payment methods explained in the chapter.

8. **Identify some of the online shopping product categories explained in the chapter.**
9. **Identify the online security measures recommended in the chapter.**
10. **Identify six other online applications explained in the chapter.**

A few years ago, a well-known computer pioneer named Grace Hopper stated that "computing is still in its infancy." Her statement remains true today. Each day new, faster, and more powerful computing devices and software are being introduced and their uses continue to expand. Today, we have the Internet, the World Wide Web, and electronic commerce, and most computer professionals are likely to agree that all three are still in their infancy stages.

You have learned that **electronic commerce**—one of the fastest growing uses of the Internet—is the buying and selling of products and services electronically over the Internet. By using the Internet, businesses can advertise and market products and services worldwide, reduce costs, simplify ordering procedures, speed up the delivery of products and services, and simplify and speed up payments for goods and services sold.

Electronic commerce represents a new way of doing business. Using the Internet, retailers can sell goods and services to customers and, in return, receive payments, businesses can conduct normal business activities with other businesses including suppliers of raw materials, and governments can provide services to citizens easily, quickly, and efficiently.

Many companies now use the Web to conduct normal business activities. Manufacturers use it to search out new raw material sources, to locate suppliers, and

E-Commerce Leaders

Jerry Yang and David Filo

The phrase "Web portal" was virtually unheard of until only about two years ago. Today it is a common phrase among Web enthusiasts and millions of users who regularly use Web portals such as Yahoo!, AltaVista, Infoseek, and Lycos to search for, and find, useful information at Web sites around the world.

A Web portal is a software program that opens the door to the World Wide Web. In some parts of the world, people use the word "portal" in place of the word "door" or "doorway." Thus, a Web portal may be thought of as a doorway to the vast storehouse of documents available to us on the Web.

One of the largest, most popular, and most successful Web portals is called Yahoo! Yahoo! was created in early 1994 by two Stanford University graduate students, Jerry Yang and David Filo, when the Web consisted of only a few hundred sites. Yahoo! began as a hobby but soon grew into a successful business as a result of Yang and Filo's marketing and technological talents.

Still in their early 30s, Yang and Filo are competitive individuals. They've continued to expand Yahoo!'s services at a brisk pace, moving from its meager beginning as a simple directory into a full-featured Web service that can retain user attention for long periods of time. During 1998, Yahoo! added several new services including messaging, a gaming hub, auction services, Internet telephone, and many special-interest clubs. The company now offers Internet access and markets its own credit card. It's main goal is to maintain Yahoo!'s position as the leader among Web portals.

Yahoo! has grown to a point where the worth of the company is approximately $11 billion. Yang and Filo represent two notable pioneers whose contributions are enjoyed by Web users around the world.

to attract potential employees. Retailers are able to find new markets for their products and services and to check on competitors. Mail-order businesses can obtain information about shippers and other means for distributing their products and services.

The Internet and the Web offer users applications and opportunities that were unimagined only a few years ago. Internet, Web, and electronic commerce technologies allow you to travel the world electronically. From the comfort and convenience of your own home or office, you have immediate access to a vast storehouse of information, education, and news. You can conduct a variety of activities, including banking, investing, and a host of others.

In the following sections, we will examine several activities and opportunities that are now available because of innovative developments in electronic commerce technologies. As you learn about these activities and opportunities, you are encouraged to visit some the sites identified in the chapter. Visiting these sites will help you learn how businesses and organizations are using this technology to make your life as a consumer easier and more productive.

This chapter focuses on business applications with customers. Any business, large or small, can use the Internet to sell its products or services to consumers. Almost any product or service can be marketed and sold or purchased online by using the Internet. In the sections that follow, we examine some of these companies and the kinds of products and services made available for purchase by consumers.

Electronic Commerce Growth and Structures

Online shopping, also called **electronic shopping** or **e-shopping,** is using a computer, modem, and Internet access to locate, examine, purchase, sell, and pay for products over the Internet. Online shopping can be worldwide or local. **Worldwide online shopping** means that a customer goes online to find the best buys regardless of the location of the seller. For example, the shopper may visit Web sites in England to find a particular wool sweater. **Local online shopping** is limited to specific Web sites located in close proximity to the customer.

As more and more consumers, called **electronic shoppers** or **e-shoppers,** flock to the Internet as time and convenience become more important, electronic commerce between businesses and consumers will continue to grow at an accelerated rate. Companies that combine Web marketing strategies with traditional approaches are sure to see improvements in sales and performance.

Electronic commerce is expanding so rapidly in the United States that President Clinton has appointed an e-commerce czar to monitor and make recommendations for future growth. The results of a recent study (Figure 4.1) indicate that annual worldwide online sales will increase from $211 billion in 1998 to $954 billion in 2001.

The 1998 Christmas season saw a boom in online sales. Among online shoppers, the most popular product categories, in order, were (1) toys, (2) clothing, (3) books and music, (4) electronics and videos, and (5) flowers, candy, and cards.

It was widely reported that during the 1998 season online sales rose 320 percent compared to online sales for the previous season. Much of the increase was due to online catalog shopping. Several online stores reported increased sales during the 1998 Christmas season. Intimate Brands, Inc., the parent company of Victoria's Secret, reported that online sales helped fuel strong sales in the fourth quarter of 1998. Lands' End, which has had an online store since 1995, broke its all-time online traffic record on December 9, 1998. The company reported that, for the first time, online sales of women's items equaled that of men's items sold. Other companies also reported similar gains in online sales.

FIGURE 4.1
Worldwide Growth in Annual E-Commerce Sales

Research indicates that worldwide electronic commerce sales will increase rapidly by 2001. Efforts are under way to encourage growth and to ensure safety for online businesses and customers.

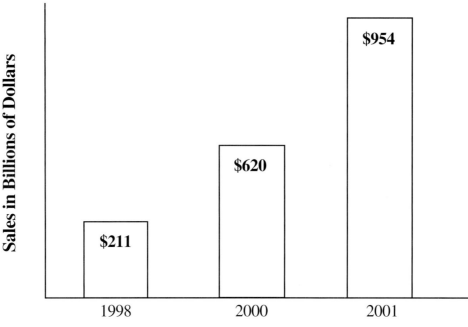

Source: PC Magazine, February 9, 1999, p. 30.

America Online, Inc., reported that on its highest sales date, December 17, 1998, sales exceeded $36 million compared with its highest sales date during the 1997 season when sales reached only $1 million. During the 1998 season, toy sales increased by 86 percent and apparel sales rose by 73 percent.

Virtual Storefronts

Today, thousands of businesses, organizations, and even individuals use the Internet to sell products and services. They begin by connecting their computers and networks to other networks throughout the world. Once connected, they design Web pages containing information about their products and services. The Web pages are then stored on a network server. Any individual with a computer and Internet access can then access the stored pages by entering the address of the specific Web site. For example, an individual can access and view pages by typing the address (URL) for CompUSA's Web site (http://www.compusa.com). CompUSA is a leading retailer of computer hardware and software products and supplies. After typing the URL, CompUSA's home page will be displayed on the user's screen, as shown in Figure 4.2.

The home page for many businesses contains links to other pages available for viewing. CompUSA's home page in Figure 4.2 contains several links to other pages that provide viewers with additional detailed information about specific products and services. A link is usually underlined or in a different color, such as red or blue. Clicking on a link accesses the selected page. For example, by selecting (clicking on) the Modems link, a user can view specific information about modems offered by the company.

As is true for home pages of many companies, CompUSA's home page serves as a virtual storefront. What is a virtual storefront? Webster's dictionary defines

FIGURE 4.2
CompUSA Home Page

the word *virtual* as "existing or resulting in effect or essence though not in actual fact, form, or name" and defines *storefront* as "a room or suite in a store building at street level." Thus, a storefront is an entrance, or entryway, into a store. A **virtual storefront** is a computerized storefront (entryway) through which potential customers can enter to view, and possibly purchase, the company's products and services. Many retailers maintain their own virtual storefronts by regularly updating information about new and existing products and services and by providing up-to-date ordering information and forms.

Electronic Shopping Malls

Some companies do not have their own virtual storefronts but rather offer their products and services through electronic shopping malls, such as Netmarket (Figure 4.3). An **electronic shopping mall** is an online mall with many electronic stores offering for sale a variety of goods and services, such as computers, clothing, sporting goods, greeting cards, books, and flowers. After accessing an electronic shopping mall, a customer can locate a product or service by choosing the type of product or service or by choosing the store offering the product or service.

Examine Netmarket's home page in Figure 4.3. You will notice links to categories of products and services, such as Apparel or Babies, Kids, & Toys. By moving through the mall's pages, chances are you will be able to locate specific products and brands of interest to you.

Thousands of online shoppers find electronic shopping malls fascinating. A huge inventory of products and services can be located and purchased, often at discounted prices. For many online shoppers, these malls represent a new and exciting way to shop for a variety of items. One site, for example, the Internet Mall, shown in Figure 4.4, hosts more than 27,000 stores and markets itself as the world's largest virtual shopping mall.

FIGURE 4.3

Netmarket Home Page

FIGURE 4.4

Internet Mall Home Page

Most electronic shopping malls allow anyone to make purchases. However, some offer lower prices to members. A user can become a member by signing up at the mall's Web site and paying a fee.

FIGURE 4.5
Lands' End Home Page

Online Catalogs

Each week thousands of shopping catalogs are delivered to homes around the world and thousands more are made available to shoppers at various locations, including retail stores, barbershops, beauty salons, specialty shops, and even on commercial airplanes. For many retailers, including L.L. Bean, Lands' End (Figure 4.5), and J.C. Penney, catalogs provide customers with a convenient way to learn about available products, just as physical store displays allow customers to see and examine products for sale.

For retailers and customers alike, catalogs provide a convenient way to shop. Catalogs are the marketing backbone for many retailers. After finding a desired product in a company catalog, a customer can make a purchase by placing a telephone call to the seller, identifying the product, and providing the company with purchase information including the customer's name, address, and credit card number.

Many retailers have already put catalogs on the Web, and customers can browse through them and make purchases (Figure 4.6). For some companies, online catalogs have proven quite successful. For example, SkyMall Inc., a well-known in-flight catalog, experienced a dramatic increase in sales after placing its catalog online. From 1997 to 1998, the company's online sales increased 600 percent—to $2.1 million. Reel.com, an online movie site, experienced a 700 percent increase in sales from 1997 to 1998.

Intelligent Shopping Agents

In recent months, specialized software has been developed to aid shoppers seeking bargain prices or additional product information. These programs, called **intelligent shopping agents,** aid shoppers in searching the Web for the

FIGURE 4.6

CatalogCity Home Page

lowest-priced products. Intelligent shopping agents are sometimes integrated into search programs so that they act automatically when an online search is executed.

One example is an agent called Jango that Excite purchased from Netbot and integrated into Excite's Shopping Channel to give Excite shoppers a convenient and powerful resource for finding, evaluating, and purchasing products online. Jango works automatically when the Excite search engine is accessed and a search for a specific product is executed.

Here's how it works. When the Excite search engine is activated, Excite displays several categories of products from which a shopper can make a selection. For example, the Computer Hardware category includes Desktops, Laptops, Modems, Monitors, Printers, Peripherals, and Scanners. Clicking on Printers results in a dialog box for the shopper to enter specific printer information, including manufacturer, model, kind, and color. After entering the required information, the shopper can choose to find prices or find reviews about the product. By choosing to find prices, a thorough search of online stores offering the product is made. A list of stores offering the product is displayed along with other useful information including the product's price. By clicking on the price column heading, the list is sorted with the stores offering the lowest prices listed first (Figure 4.7). A shopper can readily identify sellers offering the lowest prices. By clicking on the name of the store, a shopper can conveniently place an order for the product.

Intelligent shopping agents can perform continuous comparison shopping across several electronic marketplaces, presenting only the best of the best. They also do periodic scans for new products or closeout items. As shopping increases on the Web, we will see intelligent-agent technology routinely available to the online shopper. Intelligent shopping agents save the shopper valuable time and effort. And, we may expect significant improvements to be made in these technologies in the future.

The potential use for intelligent shopping agents is not limited to finding online products. Their use is already being extended to include database searches, travel scheduling, vacation planning, and many other areas in which information searches are necessary.

FIGURE 4.7

List of Stores, Products, and Prices

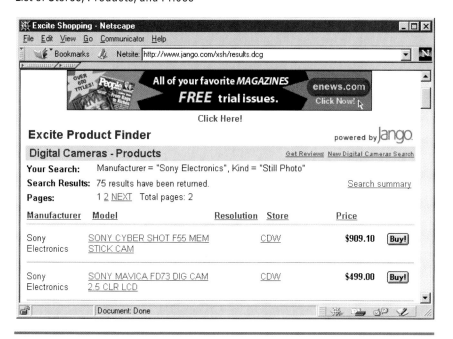

Some online merchants are unhappy with intelligent shopping agents and are engaged in efforts to block their use using firewalls. These merchants do not want to be evaluated solely by price, preferring instead to be evaluated on the basis of other criteria including customer service and product quality.

Online Payments

Financial institutions play a major role in electronic commerce. We can view banks in two different ways. First, they are actually electronic shopping malls themselves, offering a variety of financial products and services at various prices. You can shop banks for rates and services much like you shop grocery stores. Figure 4.8 highlights several types of customer banking activities.

Payments for goods and services purchased online can be made in a variety of ways including the use of credit accounts, credit cards, traditional payments, or by providing a personal identification number (PIN). Some companies are developing technologies that allow for small purchases, although most of these efforts have met with little success.

Credit Accounts

Some online sellers will allow a qualified customer to open a credit account the same way local retailers often provide credit for customers. A **credit account** represents a promise by the customer to pay for online purchases upon receipt of a periodic statement from the seller. When online purchases are made, each purchase is charged to the customer's credit account. Customers having a credit account receive regular statements showing the balance owed during the period, such as the previous month. Upon receipt of a statement, the customer sends a check to pay for purchases made during the period.

FIGURE 4.8
Banking Services

Banks typically offer various customer services. One service is a customer credit card account. Once a valid credit card is obtained from the bank, a customer can use the card to make online purchases just as the customer would make at a traditional retail store.

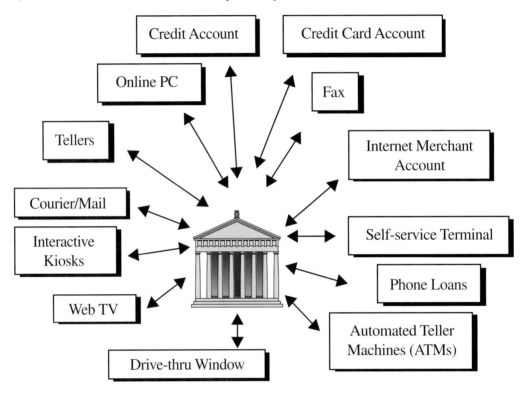

Credit Card Payments

Banks play an essential role in electronic commerce. Notice in Figure 4.8 that one of the bank's services is to offer a credit card account that allows payments to be made by credit card. You know already that a **credit card** is a small plastic card issued by a financial institution; it contains essential information that allows the customer to make credit purchases, which are then charged to the customer's account with the financial institution. When a customer pays for an online purchase using a credit card, the amount of the purchase is charged to the customer's account. Along with other charges, the amount of online purchases appears on the customer's monthly statement from the bank. Figure 4.9 illustrates a typical online form for entering credit card information and other financial data required by the seller.

Traditional Payments

Many consumers are wary of supplying personal financial data, such as credit card numbers, over the Internet. As a result, some online merchants allow consumers to pay by a more traditional means. Here's how it works. When making an online purchase, the customer can select an on-screen option that results in a phone call during which time the customer is asked whether he or she prefers to pay by check or credit card. This method results in higher cost to the merchant who must hire additional staff to handle these transactions. However, many cus-

FIGURE 4.9

A Form Used for Online Credit Purchases

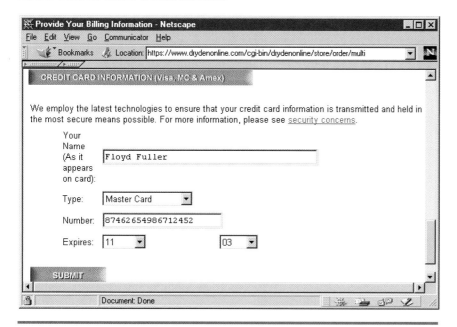

tomers prefer this method of payment due to their fear of sending personal financial data across the Internet.

Personal Identification Number (PIN) Payments

Most of us who use automated teller machines (ATMs) are familiar with the personal identification number (PIN), which identifies us as customers of the bank. Banks typically issue personal identification cards to customers, which they can use to obtain cash from the bank's ATMs. The customer uses the ATM console to enter the required information, including the customer's personal identification number (PIN) and the amount to be withdrawn.

For online purchases, a customer needs a valid credit card, such as a MasterCard or VISA. For a small processing fee, some banks will allow a customer to set up a special account for online purchases. When a purchase is made from a participating merchant, the customer supplies an encrypted PIN number that is forwarded to the bank that issued the customer's PIN and maintains the customer's account. The bank then contacts the customer to confirm the transaction. The amount of the purchase is billed to the customer's credit card account.

Many of the items we purchase are inexpensive. Items including newspapers, magazines, and greeting cards are usually paid for in cash. Just as many items you might purchase from a local retailer are cheap, some sites offer inexpensive items over the Internet. The problem is that the cost of processing the sale of inexpensive items (labor, bank charges, etc.) may exceed the value of the items sold. Several companies are experimenting with technologies to handle small transactions in a cost-effective way. Perhaps soon online shoppers will be able to make online purchases for even small purchases.

E-Commerce Technology

Voice Commerce: Next Step in Telecommunications and E-Commerce?

Over the years, problems have hindered the development of satisfactory interactive voice-recognition technology (IVR) in both telephone and Web-based applications. In telecommunications, the development of voice recognition has been limited by awkward interfaces that require users to access information through layered menus over the phone. Nearly every touch-telephone user has experienced the frustrations of having to press several numbers on the dial to contact a specific person or department, and pressing an incorrect number often can force the caller to repeat the cycle or place another call. Either can result in wasted time and increased expense.

Via an agreement with Nuance Communications Corporation in California, Edify Corporation has announced a landmark upgrade to its Electronic Workforce software that will voice-enable its self-service Workforce software. By incorporating Nuance's speech-recognition technology into its software, Edify will enable its users to offer a far more robust level of information to their customers, according to a company press release. This new version of Workforce will also give corporate developers a single environment for creating both e-commerce and voice commerce (v-commerce) applications. The inclusion of the Nuance speech technology in Edify's software will allow IT mangers to maintain only one application for both Web and phone access. A user will be able to make travel arrangements using the IVR interface and change them on the Web if necessary.

For example, First American National Bank in Nashville, Tennessee, uses the same service for Web-based and telephone access that lets users check account information. A First American customer may be told, "You have three bills to pay. The first bill is American Express for $300." Soon the user will be able to say, "Pay the American Express bill," rather than having to push a number on the phone.

Alliances between other speech companies are expected to expand the market for v-commerce and e-commerce. For example, Conversational Computing Corporation in Redmond, Washington, plans to deliver in 1999 a program that lets Web site developers conversation-enable Web sites, company officials said.

Sources: "V-commerce: The Next Frontier," *InfoWorld,* December 1, 1988, p. 45; Edify Corporation Web site at www.edify.com.

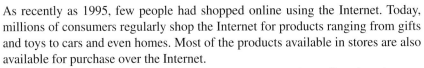

Consumer Shopping on the Internet

As recently as 1995, few people had shopped online using the Internet. Today, millions of consumers regularly shop the Internet for products ranging from gifts and toys to cars and even homes. Most of the products available in stores are also available for purchase over the Internet.

In the following sections, we will explore some popular online shopping opportunities. As we explore these opportunities, you are encouraged to visit some of the Web sites shown to learn more about opportunities that are available to you as a potential online shopper.

Automobiles

Let's face it, automobiles are expensive and many car buyers are impulsive shoppers. For whatever reason, impulsive buyers don't take time to compare products and prices before making a purchase and afterward these consumers often regret their mistakes. Before you make an expensive automobile purchase, you need to take time to compare products, features, and prices, as well as finance and other charges.

You can save time, aggravation, and money if you research and even haggle for an automobile on the Web (Figure 4.10). You can research information about automobiles at several Web sites including Autopedia (http://www.autopedia.com) and Autoweb (http://www.autoweb.com).

To find the best deal you first need to decide exactly what you're looking for. All new car manufacturers maintain their own Web sites and so do many large dealers. At a manufacturer's site (for example, Ford Motor Company's site) you can find a list of dealers near you. At a manufacturer's or at a dealer's site, you can check out the features you want. Then you can visit a general-purpose site, such as (www.consumerreports.com) where an interactive car finder can help you select a car based on criteria including price, fuel economy, and car features and accessories.

To get the best car deal, you need to know how much the dealer paid the manufacturer for the car. You can find this price at Edmund's Automobile Buyer's Guide (www.edmunds.com). Rebates and dealer incentives are also given.

After completing your research, you can go to a dealer and negotiate a deal, or you can buy the car of your dreams on the Web. At several Web sites, including Autobytel (www.autobytel.com), Autoweb (www.autoweb.com), and MicroSoft's CarPoint (www.carpoint.com), you to purchase the car of your choice.

Books, Tapes, Movies, and CDs

Many shoppers now prefer the convenience of shopping online for items like books, tapes, movies, and CDs from the convenience of their homes or offices. Almost any item that can be purchased at a book or music store can be purchased from an online seller and, in many cases, can be purchased at cheaper prices.

FIGURE 4.10
Autoweb Home Page

Amazon.com is a leading online seller of books, tapes, movies, and CDs. However, there are many companies on the Web that offer these items, including Reel (www.reel.com), Borders (www.borders.com), CDNow (www.cdnow.com), Music Boulevard (www.musicboulevard.com), and Amazon.com (www.Amazon.com), shown in Figure 4.11.

Many online sources are available on the Web from which you can purchase these items at reduced prices. When you visit one of these sites, you can browse through hundreds of available items and check out an extensive variety of titles and special deals.

Clothing

If you're used to ordering clothing from mail-order catalogs like L.L. Bean, Lands' End, J. Crew, and the Gap, you'll likely find that ordering clothing from these, or other, online merchants is just as easy and convenient. The only problem is the same problem you face when ordering from mail-order catalogs—you can't feel the fabric or try on the clothes. And like ordering from a mail-order catalog, the colors may not be the same as they appear online.

To overcome these problems, reputable online clothing merchants offer a no-questions-asked guarantee of customer satisfaction. For example, merchants like L.L. Bean (www.llbean.com) will allow you to return any purchase if you're not completely satisfied, regardless of the reason (Figure 4.12).

A few basic guidelines will aid you in choosing an online clothing merchant. Before deciding on a merchant, you can protect yourself by following these guidelines:

- *Learn the site's return policy.* Because you're not certain whether the item will fit properly or be the right color, make sure the merchant will allow you to return items for whatever reason. Otherwise, shop elsewhere.

- *Check out the company's size charts and sizing advice.* Because you cannot try on the clothing item, look for sizing charts and descriptions that allow you to better determine which size may be the best fit for you.

FIGURE 4.11

Amazon.com Home Page

FIGURE 4.12

L.L. Bean Home Page

■ *Find a site that provides detailed photos of clothing.* Never buy clothing items unseen. Sites like the Gap contain models you can virtually "dress" in clothes to determine what they look like and allow you to mix and match clothes so you can see which combinations look better together.

Department Stores and Malls

If you just want to browse through a variety of shopping locations and view various kinds of merchandise, online department stores and malls are just the place for you. Some department stores, including J.C. Penney (www.jcpenney.com), Macy's (www.macys.com) (see Figure 4.13), and Bloomingdale's (www.bloomingdales.com) offer Web sites where you can shop for a variety of items. However, most online department stores do not offer the complete selection you might find in their regular catalogs.

The home page of a typical online mall contains links to many stores where you can browse through the store's offerings and order items from individual stores. Two impressive mall sites are the Internet Mall (www.internetmall.com) and Fashionmall (www.fashionmall.com) (see Figure 4.14). Of all malls available on the Web, the Internet Mall offers perhaps the greatest variety of store links.

Food

Going to the grocery store is drudgery for some people, especially for those who have difficulty finding time for grocery shopping. In some locations, online supermarkets eliminate this problem by allowing customers to do their grocery shopping online.

If you dislike going to a grocery store and if you're fortunate to have an online grocery store in your area, online stores like NetGrocer (www.netgrocer.com), HomeRuns (www.homeruns.com), and Peapod (www.peapod.com) allow you to visit their Web sites, select the items you want, and have them delivered to your home.

FIGURE 4.13

Macy's Department Store Home Page

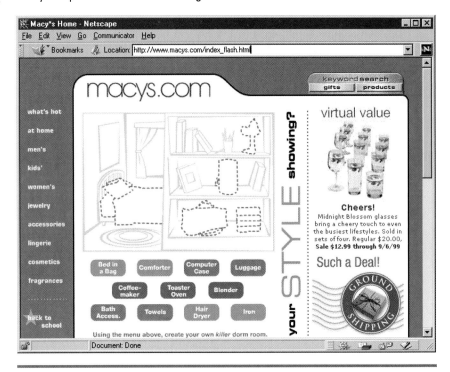

FIGURE 4.14

Fashionmall.com Home Page

NetGrocer (Figure 4.15) is probably the best-known online grocery and drug superstore. Unlike HomeRuns and Peapod, which fill your order and deliver them to you, NetGrocer pulls the items you select from a centralized warehouse and ships them to you overnight via FedEx. HomeRuns and Peapod obtain the items you order from area grocery stores and deliver them to your door.

There are limitations to online grocery shopping. You do not have an opportunity to examine specific items and some items on your list might not be available.

FIGURE 4.15

Netgrocer Home Page

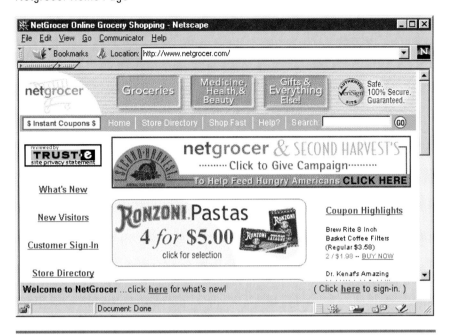

All three online grocers operate similarly. When you visit the grocer's site, you obtain a shopping cart, select a category of food items, and browse through the list of items available. You choose an item by clicking on it. You pay for items you selected by entering your credit card information on your screen and sending it to the grocer.

It may be only a matter of time before local grocery stores in your area go on-line. If you are interested in online grocery shopping, you can check with your local grocers to learn if they have future online shopping plans.

Gifts

Thousands of online stores offer a variety of gifts you can purchase. Depending on what you're looking for, you can visit any number of online department stores, specialty shops, malls, and even stores that specialize in unique gifts. Almost any gift available in a traditional store is available at a site on the Web.

Some gift shops are available only on the Web. Examples include Cybershop (www.cybershop.com), Never Forget (www.neverforget.com), and Perfect Present Picker (www.presentpicker.com).

Homes, Apartments, and Condos

If you have experience buying a home or condominium or searching for an apartment, you know how exasperating and time-consuming it can be. If you are a first-time home or condo buyer, you likely need to know how much you can afford to spend, what closing costs are, what a home inspection is, and so on. Probably every prospective home buyer can benefit from expert advice that is available on the Web.

Sites like HomeShark (www.homeshark.com), Countrywide (www.country-wide.com), and HomeAdvisor (www.homeadvisor.com) provide expert advice for prospective buyers. Advice available at these sites provides answers to basic home-buying questions.

In your preliminary research into buying a new home, you need to determine how much you can afford to pay. At some sites you can determine the amount you can afford by clicking on Financing and then selecting an option that computes the amount that you can afford. (Figure 4.16). This feature calculates the amount you can afford based on data you enter, including your present salary, outstanding debt, and your down payment. After calculating the amount you can afford, you can compare interest rates by visiting the Bank Rate Monitor site (www.bankrate.com). At this site, just click on the state in which you will obtain a mortgage to display a side-by-side listing of mortgage rates.

Several larger realty companies maintain Web sites where you can learn about homes, condos, and apartments available in specific locations. Some sites, such as the one for Century 21, contain links to member agencies in the area you select and even provide pictures, descriptions, and prices of available properties.

If you're like most people, you probably prefer not to buy a home sight unseen over the Internet, buy you can if you wish to do so. However, the information available on the Web can be quite beneficial in your search for a new residence.

Sports and Fitness

Sports and fitness stores have sprung up on the Web and you can probably find your favorite store easily. All offer a variety of sports goods such as clothing apparel, shoes, and related products.

Some stores allow you to shop online, whereas others identify traditional store locations in your area. Like online catalog stores, many online sports and fitness stores offer a return policy if you're not satisfied with your purchase (Figure 4.17).

Toys and Games

Online toy and game sites are favorites among both children and parents. At some sites, the home page contains a list of toy and game categories. After choosing a

FIGURE 4.16

Mortgage Qualification Calculator

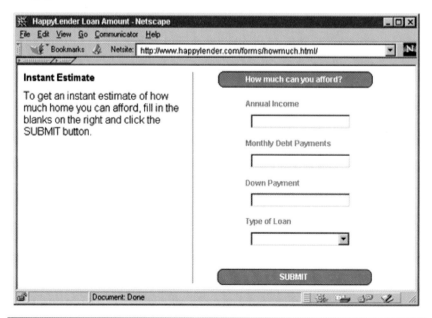

FIGURE 4.17
Foot Locker Home Page

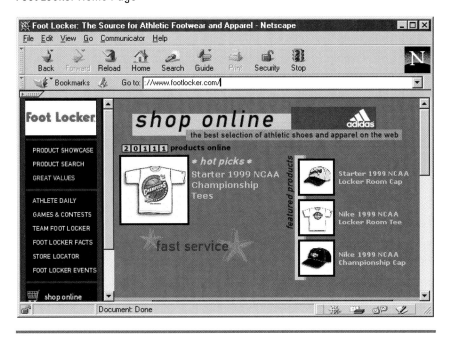

FIGURE 4.18
Toys "R" Us Home Page

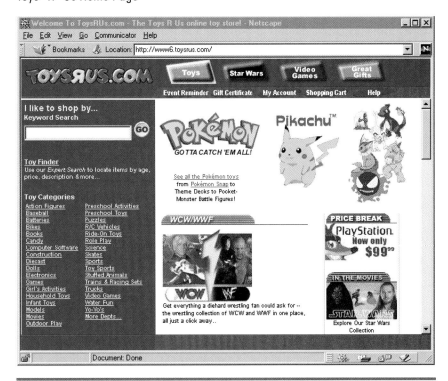

category, a list of products in the category is displayed from which you can make a selection. In Figure 4.18, notice the various toy and game categories shown on the home page.

The toysrus.com Web site is a popular toy and game site. Others include SmartKids.com (www.smartkids.com), eToys (www.etoys.com), and Holt Educational Outlet (www.holtoutlet.com).

Tickets

If you've ever stood in a long line waiting to buy tickets for a play, movie, concert, or ball game, you know how exasperating it can be especially after you've arrived at the ticket window only to learn that all tickets have already been sold. Alas! With online ticket shopping, you can easily and quickly purchase tickets to a favorite event.

TicketMaster (www.ticketmaster.com) and Ticketron (www.ticketron.com) are popular sites for thousands of users seeking tickets for favorite events. Tickets are available on a first-come, first-served basis. Payment can be made online by entering your credit card information. You can choose to pick up your purchased tickets at the event's box office or have them sent to you (Figure 4.19).

Travel, Cruises, and Vacations

More and more travelers and vacationers are turning to the Web to arrange for travel, cruises, and vacations. Many online sites allow you to purchase travel tickets, book cruises, and obtain vacation accommodations, including lodging, amusement park admissions, and tours. Major airlines allow you to purchase a ticket online, called an **electronic ticket,** that you can pick up at the airport ticket counter.

Many online travel sites offer complete travel services, whereas others offer only limited services. At sites like The Trip (www.thetrip.com) and Travelocity (www.travelocity.com), you can obtain comprehensive travel information including descriptions of your intended destinations in addition to ticket purchases (Figure 4.20).

FIGURE 4.19

TicketMaster Home Page

FIGURE 4.20
Travelocity Home Page

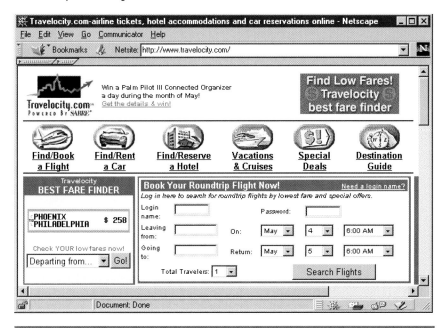

Some travel sites offer discounts on some services including tickets, lodging, and food. For example, at the Hotel Discounts site (www.hoteldiscounts.com), you can obtain discounts available at specified hotels in the area you plan to visit. Cruise line sites, including Carnival Cruise Lines and Caribbean Cruise Lines, frequently offer discounts at their sites to customers who book arrangements early, and even late if a particular cruise is not sold out.

Finding an Online Store or Web Site

If you're looking for a specific online store or Web site, you may be able to find it by typing the letters *http,* followed by a *colon, two slashes,* the letters *www,* a *period,* the *name of the store,* a *period,* and finally the letters *com.* For example, typing the address http://www.jcpenney.com will take you to J.C. Penney's on-line store.

You may be able to find the store you want using Excite's shopping guide at http://www.excite.com/shopping. This guide lists hundreds of sites by category, such as Automobiles and Home and Garden. Yahoo! (http://www.yahoo.com) and Lycos (http://www.lycos.com) offer similar guides.

Online Security

A major concern of online shoppers is the security of personal and financial information traveling across the Internet. It is commonly known that information, including encrypted information, sent across the Internet may be intercepted and misused by unauthorized persons. To prevent others from intercepting and misusing personal and financial information, businesses and banks use a variety of technologies and methods to safeguard this information. Sites vary in the level of security offered. Data encryption, or scrambling of electronic signals, is one method of security used today.

When you shop the Internet, you need to be aware that online shopping is somewhat different than traditional shopping in which you visit stores to find the items you want. Traditional shopping allows you to carefully examine items and ask questions. While shopping online, you are considering purchasing items without first examining them. Moreover, you are dealing with a "faceless" merchant you do not personally know and whom you cannot personally question. Although online shopping is relatively safe, you need to be careful. The adage "better safe than sorry" is good advice when shopping online. You can protect yourself by being informed. Here is a list of useful tips you should keep in mind when shopping online:

■ *Make your online purchases at secure sites.* Many sites provide greater security by using encryption technology to scramble your credit card information so that only authorized personnel at the site can read it. When you enter a secure site, you'll get a pop-up notice in your browser, and then an icon of a locked lock will appear at the bottom left of your screen. A locked (closed) lock means the site is secure. An unlocked (open) lock means the site is not secure.

■ *Learn about the privacy policy of shopping sites before you buy.* Before making an online purchase at a specific site, ask what information the company gathers, how that information will be used, and whether the company shares that information with others, such as a company that compiles and sells mailing lists.

■ *When filling out forms such as order forms, provide only necessary information.* Some forms ask you for more information than is needed. On some forms, an asterisk is placed beside questions that you must answer. A good rule is to answer only those questions that must be answered to accurately order, pay for, and receive the product.

■ *Do not give out your social security number or checking account number.* There's no legitimate reason a site needs to know these numbers. If you're paying with a credit card, you will be asked for your credit card number. Remember to provide only information the company actually needs.

■ *Shop at sites that follow privacy rules from a privacy watchdog such as TRUSTe.* TRUSTe (www.truste.org) is a nonprofit group that serves as a watchdog for Internet privacy. It allows sites to post an online seal if the site adheres to TRUSTe's Internet privacy policies. These policies are designed to protect both the company and the customer (Figure 4.21).

■ *Be aware of potential Internet scams.* The U.S. Consumer Gateway (www.consumer.gov) reports on Internet scams and tells you what actions the Federal Trade Commission (FTC) has taken against Internet scam artists. The Internet Fraud Watch, run by the National Consumers League (www.fraud.org), is a great source as well. Learn about potential Internet scams and don't allow yourself to become a victim (Figure 4.22).

Other Online Applications and Opportunities

Although online shopping is perhaps the most enticing electronic commerce activity, many other online applications and opportunities are available to consumers. Businesses are flocking to the Internet to provide a variety of useful and unique products and services. In the following sections, some of the more popular online activities are identified.

FIGURE 4.21
TRUSTe Home Page

FIGURE 4.22
National Fraud Information Center Home Page

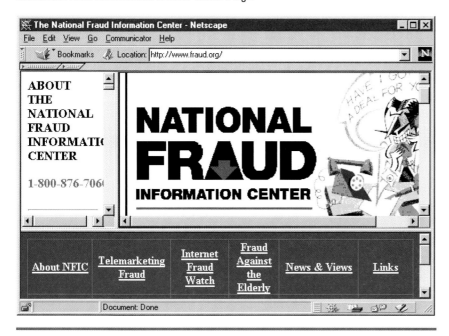

Online Information and News

An increasing number of users are turning to the Internet for breaking news. A study of 2,200 users in the United States by Juniper Communications, a leading Internet research company, revealed that 12 percent of the users surveyed get their news over the Internet. The study found that 61 percent of those surveyed

FIGURE 4.23

The New York Times Home Page

read national and international news online, 39 percent read business news, 34.4 percent read sports news, 31.3 percent access entertainment news, 25.9 percent read local news, and 20.6 percent read technology news.

Online information and news is current news provided by news organizations to users having access to the Internet. Many news organizations, including television networks, news services, newspapers, and magazine publishers, maintain sites where the latest news stories are available for reading (Figure 4.23).

If it's local news you're interested in, chances are your local newspaper or television station may have a Web site you can visit for local news. For example, North Carolina's *Winston-Salem Journal* site (Figure 4.24) provides local news stories for the area served by the newspaper.

Online Education

Today, educational opportunities abound on the Internet. **Online education** allows a user to study a particular subject or course by using a computer and a modem to access course information and materials available from publishers' Web sites. A user can visit a publisher's Web site and choose from a list of available courses for a fee. For example, a visitor to The Dryden Press site can easily choose any online course offered (Figure 4.25).

At Dryden's Web site, you can purchase a printed copy of a book or register for an online course. The procedure for registering for a DrydenOnline course is simple. After accessing the DrydenOnline site, you click on *Bookstore,* click on the Information Systems bookrack, click on Online Courses to display a list of online courses and fees, and click on the course you want. From there, you simply follow the instructions to register and pay for the course. You will be issued a password to access the course for which you registered.

Online courses are gaining in popularity because they are relatively inexpensive (no tuition charges) and you can study in your home or office and at your

FIGURE 4.24
Winston-Salem (N.C.) *Journal* Home Page

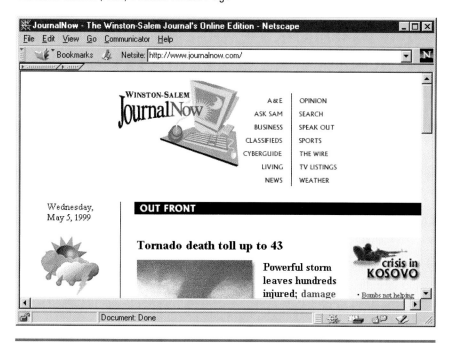

FIGURE 4.25
DrydenOnline Home Page

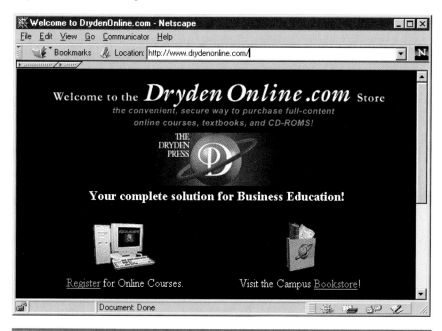

convenience. These advantages make online courses attractive for students and working individuals.

Some manufacturers have begun introducing small hand-held wireless devices to which books can be downloaded. These devices, called **e-books,** are about the size of a flat paperback book and contain memory and a screen for displaying pages. One of the devices, available from NuvoMedia, Inc., of California, is shown in Figure 4.26.

Online Banking

Online banking offers customers traditional banking services over the Internet from the convenience of a customer's own home or office. Many banks and other financial institutions, such as credit unions, now offer online banking services to customers that have Internet access. Online banking requires that special software be installed on the customer's computer.

Online banking, also called Internet banking, offers two main advantages over traditional banking. First, some banks that provide online banking allow customers to pay bills online—a service sometimes called **digital bill paying.** With digital bill paying, a customer can pay bills electronically in less time that it takes to prepare a check for mailing, and the fees are usually less than the cost of mailing printed checks. Second, online banking allows you to check your account balances at anytime instead of having to wait until you receive your monthly statement or visit an ATM machine.

Some banks provide a demonstration of online banking at their Web sites. For example, an online guided demo at the Republic Bank and Trust Company's site provides details of the bank's online services and allows a user to sign up as an online customer (Figure 4.27).

You can learn more about online banking by visiting your bank and learning how your bank's online banking system works or by visiting the bank's Web site. If you're concerned about security, question a bank employee about security measures.

Online Investing

Online investing refers to using a computer and Internet access to purchase or sell stocks, bonds, commodities, insurance, or other financial assets including mutual funds and annuities. Today, we are experiencing a virtual explosion of online investment opportunities.

FIGURE 4.26

NuvoMedia Electronic Book

FIGURE 4.27

Republic Bank and Trust Company Online Banking Web Page

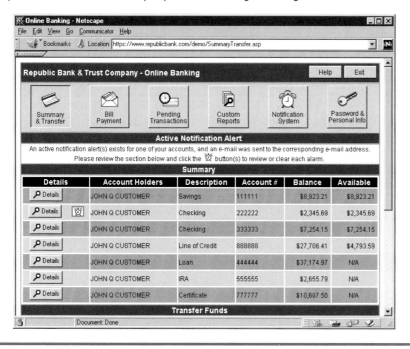

Until recently stock and bond traders, insurance companies, mutual funds, and other investment firms were reluctant to embrace the Internet as a marketing vehicle. Some still prefer to conduct business in traditional ways—that is, face to face with customers. However, competition among firms for investors has driven many of them to the Internet as a means of attracting new customers.

Many investors prefer online investing because of the convenience it offers. Investors can track stock and bond prices and trends on their computers at home or at the office. They can obtain quotes around the clock, receive up-to-the-minute analyses of investment opportunities, and get advice from trading companies. Moreover, online traders offer cheaper fees.

Several investment companies are taking advantage of the Internet to provide customers with online investment opportunities. Two notable examples are Charles Schwab (www.schwab.com) and E*Trade (www.etrade.com). At their Web sites, both companies explain the services available, provide instructions for opening an account, and identify a variety of investment opportunities available to customers. Both provide information about specific stocks, bonds, mutual funds, and other investments. For example, a visitor to E*Trade's Web site (Figure 4.28) can enter the market symbol for a particular stock and immediately obtain that stock's most recent price quotation.

There is little doubt that more investment companies will find their way to the Internet as competition for investors intensify. As this occurs, online investors can expect improved services and more competitive investment fees.

Online Auctions

One of the more innovative online applications is that of online auctions. An **online auction** is a Web site that allows you to place a bid for a specific item. If you've ever attended a traditional auction, you probably already have an idea of how online auctions work.

FIGURE 4.28

E*Trade Home Page

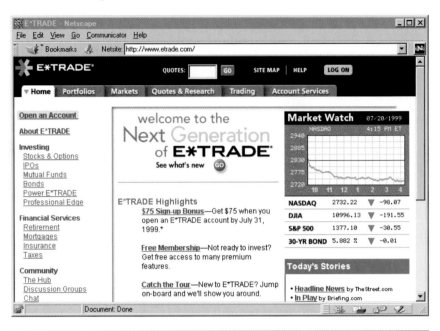

FIGURE 4.29

eBay Home Page

Two popular online auctions are uBid (www.ubid.com) and eBay (www.ebay.com). At uBid's site, you can sign up and then place a bid for any of several computer products, including desktops, portables, modems, and printers. At eBay's site, you can register online and then place a bid for a variety of products. The eBay home page (Figure 4.29) includes a list of product categories, including antiques, computers, dolls and figures, jewelry and gemstones, photo and electronics items, and sports memorabilia.

After you've selected a category, a list of specific items in that category will appear on your screen, along with the current highest bid and the closing date by which your bid must be submitted. You will be notified if yours is the winning bid. Following payment, the item will be sent to you.

Online Employment

Many companies and organizations post employment opportunities at their Web sites, and thousands of online users have turned to the Web to find jobs. Hundreds of private companies, colleges and universities (Figure 4.30), government agencies, and nonprofit organizations regularly post job vacancies at their sites, along with specific job information including job descriptions, salaries, and starting dates.

Many companies and organizations allow you to submit an application online by completing an onscreen form. You can also send your resume over the Internet to a prospective employer. You may receive notification that the company has received your application and resume.

If you're seeking employment, you can visit several sites to learn more about employment opportunities with that firm or organization. Even if you aren't seeking employment, you may want to investigate employment possibilities in your field of interest.

In this chapter we looked at some of the more popular electronic commerce applications between businesses and customers. However, space limitations made it impossible to cover all possible applications, many of which you can learn about in newspapers, magazines, and by surfing the Web on your own.

In the next chapter, we focus on business-to-business electronic commerce applications and opportunities. You will learn some ways businesses are using electronic commerce to simplify and streamline their activities and operations with other companies.

FIGURE 4.30

Appalachian State University Job List

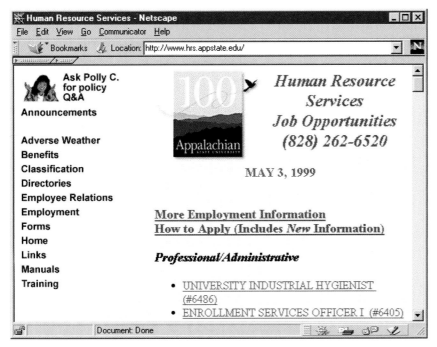

Electronic commerce, one of the fastest growing uses of the Internet, is the buying and selling of products and services electronically over the Internet. Using the Internet, businesses can advertise and market products and services worldwide, reduce costs, simplify ordering procedures, speed up the delivery of products and services, and simplify and speed up payments for goods and services sold.

Online shopping, also called electronic shopping or e-shopping, is using a computer, modem, and Internet access to locate, examine, purchase, sell, and pay for products over the Internet. An online shopper is often referred to as an e-shopper. Online shopping can be worldwide or local. Worldwide online shopping means that a customer goes online to find the best buys regardless of the location of the seller, whereas local online shopping is limited to specific Web sites located in close proximity to the customer.

A virtual storefront is a computerized storefront (entryway) through which potential customers can enter to view, and possibly purchase, the company's products and services. Many retailers maintain their own virtual storefronts by regularly updating information about new and existing products and services and by providing up-to-date ordering information and forms.

An electronic shopping mall is an online mall with many electronic stores offering for sale a variety goods and services, including computers, clothing, sporting goods, greeting cards, books, and flowers. After accessing an electronic shopping mall, a customer can locate a product or service by choosing the type of product or service or by choosing the store offering the product or service.

Special programs, called intelligent shopping agents, aid shoppers in searching the Web for the lowest-priced products. Intelligent shopping agents are sometimes integrated into search programs so that they act automatically when an online search is executed.

Methods for making online payments for products and services include credit accounts, credit card payments, and personal identification number (PIN) payments.

As recently as 1995 few people had shopped online using the Internet. Today, millions of consumers regularly shop the Internet for products ranging from gifts and toys to cars and even homes. Most of the products available in stores are also available for purchase over the Internet.

If you're looking for a specific online store or Web site, you may be able to find it by typing the letters *http,* followed by a *colon, two slashes,* the letters *www,* a *period,* the *name of the store,* a *period,* and finally the letters *com.*

Currently there is concern about privacy, security, and theft of financial data on the Web. Different sites offer different degrees of security and protection. Data encryption, or scrambling of electronic signals, is a way of improving security.

Although online shopping is perhaps the most enticing electronic commerce activity, many other online applications and opportunities are available to consumers. These include online information and news, online education, online banking, online investing, online auctions, and online employment.

KEY TERMS

credit account (107)
credit card (108)
digital bill paying (124)
e-book (123)
electronic commerce (100)
electronic shopper (e-shopper) (101)
electronic shopping (e-shopping) (101)

electronic shopping mall (103)
electronic ticket (118)
intelligent shopping agent (105)
local online shopping (101)
online auction (125)
online banking (124)
online education (122)

online information and news (122)
online investing (124)
online shopping (101)
virtual storefront (103)
worldwide online shopping (101)

END-OF-CHAPTER ACTIVITIES

Matching

Match each term with its description.

a. electronic shopping mall
b. electronic ticket
c. online auction
d. online shopping

e. credit card
f. virtual storefront
g. beware of potential Internet scams

h. intelligent shopping agent
i. online education
j. online banking

_____ **1.** Using a computer and modem to access information and materials from publisher Web sites.

_____ **2.** A computerized entryway through which potential customers can enter to view, and possibly purchase, the company's products and services.

_____ **3.** Using a computer, modem, and Internet access to locate, examine, purchase, sell, and pay for products over the Internet.

_____ **4.** One of the guidelines you should follow to protect yourself when using the Internet.

_____ **5.** A method of paying for products or services purchased over the Internet.

_____ **6.** A ticket purchased over the Internet.

_____ **7.** A location on the Web that consists of many electronic stores.

_____ **8.** A Web site that allows you to bid for a specific item.

_____ **9.** A special program that aids shoppers in searching the Web for the lowest prices.

_____ **10.** Traditional banking services over the Internet between a bank and customer.

Review Questions

1. Electronic commerce is becoming increasingly popular for both individuals and businesses. What are the main reasons for this increasing popularity?

2. What is online shopping and is there a difference between worldwide online shopping and local online shopping.

3. What is a virtual storefront?

4. How do electronic shopping malls make it possible for a shopper to find a desired product or service?

5. What is an online catalog? Identify two addresses where you can access an online catalog.

6. What is an intelligent shopping agent?

7. Identify two ways or methods for making online payments for products.

8. Identify five categories of products or services that can be purchased over the Internet.

9. Identify five ways to protect yourself as an online shopper.

10. What is online education and why is online education gaining in popularity among certain groups of users?

Activities

1. Using your browser, try to find three online stores near you. Examine each store's site. Prepare a written report of each site. In your report, indicate whether a site is attractive, secure, informative, and includes links to other useful sites.

2. This activity involves using the intelligent shopping agent Jango to search online stores and find a specific product and the price of the product at each store. Using your browser, type *http:www.jango.com* in the address box to access Jango's home page, on which product categories are listed. Select a category to display a dialog box. In the boxes, enter the required product information, including manufacturer. (*Note:* The more specific the information, the more successful your search will be.) Click on the Find Prices button. A list will appear that contains online store names and the prices they charge. Examine the list. Make a note of the store offering the lowest price.

3. Visit the Web site for The Dryden Press at (http://www.drydenonline.com) and select the Online Courses feature (option). Prepare a written list of available online courses. On your list, indicate one course in which you might have a particular interest.

4. Visit an online auction, such as eBay. While at the site, choose three items available for bidding. Prepare a brief report that includes the items you selected and the most recent bid for each of the three items.

5. This is a group activity. Your instructor will arrange class members into groups with a small number of students in each group. The Internet addresses for some online shopping sites follow. Each member of a group will be assigned the task of visiting one of the listed sites. While at the site, prepare a critique of the site, including your evaluation of the site's home page and other pages accessible by using the available links. Also, note whether the site offers visitors greater security by displaying a notice or a seal, such as a TRUSTe seal.

ONLINE SHOPPING SITE:	INTERNET ADDRESS:
CompUSA	http://www.compusa.com
Dell Computer	http://www.dell.com
IBM	http://www.ibm.com
Gateway	http://www.gateway.com

Business-to-Business Applications

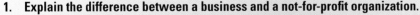

AFTER COMPLETING THIS CHAPTER, YOU WILL:

1. Explain the difference between a business and a not-for-profit organization.
2. Name four factors of production and the type of payment earned by each factor.
3. Identify the five management functions explained in the chapter and explain the meaning of each function.
4. Explain why information is sometimes referred to as the lifeblood of a business or an organization.
5. Identify the five organizational goals presented in the chapter and explain the importance of each goal.
6. Explain the nature of an information system and why it is important to the success of a business or organization.
7. Explain the meaning of the term *value chain*.

8. Briefly explain the nature of electronic data interchange (EDI) and how EDI can be used to save valuable time and money.

9. Briefly explain the difference between financial EDI and automated clearinghouse (ACH) transfers.

10. Identify two businesses that were presented in the chapter and tell how each company uses electronic commerce to improve the company's business operations.

The American economy is based on the concept of a free market system. A **free market system** is a type of economy in which private individuals and companies can produce and sell products and services with minimal government involvement.

A free market system allows for open competition in which each business can compete with other businesses to pursue its goals and objectives and to be rewarded for its efforts by earning profit. As a result, the American economy is truly the envy of other economies around the world.

Electronic commerce is playing an ever-increasing role in business-to-business applications. More and more, businesses and other types of organizations are taking advantage of the opportunities available with modern electronic commerce technologies. Their doing so benefits not only the business or organization itself but also consumers and the general public.

In the previous chapter, we examined several business-to-customer applications that allowed some businesses to experience remarkable success. In this chapter, our attention will focus on business-to-business applications that allow businesses to improve operations with other companies, including suppliers, customers, and others with which a firm conducts business activities.

Recognizing that not every student has an educational background in business subjects, this chapter begins with a brief explanation of basic business terminology and some business fundamentals. Afterward, business-to-business applications involving electronic commerce technologies, activities, and applications are presented. Here you will gain valuable insight into the ever-increasing importance of electronic commerce in our dynamic business world.

Business Terminology and Activities

Earlier in this book you encountered some business terminology and activities with which some of you may have already been familiar. However, for those with little or no prior business education and training, the following sections identify important business terms and activities. An understanding of these terms and activities will make it easier for you to understand business-to-business transactions in electronic commerce.

What Is a Business?

When you hear the word *business,* what image comes to your mind? The word brings forth different images for different people. To some, it brings to mind one's job or employment situation. To others, it brings to mind a retailer that sells products to consumers. To some, it brings to mind a broader image of the millions of companies that make up the economy. This broad image is an all-inclusive one that encompasses all kinds of enterprises and their activities.

A **business** is a profit-seeking enterprise that engages in numerous activities to provide products and services to consumers in an economic system. These products and services are provided to consumers, like you and me, and to other businesses and organizations. Some businesses provide tangible goods, such as food, clothing, television sets, computers, and automobiles. Others provide nontangible services, such as insurance, travel services, health services, and car rentals.

Today's global economy consists of businesses of various types and sizes. There are single-owner businesses, partnerships, and corporations. Any of them can be large or small. Some are retailers, some are service companies, and others are manufacturers. Regardless of type or size, any business must obtain and use certain inputs, called the *factors of production,* in order to provide products and services to the public and to other businesses and organizations.

Factors of Production

The driving force behind any kind of business is profits. **Profit** is the reward for businesspeople, called **entrepreneurs,** who take risks by combining capital (including money, machinery, and equipment), employees, materials, and other resources to produce the products and services wanted and needed by other members of society, including individuals, households, government, and other businesses. Elements that are combined to produce products and services are called the **factors of production,** and payments must be made to the supplier(s) of each factor, as shown in Figure 5.1

Profits are not earned automatically. Just because an entrepreneur assumes risks does not guarantee success. Profits represent rewards to entrepreneurs who are successful. Many businesses fail for various reasons. One only needs to travel a short distance to find at least one business that failed and is no longer in operation. Occasionally, we find stores with windows boarded up or plants that are closed.

Natural resources are inputs that are used in their natural states, including land, forests, and mineral ore deposits, such as oil. For example, a gold mining company may excavate 10 or more tons of earth to obtain one ounce of gold. One bale of cotton is used to produce up to 100,000 filters used in coffeemakers. Payment for these resources is called **rent.**

Human resources include workers at all levels, such as production workers, clerks, managers, technicians, and accountants. Self-employed insurance agents, real estate agents, electricians, plumbers, and accountants are also examples of human resources. Payment for human resources is called **wages.**

FIGURE 5.1

Factors of Production and Payments to Each Factor

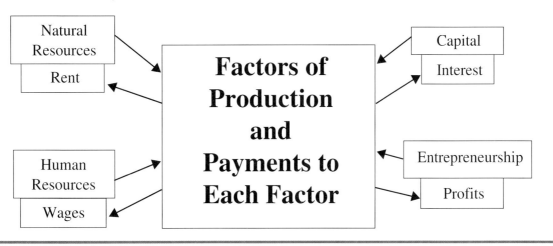

Another important factor of production is **capital,** which includes money, physical facilities, information, technology, and equipment. Equipment may include assembly-line machinery, computers, cash registers, farm tractors, or other types of physical resources. Payment for capital is **interest.** For example, if you borrow money from a bank to obtain machinery, you pay interest on the borrowed money.

Although profit is the primary driving force of businesses, most businesses recognize that they have social and ethical obligations to society. To achieve success, businesses must treat employees fairly, pay taxes, obey the laws, refrain from polluting the environment, and provide products and services that are safe. Companies that continually ignore their social and ethical responsibilities do so at the risk of failure.

Not-for-Profit Organizations

An organization that is formed and exists for purposes other than to earn profits is a **not-for-profit organization.** Not-for-profit organizations exist in both the public and private sectors of our economy, and they play important roles in our society (Figure 5.2).

FIGURE 5.2
Some Not-for-Profit Organizations

Churches and Other
Religious Organizations

Emergency Services

Charitable Medical and
Health Care Services

Performing Arts and Other
Cultural Organizations

Libraries

Private Nonprofit Educational
Colleges, Schools, and Institutions

E-Commerce Technology

Selling Music over the Internet

Like thousands of other products, many businesses and Internet users knew it would be just a matter of time before big companies would begin selling music by allowing customers to download it from the Internet. It seems that time has now arrived. The big companies want to sell tunes directly to consumers and transmit the product instantly to personal computers.

Soon, music lovers won't have to wait in line at a music store for the latest release from recording artists such as the Backstreet Boys, Whitney Houston, Will Smith, or Britney Spears. Consumers will be able to just click on the right buttons on their PCs, wait about three minutes for the download, and boogie.

Music lovers in the United States will spend about $12 billion this year. So no wonder the big companies look at the digital future with a combination of fascination and fear. Universal Music, Warner Music, Sony, BMG, and EMI, along with their partner IBM, have announced new technology that makes it easier for companies to track and control music and sales over the Web. Testing of the new system began in San Diego in the spring of 1999. With high-speed Internet connections from the Time Warner cable system, about 1,000 families participated in a nine-month test that enabled them to buy recordings from about 2,000 album choices.

At a special Web site, participants will be able to download and charge to their credit cards albums or singles. The companies haven't decided what titles they'll offer or how much they'll charge.

Music companies are seeking ways to increase their profits. If the system works as companies are hoping it will, direct sales mean they could keep the music store's share of a typical sale (currently about 40 percent of the average $13.50 retail price for a compact disc). Also, they could eliminate the cost of making and packaging a typical CD (currently about 75 cents per disc). Distributors also may be able to improve profit margins from sales of older recordings that currently account for about 70 percent of online music sales.

The big companies have other reasons for wanting the trial to work. Some cable companies want subscribers to pay premium prices for high-speed Internet connections. Music companies want to curb music piracy now occurring on the Internet. IBM is convinced that its software will deter, and possibly prevent, hackers from making copies of downloaded music and offering it for free on the Internet. The IBM system encrypts downloaded music so it cannot be copied and resold to others. Manufacturers of portable electronic devices, such as Sony, want to make new devices capable of storing downloaded music.

Music downloaded from the Internet offers great potential for all companies and recording artists involved. If the technology proves successful and if music downloading becomes popular with users, the music industry could experience the most revolutionary change in its history.

Source: USA Today, February 9, 1999, p. 6B.

Not-for-profit organizations that exist in the public sector include local charities, public schools, public hospitals, libraries, and zoos. One example is a local charity established to aid a family whose home was destroyed by fire. Not-for-profit organizations that exist in the private sector include museums, charities, religious organizations, and theaters. An example might be a local theater established and operated for the purpose of providing cultural opportunities to performers and patrons.

It is important to know that both for-profit and not-for-profit organizations engage in business-type activities. Both types require the use of the factors of production and both must operate efficiently. To be successful, both types rely on expert and efficient management and must provide high-quality products and services. Both types of organizations may actively engage in electronic commerce.

To be effective, electronic commerce applications, as well as standard business applications, require effective and innovative management practices. Successful managers perform essential management functions, each of which is described in the following sections.

Management Functions

Management may be defined as the attainment of organizational goals in an effective and efficient manner through planning, organizing, leading, and controlling organizational resources (Figure 5.3). Successful managers are those that get things done through their organizations.

Planning is the management function of identifying and defining future organizational goals and deciding on the tasks and resources needed to complete the tasks and achieve the organizational goals. To be successful and to avoid mistakes and potential problems, companies wanting to engage in electronic commerce should develop and implement detailed plans carefully and deliberately.

Organizing is the management function of assigning tasks, delegating authority to individuals who perform the tasks, and allocating resources needed to perform the tasks. To achieve organizational goals, sufficient resources must be available and should be allocated to those charged with completing assigned tasks.

Leading is the management function that involves the use of influence to motivate employees to achieve the organization's goals. A successful leader is able to create a wholesome working environment in which employees want to perform at their highest level.

Controlling is the management function of monitoring employee performance and activities, keeping the organization on track toward its goals, and making corrections and adjustments as needed. While pursuing a specific goal, changes and adjustments are sometimes needed. A properly controlled organization operates within a framework in which changes and adjustments are made when necessary.

FIGURE 5.3

Management Functions

Planning
Organizing
Leading
Controlling

Many companies are now successfully engaged in electronic commerce because the management functions were implemented and practiced. Others are now in the process of implementing already-developed plans and strategies. Still others are in the process of developing their electronic commerce plans and strategies. Good management is indeed a key to success for any organization with electronic commerce ambitions.

Organizational Structure

The American economy consists of businesses of various kinds, sizes, and structures. They include retailers, service companies, manufacturers, and others. Some are small one-owner businesses while others are large corporations with thousands of employees and with sales in the billions of dollars.

A small business may consist of a single owner who performs virtually all functions and activities of the business, including ordering products for resale, employing and managing workers, maintaining business records, and serving customers. In short, specialized personnel and departments typically found within large businesses may be nonexistent in smaller businesses.

Large businesses are often organized into specialized departments with clearly defined goals and objectives. Highly trained managers supervise skilled employees who are assigned specific tasks. Figure 5.4 illustrates the way in which a manufacturing company may be structured into several departments to achieve the organization's goals and objectives by performing assigned tasks effectively and proficiently. An actual manufacturing company may have more or fewer departments

FIGURE 5.4

Possible Manufacturing Company Departments

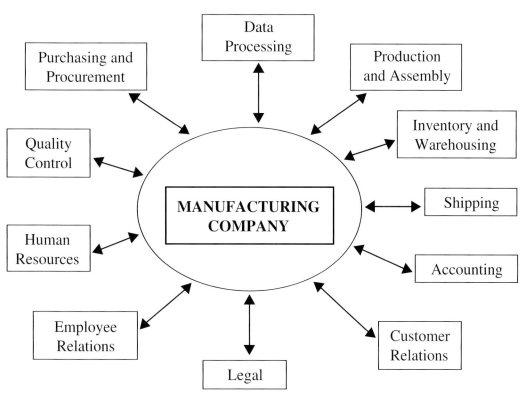

than those shown in the illustration and the actual department names may be different than those shown.

Information: Lifeblood of Business

Information, often called the *lifeblood* of a business or an organization, is data that have been processed so as to make them useful for a specific purpose, such as making a decision. To be useful, information must be accurate, complete, and timely.

If we could measure it, the amount of information consumed throughout the world would be staggering. Each day on a worldwide basis people make trillions upon trillions of decisions. Some decisions, such as what to eat for lunch, are more or less commonplace. Many decisions, including the quantity of a particular product a firm should produce, are arguably more important. Many decisions, including choosing a supplier of raw materials to be used in production, have financial consequences. The basis of all these decisions is information.

Computers, networks, and the Internet have changed the way people, businesses, and organizations obtain information. In general, these technologies allow people to obtain information that is more current, more accurate, and more accessible. Modern computer technologies have changed the information-gathering and decision-making behaviors of people, businesses, and organizations throughout the world, and these changes continue to occur. From a business perspective, the Internet provides almost instant access to customers, suppliers, competitors, government agencies, and markets anyplace in the world (Figure 5.5).

Business Communications

Communication can be defined as a meaningful exchange of information. Everyone is familiar with oral and written communication because oral and written messages are regularly used in a person's daily activities. Oral communica-

FIGURE 5.5

Worldwide Access via the Internet

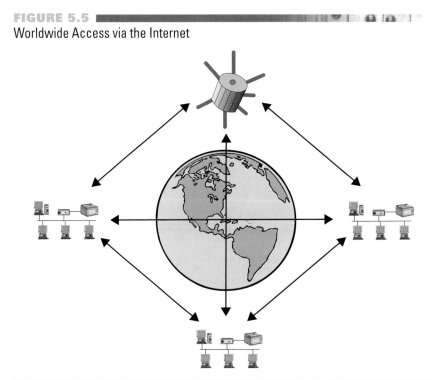

tion is practiced when two or more people engage in a conversation. Written communication is practiced when one person sends a letter or memo to another person. A variety of familiar communications devices, media, and technologies are often used for oral and written communications between individuals and groups, as shown in Figure 5.6.

More and more, information is now being transmitted and received electronically using combinations of computer technologies and communications technologies, collectively called **telecommunications.** These newer technologies include computer hardware and software, networks, and the Internet and the World Wide Web, which help make electronic commerce possible (Figure 5.7). They allow fast, efficient, and cost-effective communications within an organization,

FIGURE 5.6

Traditional Communications Methods

| Verbal Person-to-Person | Telephones | Cell Phones |

| Conferences and Meetings | Memos | U.S. Postal |

| Fax Machines | Audio-Visual Presentations | Pagers |

FIGURE 5.7
Electronic Commerce Communications Methods

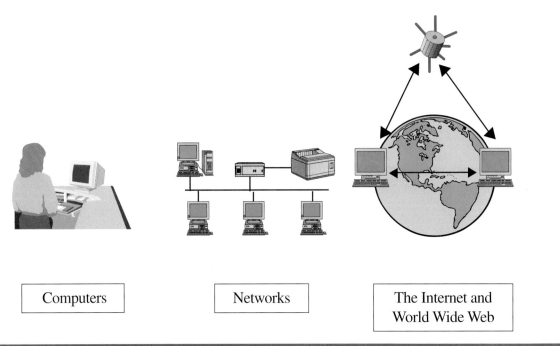

| Computers | Networks | The Internet and World Wide Web |

between organizations, and between individuals, companies, and agencies throughout the world.

Fast, effective, and efficient communication is essential to business. In a business environment, communication with the marketplace, and especially with customers, allows a company to learn what products or services customers want and the changes they would like to see in existing and new products and services. Communication makes it possible for managers to inform employees about changes in policies and procedures. Communication among engineers, production workers, suppliers, and marketers enables a company to design and produce products that customers want. Communication through advertising is intended to persuade customers to buy the company's products. Equally important, effective communication among and between all departments within an organization results in increased productivity. Just as you must have the information you need to perform your activities, each department requires information to perform its assigned tasks. For example, personnel cannot ship products to customers before receiving authorization from the accounting department. Personnel in the production and assembly department rely on reports prepared by quality control inspectors in order to produce high-quality products. After performing periodic inspections and tests, quality control personnel submit inspection and test data to the data processing department for statistical analysis. Test results and recommendations are made available to management in the production and assembly department. Decisions concerning appropriate action can then be made.

Some communications are internal while other communications are external. **Internal communications** are those that occur *within* an organization. Examples include memos, departmental meetings, training sessions, and phone conversations. More recently, electronic mail has become popular as a means of communicating internally. Electronic mail (e-mail) is the use of a computer network to send and receive messages. Some e-mail systems are strictly local, providing communication services for users of a local area network. Other e-mail systems are linked to the Internet to allow messages to be transmitted and received across national boundaries.

External communication is the exchange of useful information between an organization and its audiences. Examples of company audiences include other businesses, customers, suppliers, the general public, and governmental agencies. External communication allows a company to continue functioning properly, to maintain good customer relationships, and to locate and communicate with suppliers of raw materials.

For both internal and external communications, businesses continue to use traditional communications media such as the U.S. Postal Service, telephones, and human messengers. In addition, more and more businesses now are using modern communications media and software, computers, networks, and the Internet and the Web because of the advantages of using these technologies.

Organizational Goals and Objectives

To be successful, every business must establish and meet goals and objectives to achieve high standards of performance. For all organizations, high performance in efficiency, service, quality, productivity, and profitability is critical. Achieving high performance levels in each of these areas provides a business with a distinct advantage over its competition and enables the business to prosper.

Many private companies have embraced the Internet as a means for improving performance. Some firms, including large corporations, continue to conduct their activities by traditional means as though the Internet does not exist. Others, however, now conduct many of their business activities and operations via the Internet in order to improve overall performance in all areas of their operations. In the following paragraphs, we look briefly at the areas of efficiency, service, quality, productivity, and profitability in which performance levels are particularly important (Figure 5.8).

FIGURE 5.8
Organizational Performance Criteria

Efficiency

Service

Quality

Productivity

Profitability

Efficiency

The term **efficiency** refers to the allocation of resources required to achieve specific organizational goals. Each unit of a resource has a cost. If the cost of the resources is excessive, a company can easily incur costs that exceed the value of the output. This obviously would not be an efficient use of valuable resources.

Unemployment and underemployment of resources can be a serious problem for a company. **Unemployment** refers to a lack of resources necessary for the successful completion of a project. An example of unemployment would be an inadequate staff of programmers needed to update a company's computer programs that are not Y2K compliant—that is, existing programs cannot read and process dates after the year 1999. **Underemployment** refers to resources that are not employed in their most efficient uses. For example, a trained and skilled engineer employed as an assembly-line worker or a plant custodian who had been educated and trained as an elementary school teacher might be considered underemployed. Unfortunately, both unemployment and underemployment exist within many business enterprises.

Service

The term **service** refers to the intangible tasks that satisfy consumer or business needs. Good service results in goodwill. *Goodwill* may be defined as the desire of a consumer or business to want to do business with an organization with which the consumer or business is treated well. If you have been treated unfairly by a retailer, chances are that you prefer not to do business with that same retailer in the future.

Everyone associated with a business should expect good service. An airline passenger who has been treated rudely by a reservations agent or member of the flight crew may prefer to travel with a different airline in the future. A consumer who purchases a defective product expects courteous treatment when returning the product. An employee who is harassed by a supervisor may seek employment elsewhere. An individual making an expensive long-distance telephone call to a company may become frustrated by having to spend valuable time and money while pressing a long series of buttons before being connected to someone who can assist the caller.

Good service is the hallmark of a well-organized and well-managed organization. Customers, suppliers, and others are sensitive to how they are treated. The service they receive has a significant influence on their future relationship with the organization.

Quality

Quality refers to the value (or perceived value) of a firm's products and services. Everyone expects products and services purchased to be of value, at least in proportion to the prices paid. Organizations that provide low-quality products and services should expect sales to decline as customers associate product and service quality with price.

Chances are that you have purchased a product only to discover its quality to be less than expected. If so, you probably would not purchase that same product in the future. Some companies provide products or services that are inferior in quality. The problem may result from poor quality-control standards. Regardless of the reasons, companies providing inferior products or services often experience declining sales.

America Online Inc.

Until the mid-1980s, most personal computers were used in isolation. The typical view many people had was that users were basically computer nerds who interacted with computers rather than with people. That image has changed primarily because of the emergence of modern online subscriber services that allow a user to connect a personal computer to a large mainframe computer and, in turn, to networks around the world. America Online (AOL) is one of these services.

Founded in 1985 by Steve Case, America Online Inc., is the world's largest and fastest growing Internet subscriber service with more than 15 million subscribers worldwide, of which more than 12 million reside in the United States. Under chair and CEO Case and chief operating officer Bob Pittman, America Online is a leader in developing the new interactive media.

If you have a modem and use an Apple Macintosh or a personal computer with Windows, getting an account with America Online is easy. After contacting the company, AOL will send you a free copy of its software, which will manage your modem settings and the connection specifications necessary to begin your membership. After you've installed the software and answered the questions on your screen, connecting your computer to AOL is as easy as clicking a button.

Once you're connected to AOL, the interface you work with is quite user-friendly. When you access AOL, windows and colorful icons appear that you can activate by pointing and clicking. AOL offers users many services. Windows and items that appear on the screen are organized in a convenient manner so you can find the items you want quickly and easily.

America Online, one of the largest and fastest growing online services, may best be described as an electronic community. Its windows and icons are easily activated by pointing and clicking.

Each window appearing on your screen offers several choices of what to do or where to go next. For example, when you first log on (access AOL), you have the choice of reading some top news stories of the day, checking to see if you have received any electronic mail messages, or going directly to the Departments section. If you select Departments, you will see a window of choices including travel, sports, and entertainment.

America Online is more than just a storehouse of information. It more closely resembles an online community. An AOL subscriber can send and receive electronic mail messages, participate in one or more of several forums in which topics of interest to certain users and groups are discussed, and post notices to other members.

If you are interested in trying America Online, you can do so without charge during a trial period by accessing America Online's Web site at www.aol.com.

Productivity

The relationship between the value of products and services produced and the cost incurred in producing them is called **productivity.** Productivity can be measured by dividing the value (price) of the output by the cost of the inputs. If the cost of the inputs exceeds the value of the outputs, the producer incurs a loss because the ratio is less than one. An increasing ratio means that productivity is increasing.

A low level of productivity can result from several factors. For example, poorly trained workers, poor management, an inadequate supply of raw materials, poor scheduling, and a high rate of employee absenteeism can lower productivity. A high level of productivity requires a team effort to assure an acceptable ratio between the cost of inputs and the value of outputs.

Profitability

Profitability refers to a firm's ability to earn profits, which represent the difference between the revenues derived from the sale of products and services and the costs of producing the products and services. Profitability is essential if a firm is to survive in the long term. Although a particular firm may lose money for a period of time, it cannot continue to do so indefinitely.

Companies are continually seeking ways to improve profitability. One popular way is to reduce or eliminate wasted resources. For example, a secretary who retypes a letter several times before producing one that is error-free wastes expensive time. A factory worker who cuts wooden boards into incorrect lengths wastes expensive lumber. Conversely, a carefully planned and implemented advertising campaign that increases sales raises the level of productivity.

To achieve success, an organization must establish and carefully monitor specific goals and objectives. Information systems can assist management in monitoring and evaluating a company's performance to determine whether it meets its established goals and objectives.

Today's Worldwide Business Environment

No business can operate successfully in a vacuum. Instead, a business operates in an interdependent environment that includes other businesses, organizations, and groups. Business decisions and actions are dependent on decisions and actions of other firms.

Although some decisions and actions may be strictly internal with little, if any, impact on those outside the organization, many decisions and actions greatly affect others outside the organization and even the organization itself, just as decisions and actions by one member of a family can affect other family members as well. For example, an employed individual earns a salary that, in turn, may be used to pay taxes, purchase products and services, invest, and put into a savings or retirement account. The individual's decisions and actions have an impact on others including taxing agencies (e.g., the IRS), retailers, manufacturers, banks, and savings institutions. Although this is a relatively simple illustration involving a single individual, it illustrates the complexity of the environment within which businesses must operate (Figure 5.9).

In recent years, the advancement of technology and the expansion of many businesses into international markets have resulted in a business environment that has become global in scope. While continuing its activities within the organization as well as activities with other organizations in this country, many businesses

FIGURE 5.9

Worldwide Business Environment

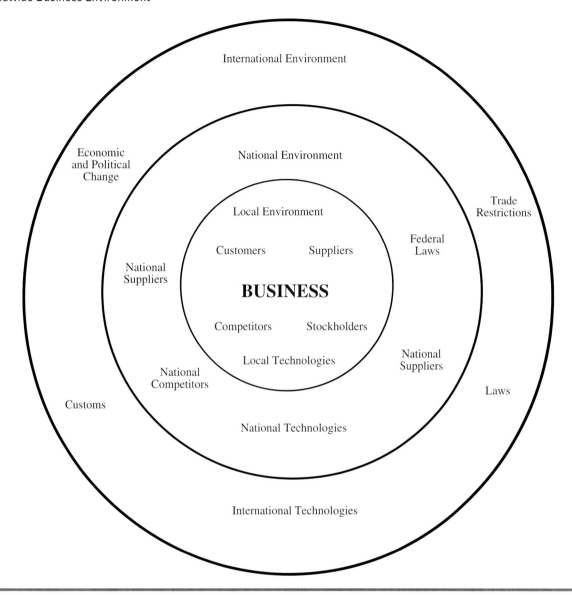

now must be able to respond appropriately to international businesses and organizations, politics, laws, and customs. Advances in technologies make it possible for firms to conduct business more easily and efficiently, both domestically and internationally.

The business environment can be divided into three categories: the local environment, the national environment, and the international environment. The **local environment** encompasses local customers, suppliers, competitors, stockholders, and local regulators with which the business must interact on a local basis. For example, a business must adhere to fire safety regulations. Internally, the business must also interact with managers, employees, and departments.

The **national environment** is broader in scope and the business must interact with national suppliers, federal agencies, competitors, and national regulators. For example, at a national level the business must interact with federal agencies (including the Social Security Administration, the Occupational Safety and Health

Administration, as well as others). Nationally, the business interacts through competition with competitors and purchases inputs from national suppliers.

In recent years, many businesses have expanded their operations internationally by locating business establishments in other countries. With the passage of restriction-easing legislation, such as the North American Free Trade Agreement (NAFTA), several American companies have expanded their operations into Mexico. Due to the expansion, many firms now operate in an **international environment** that subjects them to international laws and restrictions and to international customs and changes.

The development and implementation of advanced electronic communications and computer technologies including the Internet, the World Wide Web, and electronic commerce technologies have made it possible for organizations to expand and function worldwide. Without modern communications and computer technologies and equipment, worldwide expansion by many organizations may not have been possible.

Business Information Systems

You have learned that information is the lifeblood of business because managers need information to make decisions vital to the success of a business. Due to the huge volume of data that must be processed, all but the smallest business enterprises use computers to process data into useful information. A small business might use a single computer to satisfy its processing needs. However, a large company frequently makes use of complex computer information systems in order to be competitive in the marketplace.

An **information system** can be defined as a set of interrelated components working together to collect, retrieve, process, store, and distribute information needed for the successful planning, control, coordination, analysis, and decision making in a business or other organization. Before computers became available, this was accomplished manually by managers and employees who spent long periods of time converting raw data into useful information. Today, this is accomplished with the use of computer technologies called **computer information systems.**

Today, the activities, operations, and decisions of most businesses extend beyond local boundaries. In addition to its local environments, a firm must also function effectively in an **external environment** that includes entities outside the organization such as individuals and groups, suppliers, competitors, agencies, and technologies (Figure 5.10). For this reason, information systems today are much broader than in the past. No longer do computers operate in isolation on desktops. They now operate as part of a network that may be connected to other networks via the Internet. By being connected to the Internet, networks span computers and networks around the world.

Electronic commerce, also referred to as **electronic business** or **e-business,** involves the use of computer and communications technologies that allow a business or an organization to improve its performance levels. Electronic commerce has emerged as a result of the Internet and the Web. Continuing developments and refinements in electronic commerce provide new opportunities for businesses and organizations to improve efficiency, service, and quality, and to increase productivity and profitability. Greater achievements in these performance goals are made possible with the Internet and the Web. Later in this chapter, we will explore cases in which companies and organizations use available technologies to enhance their positions in a competitive environment.

FIGURE 5.10
External Environment

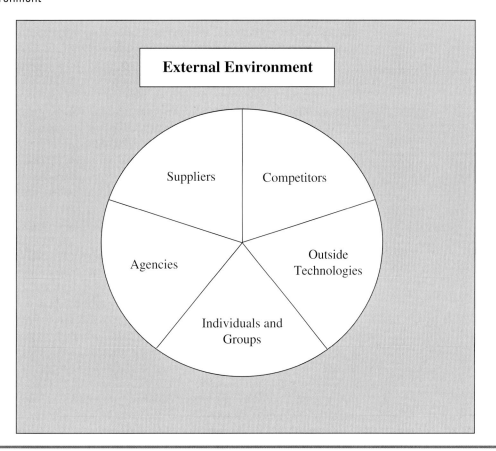

Value Chains

The management of both internal and external business operations has been changing for many businesses, particularly for businesses that have dealings with other businesses on a worldwide basis. The primary reasons for changes in operating strategies are to reduce operating costs and to improve performance in the five areas explained earlier. Today, there is a greater awareness by companies of the interdependence of activities, functions, and operations both internally and externally that can be managed more effectively by means of information systems. This awareness is known as the concept of value chains.

The concept of **value chains** is one in which a business firm is viewed as a series of basic, or *chain,* activities each of which adds value to the firm's products or services. For example, a retailer adds value to products by making the products available to customers in a timely manner. A manufacturing company adds value to its products during each phase of the manufacturing process. A service company adds value by providing services in a friendly and timely manner, such as an airline that arranges arrival and departure schedules that accommodate passenger needs. Computerized information systems can aid a firm in performing its activities at a lower cost than competitors and by providing customers with added value to the products and services it provides.

Electronic commerce technologies allow manufacturing firms to streamline their manufacturing processes by employing and linking (integrating) automated manufacturing systems using computer and communications technologies. The purpose of these integrated systems is to make the information produced by one system immediately available for use by other systems. This allows companies to respond more rapidly to customers, suppliers, employees, and others needing information. For example, an automobile manufacturer is able to transmit purchase orders for parts electronically from its computer system to suppliers' computer systems and to track the status of the purchase orders at any time. Upon receipt of the purchase orders, suppliers prepare and deliver the ordered supplies to the manufacturer's automobile assembly lines at the exact time they are needed, thereby keeping the manufacturer's costs to a minimum. Systems such as this that eliminate the need to maintain large inventories by providing materials for production at the exact time they are needed are called **just-in-time (JIT) production systems** (Figure 5.11).

Electronic commerce applications are not limited to manufacturing. Retailing companies, investment firms, stock brokerage firms, transport companies, common carriers, and other types of businesses and organizations also engage in electronic commerce applications. In the retailing field, many companies use similar systems for managing inventories. Employees at stock brokerage firms use computers linked to computer systems at major stock markets to obtain information about specific stocks and market trends. They are able to obtain up-to-the-minute quotations and changes in market conditions immediately when they occur. Travel agents can use their computers to make travel arrangements and purchase tickets for customers. Companies can send out announcements about company events and job openings. A job applicant can apply for employment positions online by filling out an electronic employment application on a computer screen and sending it over the Internet to the company or organization. The point is that electronic commerce applications and practices are being implemented around the world by a variety of businesses, organizations, and agencies using modern electronic commerce and telecommunications technologies.

FIGURE 5.11

Example of a JIT System

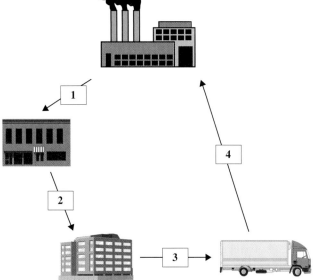

Electronic Data Interchange (EDI)

In addition to traditional communications methods explained earlier, businesses also use telecommunications technology, including electronic mail, fax machines, teleconferencing, videoconferencing, voice mail, and pagers, to communicate with dispersed individual plants, suppliers, agencies, and others. These technologies allow for fast, efficient, and low-cost communications, enable people to make decisions more quickly, and provide for an accelerated production of products and services.

Despite the value of these technologies, none are suitable for exchanging business documents and forms required in routine business transactions. The electronic exchange of business documents and forms is accomplished by means of a telecommunications technology called electronic data interchange (EDI).

Electronic data interchange (EDI) is the direct computer-to-computer capability to transfer business forms and documents from one computer to another computer. Many large companies use EDI for routine transactions, including billing and purchase orders. In situations involving repeat business, such as a manufacturing company ordering materials from suppliers, EDI is a standard way of doing repeat business. When compared to transactions involving paper documents, EDI offers some distinct advantages, including the following:

- Transaction costs are reduced.

- Time required for transmitting forms and documents is reduced.

- The volume of paper flow is reduced.

- Data entry errors are reduced because the need to reenter at the receiving end is eliminated.

- EDI offers a more reliable method for delivering documents than some other methods for sending and receiving the documents.

Some companies have developed EDI applications whereby orders from customers are automatically created, processed, and shipped without human intervention. For example, a company's EDI system may be designed to automatically notify vendors when the inventory decreases to a certain level. Upon notification, vendors process the orders and send the products to the company to replenish its inventory. Figure 5.12 illustrates how EDI streamlines inventory ordering.

EDI is an electronic communications protocol standard developed by The Data Interchange Standards Association for the exchange of business documents, such as purchase orders, invoices, and other business documents. EDI uses field codes, such as BT for Bill To or ST for Ship To, and specifies the format in which data are being transmitted electronically. The EDI protocol allows companies to exchange documents electronically by ensuring that all EDI-based communications have the same data in the same place.

The EDI communications standard is used for a variety of electronic business applications. Although it was initially developed to facilitate business transactions and shipping among businesses, its use has expanded to include other kinds of applications, mainly because of the need to expedite transactions and reduce cumbersome paperwork.

International trade is a rapidly growing market segment, particularly for many large businesses, and involves the creation and transmission of numerous documents. It has been estimated that a typical international trade transaction may involve up to 30 different parties, 60 original documents, and 300 document copies. By using EDI to streamline procedures and reduce the volume of paper documents, international trading firms can gain significant savings.

FIGURE 5.12
Electronic Data Interchange (EDI)

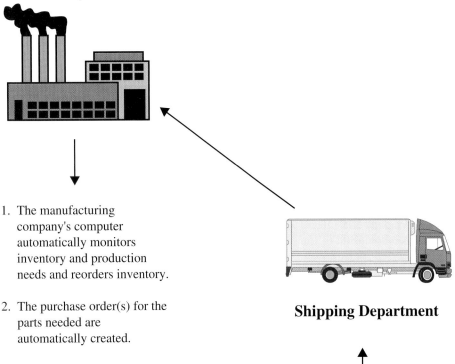

Manufacturing Company

Shipping Department

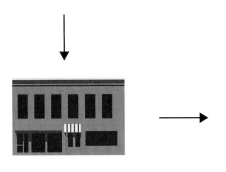

Parts Vendor

1. The manufacturing company's computer automatically monitors inventory and production needs and reorders inventory.

2. The purchase order(s) for the parts needed are automatically created.

3. The manufacturer's computer transmits the purchase online to the vendor's computer.

4. The vendor's computer automatically processes the purchase order.

5. The vendor's computer automatically routes the purchase order to the shipping department.

6. The products are located, shipped to the manufacturing company, and the vendor's computer automatically creates a bill and sends it electronically to the manufacturer.

Electronic Payments and Transfers

The exchange of products and services is accompanied by financial payments. Traditionally, payments were made by creating and sending checks to the suppliers of the goods and services.

Financial EDI

Many businesses use a form of EDI technology, called financial EDI, to transmit payments electronically. **Financial EDI** technology provides for the electronic transmission of payments and associated remittance information between a payer, payee, and their respective banks. It allows businesses to replace the labor-intensive activities of producing, mailing, and collecting checks through the banking system with the automated and electronic transmission and processing of instructions for payment. Thus, delays inherent in processing checks are eliminated because both the payer's and payee's bank accounts can be processed and updated the same day.

The use of financial EDI technology is also spreading quickly to other areas. Health care providers, including hospitals, doctor's offices, ambulance services, and others, use computers and financial EDI technologies to bill private insurance companies and government agencies, such as Medicare, for patient services. In turn, some insurance companies and government agencies use EDI technologies to remit payments for patient services.

Automated Clearinghouse (ACH) Transfers

An **automated clearinghouse** is an automated entity established for the purpose of transferring funds electronically from one account to another. Some large banks have established their own private clearinghouses, whereas other smaller banks have joined together to form clearinghouses that serve member banks. In either situation, the clearinghouses perform the same function and offer the same, or similar, services.

Here is a simplified explanation of how payments are made using an automated clearinghouse. When payments are made for purchased goods, the purchaser transmits payment information to the purchaser's bank, which validates the purchaser's account and processes the information. The purchaser's bank transmits the information to the clearinghouse, where the purchaser's account is again validated. The clearinghouse electronically notifies the purchaser's bank that funds have been transferred from the purchaser's account to the seller's account at seller's bank and notifies the seller's bank of the transfer. Finally, both the purchaser and the seller are informed by their respective banks that the financial transfer has been completed (Figure 5.13).

FIGURE 5.13

Automated Clearinghouse (ACH) Transfers

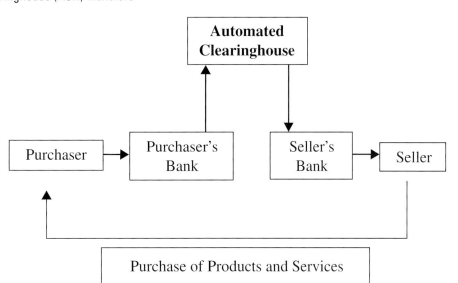

Business-to-Business Applications: Some Examples

Every business conducts business activities within its own organization and with others, including customers, suppliers, and government agencies such as the Occupational Safety and Health Administration and various taxing agencies. Without electronic commerce capabilities, the sheer volume of documents and the cost of transmitting them would, in some cases, be enormous. Keep in mind that the term *business-to-business* refers to applications within a business and to applications between businesses.

Fortunately, electronic commerce technologies enable companies to streamline many routine activities. These technologies allow companies to manage both internal and external operations more efficiently, maintain quality-control standards, manage inventories, and perform management functions more effectively. Performance standards can be much more accurately measured and achieved than would be possible using older, more traditional methods.

At present, business-to-business applications represent the largest and fastest-growing segment of electronic commerce. According to International Data Corporation, the value of procurements in U.S. manufacturing will reach $50 billion by 1999 and increase to $300 billion during the year 2002. Dataquest, a private research firm, predicts an increase in projected worldwide purchases of procurement software from $95 billion in 1999 to $470 billion in 2003.

In the following sections, we will look at specific companies in which electronic commerce technologies are used to enhance internal performance and situations in which electronic commerce technology is used to improve operations with other firms with which a firm conducts business, such as suppliers. We will see how the companies are using electronic commerce to control business operations and improve performance.

The Automotive Network eXchange (ANX)

Chrysler, General Motors, and Ford have banded together to build a system that links them with their suppliers through a virtual private network called the **Automotive Network eXchange (ANX).** The goal is to save billions of dollars in inventory costs. Deliveries of materials are coordinated and shipped to assembly plants as they are needed. This provides for a more efficient management of inventories and for reduced inventory storage costs. The system also routes deliveries and even helps coordinate design and manufacturing processes.

Boeing's Customer Inventory System

The Boeing Company, located in Seattle, Washington, is the world's largest producer of commercial airplanes (see Figure 5.14). Annual company sales exceed $35 billion. Electronic commerce helped Boeing establish closer relationships with a larger group of potential partners, suppliers, and customers.

Boeing has implemented a system that allows its customers to order airplane parts directly from the company's inventory stock. Idle planes are a big expense, and the bigger the plane, the bigger the expense. It costs about $1,000 a minute to have a large plane like the model 747, with a purchase price of $175 million, on the ground when it is scheduled to be flying! To minimize this expense, Boeing has implemented a new, online system that allows more than 1,000 customers to quickly locate, order, and track shipments of aircraft spare parts, using electronic commerce technology, the Web, and the Internet.

FIGURE 5.14

The Boeing Company Home Page

Using the Boeing PART Page (a secure, password-protected Web site), a customer interactively queries Boeing's spare parts database. By typing in the part number, a customer can then order that part and locate the closest stocking warehouse. The Boeing Web site also includes hot links to many cargo carriers so that a customer can track a parts shipment even while it's en route.

Boeing sells more than $1 billion of aircraft spare parts annually from an inventory of more than half a million different items. Boeing's system has been a huge success.

Wal-Mart's EDI Inventory System

In 1974 Wal-Mart began streamlining its inventory control system by installing a systemwide computer network that linked the company's corporate headquarters, individual stores, and the company's distribution centers. To better manage its huge inventories, Wal-Mart had fully implemented its companywide just-in-time (JIT) inventory system by 1977.

The largest and most successful applications of Wal-Mart's inventory control system links company stores, suppliers, distributors, and corporate headquarters in a communications network. Information flows from any source to any destination on a need-to-know basis. The advantages gained with this system include a reduction in delivery time from five days to just one day, increased sales, and the lowest costs and highest profit margins of any retailer in the United States.

Wal-Mart uses electronic data interchange (EDI) to electronically link the company to its suppliers. EDI has enabled the company to reduce the amount of paperwork by using standard electronic communications processes and documents for sending purchase orders, shipping lists, invoices, and payments from one computer to another. Using EDI technology, Wal-Mart has also been able to lower its operating costs, eliminate delays in ordering, shipping, and receiving, obtain more accurate pricing and inventory information, and increase system responsiveness to customer needs. Electronic funds transfer (EFT) systems linked to the company's EDI system allow payments to be electronically credited to suppliers' bank accounts. These systems now connect the company to its 1,500 largest suppliers.

Wal-Mart's systems have benefited everyone. Products are available when customers want them, suppliers can control their product flows, and Wal-Mart has reduced its inventory costs. Data are entered into the system only one time and then are manipulated as necessary to process inventory. This efficiency translates into lower costs and the resulting savings are passed on to the consumer.

Wal-Mart's system includes one of the world's largest database systems. This system makes it possible for the company to keep track of each customer and business transaction. The ability to keep track of each transaction enables the company to maintain up-to-date records and to establish customer profiles to better serve its customers.

United Parcel Service (UPS)

UPS is the world's largest express package distribution company, delivering more than 12 million packages daily. With a package volume that is more than the U.S. Postal Service, FedEx, and Airborne combined, UPS needed to develop a sophisticated technology backbone to provide quality service to customers. UPS invests more than $1 billion annually in its technology infrastructure—more than the company spends on trucks. It also maintains the world's largest private database, one that is larger than that of the U.S. Census Bureau.

The consumer delivery market comprises 20 percent of the company's operations, with business-to-business shipments representing the other 80 percent. In both markets, the information that pertains to a given package, from it's location in the system to how much it will cost to send to the exact time that it is delivered to the customer, has become more and more important.

Personal computers are located at each UPS customer services center. Information obtained from customers who call to request that a package be picked up or traced is entered into a PC by a company employee. UPS drivers use handheld, battery-powered electronic devices to capture and store customer signatures, scan bar codes for product and destination information, and to display delivery routes. The captured information is transmitted to the company's computer network. Information captured from package shipping labels is used for tracking packages. UPS employees can bring the information up on their computers and inform customers about the status of shipments.

Customers can schedule their own shipments and track their packages themselves using a special kind of software made available by the company on the Web. To track a shipment, a customer can simply access the UPS Web site, click the Tracking button, type a tracking number, and then click the Track button (Figure 5.15).

UPS is using electronic commerce technologies to meet the company's goals and objectives. The systems and applications described here provide greater efficiency, enhance service quality, improve productivity, and increase the company's profits. Electronic commerce is an important and integral part of the company's business operations.

FIGURE 5.15

Tracking Option at the UPS Web Site

The Status of Business-to-Business Applications

Electronic commerce technologies are now being used by thousands of businesses and organizations and are being explored by thousands of others. Intense and growing competition is a catalyst causing many businesses to examine their futures and to consider how they might use electronic commerce to remain competitive and achieve high performance levels in every area of both their internal and their external operations.

Today's businesses operate in an ever-expanding global market in which competition exists locally and from countries abroad. Unfortunately, many foreign businesses are faced with extremely limited electronic commerce opportunities due, in part, to their having to operate in a technologically limited environment. For example, several Middle Eastern countries lack the technological and communications structures that are already in place in the United States and in many other highly developed countries. Despite this enormous disadvantage, businesses located in these countries may be forced to discover ways to be competitive with firms having fast and easy access to global markets.

In technologically developed countries, such as the United States, Canada, Japan, and several western European countries, the availability of electronic communications systems and access to the Internet, the Web, and electronic commerce technologies have allowed thousands of businesses to take advantage of available electronic commerce opportunities. Many are continually exploring new ways in which they can use electronic commerce technology to streamline operations, improve services, and increase profits.

Each day, many retailers that for decades marketed their products in traditional ways are going online to market a larger variety of products at less cost and to a larger market. In addition to offering products in stores, companies like Sears, J.C. Penney, Apple, CompUSA, and National Brands now have Web sites where consumers can browse catalogs and purchase products online. Almost any product or service can now be purchased over the Internet.

Electronic commerce technologies have experienced perhaps their most extensive uses in business-to-business applications. Most, if not all, businesses now use electronic commerce for communications within the business and with others outside the business, including suppliers, regulating agencies, taxing agencies, customers, and shipping companies. By using electronic data interchange (EDI) and other technologies, firms are able to create and transmit electronic forms to reduce the flow of paperwork and to better manage inventories. This results in lower operating costs and increased profits.

The present status of business-to-business applications is promising for business in general. Electronic commerce technologies are being embraced by many businesses at a growing pace. New developments are being introduced almost daily.

In their early stages, the Internet and the World Wide Web were, for many users, a novelty. Today, there is worldwide excitement about electronic commerce and the tremendous potential it holds for everyone. Perhaps what we've seen thus far is only the tip of the iceberg.

You've learned about electronic commerce as it is used to improve business-to-customer applications and business-to-business applications. In the next chapter, you will learn about ways in which electronic commerce allows federal, state, and local governments to serve members of society more effectively and efficiently.

SUMMARY

Electronic commerce is playing an ever-increasing role in business-to-business applications. More and more, businesses and other types of organizations are taking advantage of the opportunities available with modern electronic commerce technologies.

A business is a profit-seeking enterprise that engages in numerous activities to provide products and services to consumers in an economic system. Products and services are made available to consumers, like you and me, and to other businesses and organizations.

Today's global economy consists of businesses of various types and sizes. Regardless of type or size, any business must obtain and use certain inputs, called the factors of production, in order to provide products and services to the public and to other businesses and organizations.

The driving force behind any kind of business is profits. Profit is the reward for businesspeople, called entrepreneurs, who take risks by combining capital (including money, machinery, and equipment), employees, materials, and other resources to produce the products and services. Elements that are combined to produce products and services are called the factors of production, and payments must be made to the supplier(s) of each factor. Natural resources are inputs that are used in their natural states, including land, forests, and mineral ore deposits such as oil. Payment for these resources is called rent. Human resources include workers at all levels including production workers, clerks, managers, technicians, and accountants. Payment for human resources is called wages. Capital includes money, physical facilities, information, technology, and equipment. Payment for capital is interest.

Management may be defined as the attainment of organizational goals in an effective and efficient manner through planning, organizing, leading, and controlling organizational resources.

Information, often called the lifeblood of a business or an organization, is data that have been processed so as to make them useful for a specific purpose, such as making a decision. To be useful, information must be accurate, complete, and timely.

Communication can be defined as a meaningful exchange of information. More and more, information is now being transmitted and received electronically using combinations of computer technologies and communications technologies, collectively called telecommunications. Internal communications are those that occur *within* an organization. Examples include memos, departmental meetings, training sessions, and phone conversations. External communication is the exchange of useful information between an organization and its audiences.

To be successful, every business must establish and achieve goals and objectives in order to achieve high standards of performance. For all organizations, high performance in efficiency, service, quality, productivity, and profitability is critical.

An information system can be defined as a set of interrelated components working together to collect, retrieve, process, store, and distribute information needed for the successful planning, control, coordination, analysis, and decision making in a business or other organization. Today, this is done using computer information systems.

Electronic commerce, also referred to as electronic business or e-business, involves the use of computer and communications technologies that allow a business or an organization to improve its performance levels. Electronic commerce has emerged as a result of the Internet and the Web. Continuing developments and refinements in electronic commerce provide new opportunities for businesses and organizations to improve efficiency, service, and quality, and to increase productivity and profitability.

Today, there is a greater awareness by companies of the interdependence of activities, functions, and operations both internally and externally that can be managed more effectively by means of information systems. This awareness is known as the concept of the value chain, in which a business firm is viewed as a series of basic, or chain, activities each of which adds value to the firm's products or services.

Electronic data interchange (EDI) is the direct computer-to-computer capability to transfer business forms and documents from one computer to another. The exchange of products and services is accompanied by financial payments. Financial EDI technology provides for the electronic transmission of payments and associated remittance information between a payer, a payee, and their respective banks. An automated clearinghouse is an automated entity established for the purpose of transferring funds electronically from one account to another.

Electronic commerce technologies are now being used by thousands of businesses and organizations, and are being explored by thousands of others. Intense and growing competition is a catalyst causing many businesses to examine their futures and to consider how they might use electronic commerce to remain competitive and achieve high performance levels in every area of both their internal and their external operations.

KEY TERMS

automated
  clearinghouse (151)
Automotive Network
  eXchange (ANX)
  (152)
business (132)
capital (134)
communication (138)
computer information
  systems (146)
controlling (136)
e-business (146)
efficiency (142)
electronic business
  (146)
electronic commerce
  (146)
electronic data
  interchange (EDI)
  (149)
entrepreneur (133)
external
  communication (141)

external environment
  (146)
factors of production
  (133)
financial EDI (150)
free market system
  (132)
human resources (133)
information (138)
information system
  (146)
interest (134)
internal
  communications
  (140)
international
  environment (146)
just-in-time (JIT)
  production system
  (148)
leading (136)
local environment (145)
management (136)

national environment
  (145)
natural resources (133)
not-for-profit
  organization (134)
organizing (136)
planning (136)
productivity (144)
profit (133)
profitability (144)
quality (142)
rent (133)
service (142)
telecommunications
  (139)
underemployment (142)
unemployment (142)
value chain (147)
wages (133)

END-OF-CHAPTER ACTIVITIES

Matching

Match each term with its description.

a. information
b. value chain
c. financial EDI
d. management
e. EDI

f. communication
g. automated
  clearinghouse
h. information system

i. interest
j. controlling
k. profitability
l. business

_____ **1.** The direct computer-to-computer capability to transfer business forms and documents from one computer to another.

_____ **2.** Payment for the use of capital.

_____ **3.** A set of interrelated components working together to collect, retrieve, process, store, and distribute information needed for the successful planning, control, coordination, analysis, and decision making in a business or organization.

_____ **4.** A profit-seeking enterprise that engages in numerous activities to provide products and services to consumers in an economic system.

_____ **5.** A concept in which a business firm is viewed as a series of activities, each of which adds value to the firm's products and services.

_____ **6.** A meaningful exchange of information.

_____ **7.** A function of management.

_____ **8.** A technology that provides for the electronic transmission of payments and associated remittance information between a payer, a payee, and their respective banks.

_____ **9.** An automated entity established for the purpose of transferring funds electronically from one account to another.

_____ **10.** The attainment of organizational goals through planning, organizing, leading, and controlling.

_____ **11.** A performance standard.

_____ **12.** Often called the lifeblood of a business or an organization.

Review Questions

1. Explain the meaning of the term _business._

2. What are the four factors of production explained in the chapter and what is the payment made to each factor?

3. Explain what is meant by a not-for-profit organization and give some examples.

4. Identify and define the functions of management explained in the chapter and briefly define each function.

5. What is information?

6. Distinguish between the terms _communication_ and _telecommunications._

7. List five areas in which performance levels are particularly important to a business.

8. Explain the meaning of the term _information system._

9. Explain the nature of a business value chain and give a few examples of value chains.

10. What is electronic data interchange (EDI), and what are some of the advantages of using this technology?

Activities

1. Computers in the computer lab at your school may be linked in a network with access to the Internet. If so, access the Internet using one of the computers in your school's computer lab. Using a search engine to search the Web, locate and read five articles containing information about electronic commerce business-to-business applications. Prepare a brief written summary of each article.

2. Using one of the computers in your school's computer lab, perform a search on the Web. Locate and read three articles containing information about electronic data interchange (EDI). After you've finished reading the three articles, use the information you found in the articles to write a new article about EDI.

3. Numerous computer magazines contain articles about business-to-business applications using electronic commerce technology. Most of these printed magazines are also online and available to you on the Web. Here is a list of some popular magazines that are available online:

MAGAZINE NAME	WEB ADDRESS
PCMagazine	http://www.pcmagazine.com
Infoworld	http://www.infoworld.com
PCWeek	http://www.pcweek.com
Datamation	http://www.datamation.com
Computer World	http://www.computerworld.com

For this activity, you can either search through issues of one or more of the magazines in your school's library or visit the magazine's Web site. Find two articles about business-to-business applications using electronic commerce technology. After carefully reading the articles, prepare a written summary of each article.

4. The home page of many companies contains links to other pages that identify job opportunities with the company and links to application forms that allow users to apply for the jobs listed. Visit three company Web sites. At each site, find one job in which you might be interested. Using a link (if available), access the company's application for employment form. Prepare a written report that includes information about a specific job and the kind of information required on the job application form.

5. This is a team project. Your instructor will divide the class into groups with four or five students on each team. It is possible that there are businesses in your area that are actively engaged in business-to-business electronic commerce activities. Each team member will visit one local company in the area and find out if the company is engaged in electronic commerce activities. If so, learn about specific ways the company uses electronic commerce to improve its operations. Following your visit, prepare a brief written report of your findings. These reports will be merged into a team report that will be turned in to your instructor.

CHAPTER SIX

Government-to-Society Applications

AFTER COMPLETING THIS CHAPTER, YOU WILL:

1. Explain the federal government's Framework for Global Electronic Commerce.
2. Identify the five main principles to guide government support for the evolution of economic commerce.
3. Define the term *procurement* and tell why procurement is an important government activity.
4. Identify five federal government Web sites covered in the chapter and briefly explain how each site allows a user to learn about the department or agency's involvement in electronic commerce.
5. Explain the primary purpose of the Smithsonian Institute's Web site.
6. Select one federal Web site and explain how a visit to this site might prove to be of particular interest and use to you.
7. Explain briefly the purpose(s) of various state Web sites.
8. Explain briefly the purpose(s) of regional and local government Web sites and identify ways in which these governments are using electronic commerce technologies.

Elected officials, business leaders, and scholars have long recognized the importance of free trade among trading partners around the world. Many economists argue that free trade benefits everyone. Without trade barriers, companies are free to compete for customers anyplace in the world and consumers can purchase a wider variety of products and services at competitive prices. The result is that valuable resources are allocated to the production of products and services that consumers want and can better afford.

Federal, state, and local governments are now among the strongest supporters and users of the Internet and of electronic commerce applications. In this chapter you will learn ways in which these governments use electronic commerce to streamline their operations. We begin by examining the current position of the federal government regarding electronic commerce and its future plans for ensuring the continuing growth of this important technology.

A Framework for Global Electronic Commerce

Recognizing the potential of the Internet and the importance of electronic commerce in a global environment, the U.S. federal government has assumed a leadership role in promoting the worldwide use of the Internet for commercial purposes. With input from various federal departments and agencies and with the cooperation of the private sector, the federal government, under the leadership of Vice President Albert Gore, has prepared a strategy to help accelerate the growth of global commerce across the Internet. Under Gore's leadership, a federal interagency working group has prepared a document, titled "A Framework for Global Electronic Commerce," which describes the federal government's position regarding electronic commerce. The document outlines the administration's strategy for fostering increased business and consumer confidence in the use of networks for electronic commerce. The document lists five main principles to guide government support for the evolution of electronic commerce (Figure 6.1).

The document also includes recommendations about nine key areas where international efforts are needed to preserve the Internet as a nonregulatory medium (Figure 6.2). The federal government is committed to promoting the nine essential recommendations worldwide to ensure the continuing expansion of the Internet and the future growth of electronic commerce on a worldwide basis.

Federal, state, and local governments have a responsibility to promote the public welfare. Included is the obligation to promote future competition that can be achieved more easily by freeing the Internet from bureaucratic domination and by ensuring that Internet, the Web, and electronic commerce technologies are freely available for use by everyone. This includes private citizens, businesses, organizations, and even government itself. The leadership provided by the federal government has allowed Internet, Web, and electronic commerce technologies to flourish throughout the world. Moreover, governments at all levels—federal, state, and local—are using these technologies to serve the public interests in ways similar to those used by businesses to serve customers.

Government Involvement in Electronic Commerce

In previous chapters we explored many ways in which individuals, businesses, and organizations are involved in both Internet and electronic commerce applications. We learned that many businesses maintain Web sites to advertise, promote,

FIGURE 6.1

Five Principles That Guide Government for Electronic Commerce

1. *The private sector should lead.* The Internet should develop as a market-driven arena, not as a regulated industry. Even where collective action is necessary, governments should encourage industry self-regulation and private sector leadership where possible.

2. *Governments should avoid undue restrictions on electronic commerce.* In general, parties should be able to enter into legitimate agreements to buy and sell products and services across the Internet with minimal government involvement or intervention. Governments should refrain from imposing new and unnecessary regulations, bureaucratic procedures, or new taxes and tariffs on commercial activities that take place via the Internet.

3. *Where governmental involvement is needed, its aim should be to support and enforce a predictable, minimalist, consistent, and simple legal environment for commerce.* Where government intervention is necessary, its role should be to ensure competition, protect intellectual property and privacy, prevent fraud, foster transparency, and facilitate dispute resolution, not to regulate.

4. *Governments should recognize the unique qualities of the Internet.* The genius and explosive success of the Internet can be attributed in part to its decentralized nature and to its tradition of bottom-up governance. Accordingly, the regulatory frameworks established over the past 60 years for telecommunication, radio, and television may not fit the Internet. Existing laws and regulations that may hinder electronic commerce should be reviewed and revised or eliminated to reflect the needs of the new electronic age.

5. *Electronic commerce on the Internet should be facilitated on a global basis.* The Internet is a global marketplace. The legal framework supporting commercial transactions should be consistent and predictable regardless of the jurisdiction in which a particular buyer and seller reside.

and sell products and services, and for a variety of other purposes including the management of inventories and the recruitment of employees. Customers use these sites for various reasons including purchasing products and services and applying for employment. Other individuals visit Web sites simply to obtain information, such as weather reports and stock market quotations. Thousands of Web sites are devoted primarily to applications between businesses and customers and to applications between businesses and other businesses.

In this chapter we examine ways in which governments are using the Internet, the Web, and electronic commerce technologies to serve constituents. You will learn that governments are now using these technologies for a variety of applications. Federal department and agency Web sites have been established to provide citizens and others with information about passed and proposed legislative activities, statistics, and services. All states currently maintain Web sites that provide visitors with a wealth of information about the state, including academic and cultural opportunities, population and growth statistics, taxes, and much more. Local governments have established Web sites to promote their communities and to recruit business and industry.

FIGURE 6.2

Nine Recommendations Based on the Five Principles

The principles described in Figure 6.1 guide the recommendations listed here.

1. *Tariffs and Taxation.* The Internet should be declared a tariff-free environment whenever it is used to deliver products and services. The Internet is a truly global medium, and all nations will benefit from barrier-free trade across it.

   No new taxes should be imposed on Internet commerce. Existing taxes that are applied to electronic commerce should be consistent across national and subnational jurisdictions and should be simple to understand and administer. State and local governments should cooperate to develop a uniform, simple approach to the taxation of electronic commerce, based on existing principles of taxation.

2. *Electronic Payment Systems.* The commercial and technological environment for electronic payments is changing rapidly, making it difficult to develop policy that is both timely and appropriate. For these reasons, inflexible and highly prescriptive regulations and rules are inappropriate and potentially harmful. In the near-term, case-by-case monitoring of electronic payment experiments is preferable to regulation.

3. *Uniform Commercial Code for Electronic Commerce.* In general, parties should be able to do business with each other on the Internet under the terms and conditions they agree on. Private enterprise and free markets have typically flourished, however, where there are predictable and widely accepted legal principles supporting commercial transactions.

   The United States supports the development of an international uniform commercial code to facilitate electronic commerce. Such a code should encourage governmental recognition of electronic contracts, encourage consistent international rules for acceptance of electronic signatures and other authentication procedures, promote the development of alternative dispute resolution mechanisms for international commercial transactions, set predictable ground rules for exposure to liability, and streamline the use of electronic registries.

4. *Intellectual Property Protection.* Commerce on the Internet will often involve the sale and licensing of intellectual property. To promote electronic commerce, sellers must know that their intellectual property will not be stolen and buyers must know that they are obtaining authentic products. Clear and effective copyright, patent, and trademark protection is therefore necessary to guard against piracy and fraud. The recently negotiated World Intellectual Property Organization (WIPO) treaties for copyright protection should be ratified. Issues of liability for infringement, application of the fair use doctrine, and limitation of devices to defeat copyright protection mechanisms should be resolved in a balanced way, consistent with international obligations.

   The government will study and seek public comment on the need to protect database elements that do not qualify for copyright protection, and, if such protection is needed, determine how to construct it.

   The administration will promote global efforts to provide adequate and effective protection for patentable subject matter important to the development of the Global Information Infrastructure (GII) and establish standards for determining the validity of patent claims.

Many federal, state, and local governments are now actively involved in electronic commerce applications. An important activity of every government is procurement. The term **procurement** refers to the act of acquiring, or obtaining, products and services. To function effectively, every government must have the necessary resources, including products, services, and employees. Authorized companies visiting some of these sites can offer contract bids by filling out electronic bid forms and sending them to the appropriate department or agency. In business, the term **bid** refers to an attempt to acquire, win, or obtain something of value. A person or business offering a bid does so to acquire, win, or obtain something of value, such as a contract to sell products or services to another entity, such as a government agency.

The administration also will work globally to resolve conflicts that arise from different national treatments of trademarks as they relate to the Internet. It may be possible to create a contractually based, self-regulatory regime that deals with potential conflicts between domain name usage and trademark laws on a global basis.

The administration will review the system of allocating domain names to create a more competitive, market-based system and will seek to foster bottom-up governance of the Internet in the process.

5. *Privacy.* It is essential to assure personal privacy in the networked environment if people are to feel comfortable doing business across this new medium.

Data gatherers should tell consumers what information they are collecting and how they intend to use it. Consumers should have meaningful choice with respect to the use and reuse of their personal information. Parents should be able to choose whether or not personal information is collected from their children. In addition, redress should be available to consumers who are harmed by improper use or disclosure of personal information or if decisions are based on inaccurate, outdated, incomplete, or irrelevant personal information.

The administration supports private sector efforts now under way to implement meaningful, user-friendly, self-regulatory privacy regimes. These include mechanisms for facilitating awareness and the exercise of choice online, private-sector adoption of and adherence to fair information practices, and dispute resolution protocols. The government will work with industry and privacy advocates to develop appropriate solutions to privacy concerns that may not be fully addressed by industry through self-regulation and technology.

6. *Security.* The GII must be secure and reliable. If Internet users do not believe that their communications and data are safe from interception and modification, they are unlikely to use the Internet on a routine basis for commerce. The administration, in partnership with industry, is taking steps to promote the development of a market-driven public key infrastructure that will engender trust in encryption and provide the safeguards that users and society will need.

7. *Telecommunications Infrastructure and Information Technology.* Global electronic commerce depends on a modern, seamless, global telecommunications network and on the "information appliances" that connect to it. In too many countries, telecommunications policies are hindering the development of advanced digital networks. The United States will work internationally to remove barriers to competition, customer choice, lower prices, and improved services.

8. *Content.* The administration encourages industry self-regulation, the adoption of competitive content rating systems, and the development of effective, user-friendly technology tools (such as filtering and blocking technologies) to empower parents, teachers, and others to block content that is inappropriate for children.

The government will seek agreements with trading partners to eliminate overly burdensome content regulations that create nontariff trade barriers.

9. *Technical Standards.* The marketplace, not governments, should determine technical standards and other mechanisms for interoperability on the Internet. Technology is moving rapidly, and government attempts to establish technical standards to govern the Internet would only risk inhibiting technological innovation.

Individuals seeking employment can read and respond to employment notices posted at government sites. Companies interested in relocating or building a new plant can learn about existing opportunities available in various geographical locations. Most government Web sites are updated periodically with new or additional information.

Just as individuals, businesses, and organizations are finding new ways for using electronic commerce technologies, governments are discovering new ways in which the Internet, the Web, and electronic commerce can be used to serve the public. Keep in mind that the technologies now in use are still relatively young and that new and improved technologies are frequently being introduced that will benefit everyone.

E-Commerce Technology

Electronic Ink

Electronic ink, or e-ink, is a new technology that could have a big effect on newspapers, books, and signs. Originally developed at the Massachusetts Institute of Technology and produced by E-Ink of Cambridge, Massachusetts, some stores, including some J.C. Penney stores, will soon begin using e-ink in display signs.

Electronic ink is real ink on paper or a similarly thin display. The main difference between standard ink and e-ink is that the latter can be changed just like letters on a computer screen or theater marquee. One of the company's goals is to make a book that looks and feels exactly like today's standard printed books, except the contents of books using e-ink could be changed by downloading new material onto the paper.

The first sign to use e-ink is about as thick as the brim of a baseball cap and consumes less energy than a light bulb. The sign is located in the sports clothing department in a J.C. Penney store located in Marlborough, Massachusetts. To a shopper, it looks like a large printed sign. But every few seconds the sign changes. Unlike a typical electronic display, e-ink looks the same from any angle and in any light. The retailer also plans to install e-ink signs in the company's Dallas and Chicago stores.

E-Ink, still a private company, continues to drive toward books and newspapers. For instance, e-ink eventually could make it possible to buy one copy of a newspaper, then have it updated via radio signals each morning.

Here's how e-ink works. A sign with a built-in pager is coated with millions of tiny capsules. Inside each capsule is a dark liquid and hundreds of white balls that respond to electrical charges. Charged one way, they float to the top and make the "ink" white. Charged another way, they sink and make the visible part of the capsule black. Charged in a pattern, they form letters. To change the sign, Penney messages E-Ink, which sends changes to the paper.

Perhaps e-ink or a similar technology might someday find its way to the Internet. Imagine a technology that might allow Web pages to be changed simply by sending electrical charges to characters contained on a page. New and innovative technologies are emerging at a frantic pace.

In the following sections, we will visit selected federal government Web sites to learn ways in which departments, agencies, and commissions are using Internet, Web, and electronic commerce technologies in their efforts to serve the public. As you visit the home pages of various sites, you may notice links to other pages and documents you may also want to see.

Federal Government Web Sites

Almost all federal departments, agencies, and commissions have established and maintain sites on the World Wide Web. Each site is designed to serve the interests and needs of visitors. For this reason, information varies from site to site. For security purposes, the amount of information available at some sites is limited, or restricted to authorized persons, whereas information at other sites is more extensive.

Some early federal sites we will visit are designed primarily to provide information to the viewing public. Afterward, we will examine other federal sites that, in addition to information, provide individuals and businesses with an electronic vehicle for conducting business activities with the government.

As you view sites designed mainly to inform the public, keep in mind that, by providing information, the government is providing a service to citizens just as businesses provide services to customers. In this sense, **service** may be defined as the provision of information and assistance to the public.

United States Mint

A federal site, and one that has become more popular recently, is the **U.S. Mint.** A single Web site (Figure 6.3) serves the two mint locations at Denver, Colorado, and Philadelphia, Pennsylvania.

By scrolling down the U.S. Mint's home page, you will find links to other pages. For example, clicking on the Product Catalog link accesses a comprehensive catalog containing descriptions and illustrations of mint products, including special coins and coin sets, commemoratives, bullion, and medals. Links are available to other useful and informative pages and documents. For example, the History link displays a document that summarizes the history of the U.S. Mint and the Jobs link accesses and displays information about employment opportunities with the U.S. Mint. A link to information about the 50 State Quarters program is of special interest to many collectors. Information about this program is provided, along with detailed instructions for ordering individual coins and sets. Some of the early state coins are already becoming scarce, as collectors seem eager to obtain these unusual coins that appear likely to become valuable collector items.

United States Senate

Another informative federal Web site is the U.S. Senate site (Figure 6.4). Here visitors can learn about the Senate, legislative activities, and Senate committees,

FIGURE 6.3

U.S. Mint Home Page

FIGURE 6.4
U.S. Senate Home Page

and they can obtain the names and addresses of senators from each state. History enthusiasts can learn the history of the U.S. Senate and art lovers can view some historical art.

Visitors can contact a senator to express their views on any pending legislation or about other matters. Some, if not all, senators welcome opinions and comments from their constituents, especially on controversial topics. They want to learn the feelings and opinions of their constituencies so they can better serve them. They are elected, after all, by the voters they serve.

United States House of Representatives

Similar to the Web site of the U.S. Senate, the House of Representatives site provides visitors with information about members, committees, and legislative activities. A link to the House Directory provides the names and addresses of members a visitor can use to locate and contact representatives (Figure 6.5).

The home page contains links to other pages. For example, the House Operations link provides legislative information on a variety of activities and other topics. This is a useful site for students wanting to learn about the House and its ongoing activities.

Library of Congress

The **Library of Congress** Web site offers a vast reservoir of online information on almost every imaginable topic from the time this country was founded to the present (Figure 6.6). Documents, photographs, movies, and sound recordings are available that tell the history of the United States.

A brief description of almost every copyrighted book, document, and other publication is available online at the Library of Congress site. For example, you can learn whether a particular book or document is available by clicking on the Search the Catalog button then entering information into the search box. If available, a brief description of the book or document will be displayed on the screen.

FIGURE 6.5

U.S. House of Representatives Home Page

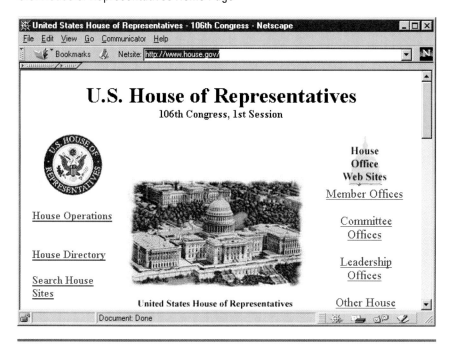

FIGURE 6.6

Library of Congress Home Page

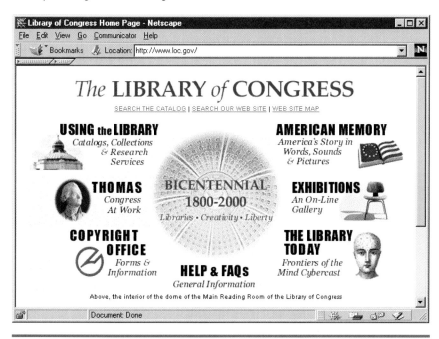

Smithsonian Institution

If you've ever visited the Smithsonian Institution in Washington, D.C., you may have felt somewhat overwhelmed by the vast number of interesting and impressive exhibits. The primary purpose of the **Smithsonian Institution** is to preserve the history of the United States by conserving and displaying to the public items of historical importance.

FIGURE 6.7

Smithsonian Institution Home Page

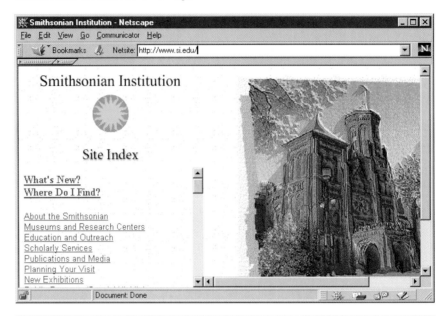

The Internet has made it possible for you to visit the Smithsonian without leaving the comfort of your own home. Although a stop at the Smithsonian's Web site cannot completely replace a physical visit, the site offers viewers a useful alternative (Figure 6.7).

A wealth of information awaits you at The Smithsonian Institution's Web site. The home page contains a site index that allows you to jump from location to location to view various exhibits. You can examine photographs of Charles Lindbergh's *Spirit of Saint Louis* aircraft, the *Mercury* spacecraft, old automobiles such as the *Stanley Steamer,* and more. Simply stated, the Smithsonian is a treasure of historical information for learning and enjoyment.

National Zoo

For users interested in learning about animals, the **National Zoo's** Web site is a fascinating site to visit (Figure 6.8). This site offers views of the zoo, as well as a large inventory of animal photographs and information about each animal in the zoo.

The zoo's home page contains a list of animal categories, such as bears and birds. After choosing a category, a dialog box allows a user to indicate which animal he or she would like to research. Along with a photo of the animal, a brief description allows the user to learn about the animal's physical characteristics, natural habitat, feeding habits, and more. Because several animals housed in the zoo are endangered, they can be seen only by personally visiting the zoo or by visiting this Web site.

The following sections highlight federal department, agency, and commission Web sites that provide useful information and other services. The information and services available at each site are consistent with the primary purposes for which the department, agency, or commission was established.

FIGURE 6.8
National Zoo Home Page

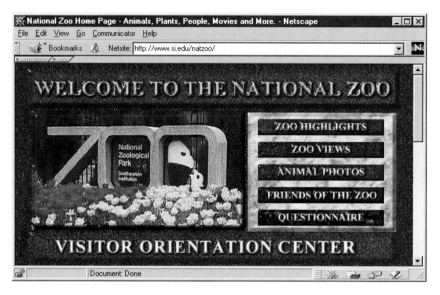

FIGURE 6.9
U.S. Department of Commerce Home Page

Department of Commerce

The **U.S. Department of Commerce** promotes job creation, economic growth, sustainable development, and improved living standards for all Americans by working in partnership with businesses, universities, communities, and workers. As stated at its Web site (Figure 6.9), the department's threefold purposes are to do the following:

1. Build for the future and promote U.S. competitiveness in the global market-place by strengthening and safeguarding the nation's economic infrastructure.

2. Keep America competitive with cutting-edge science and technology and an unrivaled information base.

3. Provide effective management and stewardship of the nation's resources and assets to ensure sustainable economic opportunities.

The department's home page contains links to documents that identify ways in which the department is engaged in electronic commerce applications. For example, a business considering opportunities available in a particular geographical location can obtain area census data by clicking on the link to the Bureau of the Census where this information is available. Numerous other links provide access to other kinds of economic information including national, regional, and local statistics useful to businesses in strategic planning. Hundreds of individuals and businesses regularly visit this site to obtain information and to communicate with the department. One who is interested in employment with the department can learn about available opportunities by clicking on the Opportunities link.

Department of Defense

The U.S. Department of Defense Web site, called **DefenseLINK,** is the starting point for finding military information online (Figure 6.10). Located in the Pentagon, the department's mission is to provide the military forces with information needed to deter war and to protect the security of the United States.

Although the value of this site may not be readily apparent to some viewers, the home page includes links to a variety of useful information. For example, a retiring veteran who has lost his or her copy of military document DD-214, the document that verifies the retiree's military service, can obtain another copy which, when sent to the Social Security Administration, provides the retiree with additional retirement income.

An individual wanting to enlist in a branch of the military service can begin the enlistment process by contacting the department at this site. A visitor to the site can view department contracts with commercial companies. An authorized

FIGURE 6.10

U.S. Department of Defense Home Page

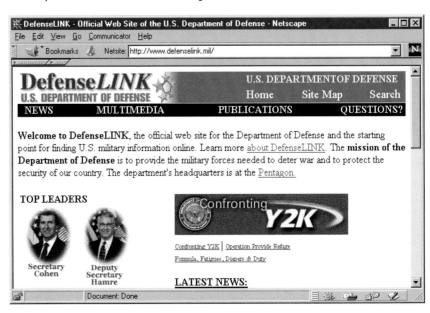

commercial bidder can learn about contracts available for bid and can submit a bid on behalf of the company represented by the bidder.

Department of the Interior

The mission of the **U.S. Department of the Interior** is to protect and provide access to the nation's natural and cultural heritage and to honor its trust responsibilities to Native American tribes. The department's Web site offers the latest news about the department's ongoing activities for carrying out its mission (Figure 6.11).

Responsibility for maintaining the nation's national parks rests with the **National Park Service**—an agency within the Department of the Interior. A visitor to the agency's Web site can view selected photos of national parks and can learn about other agencies within the Department of the Interior, including the U.S. Geological Survey, the Bureau of Indian Affairs, the Bureau of Land Management, and the U.S. Fish and Wildlife Service. A visit to this site is a special attraction for students and others who are interested in learning about natural resources throughout the United States.

The department regularly contracts for, and purchases, a variety of products and services and offers employment opportunities for job seekers with the department. A link at the department's home page allows a user to learn how to become an authorized vendor and outlines the procedure for conducting business with the department.

Department of Labor

The **U.S. Department of Labor** is charged with the mission of preparing the American workforce for new and better jobs and of ensuring the adequacy of America's workplaces. Within its mission is the responsibility for the administration and enforcement of more than 180 federal statutes. Every American worker

FIGURE 6.11
U.S. Department of the Interior Home Page

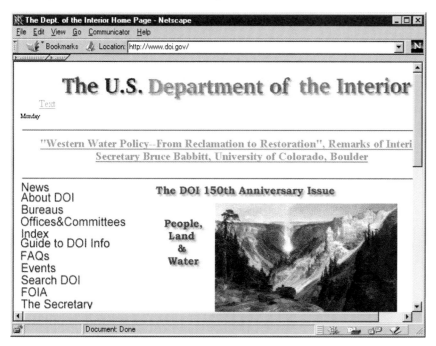

needs to be aware of basic federal laws and regulations that affect individual workers, as well as those that affect the labor force in general, such as the Fair Labor Standards Act (also known as the Minimum Wage Act).

The department provides and maintains a Web site to offer a wealth of information for the public (Figure 6.12). Its home page contains links that will allow users to learn more about major statutes, grants and contracts, and employment opportunities. By selecting the link to Grant and Contract Information, for example, a user can read about current grants, as well as grants for which the user can apply. Also, authorized bidders can learn about contracts available for bidding and can submit their own bids for announced products, services, and projects.

By clicking on the Job Openings at the Department of Labor link, a user can learn about employment opportunities from an extensive list of posted jobs and a description of each job along with specific job requirements. A visitor will quickly notice an extensive list of job openings for statisticians, as the preparation of statistical reports is an ongoing activity within the department.

National Aeronautics and Space Administration (NASA)

The primary mission of the **National Aeronautics and Space Administration (NASA),** as stated on its Web site home page, is "to conduct safe and timely flight research for the discovery, technology development, and technology transfer for U.S. Aeronautics and Space Preeminence." Most people know already that NASA is actively involved in space exploration and news media regularly cover NASA events, such as flights involving shuttle aircraft.

Fewer people are likely to be aware of NASA's involvement in electronic commerce applications. NASA has an active **Office of Procurement** that posts and maintains procurement pages that are interconnected into a system, called the **NASA Acquisition Internet Service (NAIS),** which allows NASA and commer-

FIGURE 6.12

U.S. Department of Labor Home Page

cial companies to conduct business transactions online. At NASA's Office of Procurement home page, authorized businesses can learn about business opportunities available with NASA. A link on this page allows representatives of authorized companies to access center procurement sites where specific business opportunities, including bid announcements, are posted. After reviewing bid specifications, an authorized company can retrieve online bid forms, fill in the required data, and transmit the forms to NASA (Figure 6.13).

Equal Employment Opportunity Commission

Discrimination is both a social and economic problem in our society and around the world. Discrimination may be based on various factors, including gender, race, religion, and age.

In the 1960s, Congress enacted legislation authorizing the establishment of the **Equal Employment Opportunity Commission (EEOC).** The mission of the EEOC, as stated at its Web site, is "to promote equal opportunity in employment through administrative and judicial enforcement of the federal civil rights laws and through education and technical assistance" (Figure 6.14).

The EEOC home page includes links to other useful sites and pages. By clicking on the Filing a Charge link, any past or present worker can retrieve an online form that can be used to file a discrimination complaint against an employer with the commission. Thousands of complaints have been filed in this manner. After a complaint has been filed, the commission will notify the employer and investigate the complaint. Results of the investigation will be shared with the person or group that filed the complaint. Offenders may be fined, subjected to litigation, or the case may be settled by mediation.

Like other federal departments, agencies, and commissions, employment opportunities are available at EEOC for qualified individuals. The EEOC home page includes a Jobs at EEOC link to listings of available jobs.

FIGURE 6.13

NASA's Office of Procurement Home Page

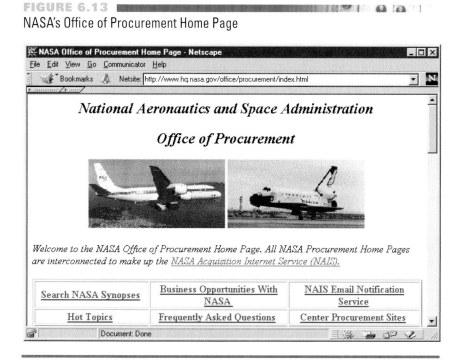

FIGURE 6.14
Equal Employment Opportunity Commission Home Page

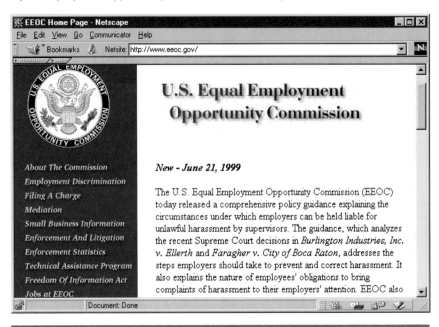

Federal Trade Commission

The primary responsibility for enforcing federal consumer protection laws rests with the **Federal Trade Commission (FTC).** The commission also works to enhance the smooth operation of the marketplace by eliminating acts or practices that are unfair or deceptive.

Like other federal departments, agencies, and commissions, the FTC maintains a Web site to provide users with information (Figure 6.15). Links on the FTC's home page allow a user to quickly jump to FTC offices and branches, to other sites, and to read about cases in which the commission has a special interest.

The FTC conducts its electronic commerce operations online through its acquisitions branch, which can be accessed by clicking on the Acquisitions Branch link on the home page. Through the acquisitions branch, the FTC purchases products and services for its headquarters and its 10 regional offices located throughout the United States. Examples of products and services purchased are information technology supplies and services, expert witness services, and management and administrative support services. Through the Acquisitions Branch, the FTC can be contacted and products and services offered.

Social Security Administration

The mission of the **Social Security Administration (SSA),** as stated at its Web site, is "to promote the economic security of the nation's people through compassionate and vigilant leadership in shaping and managing America's social security programs." The SSA publishes a list of publications available to citizens who submit an online request (Figure 6.16).

The SSA is actively involved in electronic commerce activities. Its home page contains links to pages that describe these activities. An important link is Selling to SSA. Here, procurement opportunities are explained and additional links are provided that allow a user to find out how to do business with the SSA. A list of current solicitations and bidder announcements is available for viewing.

FIGURE 6.15
Federal Trade Commission Home Page

FIGURE 6.16
Social Security Administration Home Page

The SSA purchases a variety of products and services online from authorized vendors. Any person or business wanting to sell products and services to the SSA can offer bids after becoming registered as an authorized vendor.

Small Business Administration

A wealth of information and opportunities await visitors to the Web site of the **Small Business Administration (SBA).** The mission of the SBA is to encourage policies that support the development and growth of American small businesses.

The SBA's Web site (Figure 6.17) is perhaps the most impressive federal site. A comprehensive library of SBA publications, forms, reports, statistics, and more await users. A click on the Outside Resources button displays a matrix of useful links to resources, including jobs, franchising opportunities, business schools, procurement, and other resources. Selecting the Procurement option allows a user to learn about doing business with the SBA and with other departments, agencies, and commissions.

A link at the SBA site displays a list of documents with general and specific information about electronic commerce. For example, selecting the Electronic Commerce Resource Centers option automatically moves a user to the FedWorld Information Network home page. Here, the user can click of the Table of Contents option to view a list of documents offering explanations on topics including the Internet, the World Wide Web, electronic commerce, and electronic data interchange. For users interested in learning more about these and other topics, a visit to this location represents time well spent.

Veterans Administration

A visit to the Web site of the Veterans Administration (VA) may be of little value unless the visitor is a veteran of military service. However, for veterans a visit may prove quite beneficial because many veterans, dependents of veterans, and their children are entitled to special benefits available through the VA.

The home page of the VA's Web site (Figure 6.18) contains links to benefits, special programs, data, medical information, and procurement. For example, accessing the Benefits link causes information to be displayed that describes the benefits available to veterans and their families. Clicking on the Procurement link retrieves information that explains the procedure used by the VA for acquiring products and services, including the procedure for obtaining products and services

FIGURE 6.17

Small Business Administration Home Page

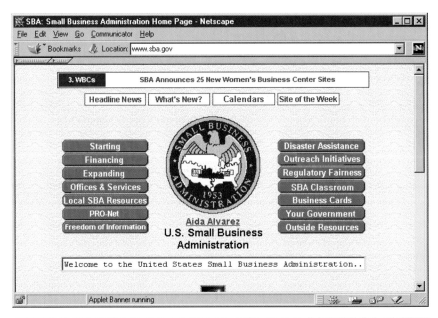

FIGURE 6.18
Veterans Administration Home Page

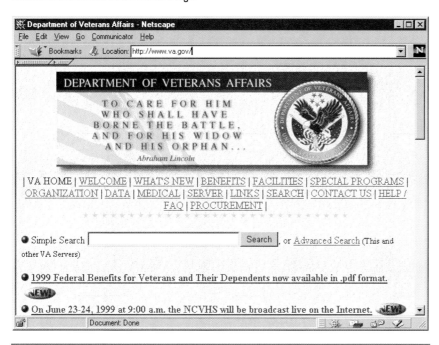

online. A link at this location allows a user to view lists of products and services being advertised for bidding.

A user can contact the VA using the VA Web site. For example, a veteran needing a copy of the veteran's form DD-214 (discharge form) can obtain a copy by contacting the VA via its Web site.

Internal Revenue Service

Millions of American taxpayers and tax preparers now file tax returns electronically by accessing one or more electronic tax forms, filling in the forms, and sending them over the Internet to the Internal Revenue Service. Theoretically, this allows individual taxpayers and companies to receive refunds sooner than by filing returns by mail.

The mission of the **Internal Revenue Service,** as stated at its Web site, is to "provide America's taxpayers top quality service by helping them understand and meet their tax responsibilities and by applying the tax law with integrity and fairness to all."

When a user first accesses the IRS Web site, the home page appears that contains a photograph or image of a mailbox (Figure 6.19). The image is the gateway to information and forms available at the site. A click on the mailbox displays another page containing links to taxpayer information and forms. A single click on the Forms & Pubs option causes a list of tax forms to appear from which you can make a selection.

To retrieve and view a specific tax form, you need special software, such as Adobe's Reader, installed on your computer. This can be a problem for some taxpayers that do not have this software. Information, including publications and forms, is updated frequently because Congress frequently changes the tax laws.

FIGURE 6.19

Internal Revenue Service Home Page

In the preceding sections we have examined several federal department, agency, and commission Web sites. Space limitations prevent us from examining every site. However, there are other federal sites that provide useful information and electronic commerce applications.

State Governments and Electronic Commerce

Governments of the various states maintain Web sites designed to inform and assist users. Several states are promoting electronic commerce as an efficient and cost-effective way to conduct business and are actively engaged in electronic commerce activities. However, some states have taken a more active role than others. In the following sections, we will examine a few of these sites and learn how state governments are using the Internet and Web to serve the public and to facilitate electronic commerce applications.

State of North Carolina

The state of North Carolina is a leading promoter and user of electronic commerce as a means of serving the public and conducting business activities with vendors. The state's home page (Figure 6.20) emphasizes this fact.

North Carolina maintains a Web site to provide a variety of information and assistance to the public. Its home page contains several links that enable a user to locate almost any needed information, including a link to useful business information. For example, clicking on the Business Info. link causes an index of topics to appear on the user's screen. Each option is a link to detailed information on the topic. A click on the Purchase & Contract topic displays the Purchase & Contract page that also includes a list of options, one of which is the Forms option. A click on the Forms option displays a list of forms arranged by category. An authorized

Andrew S. Grove

Andrew S. Grove was born in Budapest, Hungary, in 1936. He graduated from the City College of New York in 1960 with a bachelor's degree in chemical engineering, and he received his Ph.D. from the University of California, Berkeley, in 1963. Upon graduation, he joined the research and development laboratory of Fairchild Semiconductor and became assistant director of research and development in 1967.

In July 1968, Grove participated in the founding of Intel Corporation.

In 1979, he was named its president, and in 1987 he was named chief executive officer. In May 1997 he was named chairman and CEO. In May 1998 he relinquished his CEO title to Craig Barrett.

Grove has written more than 40 technical papers and holds several patents on semiconductor devices and technology. For six years he taught a graduate course in semiconductor device physics at the University of California, Berkeley. He currently is a lecturer at the Stanford University Graduate School of Business, teaching a course titled "Strategy and Action in the Information Processing Industry."

His first book, *Physics and Technology of Semiconductor Devices* (John Wiley and Sons, 1967), has been used at many leading universities in the United States. His book *High Output Management* (Random House, 1983, and Vintage, 1985) has been translated into 11 languages, and has recently been updated and reissued by Vintage Books. His book *One-on-One with Andy Grove* was published by G.P. Putnam's Sons in June 1987 and by Penguin in 1989. His latest book, *Only the Paranoid Survive,* was published by Doubleday in September of 1996. An author of articles published in *Fortune, The Wall Street Journal,* and *The New York Times,* he has written a weekly column on management that was carried by several newspapers, and a column on management for *Working Woman* magazine.

Grove has been elected a fellow of the Institute of Electrical and Electronics Engineers (IEEE) and a member of the National Academy of Engineering. In 1985 he was awarded an honorary doctor of science degree by the City College of New York, and in 1989 he was awarded an honorary doctor of engineering degree from Worcester Polytechnic Institute. He is a recipient of many awards, including the 1987 Engineering Leadership Recognition Award from the IEEE. In 1993 he received the AEA Medal of Achievement, and in March 1994 was elected a fellow of the Academy of Arts and Sciences. In January 1995 Grove was awarded the Heinz Family Foundation Award for Technology and the Economy and was selected to give the opening keynote speech for Telecom '95 in Geneva in October of 1995.

In 1997 Grove gave the keynote speech at the World Economic Forum in Davos, Switzerland, and was presented the Cinema Digital Technologies Award at the Cannes Film Festival in May. In September he received the CEO of the Year award from *CEO* magazine.

In December 1997, Grove received the Technology Leader of the Year Award from *Industry Week* and was named *Time* magazine's Man of the Year.

Source: Intel Corp. Web site, www.intel.com.

vendor can retrieve and display the appropriate electronic form by clicking on its title. Once retrieved and displayed on the user's screen, a vendor can offer a bid for advertised products or services by entering the required information and transmitting the form over the Internet to the appropriate state agency.

FIGURE 6.20

State of North Carolina Home Page

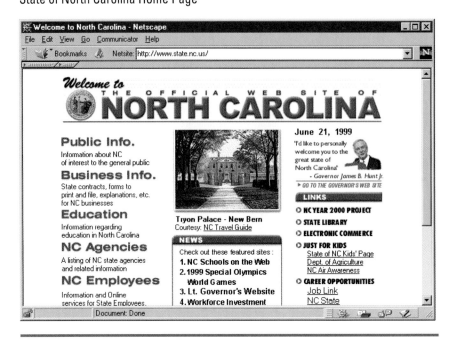

For new vendors, other forms are listed that explain the requirements for becoming an authorized vendor. Each year, hundreds of businesses become authorized agents by completing online forms and sending them to the state. After completing this process, firms that have obtained approval are eligible to submit bids to the state for advertised products and services.

State of Florida

Florida's Web site appears to be geared toward electronic commerce applications. Like Web sites of other states, the Florida site contains links to a variety of information residents and others may find useful (Figure 6.21).

The Florida site offers easy navigation to the state's electronic commerce involvement. At the bottom of the home page is a special Purchasing DIRECT link, which, when activated, causes a page titled "Purchasing DIRECT" to be displayed. Two links on this page are noteworthy. One is a Purchasers link, which accesses information that describes the procedure for purchasing products offered by the state. The other is a Vendors link, which, when activated, displays a page containing links to important documents of special interest to vendors wanting to do business with the state.

Clicking on the Vendors link displays a page titled "Visitors' Center." This page contains a list of links to important information and online forms. A Visitor Bid System link accesses information that clearly explains the procedure for becoming an authorized vendor and allows a user to view advertisements for products and services the state of Florida is anticipating purchasing. A separate link beneath the Vendor Bid System link is the Download Vendor Forms link for downloading electronic forms including a vendor application form that can be completed and returned to the state. Other forms include forms needed to place bids for products advertised. Anyone interested in doing business with the state should carefully read and examine all the documents listed on the Visitor Center page. All are clearly written and understandable.

FIGURE 6.21
State of Florida Home Page

Visitors to the state of Florida Web site will find other online applications. The site makes it possible for job seekers to download electronic application forms that can be filled out and returned, consumer protection information, and much more. In short, a visitor to the state of Florida Web site will learn ways in which the state uses electronic commerce technologies to better serve the public efficiently and effectively.

State of Colorado

Like other state Web sites, Colorado's home page contains links to categories of information (Figure 6.22). The Business Information category offers links to business-related topics including state government purchasing opportunities—BIDS, links to business directories, chambers of commerce, taxes, and state agency resources.

By clicking on the State Government Purchasing Opportunities—BIDS link, a user can view another page titled "Division of Purchasing and State Buildings," with links to various types of information. For a viewer interested in electronic commerce, the Colorado BIDS for Goods and Services link displays additional links, one of which is How to Use Bids. This document clearly explains the procedure for becoming an authorized vendor along with detailed instructions for submitting bids to the state for the sales of goods and services.

State of Arizona

The home page at Arizona's Web site (Figure 6.23) allows a visitor to quickly learn about the state's electronic commerce initiative. A click on the Doing Business with the State link at the bottom of the home page causes another page, titled "Arizona Procurement Information eXchange" (AZPIX), to appear on the user's screen. At the left side of the page is an index of useful business links.

For a person or business wanting to do business with the state, two Index links are of special importance. Clicking on the How to Do Business link causes

FIGURE 6.22

State of Colorado Home Page

FIGURE 6.23

State of Arizona Home Page

information to be displayed that explains the procedure for becoming an authorized vendor and for conducting business activities with the state. The Vendor Information link allows a user to read about products and services the state wants to purchase. Here, a vendor can download bid submission forms that can be filled in and transmitted electronically to the state.

In the preceding sections we looked at selected state government Web sites. For persons interested in viewing other state sites, Figure 6.24 is an alphabetical list of states along with each state's Internet address.

FIGURE 6.24

State Government Internet Addresses

A list of Internet addresses for the 50 states. These addresses allow you to access state government Web sites. At each site, you can learn about the state and about ways in which each state government is engaged in electronic commerce activities.

STATE	INTERNET ADDRESS
Alabama	http://www.state.al.us
Alaska	http://www.state.ak.us
Arizona	http://www.state.az.us
Arkansas	http://www.state.ar.us
California	http://www.state.ca.us
Colorado	http://www.state.co.us
Connecticut	http://www.state.ct.us
Delaware	http://www.state.de.us
Florida	http://www.state.fl.us
Georgia	http://www.state.ga.us
Hawaii	http://www.state.hi.us
Idaho	http://www.state.id.us
Illinois	http://www.state.il.us
Indiana	http://www.state.in.us
Iowa	http://www.state.ia.us
Kansas	http://www.state.ks.us
Kentucky	http://www.state.ky.us
Louisiana	http://www.state.la.us
Maine	http://www.state.me.us
Maryland	http://www.state.md.us
Massachusetts	http://www.state.ma.us
Michigan	http://www.state.mi.us
Minnesota	http://www.state.mn.us
Mississippi	http://www.state.ms.us
Missouri	http://www.state.mo.us
Montana	http://www.state.mt.us
Nebraska	http://www.state.ne.us
Nevada	http://www.state.nv.us
New Hampshire	http://www.state.nh.us
New Jersey	http://www.state.nj.us
New Mexico	http://www.state.nm.us
New York	http://www.state.ny.us
North Carolina	http://www.state.nc.us
North Dakota	http://www.state.nd.us
Ohio	http://www.state.oh.us
Oklahoma	http://www.state.ok.us
Oregon	http://www.state.or.us
Pennsylvania	http://www.state.pa.us
Rhode Island	http://www.state.ri.us
South Carolina	http://www.state.sc.us
South Dakota	http://www.state.sd.us
Tennessee	http://www.state.tn.us
Texas	http://www.state.tx.us
Utah	http://www.state.ut.us
Vermont	http://www.state.vt.us
Virginia	http://www.state.va.us
Washington	http://www.state.wa.us
West Virginia	http://www.state.wv.us
Wisconsin	http://www.state.wi.us
Wyoming	http://www.state.wy.us

Local Governments and Electronic Commerce

Some local governments are already using the Internet and electronic commerce technologies to conduct business activities. However, some smaller local governments are just starting to recognize electronic commerce as an effective and cost-saving technology. Some already have the necessary technologies in place but lack the professional expertise for implementation.

Federal and state authorities are helping local governments by providing physical and human resources and by assisting local governments in the development, implementation, and operation of electronic commerce technologies. Some federal and state agencies provide funds in the form of grants to local governments wanting to establish electronic commerce capability and to use this capability to improve public services and to streamline business activities. Eventually, electronic commerce capability may enable even small local governments to operate as effectively as their larger counterparts.

In this chapter we learned how governments are using electronic commerce to improve operations to better serve the public. By now you may be wondering how an individual, business, or organization can establish a presence on the World Wide Web and become actively involved in electronic commerce. The following chapter is devoted to this topic and explains how a person, business, or organization can establish a presence and can use available electronic commerce technologies for a variety of personal and business applications.

SUMMARY

Federal, state, and local governments are among the strongest supporters and users of the Internet, the Web, and electronic commerce applications. Recognizing the potential of the Internet and the importance of electronic commerce in a global environment, the United States federal government has assumed a leadership role in promoting the worldwide use of the Internet for commercial purposes.

A federal interagency working group has prepared a document, titled "A Framework for Global Electronic Commerce," which describes the federal government's position regarding electronic commerce purposes. The document outlines the federal administration's strategy for encouraging the use of networks for electronic commerce. The document lists five main principles to guide government support for the evolution of electronic commerce and includes recommendations about nine key areas where international efforts are needed to preserve the Internet as a nonregulatory medium.

Federal, state, and local governments have a responsibility to promote the public welfare. Included is the obligation to promote future competition that can be achieved more easily by freeing the Internet from bureaucratic domination and by ensuring that Internet, Web, and electronic commerce technologies are freely available for use by everyone. Leadership by the federal government has allowed Internet, Web, and electronic commerce technologies to flourish throughout the world. Moreover, governments at all levels—federal, state, and local—are using these technologies to serve the public interest in ways similar to those used by businesses to serve customers.

Federal department and agency Web sites have been established to provide the public with information about legislative activities, statistics, and services. All states currently maintain Web sites that provide visitors with information about the state, including academic and cultural opportunities, population and growth statistics, taxes, and much more. Many local governments post Web sites to promote their communities and to recruit business and industry.

Many federal, state, and local governments are actively involved in electronic commerce applications. An important activity at every government level is procurement, a term that refers to the act of obtaining products and services. Authorized vendors visiting some of these sites can offer contract bids by filling out electronic bid forms and sending them to the appropriate department or agency. In business, the term *bid* refers to an attempt to acquire, win, or obtain something of value. A person or business offering a bid does so to acquire, win, or obtain something of value, such as a contract to sell products or services to another entity, such as a government agency.

Individuals seeking employment can read and respond to online employment notices posted at government sites. Companies interested in relocating or building a new plant can learn about existing opportunities available in various geographical locations.

Almost all federal departments, agencies, and commissions have established and maintain sites on the World Wide Web. Each site is designed to serve the interests and needs of visitors. For this reason, the information varies at each site. For security purposes, the amount of information available at some sites is limited or restricted to authorized persons. By providing information, the government is offering a service to citizens just as businesses provide services to customers. In this sense, *service* may be defined as the provision of information and assistance to the public.

Governments of the various states maintain Web sites designed to inform and assist users. Several states are promoting electronic commerce as an efficient and cost-effective way to conduct business and are actively engaged in electronic commerce activities.

Some large local governments use the Internet and electronic commerce technologies to conduct business activities. Some smaller local governments are just starting to recognize electronic commerce as an effective and cost-saving technology. Some already have the necessary technologies in place but lack the professional expertise for implementation.

Various federal and state authorities are now aiding local governments in this area by providing physical and human resources and by assisting local governments in the development, implementation, and operation of electronic commerce technologies. Some federal and state agencies provide funds to local governments wanting to establish electronic commerce capabilities and to use the capabilities to improve public services and to streamline business activities.

KEY TERMS

bid (165)
DefenseLINK (172)
Equal Employment
  Opportunity Commission (EEOC) (175)
Federal Trade Commission (FTC) (176)
Internal Revenue
  Service (179)
Library of Congress
  (168)
NASA Acquisition Internet Service (NAIS)
(174)
National Aeronautics
  and Space Administration (NASA) (174)
National Park Service
  (173)
National Zoo (170)
Office of Procurement
  (174)
procurement (165)
service (167)
Small Business Administration (SBA) (177)
Smithsonian Institution
  (169)
Social Security Administration (SSA) (176)
The U.S. Mint (167)
U.S. Department of
  Commerce (171)
U.S. Department of
  Labor (173)
U.S. Department of the
  Interior (173)

END-OF-CHAPTER ACTIVITIES

Matching

Match each term with its description.

a. bid
b. U.S. Mint
c. Library of Congress
d. procurement
e. Smithsonian Institution

f. EEOC
g. National Zoo
h. Department of Labor
i. Bureau of Indian Affairs

j. Federal Trade Commission
k. Defense LINK
l. IRS

_____ **1.** The act of acquiring, or obtaining, goods and services.

_____ **2.** A federal commission charged with promoting equal opportunity in employment through administrative and judicial enforcement of federal civil rights laws and through education and technical assistance.

_____ **3.** Its purpose is to preserve the history of the United States by conserving and displaying to the public items of historical importance, including the *Spirit of Saint Louis* aircraft.

_____ **4.** A commission that works to enhance the smooth operation of the marketplace by eliminating acts or practices that are unfair or deceptive.

_____ **5.** An agency within the Department of the Interior.

_____ **6.** A federal agency that produces coins.

_____ **7.** A federal Web site that taxpayers can use to access, fill out, and transmit electronic tax forms.

_____ **8.** The name of the Web site of the Department of Defense.

_____ **9.** A Web site that offers a reservoir of online information on almost every imaginable topic from the time this country was founded to the present.

_____ **10.** A Web site that offers a large inventory of animal photographs and information about each.

_____ **11.** Its mission is to prepare the American workforce and to ensure the adequacy of America's workplaces.

_____ **12.** An attempt to acquire, win, or obtain something of value.

Review Questions

1. Briefly explain the purpose of the document titled "A Framework for Global Electronic Commerce."
2. Identify three federal government Web sites that were presented in the chapter.
3. Briefly explain the mission of the U.S. Department of Labor.
4. Briefly explain how a person can use the EEOC site to file a charge of discrimination against an employer.

5. At the state of North Carolina Web site, explain the procedure a vendor should follow to submit a bid to the North Carolina state government.

Activities

1. Using a computer in your school's computer lab, visit the U.S. Mint site at http://www.usmint.gov. On the U.S. Mint home page, can you find out how coins are made? If so, follow the links through the production process. Prepare a written report that includes the details of your visit.

2. Using a computer in your school's computer lab, visit one of the federal government Web sites presented in the chapter. While viewing the site, prepare a written of list of features you like about the site and a list of features you do not like (or believe could be improved).

3. Almost all the federal government Web sites presented in the chapter provide useful information about job and career opportunities. Visit one federal department, agency, or commission Web site to learn about employment opportunities with the department, agency, or commission. Prepare a written list of the job opportunities you find, and indicate whether an individual is allowed to submit an employment application online using the Internet.

4. In the chapter, Figure 6.24 contains Internet addresses for the 50 states. Using the address provided, visit the state government site of your state. Prepare a brief written critique of the site. Include a list of services provided at the site, such as employment opportunities. Also include statements that identify your state government's involvement in electronic commerce applications.

5. This is a team project. Your instructor will divide the class into groups (teams) with four or five students on each team. Each student in each group will visit one federal government Web site. At the site's home page, identify and prepare a written list of all links to business information. Click on each link and examine the information displayed. If the state is actively involved in electronic commerce, prepare a written summary of the ways in which the state is involved in electronic commerce activities. When you have finished, prepare a written group report explaining how all states examined by group members are using electronic commerce, such as information, recruitment, and procurement.

Establishing Your Presence in Electronic Commerce

AFTER COMPLETING THIS CHAPTER, YOU WILL:

1. Explain the nature of a Web site.
2. Explain the main difference between a personal, company, organizational, and governmental Web site.
3. List five main steps in Web page construction.
4. Identify two tools that can be used to create Web pages.
5. List and explain some basic design rules.
6. Explain why it is important to keep the visitor in mind when developing a Web site.

7. **Identify several Web page components.**
8. **Identify several media considerations for constructing Web pages.**
9. **Explain the nature of a Web host and identify three Web host options.**
10. **Identify various options for publishing a Web site.**
11. **Explain ways in which a Web site can be promoted and publicized.**
12. **Discuss the importance of maintaining your Web site and identify ways for keeping your site attractive and current.**

Chances are that you are already an Internet user and have visited many Web sites. During your visits, perhaps you noticed that various sites look different and appeal to different individuals and groups. Some sites were designed for casual visitors simply seeking information, such as newspaper, magazine, and nonprofit organization sites. For example, a site such as the one by *USA Today* is designed to provide information for viewers. Business sites are designed to capture customer interest and to persuade customers to purchase products and services. Individuals and groups create and maintain sites that enable them to communicate with other individuals and groups.

Anyone wanting to do so can create a site on the World Wide Web for whatever purpose he or she chooses. Thousands of individuals, companies, and organizations have already done exactly that. If you spend a few minutes browsing the Web, you will likely visit various Web sites that are quite distinct in both design and content. Some are impressive and quickly capture your attention. Others are poorly designed and offer little, if any, value to the visitor. You may return again and again to those sites that are attractive and informative, but you may never return to sites that offer little of value.

The Internet and the Web make it possible for any individual, business, or organization to establish a presence in the dynamic field of electronic commerce. The range of applications is virtually unlimited. You can create a Web site to sell a single product, such as birdhouse, or one highlighting your employment qualifications that can be examined by potential employers. A company can create a home page with links to other pages that describe a variety of available products.

This chapter describes some important concepts for those wanting to establish a presence on the Web for whatever purpose. After learning the information presented in the chapter, you can proceed to establish your presence, just as thousands of others have already done. Establishing your presence might prove to be an interesting and relatively inexpensive way for you to begin and maintain communication with other people around the world.

What Is a Web Site?

You learned in Chapter Three that the World Wide Web (called the Web) is a global system of accessible computer networks linked in a way that allows a user to jump from one place on the Web to another. Each network includes a special server, called a **Web server,** on which Web documents and pages are stored. A **Web document** is an electronic document stored on a Web server (Figure 7.1). A document can contain several **Web pages,** and only one page can be viewed at a time. A Web page can be accessed and viewed using a Web browser. When a visitor accesses a Web site, the first page that appears on the computer screen is the site's **home page.** Each Web page that is stored has an address, called an **URL** (an abbreviation for **Uniform Resource Locator**). A Web page can be viewed by typing the page's URL in the browser's address box or by clicking on a link to the page.

FIGURE 7.1

A Network with a Web Server

Web pages can be created on any computer, including a personal computer, and stored on a Web server. A Web author can create and begin testing a personal Web site on any computer, such as an author's personal computer. Once the page(s) is stored on the Web server, it can be accessed and viewed by anyone who can access the World Wide Web. Web pages can also be stored on any other Web server as well. For example, your Internet Service Provider (ISP) may permit you to store pages on its server in return for being a subscriber.

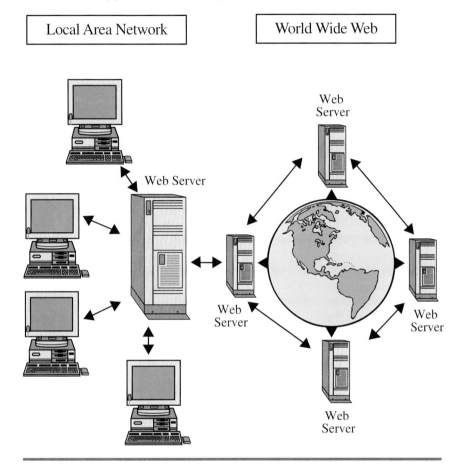

Each one of the thousands of networks owned by academic institutions, businesses, organizations, and government departments and agencies typically include one or more Web servers. Anyone who is authorized to do so can post (store) Web pages on the Web server. For example, colleges frequently allow students to create and store Web pages on the college's Web server.

A **Web site** is a collection of one or more related Web pages that are usually stored together in the same location on a Web server. For example, a retailer might store multiple catalog pages together on the company's Web server. Visitors to the site can use links on the pages to move from one catalog page to another.

Web pages are produced by individuals, called **Web authors.** Anyone can learn to be a Web author. **Web publishing** refers to the placement of Web pages on a Web server so that others can access the pages. A **Webmaster** is a trained individual responsible for managing a Web site. A Webmaster can be contacted by sending an e-mail message to the site to the attention of its Webmaster. For example, the Webmaster at Dell Computer Corporation can be contacted by sending an e-mail message to the address *webmaster@dell.com.*

Types of Web Sites

A Web author may choose to create a personal site for the author's own benefit or may be employed to create an organizational site for a business, organization, or agency. Many large companies employ trained and experienced Web authors to create company sites and to keep them current.

The following sections explain the various types of Web sites. You've already seen examples of each of the types of sites in earlier chapters. These sections present examples of each type of site for the purpose of comparison.

Personal Sites

A **personal site** is one created by an individual and posted on the Web. A personal site may exist for a variety of reasons. Some people simply want to master Web site construction. Some want a low-cost, high-technology way of communicating with a larger audience to express personal opinions or special agendas. For example, thousands of college students have created their own personal site on the school's Web server to post their resumes for potential employers to see and examine. Some simply want to meet new people and establish friendships. Some want to sell something. Many simply want to learn more about this modern technology. Some want to draw attention to themselves, to their purpose, or to their mission. For example, several presidential hopefuls have embraced the Web as a means of drawing attention to their candidacies, identifying key campaign issues, and soliciting campaign contributions. Figure 7.2 shows the personal Web site for George W. Bush, a potential Republican presidential candidate in the 2000 presidential election.

Texas Governor Bush is not the only potential candidate who is using the Web as a means of publicizing his presidential ambitions. Several others have established similar sites on the Web.

FIGURE 7.2

George W. Bush Web Site

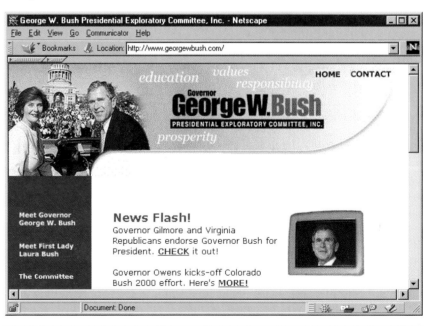

A Web author can develop a Web site using any computer, including a personal computer. Many newer computers come equipped with software that contains the tools for Web site development. After creating the pages for a site, they can be tested on any kind of computer prior to publishing them on a Web server. Basic Web publishing concepts are similar to general marketing design concepts. The main goal of both is to attract viewers' attention and to elicit favorable responses.

Company Sites

One purpose of a **company site** is to sell products and services to customers and to attract new customers. There are thousands of company sites already on the Web and hundreds more appear each week. You may already be familiar with some company sites, such as Sears, Wal-Mart, Ford Motor Company, and AT&T. Almost all large companies have gotten into the act by placing their sites on the Web. At some of these, you can purchase the company's products and services directly by completing an electronic order form. Others want to draw your attention to the company and its products and services. Some use their sites to focus customer attention on new products. Some smaller companies have discovered the Web as an inexpensive method for marketing. Whatever the purpose, many companies have enjoyed success with their sites. Figure 7.3 shows the home page of Dell Computer Corporation—a company that has experienced enormous success in selling computer products via the Web.

The Web conceals the size of the company from the visitor. When visiting a particular site, the visitor cannot determine the size of the company. On the Web, a small company may appear to be as large as a huge corporation. This tends to equalize competition among companies of various sizes. As a result, it creates an important opportunity for the small, entrepreneurial business owner. However, it may also create a risk for customers who purchase products and services from a company whose reputation is unknown. Despite the risks, many companies of various sizes are thriving in this revolutionary business environment called the Web.

FIGURE 7.3

Dell Computer Corporation Home Page

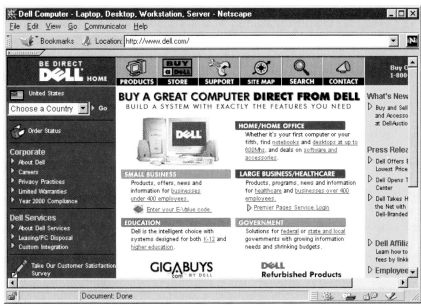

Note: Site accessed August 5, 1999.

FIGURE 7.4

Safe Kids Web Site

Organization Sites

An **organization site** is a site on the Web typically sponsored by a not-for-profit organization that promotes the organization's purposes and activities. A main purpose of many organization sites is to inform the public about the organizations and about the services they offer.

Many different organizations now have sites on the Web. The National Safe Kids organization provides information about the organization, news articles, and descriptions of the services it offers. It also encourages financial support from the public (Figure 7.4).

Similarly, the PRIDE-Omaha Inc. site informs the public about the organization's primary mission to prevent drug use by youth in the Omaha, Nebraska, area (Figure 7.5). Visitors to the site can learn about drug abuse and prevention and about what the organization is doing to promote drug awareness in the Omaha area.

Government Sites

A **government site** is one created and maintained by a unit of government—federal, state, or local. Hundreds of government sites are now available on the Web and more are being added each week.

Each government site has its own purpose and the purposes of various sites may be quite varied. Some, such as the U.S. Department of Health and Human Services site (Figure 7.6), offer a wealth of useful information for health professionals and for individuals interested in learning about various health topics and studies. The results of medical research studies are available for viewing, as well as information about various drugs and medical conditions. Departmental concerns and warnings, such as those about alcohol and drug abuse and health risks, are posted at this site.

FIGURE 7.5

PRIDE-Omaha Inc. Home Page

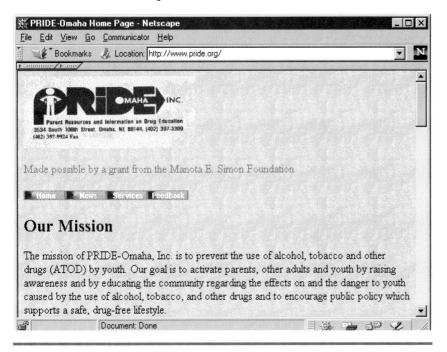

FIGURE 7.6

U.S. Department of Health and Human Services Home Page

The U.S. Department of Health and Human Services Web site contains a variety of information of interest to anyone employed in health professions and to individuals interested in learning about health topics and issues.

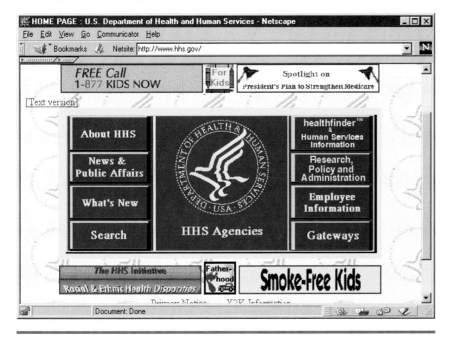

FIGURE 7.7

State of Texas Home Page

Visitors wanting to learn about the state of Texas can do so at the Texas State Web site. The home page contains links to other pages that contain information about a variety of interesting and useful topics.

All states have their own Web sites. Home pages at some state sites contain links to other pages that allow a viewer to quickly move or "jump" to another document or page. For example, the Texas State home page contains links to various other documents and pages. Clicking on the Business Information link allows a user to access information about licensing, permits, regulations, and state procurement (Figure 7.7).

The Texas home page contains links to other pages and documents of interest to many visitors. For example, the Employment link allows a visitor to quickly jump to pages containing information about state employment opportunities. The Health & Human Services link enables a visitor to quickly jump to the Texas Department of Health page where the visitor can apply for a birth certificate. Other links on the home page can be equally useful. Many states are continually upgrading their sites by offering improved information and services to visitors.

Steps in Web Page Design

Just as there are basic steps for solving other problems or completing other tasks, there are a few basic steps that should be followed when creating a Web site. For example, recall from your study of mathematics that solving a mathematical equation requires that multiplication and division be performed prior to addition and subtraction. Otherwise, the answer you get may be incorrect.

Following a few recommended steps will prove helpful as you begin creating your Web pages. Avoid the temptation of skipping over some of the steps, as you may regret it later.

Step One: Determine Your Objective

The first step is to determine your objective. Question yourself. Do I simply want to create a personal site at which others can learn about me? Do I want to share information with others? Is my (or my organization's) objective to sell products and services? Do I want to create a site that provides me with an inexpensive way to sell my products or services?

Answers to these and other questions can help you determine your objectives. Creating a Web site prior to determining your objective will likely result in a site that is poorly constructed and one that viewers will likely avoid in the future.

Step Two: Identify and Know Your Audience

After determining your objective, you need to identify your intended audience and learn as much as you can about it. Here again, ask yourself some questions. Does the audience I want to attract consist of persons with interests similar to mine? Do I want my site to attract males, females, teenagers, senior citizens, my organization's suppliers, or customers?

Knowing about your intended audience will prove helpful in designing your site. Suppose, for example, that your intended audience will be primarily female. You may decide to use pastel colors that are more attractive to females rather than darker colors, such as brown or black. Also, the pictures you select will likely include female subjects. Knowing your audience is critical for attracting members of that audience.

Step Three: Consider the Possibilities

When creating a Web site, there are unlimited possibilities. As is true for any creative process, you conjure up mental thoughts, ideas, and images. Devote considerable thought and imagination to your site—its structure, its content, and to what you want to accomplish.

Don't rely solely on your own ideas. You can get ideas from other sites available on the Web. Visit several sites that have a purpose similar to yours and those that are targeted to a similar audience. During your visits, critique the sites. How can you make your site better? Is the information offered at these sites interesting and useful? Are the colors appealing? Do the images, graphics, and pictures add significantly to the site? Use a stopwatch to determine how long it takes to download the pages. Do the pages include frames, and, if so, are they necessary? A good idea is to print copies of the pages you visit. On each page, make notes of your likes and dislikes. Refer to the notes when you begin designing your site.

As you brainstorm, capture your thoughts on paper. Take periodic breaks from your work and rest your mind. This allows your subconscious to continue working, even while you are doing other things. After a break, return to the project. You may find that you have thought of some new, even more creative ideas. Make written notes of these as well.

Step Four: Plan and Design Your Site

You are now ready to put your ideas into a workable plan. Using a pencil and paper, begin preparing a written sketch of the design for your site. Begin with your home page. Prepare a sketch of the contents, including text, graphics, links, and other features. If links are to be included, which page(s) will be linked to the home page? Prepare a sketch of each page, including the text, graphics, and features to be incorporated. Identifying each page component is similar to putting together pieces of a jigsaw puzzle. As more and more pieces are put together, a picture of your Web site will begin taking shape. Figure 7.8 shows a basic design structure for Web pages.

If this is your first attempt, be aware that your plan may be revised again and again. Don't be overly critical of your work. Being overly critical can impede your progress. Review your plan periodically and make changes when warranted. Eventually, your design will evolve into one with which you can be satisfied.

Step Five: Create the Page(s)

After completing the design, you can proceed to create the Web pages that will be posted at your site. For this, you have an abundance of options. If you are an experienced Web author, you can create your pages using a Web programming

FIGURE 7.8

Basic Design Structure for Web Pages

(a) The first page is the home page. A home page may contain a variety of features including text, graphics, colors, and links to other pages, shown as level a.
(b) Additional pages are linked to the home page.
(c) Additional pages are linked to the page shown in level b. Each page linked to a page at a higher level is in some way related to the higher level.

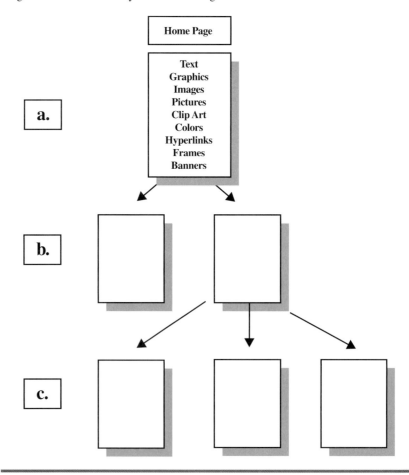

Bill Gates and Microsoft Corporation

William H. (Bill) Gates III is cofounder, chair, and chief executive officer of Microsoft Corporation, the world's leading provider of software for personal computers. He was born on October 28, 1955, and grew up in Seattle, Washington, where he attended public elementary school before moving on to the private Lakeside School in North Seattle. He began programming computers at the age of 13.

In 1973 Gates entered Harvard University. While at Harvard, he developed a version of the programming language BASIC for the first microcomputer, called the MITS Altair. Gates dropped out of Harvard in his junior year to devote his energies full time to Microsoft, a company he had started in 1975 with his boyhood friend Paul Allen. Guided by a belief that the personal computer would be a valuable tool on every office desktop and in every home, they began developing software for personal computers.

Gates's foresight and vision regarding personal computing have been the key to the success of Microsoft and the software industry. He is actively involved in key management and strategic decisions at Microsoft and plays an important role in the technical development of new products.

Under Gates's leadership, Microsoft's mission is continuously to advance and improve software technology and to make it easier, more cost-effective, and more enjoyable for people to use computers. The company is committed to a long-term view, which is reflected in its investment of some $2.6 billion for research and development during the 1999 fiscal year. The company has been quick to take advantage of opportunities created by the Internet. Gates has a substantial investment with cellular telephone pioneer Craig McCaw in Teledesic, a company that is working on an ambitious plan to launch hundreds of low-orbit satellites around the earth to provide a worldwide two-way broadband telecommunications service.

Since its inception in 1975, Microsoft's mission has been to create software for the personal computer that empowers and enriches people in the workplace, at school, and at home. Microsoft's early vision of a computer on every desk and in every home is coupled today with a strong commitment to Internet-related technologies that expand the power and reach of the PC and its users.

Microsoft products include operating systems for personal computers, server applications for client/server environments, business and consumer productivity applications, interactive media programs, and Internet platform and development tools. Microsoft also offers online services, sells personal computer books and input devices, and researches and develops advanced technology software products.

language, such as HTML (explained later). Another option is to use a Web authoring program, such as Microsoft's FrontPage 98, to create the pages. Still another option is to employ a professional to create the pages using the design you developed in Step Four.

Web authoring programs are often used by those interested in establishing an individual Web site. Experienced programmers often use Web languages for creating Web pages. Professional Web authors are frequently employed by businesses and organizations to create Web pages.

Amateurs most often use Web authoring programs to create Web pages. Most programs are relatively easy to learn and use. Many colleges and schools offer courses to students wanting to learn a particular program, such as Microsoft's FrontPage 98 or Macromedia's Dreamweaver. Using a Web authoring program can help you create informative and attractive pages.

Tools for Creating Web Pages

As stated earlier, you have options for creating Web pages. You can employ a Web professional to create your pages based on the plan and design you develop. If you are knowledgeable in the use of a Web programming language, you can use the language to create the pages. The other option is to use a software program that makes it easier for both experienced and inexperienced authors to create Web pages. These options are explained in the following sections.

Web Languages

Web pages are hypertext documents. A **hypertext document** contains highlighted text that connects to other Web pages and Web sites. You can select highlighted text on a Web page to access and display a page located on the same computer or another computer in another city or country.

HyperText Markup Language (HTML) is a language in which most Web pages are written. The program includes an editor, called the **HTML editor,** that allows a user to insert HTML tags in pages. **HTML tags** are codes embedded within the text on Web pages to identify how text, links, and images are to be displayed on the pages. These codes define the content, layout, and characteristics of your Web site. HTML sets the size and location of your text, the size and location of your graphics, your background colors, and links to other sites, sounds, animation, and even video clips. Figures 7.9 and 7.10 show a Web page and the HTML code used to create the page.

FIGURE 7.9

Watauga Medical Center Home Page

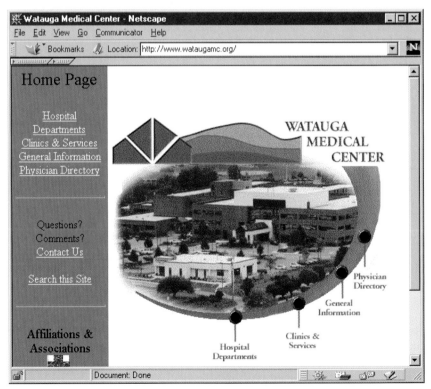

FIGURE 7.10
Watauga Medical Center Home Page HTML Tags

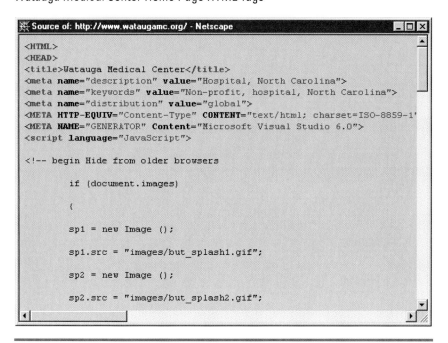

In recent years, new languages with exceptional capabilities have been introduced. These languages, such as VRML and XML, are rapidly gaining popularity. **VRML** (an abbreviation for **Virtual Reality Modeling Language**), is a Web language that allows a user to create three-dimensional objects and environments, called *VRML worlds.* More and more companies and organizations are embracing VRML because of the effectiveness. VRML is used by entertainment companies to create movies and games, and by companies to show their products. This allows a potential customer to walk around products and view them from any angle. You can see an example of VRML at the Teldor Cable Company site, http://www.netvision.net.il~teldor/vrml.html. Figure 7.11 shows a product in three-dimensional form.

A new Web language, called **eXtensible Markup Language** (**XML**) is gaining widespread acceptance among Web users and site developers around the world. XML is essentially a subsct of IBM's SGML (Standard Generalized Markup Language) and it bridges the gap between SGML and the somewhat limited capabilities of HTML (HyperText Markup Language). XML, in its earliest form, was developed in 1996 when the World Wide Web Consortium (W3C) commissioned a group of markup language experts, organized and led by Sun Microsystems' Jon Bosak, to deal with the limitations of HTML. At present, W3C is attempting to develop an acceptable standardized XML version.

Web Authoring Software

You can purchase a variety of Web authoring programs and editors that guide you through the construction of your Web pages. These programs supply the HTML instructions that are needed to create your text and graphic designs. Some include libraries and templates that allow you to create pages easily and quickly. Using a commercial Web authoring program is likely to be easier, especially for beginners.

FIGURE 7.11

A Product Shown in Three-Dimensional Form

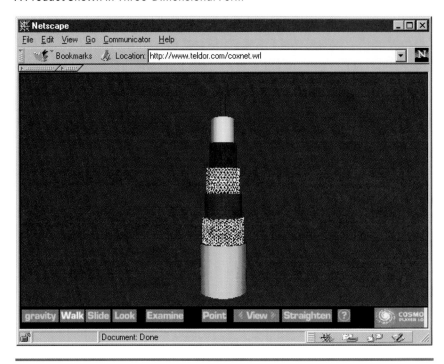

Several good Web authoring programs are available for purchase, including Microsoft's FrontPage 98 (Figure 7.12) and Macromedia's Dreamweaver 2.1. If you're thinking about buying one of these, consider buying a copy "off the shelf" rather than downloading a copy from the company. By doing so, you will have a complete hard copy of all printed materials, including a user's manual to which you can refer for help.

Most programs come with special features including clip art, pictures, and detailed instructions. Your program may also include an HTML editor for creating text that you can insert into your pages. Special features allow you to insert links to additional pages and to documents at other Web sites.

If you are inexperienced, you can use the HTML editor contained in Microsoft Word 7.0 and in other programs, which allows you to simply type the text and then convert what you've typed into HTML. Several word processor programs also allow you to type text that the editor can automatically convert into HTML format and to specify what you type as a link. Most also include other useful features for creating Web pages.

Web site development is a powerful skill that is in great demand by employers. You can improve your skills with practice. The World Wide Web is huge and is growing larger. New Web software products and services are being introduced almost daily. Although it is virtually impossible to know everything about Web site creation, the goal of this chapter is to help you get started in this dynamic and growing field.

The size and scope of various types of Web sites may be quite different, but many of the construction processes are the same. In later sections, some basic Web authoring concepts are presented to help you create pages that capture and hold the interest of visitors to your Web site. Web research suggests that a visitor's attention span during the first visit to a site is only a few seconds! If your site is unattractive and of little value to viewers, they will quickly stop downloading your pages and move on to another site.

The following sections present some basic design rules. Study them carefully! Adhering to these rules can help you create a Web site that people will likely want to visit and to tell others about.

FIGURE 7.12

FrontPage 98 Software Package

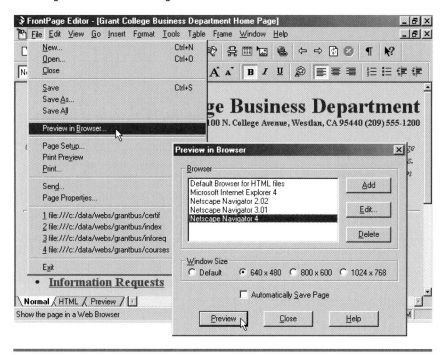

Some Basic Design Rules

As you begin to think about designing a Web site, keep in mind that your goal is to attract viewers. While viewing your site, you want visitors to be impressed with what they see. Some basic design rules will help attract viewers to your site and to impress them during their visit:

- *Make your page(s) concise.* Do not clutter your pages with too much text or other features, such as images and graphics. When necessary, include bulleted lists.

- *Make your pages easy to read.* A visitor to your site should be able to read all the pages easily. Avoid using words and terms that are unclear to a reader. In short, use simple words and terms that are easily understood to an average reader and use plenty of white space. Otherwise, a reader will quickly move to another site.

- *Make it easy for a viewer to navigate your site.* On your home page, let a reader know how to navigate through your site. Navigation is made easier with icons and by including a name with an icon to let your reader know what the icon means. For sites with multiple pages, include links to other pages that are easily understood.

- *Make your Web pages interesting.* Include text, graphics, and other features on your pages, especially on your home page, that will immediately capture reader interest. Various type sizes, boldface text, graphics, and color can be used for emphasis.

- *Design your pages so that they load easily and quickly.* Some Web page authors make the mistake of including too many large graphics on their Web pages. Pages containing large graphics slow down page retrieval. Pages with smaller graphics will load more quickly.

■ *Use frames only when necessary.* Web browsers allow the browser window to be divided into separate areas called **frames.** Although frames can be useful, some viewers find them confusing.

■ *Minimize the use of animation.* If you've visited sites that contained headline Java applets, you probably noticed rectangular boxes with blinking or flashing text. Some users find this distracting and even irritating. Unless animation serves a useful purpose, avoid the temptation to include animation (moving text or characters) in your Web pages.

■ *Test your site thoroughly.* It is disastrous to post Web pages that contain errors or mistakes. Doing so destroys a site's credibility. Take time to proofread and examine all text and images before posting the pages. Have other people proofread and critique your work.

■ *Link other sites to your site.* If your purpose is to attract visitors to your Web site, you might try to persuade others to include a link to your site at their sites. This can attract more visitors to your site, particularly when the other sites are popular.

Designing Your Site for Success

This section focuses on specific design and content issues for a Web site. Key topics include the visitor, the content, the site structure, and color. Collectively, these factors influence the success of your site.

Site Visitors

Always keep in mind the viewers that may be attracted to your site and, equally important, the purpose of your site. Is the purpose of your site to educate, to sell, to inform, to persuade, to motivate, or to affect behavior? As you build your site, be mindful of your visitors (or customers). Try to envision who they are, their age, their occupation or profession, and why they visit your site. Decide what you want a visitor to do during and after a visit. Try to determine how long you want them to remain at your site and what you want them to learn during a visit. Knowledge of these and other factors can prove valuable as you design your Web site.

First-time visitors tend to form impressions quickly. The success of any Web site rests on the site's ability to attract, capture, and retain a visitor's interest. The appearance and usefulness of your site is critical. Moreover, you must make it easy for visitors to navigate your site as they move about from topic to topic and from page to page. Carefully inserted and positioned links can aid a visitor in navigating your site. Visitors are favorably impressed when pages can be downloaded easily and quickly. These are a few of the "hooks" that will draw visitors to your site.

Site Content

The content of your site should be a major concern. Above all, the content must be accurate and up to date. Other considerations are subordinate to content, as their purpose is to convey, support, and enhance the essential information. Content should be relevant, prioritized, easy to use and understand, and easy to navigate, with the result being that visitors will leave with the feeling that their visit was productive.

Other features (colors, images, etc.) are used to focus attention on the content. Position the most important and most useful content first, followed by content that is less important. Include links to other useful and relevant pages and sites.

FIGURE 7.13

Links to Other Pages at Your Site

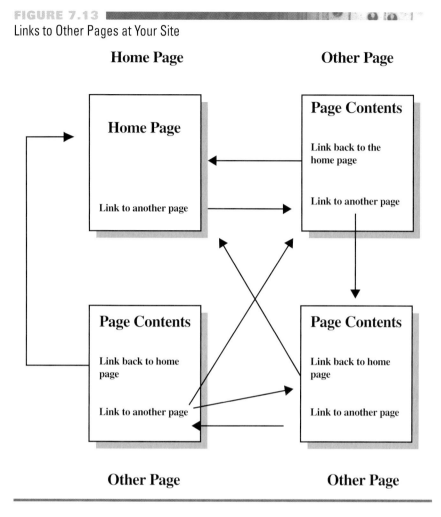

Home Page   Other Page

| Home Page | Page Contents |
| Link to another page | Link back to the home page

Link to another page |

| Page Contents | Page Contents |
| Link back to home page

Link to another page | Link back to home page

Link to another page |

Other Page   Other Page

Site Structure

Keep the structure of your site simple. Imagine your site's structure as the table of contents for your site. Include the topics and items that will appear on your site's home page. Include title headings for key topics and items. If your site will consist of multiple pages, decide which topics and items will appear on the home page and which will appear on other pages. Insert links that allow a visitor to jump to other topics, items, and pages. The menu should be as brief as possible.

If your home page contains links to other pages at your site, be sure to include a link on those pages that allows a visitor to return to your home page. Also, include links to other pages at your site, or to pages at other sites that you want your visitors to be able to access quickly. Notice in Figure 7.13 that visitors can easily navigate your site by moving from page to page and then return to your home page.

Pages found at a Web site typically contain basic elements. The following elements may be included on a site's home page or on other pages. The home page in Figure 7.14 contains some of these elements:

- Name of Webmaster, site author, or contact person
- Possible links to other home pages
- Organization name (if applicable)

FIGURE 7.14

Home Page with Elements

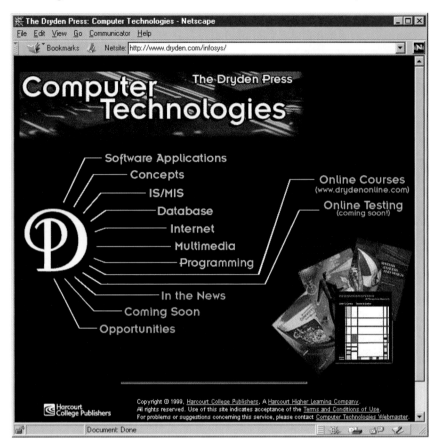

- ■ Logo or seal of the organization
- ■ Date of creation or last revision
- ■ Statement of copyright
- ■ Privacy statement
- ■ The URL or address of the document
- ■ Links to other related pages at your, or another, Web site
- ■ Contact information (e-mail, fax, phone)

Site Color and Emotion

The use of color is an important consideration in Web site design. Certain colors are known to elicit particular emotions. For some individuals, black signifies terminal, complete, done, and death. Blue elicits thoughts of deity, the sky, water, and optimism. For some, red conjures up images of fear, stopping, blood, and desire. Green communicates life, growth, newness, and wealth. Yellow brings to mind warmth, a new day, or the sun. If you have doubts regarding color combinations, solicit opinions from other people.

Other color considerations include tints, hues, and intensities. A combination of green and red may confuse a viewer. Many people are colorblind and are unable to distinguish between red and green. This is why traffic lights have the red light positioned at the top and the green light at the bottom.

Web Page Components

Visitors to your Web site will quickly notice the components of your Web pages. The most obvious component is the text, but other multimedia components may be included to support the information presented on the pages. The term **multimedia** refers to a combination of sound, images, and graphics, in addition to text. Pages at most Web sites include a combination of text and other multimedia elements that, collectively, can render the site more informative and attractive.

Both visual and sound elements can add to a page's appeal when used tastefully. However, too many elements can clutter your pages and distract your viewers. Also, improper elements can confuse your viewers and detract from your site's usefulness. Be aware that too many elements on a page or elements that are distracting to viewers can render your site unattractive and virtually useless.

Text consists of words, phrases, and paragraphs. Text is the most common Web page component and downloads quickly to a viewer's computer because text files are usually smaller than some other kinds of files, such as photographs and clip art. Text provides information being sought by viewers and guides viewers through your site. Choose your wording carefully. Your text must be understandable, interesting, and informative. Was the most recent newspaper or magazine commercial you saw interesting and enticing, or was it uninteresting or perhaps misleading? What was your reaction? Did the commercial cause you to react favorably or unfavorably? Web pages can have the same effect. They can cause a viewer to react favorably or unfavorably. Your objective, of course, is to elicit a favorable reaction by the viewer.

Clip art consists of figures, cartoons, and images stored on a disk or CD-ROM that can be inserted into a Web page or other document. Commercially prepared clip art libraries contain thousands of images, including people, animals, equipment, buildings, and automobiles. When used properly, clip art images can contribute significantly to the value of a Web page. Figure 7.15 shows examples of clip art images.

Digitized pictures are sometimes used to enhance Web pages. A **digitized picture** is simply an image of a person, item, or scene taken with a digital camera. A **digital camera** captures a picture (photograph) and stores it in digital format on a disk, rather than standard file. Once captured and stored, a picture can be inserted onto a Web page.

Scanned pictures and images can be added to Web pages. A **scanner** is a device that scans all or part of a printed page and digitizes the text or images in a format that can be interpreted by a computer. The scanned text or images are stored on a disk in digital form. Once stored, the text or images can be inserted onto a Web page.

You may recall from your studies of mathematics that a **graph** is a visual representation of numerical data. For some people, a graph is easier to understand and interpret than a table containing numbers. Types of graphs include pie graphs, bar graphs, and line graphs. When you want to simplify numerical data, a graph can be inserted into a Web page to make the data more understandable.

A **schematic** is a drawing that shows a procedure or relationships. For example, a schematic drawing can be used to show how a retailer processes a sale. An organizational chart shows the various levels of authority and responsibility within an organization.

Sound is multimedia in the form of words, music, or special sound effects, such as those made by automobile engines or a waterfall. Sounds can be captured and stored on a disk or CD-ROM using a sound device, such as a microphone or a sound recorder. Commercially produced sound can be purchased. However obtained,

FIGURE 7.15
Examples of Clip Art

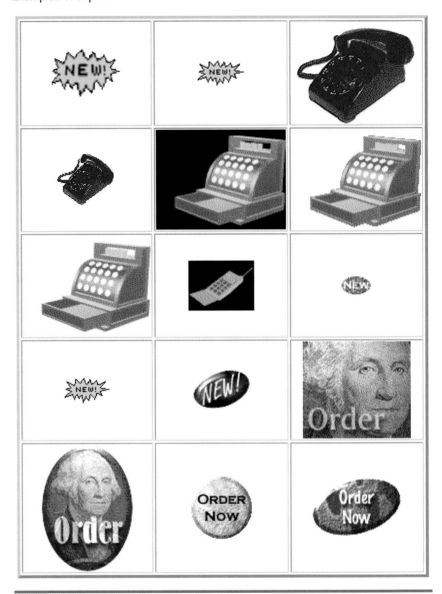

sound can be included on a Web page. Used effectively, sound can be impressive and can add to your site.

Some Web authoring programs allow you to create pages containing text and other elements that appear in three-dimensional form. In addition to height and width, the text and elements also appear to have depth. The elements, therefore, appear to be more realistic, thus the term *virtual reality.* Pages containing three-dimensional items can be quite impressive.

Some Media Considerations

Certain factors should be considered when developing a Web site. The developer has control over some factors, but little (if any) control over others.

Data consisting only of text travel across communications channels faster than other Web page components, such as images, graphics, and pictures. For this reason, developers of Web sites and pages should remember that Web pages containing several complex elements (images, pictures, etc.) will travel across communications channels and download to a user's computer more slowly than pages containing a only a few elements or text only.

The term **bandwidth** refers to the amount of data or information that can travel across a communications channel (such as a telephone line, coaxial cable, or satellite channel) during a specified period of time. Communications channels vary considerably in bandwidth. The World Wide Web uses almost all communications channels now in use. Some channels (such as satellite, coaxial cable, and fiber-optic cables) offer wider bandwidths, thereby allowing for a much faster transfer of data. Other channels (such as standard telephone lines) have slower bandwidths causing data to travel much more slowly.

Modem speed affects the speed at which Web pages can be downloaded to a user's computer. Modern computer modems are faster than older models. Modem speed is measured in thousands of bits per second (kbps). The speed of older models may be only 38 kbps, whereas newer modems can transmit or receive data up to 56 kbps.

Web pages containing graphic images and video are information intensive. They will load slowly. The longer it takes for users to retrieve your pages, the greater the probability they will terminate their visit and move on.

Most modern computers can download Web pages that contain text, clip art, schematics, and graphics. However, as noted earlier, they will download to a user's computer more slowly than pages containing only text. As you add images sound, video, animation, and other features, keep in mind that many computers may contain obsolete hardware and software and thus be unable to download these features.

Web Site Hosts

Web sites of all sizes, structures, descriptions, and purposes can be found on the World Wide Web. Sites range from small personal or business sites to very large and complex corporate sites. Developers of small personal or business sites with limited funds may prefer that their sites be stored on a Web server belonging to another person, company, or organization. Conversely, a large company or organization that has the equipment and software already installed would use its own resources for its Web site.

After a Web site has been designed and created, it must be stored on a Web server, called **Web host,** which is connected to the World Wide Web. Here, you have a variety of options. If you want your site to be available for viewing at any time, choose a host that offers visitor access every day and around the clock. Check out the fee you will be charged. Investigate Web site hosts that offer assistance to you in designing your site by providing free online tutorials.

Web Hosts for Individual and Small Business Sites

Individuals and small businesses are sometimes faced with limited funds and other resources. As a result, many of them cannot afford their own networks and Web servers. Therefore, they must find other ways for storing their Web sites and pages and making their sites available for others to see.

Most colleges and universities allow students to store personal Web pages on the school's Web server and many students are taking advantage of this free service. At these schools, students can create and store their resumes, which can be accessed and viewed by potential employers.

Many Internet service providers allow subscribers to store their sites on the provider's Web server without additional charges. Keep in mind that a subscriber is already paying a monthly access fee to the provider. Allowing subscribers to store their sites without additional charges is a service to retain current subscribers and to attract new ones.

The online service providers, such as America Online and Prodigy, offer free Web site storage to their subscribers. Each, however, does it somewhat differently. America Online allows you to upload your site if it is already coded or to download an HTML editor program to create the code for your site. Once completed, it can be uploaded and stored. Prodigy will either download an HTML editor or take you through an online tutorial to build a site.

Web Hosts for Large Business and Organization Sites

Most large businesses and organizations already have a local area network installed at their location. In addition, many already have installed hardware and software that links the business or organization's network to the Internet and the Web.

Some that already have their own network are not yet connected to the Internet and the Web, and some plan to become connected in the future. These companies and organizations have two main options. If the company or organization already employs qualified and experienced personnel, it can install its own equipment and software to link it to the Internet and the Web.

If the company or organization does not have this personnel, it can contract with another company to perform these operations—a business activity called **outsourcing.** Today, many businesses are outsourcing some of their operations to other companies that specialize in performing the operations. For example, a particular company may not have an employee staff capable of developing, implementing, and maintaining a complex Web site and may prefer to outsource this activity to another company that does have a qualified staff and the capability to handle and manage the activity.

Several companies are equipped to offer professional assistance in developing Internet and Web technologies. IBM, through its e-commerce program, offers turnkey consulting to customers. A **turnkey system** is one that the system provider designs, develops, installs, maintains, and guarantees. If the system fails to perform as expected, the system provider will make all necessary changes and corrections. Other companies also offer turnkey consulting, including AT&T, BellSouth, and MCI.

Outsourcing can bring benefits including reduced operating expenses, improved company focus on other company functions and activities, and access to capabilities the company lacks on its own, such as Internet marketing. Companies currently outsource a variety of functions such as accounting, data processing, manufacturing, and telemarketing.

Regardless of the sites size or purpose, various Web hosting options are available. The responsibility for selecting the best option rests with the individual, company, or organization wanting to establish a presence on the World Wide Web.

E-Commerce Technology

Faster Processors Mean Faster Access

Almost every PC user wants a faster computer capable of processing applications and one that provides quicker access to the Internet. Users are eager for hardware and software that allow them to complete more computing tasks in less time. The phenomenal expansion of the Internet and the World Wide Web is a major reason why users are demanding faster computers that provide them with faster access to the Internet and the Web and that allow companies to facilitate electronic commerce applications faster and more efficiently.

Computer equipment manufacturers and communications providers alike are responding to user preferences by spending billions of research and development dollars to satisfy user demand. Several have established timetables for developing and introducing new products and services.

Microprocessor producers are no exception. Intel, AMD, Cyrix, and others are busy developing faster and more advanced microprocessors that will improve PC performance and speed. Intel, the world's largest manufacturer of microprocessors, has set its own timetable through the year 2000 and beyond. The following table shows Intel's timetable for the release of new, faster, and more powerful microprocessors that may soon be appearing in new PC and other computing devices. Each microprocessor in the table is identified by its present code name.

MICROPROCESSOR CODE NAME	SPEED	APPLICATION
Intel Celeron-500	500–600 MHz	Budget desktops
Centaur WinChip 2000	500 MHz or faster	Budget desktops and notebook computers
Intel PII-700	700 MHz or faster	Power desktops
Intel Merced	Up to 800 MHz	Multiprocessor systems
Intel Willamette	1 GHz or faster	Power desktops

All of the microprocessors should be available by the year 2002. For users eager for more speed and faster Internet access, help is on the way!

Professional Web Site Developers

Many individuals, organizations, and companies are actively involved in building Web sites. The preceding sections focused primarily on individuals who are interested in creating their own Web sites and Web pages. These sections contained suggestions, instructions, and procedures for building a Web site. However, many people either lack the expertise to create a Web site or simply prefer having someone else do it for them. The following sections identify other available options for these people, organizations, or companies.

A **professional Web site developer** is an individual or group that specializes in developing Web sites and pages for customers who pay a fee for the service. These developers are trained in Web site design, development, and construction and are experienced in this field. They offer a variety of services. They can use a design you developed or work closely with you to design your site. After designing your site, they can design and construct informative and impressive pages. Using your, or another, service provider they can assist in locating a business or organization to serve as a host for your site. They will assist in registering your site so that your site's address will not conflict with that of another. Finally, a professional developer can maintain your site by keeping the information current.

A few words of caution. Just saying that one is a professional developer does not make it so. If you are considering using a professional Web developer, ask questions before you sign an agreement. Shop around. Before signing an agreement, prepare a list of services you want the developer to provide and how much each will cost. Obtain references from others who have used the same developer. If the developer requires that you sign a contact, ask to see a copy of the contract and read over it carefully, including the fine print. Make certain the contract includes all the services you expect. Avoid signing a long-term expensive contract. Equally important, insist that you be allowed to visit sites and view pages that the developer prepared. Take time to investigate a developer's previous work thoroughly. Only when you are completely satisfied should you enter into a contract or agreement with a professional developer.

Publishing and Promoting a Web Site

If you want people to visit your site, view your work, or perhaps buy your product, you need to let them know about it. You need to register your site and, to attract viewers, you should take advantage of every opportunity to promote your site. Because there is no central location where you can publicize your site, you may need to use several methods.

Publishing Your Web Site

Every Web site has a unique address, called a Uniform Resource Locator (URL). Obviously, multiple sites with the same address would be confusing. Because each site must have its own address, the problem is prevented.

When your Web site or page is complete, it must be stored on a computer available on the World Wide Web. Once stored, you can submit your site's address

FIGURE 7.16

SubmitIt! Home Page

(URL) to search engines. Most search engines have an option that allows you to submit an URL and many services can be used to submit an URL to several search engines at one time, such as the one shown in Figure 7.16. An URL can also be submitted to a subscriber's Internet service provider (ISP) or an online service such as America Online or the Microsoft Network.

The URL you submit defines the exact location of your site on the Web, much like your street address. A user wanting to access your site could do so by entering your site's address in a Web browser's address box or a search engine search box. After the URL for your site has been entered, your site's home page will be accessed and displayed on the user's computer screen.

Promoting Your Web Site

After your Web pages are available on the Web, you need to let the world know about the pages. There is no central location for publicizing your pages. Therefore, you probably need to use several promotional methods.

You can attract visitors to your site and pages by getting other people and organizations to include a link on their pages to your pages. For example, if another page on the Web contains information or ideas related to that on your pages, ask if they will include a link to your page if you will do the same by including a link on your page to theirs. This makes it easy for people reading other pages to jump quickly to yours.

Web banners are an effective way to promote Web sites. A **banner** is a rectangular graphic displayed in billboard fashion on a Web page. A banner can be any size, but many sites standardize the size. Banners provide some of the most prominent exposure possible on the Web. An interested user can quickly connect to the advertiser's site by clicking on the banner.

Many companies set aside areas on their Web pages where you can advertise your pages. The Internet Link Exchange is a company that helps you to advertise your Web pages (Figure 7.17).

FIGURE 7.17
LinkExchange Home Page

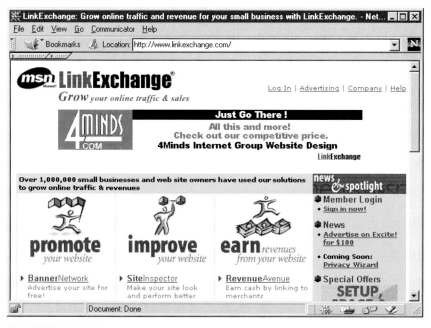

If you belong to a newsgroup, you can send an announcement of your Web pages to the group. Members will be informed about your pages, and they will likely visit your site and read information on topics of interest to them.

There are many other ways to promote your site. Radio, television, newspaper, and magazine articles and announcements frequently display addresses of Web sites and pages. Some local newspapers allow individuals to submit articles of interest to the public and to include the address of Web pages where readers can obtain additional information.

You have many options to promote and publicize your Web site and pages. Some are free, others require you to pay a fee. You can decide the best methods and media for your site. Regardless of the methods you choose, you need to publicize and promote your site to attract visitors.

Maintaining a Web Site

After creating a Web site and publishing your pages, you need to maintain your site. The information contained on your pages must be kept interesting, accurate, and current. Failure to properly maintain your site can be disastrous. Failing to maintain your site will ensure that visitors will read your pages once and never return again to your site. Properly maintained, visitors will likely return to your site to read new and stimulating information.

Businesses, organizations, and government departments and agencies periodically update their sites. Companies introduce new products and services, organizations improve their services, and government departments and agencies post new announcements of services and opportunities. For companies, organizations, and government alike, job vacancies occur almost daily. The Web offers opportunities to fill the positions.

Keep in mind that Web sites and pages can always be improved. You would not want to learn about computing using an outdated book or manual, nor would you bother to read a week-old newspaper. The same principle applies to outdated Web sites and pages. No manufacturer would bother advertising a product the company no longer manufactured.

Current information is more useful and reliable than outdated information. Including reference dates on your pages is a way to indicate that the information is new and current. Graphics and animation can sometimes date your site. These, too, should be kept current. Promote bookmarking your site—that will make it easy for users to visit. Solicit visitor input to help you assess your current coverage and to make you aware of new features that visitors might like.

You can make periodic improvements by adding new technologies to your site. As sound becomes more common in computers, consider adding sound clips to the site. As video systems become more common, consider adding video clips. Both can help convince visitors that your site incorporates the best and most efficient information vehicles for conveying your site's content. Your visitors will recognize and appreciate your efforts and are more likely to become loyal and repeat visitors and customers.

Proper maintenance will attract visitors to your site. Your goal should always be to attract viewers to your site and pages, to provide them with useful information, and to encourage them to return to your site frequently. If you can achieve your goal, visitors will return to your site again and again and will recommend your site and pages to others.

SUMMARY

The World Wide Web (called the Web) is a huge collection of unstructured objects—including Web pages—stored in network databases around the world that can be accessed and retrieved with appropriate software. Each network includes a special server, called a Web server, on which Web documents and pages are stored.

A Web document is an electronic document stored on a Web server. A document can contain several Web pages, and only one page can be viewed at a time. When a visitor accesses a Web site, the first page that appears on the computer screen is the site's home page. Each Web page that is stored has an address, called an URL (an abbreviation for Uniform Resource Locator). A Web page can be viewed by typing the page's URL in the browser's address box or by clicking on a link to the page.

A Web site is a collection of one or more related Web pages that are usually stored together in the same location on a Web server. Web pages are produced by individuals, called Web authors. Web publishing refers to the placing of Web pages on a Web server so that others can access the pages. A Webmaster is a trained individual responsible for managing a Web site.

A personal site is one created by an individual and posted on the Web. The purpose of a company site is to sell products and services to customers and to attract new customers. An organization site is typically sponsored by a not-for-profit organization; it promotes the organization's purposes and activities. A government site is one created and maintained by a unit of government—federal, state, or local.

Certain basic steps should be followed when creating a Web site. These steps are to (1) determine your objective, (2) identify and know your audience, (3) consider the possibilities, (4) plan and design your site, and (5) create the page(s). Two tools for creating Web pages are Web languages and Web authoring software. A Web developer should follow basic rules when designing Web pages and should keep in mind the importance of site visitors, site content, site structure, and color and user emotions.

In addition to text, Web pages may include multimedia elements, including clip art, pictures, schematics, and sound. Special considerations include computer capabilities, bandwidths, modem speeds, and images.

After a Web site has been designed and created, it must be stored on a Web server, called Web host, which is connected to the World Wide Web. Depending on a user's needs, a variety of Web hosts are available. Web hosts are available for individuals and small businesses and for large businesses and organizations. Some companies prefer to outsource their Internet operations. Outsourcing occurs when one business hires another business to perform tasks or functions previously handled by the company's internal staff and systems.

A professional Web site developer is an individual or group that specializes in developing Web sites and pages for customers who pay a fee for the service. Professional developers are trained in Web site design, development, and construction and are experienced in this field.

If you want people to visit your site, view your work, or perhaps buy your product, you need to let them know about it. You need to register your site and, to attract viewers, you should take advantage of every opportunity to promote your site. Because there is no central location where you can publicize your site, you may need to use several methods.

After creating a Web site and publishing your pages, you need to maintain your site. The information contained on your pages must be kept interesting, accurate, and current.

KEY TERMS

bandwidth (211)
banner (215)
clip art (209)
company site (195)
digital camera (209)
digitized picture (209)
eXtensible Markup
  Language (XML)
  (203)
frame (206)
government site (196)
graph (209)
home page (192)
HTML editor (202)
HTML tag (202)

hypertext document
  (202)
HyperText Markup
  Language (HTML)
  (202)
multimedia (209)
organization site (196)
outsourcing (212)
personal site (194)
professional Web site
  developer (213)
scanner (209)
schematic (209)
sound (209)
text (209)

turnkey system (211)
Uniform Resource
  Locator (URL) (192)
Virtual Reality
  Modeling Language
  (VRML) (203)
Web author (193)
Web document (192)
Web host (211)
Web page (192)
Web publishing (193)
Web server (192)
Web site (193)
Webmaster (193)

END-OF-CHAPTER ACTIVITIES

Matching

Match each term with its description.

a. Web publishing
b. HTML tag
c. Web server
d. company site

e. hypertext document
f. bandwidth
g. outsourcing
h. VRML

i. Webmaster
j. multimedia
k. digitized picture
l. Web site

_____ **1.** A collection of one or more related Web pages that are usually stored together in the same location on a Web server.

_____ **2.** A combination of sound, images, and graphics in addition to text.

_____ **3.** A special type of server on which Web documents and pages are stored.

_____ **4.** An image of a person, item, or scene taken with a digital camera.

_____ **5.** The amount of data that travels across a communications channel during a specified period of time.

_____ **6.** The placing of Web pages on a Web server so that others can access the pages.

_____ **7.** Contains highlighted text that connects to other Web pages and Web sites.

_____ **8.** A trained individual responsible for managing a Web site.

_____ **9.** A code embedded within the text on Web pages to identify how text, links, and images are to be displayed on Web pages.

_____ **10.** A Web language that allows a user to create three-dimensional objects and environments.

_____ **11.** A business arrangement in which a company contracts with another company to perform certain functions and operations.

_____ **12.** A Web site established for the purpose of buying and selling products and for attracting new customers.

Review Questions

1. Explain the nature of a Web document.

2. Explain the nature of a Web site.

3. Define the terms _Web author, Web publishing,_ and _Webmaster._

4. Identify and distinguish between the four types of Web sites explained in the chapter.

5. Identify the five steps in Web page design explained in the chapter.

6. Identify briefly the three Web languages explained in the chapter that can be used to create Web pages?

7. Explain briefly the nature of Web authoring software.

8. List the basic design rules that should be followed in creating a Web site and pages.

9. Identify some Web page components explained in the chapter.

10. After a Web site has been created, what two things must the site's owner do?

Activities

1. Computers in the computer lab at your school may be linked in a network with access to the Internet. If so, access the Internet using one of the computers in your school's computer lab. Using a search engine to search the Web, find and access five company Web sites. Using a pencil and paper, write the name of the company. Next, identify the kinds of products and services being offered for sale. Finally, make a list of things you find impressive about the site and a list of things you do not like.

2. Using one of the computers in your school's computer lab, visit any five Web sites you may choose. Before accessing a site, prepare a written list of the sites you will access. As you attempt to access each site, use a stopwatch to determine the amount of time it takes to download each site's home page. Write the time for each next to the name of the individual, company, organization, or agency whose site you are accessing.

3. Web pages at several sites contain a variety of multimedia elements, such as text, clip art, pictures, schematics, and sound. Using a computer in your school's computer lab, locate three sites that contain text, pictures, and sound. Prepare a written list of these sites.

4. The following list contains the addresses to five commercial Web sites. Using a computer in your school's computer lab, visit and prepare a written evaluation of each of these sites. For your evaluations, use the recommendations presented in the chapter.

COMPANY OR ORGANIZATION	WEB ADDRESS
L.L. Bean	http://www.llbean.com
Dell Computer Corporation	http://www.dell.com
The Dryden Press	http://www.dryden.com
eBay Online	http://www.ebay.com
Amazon.com Online	http://www.amazon.com

5. This is a team project. Your instructor will divide the class into groups with four or five students on each team. It is possible that there are businesses in your area that have prepared and posted Web sites on the Internet. Each team member will locate and visit one local company in the area that has a site. Interview the person responsible for the site. Learn as much as you can about how the site was created and posted on the Web and how effective (or ineffective) the site has been. Prepare written notes during your interview. After completing your interview be prepared to present an oral report in class during which you will share your findings.

Issues, Concerns, and Problems

AFTER COMPLETING THIS CHAPTER, YOU WILL:

1. Understand who controls the Internet.
2. Explain proper Internet behavior.
3. Explain how advertising can be an issue or problem for many Internet users.
4. Understand the role of government in electronic commerce.
5. Understand the problems of Internet spams and scams.
6. Discuss why pornography and obscenity are controversial Internet issues.
7. Explain why the taxation of Internet sales and use is controversial.
8. Explain the nature of a computer virus and the potential dangers caused by the spread of such viruses.

9. **Distinguish between computer hackers and computer crackers.**
10. **Explain potential problems associated with the use of mailing lists.**
11. **Tell why misinformation appearing on the Internet is a concern.**
12. **Explain what is meant by "the year 2000 dilemma."**

Throughout American history, there has never been a shortage of issues and concerns, nor is there ever likely to be one. The debates that accompany the issues focus attention on their complexity. In some cases, debates continue for many years.

Today, our society abounds with a variety of current issues and concerns. Just a sampling of the issues we face today includes equal rights, tobacco use, driving under the influence of alcohol, and the role of the military.

The development and introduction of any new technology almost always results in the emergence of issues surrounding it. The more complex the new technology, the more controversial the accompanying issues seem to be. Some individuals still argue the advantages of computers versus the disadvantages, for example.

The emergence of the Internet, the World Wide Web, and electronic commerce is no exception. Today we face a new set of issues regarding these technologies, some of which may take many years to resolve—if they can be resolved at all. This chapter focuses on some of these issues, many of which will be debated again and again in the years ahead.

Control of the Internet

The issue of controlling the Internet and the Web is a controversial one. Should government control the Internet and the Web? Should private business and organizations have control? Perhaps control should be assigned to individuals. Or maybe the Internet and the Web should be totally free of any controls. These are among the many questions being asked by people who feel that some controls and regulations are needed.

In confronting this issue, we need to keep in mind that the Internet and the World Wide Web are truly worldwide. They belong to everyone, yet no individual or country actually controls them. Governments and citizens of countries certainly have a voice in any argument dealing with their control, but the laws of different countries vary greatly in their application and meaning. Is it possible for every single country to agree to a set of standards that would apply to more than 270 million people worldwide? Even if every country would agree, would all citizens of every country abide by those standards?

The complexity of the issue of control is potentially mind-boggling. Few people like being told what they can and cannot do. To reach worldwide agreement on this issue would be remarkable. Perhaps a better solution would be to educate users to act responsibly so that the Internet will remain available to everyone. Doing so will allow users to take advantage of the full opportunities available on the Internet and the Web.

Internet Behavior

Using the Internet and the World Wide Web involves communicating with others, whether they are individuals, newsgroups, companies, agencies, or organizations. Users have a responsibility to exercise courtesy and sound judgment in their communications and dealings with others. As cliché as it may sound, a good rule to follow is the one each of us learned as a child, "Do unto others as you would have them do unto you." Perhaps the issue of Internet and Web control would be resolved if all users would practice this simple rule.

Web Ethics and Etiquette

The word **ethics** refers to personal standards involving one's behavior. Basic ethical standards in our daily interactions with other individuals, businesses, and organizations dictate that we will abide by commonly accepted ethical standards in our relationships. For example, everyone should expect us to be fair, honest, and courteous. If we are not, others in our society may regard us as being unwilling to adhere to basic ethical standards and may terminate their interaction with us.

Everyone knows there are acceptable rules of common courtesy in our relationships with other people. These rules are called **etiquette.** For example, there is table etiquette that governs our behavior while dining and classroom etiquette that governs our behavior in school.

Rules for acceptable behavior on the Internet are called **netiquette** (an abbreviation for "Net etiquette"). An important point to remember when using the Internet is that each of us is expected to be ethical and to always practice proper netiquette any time we use the Internet and the Web. In return, we should expect (and even insist) that others will abide by the same rules and make every effort to be fair, honest, and courteous.

What constitutes acceptable ethics and etiquette on the Internet and the Web? Obviously, there are disagreements. An acceptable action or statement by one person may be considered offensive to someone else. To help clarify some of the confusion on this issue, some users have posted Web pages specifying what constitutes acceptable behavior when using the Internet and the Web. One document that has gained widespread attention was developed and posted by Arlene Rinaldi at Florida Atlantic University. This document offers Ten Commandments for Computer Ethics and is shown in Figure 8.1. You can view the full document at the Internet address: http://www.fau.edu/rinaldi/ten.html.

FIGURE 8.1

Ten Commandments for Computer Ethics

1. Thou shalt not use a computer to harm other people.
2. Thou shalt not interfere with other people's computer work.
3. Thou shalt not snoop around in other people's computer files.
4. Thou shalt not use a computer to steal.
5. Thou shalt not use a computer to bear false witness.
6. Thou shalt not copy or use proprietary software for which you have not paid.
7. Thou shalt not use other people's computer resources without authorization or proper compensation.
8. Thou shalt not appropriate other people's intellectual output.
9. Thou shalt think about the social consequences of the program you are writing or the system you are designing.
10. Thou shalt always use a computer in ways that ensure consideration and respect for your fellow humans.

Source: Arlene Rinaldi, *The Net: User Guidelines and Netiquette* (Washington, D.C.: The Computer Ethics Institute).

These "commandments" apply to computer use in general and also to the Internet and the Web. The tenth commandment, in particular, addresses the issue of netiquette. Every user should always be aware of how actions, statements, and messages may be interpreted by others. Simply stated, when you are using the Internet, be aware of the potential impact of your actions by being fair, honest, polite, and courteous. On the Internet, everyone should be a **Netizen,** a term that refers to being a good citizen when using the Internet.

Electronic Communications

Almost everyone connected to the Internet uses it to communicate with others electronically. Most users send and receive e-mail messages over the Internet and many participate in LISTSERV groups, mailing lists, and Usenet activities. Some guidelines for sending and receiving e-mail messages and participating with others on the Internet are listed in Figure 8.2.

As stated earlier, good judgment and common sense should prevail on the Internet. Common courtesy and respect for other people will help ensure that the Internet remains free from government control and available for everyone to use and enjoy.

FIGURE 8.2

Some Guidelines for Electronic Communications

1. Avoid spamming on the Internet. A *spam* is any advertisement placed in an inappropriate location on the Internet, such as a posting to a newsgroup that is not involved in advertising. Under U.S. law, spamming is illegal.

2. Do not give your user ID or password to someone else.

3. Keep your e-mail messages brief and to the point.

4. Never assume that your e-mail messages are private. Other people, including your boss, may be able to intercept and read your messages.

5. An e-mail message should focus on a single point.

6. Do not use the network of your organization or institution to perform commercial work.

7. Avoid SHOUTING in your messages. Typing messages using all capital letters is considered to be SHOUTING.

8. Never use the Internet to send chain letters.

9. Be careful and professional in statements that you make in a message. An e-mail message can easily be forwarded to another person or group.

10. Be careful when using humor or sarcasm. Your humor or sarcasm may be regarded as criticism.

11. Avoid using a flame in your messages. A *flame* is an offensive statement or message.

12. Be aware of your writing style. Every message should be clear, concise, and free of grammatical errors.

Advertising on the Internet

Using the Internet and the World Wide Web for advertising is becoming big business. Most online services and Internet service providers sell advertising space and time to anyone wanting to advertise products and services. Moreover, business sites contain ads describing a variety of products, services, and special promotions.

How extensive is the practice of advertising on the Internet? According to one source, spending for advertising on the Internet is expected to reach $33 billion by 2004. The rapid surge in the popularity of the Internet and the Web may result in even greater advertising expenditures.

Some people believe advertisers are taking advantage of users by saturating the Internet with advertising. Some believe that much of the advertising on the Internet is misleading or inaccurate. Others disagree. Many who disagree believe that advertising informs the public about new products and services and that most ads placed on the Internet are accurate and helpful.

This issue, like that of potentially useless Web sites, is at best academic. With a freely accessible Internet, the amount of advertising probably will increase dramatically.

Legal Issues, Concerns, and Problems

Almost everyone is likely to agree that most businesses in our society are sincere and honest in their relationships with the public. Most of them offer products and services that are wanted and needed and make it their practice to respond appropriately to customer problems and concerns. Many use the slogan "satisfaction guaranteed or your money back" and mean exactly what they say.

Unfortunately, not all companies that solicit your business are honest. The Internet, over which electronic commerce can be conducted easily, quickly, and inexpensively, provides criminals and unsavory opportunists with a vehicle that allows them to deceive and cheat unsuspecting individuals and other legitimate businesses. For this reason, federal, state, and local governments are taking an active role to protect citizens from individuals and businesses engaged in illegal electronic commerce practices.

Role of Government

Federal, state, and local governments are aware that many questionable individuals and companies are now conducting electronic commerce activities over the Internet. Although most companies are legitimate, many take advantage of unsuspecting users by offering deals that are sometimes deceptive and even fraudulent.

The Federal Trade Commission (FTC), created by the Federal Trade Commission Act, is the federal agency responsible for regulating and overseeing companies engaged in interstate commerce—that is, companies that provide products and services across state boundaries. The FTC has the legal authority to act in the interest of all consumers to prevent deceptive and unfair acts or practices. At the state level, attorneys general typically have the same authority within the individual states. Locally, better business bureaus seek to identify those companies that engage in deceptive and unfair acts or practices.

The FTC maintains an up-to-date Web site where you can learn more about the FTC and read about companies that have engaged in illegal business practices. You can visit this site at http://www.ftc.gov. Figure 8.3 shows the FTC home page.

FIGURE 8.3

Federal Trade Commission Home Page

This site provides users with information about FTC operations as well as information about scams and other illegal Internet activities and pending investigations and litigation.

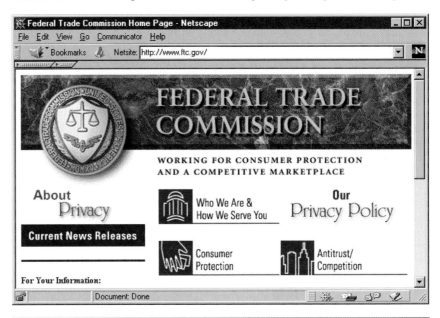

Internet Fraud

The nature of the Internet lends itself to the real potential for fraud. **Fraud** is defined by Philip B. Bergfield in *Principles of Real Estate Law* as being "a false representation of a material fact, made with knowledge of its falsity and with the intent to mislead or defraud, that is justifiably relied on by the one to whom it is made and which results in injury to him (or her) because of his reliance."

Just as there are persons or groups who defraud others face to face, through the mail, and by telephone, there are those who use the Internet to defraud innocent victims.

Internet fraud is on the increase. Victims are becoming subjected to a variety of scams and cons, ranging from requests for charitable contributions to promises of instant wealth. Fraudulent acts are illegal and punishable under the law. However, it is often difficult to locate and punish those who use the Internet to commit fraud.

The best way for an Internet user to protect against fraud is to use extreme caution when contacted by anyone asking for money, credit card numbers, or personal information about the user or anyone else. Remember the saying that "If it sounds too good to be true, it probably is!"

The Federal Trade Commission and the attorney general's office in most states investigate and prosecute fraudulent Internet activities. If you are contacted by someone on the Internet who makes unrealistic claims or offers, do not allow yourself to be pressured into sending money, giving out your credit card number, or making a commitment of any kind. Instead, you should immediately notify local law enforcement, the FTC, or the attorney general of your state.

In advertising, the FTC has clearly defined the terms *deceptive* and *unfair*. It has determined that "a representation, omission, or practice is deceptive if it is likely to mislead consumers, and affect consumers' behavior or decisions about the product or service." In addition, "an act or practice is unfair if the injury it causes, or is likely to cause, is substantial, not outweighed by other factors, and is not reasonably avoidable." The Federal Trade Commission Act prohibits unfair and deceptive advertising in any medium, including the Internet.

Two problems that occur frequently in Internet advertising are spamming and scamming. Both are potentially serious problems. As a user, you need to be aware of both kinds of problems and the difference between them, and always use caution.

Internet Spamming

A **spam** is an unwanted, unsolicited e-mail advertising message. It is a cheap way to announce and solicit purchases of products and services, and a lot of it is fraudulent and therefore illegal. A spam can be sent to thousands of people at once. This is a problem for almost everyone on the Internet. According to Jodie Bernstein, director of the FTC's Bureau of Consumer Protection, the bureau receives more than 1,000 complaints each day.

Internet Scamming

A **scam** is the deliberate attempt to cheat or defraud the public by false or misleading claims about products or services being offered. The accessibility and vastness of the Internet makes it a vehicle of choice for many scammers who prey on unsuspecting and vulnerable individuals. If you receive a message advertising a product, service, or opportunity that sounds too good to be true, be aware that it probably is too good to be true.

Bulk-mail scam messages sent to Internet users are called **spam-scams.** These messages typically offer users a chance to get rich quick or offer something for nothing. You should be wary of these kinds of schemes.

At its Web site, the Federal Trade Commission has posted a list of 12 types of spam-scams the commission culled from more than 150,000 consumer complaints. These are listed in Figure 8.4.

Pornography and Obscenity

The freedoms provided by the Internet have resulted in a virtual avalanche of bad publicity in recent months. Considerable concern has been expressed concerning the pornographic and obscene information available on the Internet, including text, pictures, and language. This problem is now being extended to electronic commerce as some companies now offer graphic pornographic pictures and images for sale over the Internet.

Although information of this type constitutes only a tiny fraction of what is available on the Internet, any amount can prove controversial. Some individuals, groups, and organizations have placed pressure on politicians for legislation making it illegal for anyone to put pornographic or obscene materials on the Internet. Therein is the issue. Should laws be enacted to regulate, and perhaps prohibit, pornography and other information considered obscene?

In response to outcries by some individuals and groups, Congress enacted the Communications Decency Act in 1996 to ban the use of these materials from the Internet. Soon after its passage, the United States Supreme Court ruled the act to be unconstitutional on the grounds that it violates free speech. Another attempt was made in 1998 to enact legislation regulating these practices. Like earlier attempts, the courts also ruled this legislation to be unconstitutional. Despite the ruling, some people and organizations continue to press for legislation to ban certain kinds of information from the Internet. Congressional actions to ban or restrict pornography on the Internet seem to coincide with popular elections.

FIGURE 8.4

12 Most Common Types of Spam-Scams

Scams have become so widespread on the Internet that the Federal Trade Commission has posted the 12 most common types of scams at its Web site, each of which is explained briefly by Jodie Bernstein, director of the FTC's Bureau of Consumer Protection. You should be careful to avoid becoming a victim of fraudulent scams that can result in losing your money and wasting your time. Remember, if it sounds too good to be true, it probably is!

Business Opportunity Scams—Most of these scams promise a lot of income for a small investment of time and money. Some are actually old-fashioned pyramid schemes camouflaged to look like something else. "Consumers should be careful of money-making schemes that sound too good to be true," said Bernstein. "They usually are."

Making Money by Sending Bulk E-Mailings—These schemes claim that you can make money sending your own solicitations via bulk e-mail. They offer to sell you lists of e-mail addresses or software to allow you to make the mailings. What they don't mention is that the lists are of poor quality; sending bulk e-mail violates the terms of service of most Internet service providers; virtually no legitimate businesses engage in bulk e-mailings; and several states have laws regulating the sending of bulk e-mail.

Chain Letters—These electronic versions of the old-fashioned chain letters usually arrive with claims like, "You are about to make $50,000 in less than 90 days!" "But you don't," said Bernstein, "and these electronic chain letters are every bit as illegal as the old-fashioned paper versions."

Work-at-Home Schemes—E-mail messages offer the chance to earn money in the comfort of your own home. Two popular versions pitch envelope stuffing and craft assembly. But nobody will really pay you for stuffing envelopes, and craft assembly promoters usually refuse to buy the crafts claiming the work does not meet their "quality standards."

Health and Diet Scams—These offer "scientific breakthroughs," "miraculous cures," "exclusive products," "secret formulas," and "ancient ingredients." Some come with testimonials from "cured" consumers or endorsements from "famous medical experts" no one's ever heard of. "These bogus cure-alls are just electronic snake oil," said Bernstein.

Easy Money—Offers such as "Learn how to make $4,000 in one day," or "Make unlimited profits exchanging money on world currency markets," appeal to the desire to "Get-Rich-Quick." "If making money was that easy, we'd all be millionaires," Bernstein said.

Get Something Free—The lure of valuable, free items—like computers or long-distance phone cards—gets consumers to pay membership fees to sign up with these scams. After they pay the fee, consumers learn that they don't qualify for the "free" gift until they recruit other "members." "These scams are just low-down, high-tech pyramid schemes," Bernstein said.

Investment Opportunities—These scams may tout outrageously high rates of return with no risk. Glib, resourceful promoters suggest they have high-level financial connections; that they're privy to inside information; or that they guarantee the investment. To close the deal, they may serve up phony statistics, misrepresent the significance of a current event or stress the unique quality of their offering. But they are not unique. They're just like the other scams.

Cable Descrambler Kits—For a small initial investment you can buy a cable descrambler kit so you can receive cable without paying the subscription fees. "There are two small problems with these schemes," Bernstein said. "The kits usually don't work and stealing cable service is illegal."

Guaranteed Loans or Credit, On Easy Terms—Some offer home-equity loans, even if you don't have any equity in your home. Others offer guaranteed, unsecured credit cards, regardless of your credit history. The "loans" turn out to be lists of lending institutions and the credit cards never arrive.

Credit Repair Scams—These scams target consumers with poor credit records. For an up-front fee, they offer to clear up a bad credit record—for a fee—or give you a completely clean credit slate by showing you how to get an Employer Identification Number. "No one can erase a bad credit record if it's accurate and using an Employer Identification Number to set up a new credit identity is against the law," Bernstein said.

Vacation Prize Promotions—Like their snail mail counterparts, these e-mail "Prize Promotions" tell consumers they've been selected to receive a "luxury" vacation at a bargain-basement price. But the accommodations aren't deluxe and upgrades are expensive.

Source: Federal Trade Commission, http://www.ftc.gov/opa/1998/9807/dozen.htm

The vastness of the Internet virtually guarantees that any legislation, even if determined to be constitutional, would probably not be enforceable. No foreign government can be forced to abide by laws of the United States. Moreover, material regarded as pornographic by some individuals may be regarded as art by others.

Almost everyone agrees that pornographic and obscene materials should not be made available to children. Congress is taking steps to ensure that certain kinds of materials are banned from viewing by children. Similar actions, such as the development of a special TV chip called the "V" chip, are being discussed concerning objectionable materials on television. The assumption is that such a chip, if and when developed, would allow parents to screen and block specific programs and materials from being shown on their television sets.

Congress and state legislatures are being pressured to increase penalties for those who put child pornography on the Internet. Almost everyone agrees that such pornography has no rightful place on the Internet and that offenders should receive severe punishment.

The issues of pornography and obscenity will probably be discussed and debated in the months and years ahead. Concern surrounding these issues is real and sensitive. The solution may lie in software that will enable parents to make sure their children cannot see material that is objectionable. Some companies already produce this kind of software. Products including CyberPatrol and SurfWatch analyze the information at Web sites and prohibit children from viewing unsuitable material. Also, some of the larger online services, including Microsoft Network and America Online, have the capability to block access to objectionable Internet material. Other groups are working to develop technologies and methods for barring access to sites and materials considered inappropriate for viewing by children.

Some businesses are concerned with materials that may be viewed by employees during company time, as they fear that the display and viewing of sexually explicit pornographic materials by some employees may be viewed as a form of sexual harassment. To eliminate this problem, some businesses have installed software on their network servers to block the reception of these materials.

Software is available that makes it possible to tell what users view on the Internet. For example, some software keeps track of the addresses of all Web sites and pages viewed by users of a network. This allows a supervisor or manager, for example, to visit those sites and see the same pages the employee has seen.

Taxation on Internet Sales and Use

There is considerable concern about attempts by some state governments to levy taxes on Internet users. Suggestions and recommendations include levying sales taxes on products and services purchased over the Internet and imposing a user tax each time one accessed the Internet.

Government interest in any Internet taxes should be obvious. Such taxes would bring millions of dollars in new taxes into government coffers. States argue that these new tax revenues would enable them to improve education, build new roads, and improve and expand government services.

Opponents argue that such taxes are unconstitutional and would create many problems. Companies doing business on the Internet argue that taxing the sales of products and services would reduce sales and therefore slow the development and growth of electronic commerce while still in its infancy. Users argue most states typically do not levy taxes on the sale of products and services across state boundaries. Another argument is that users should not be charged a user fee just for being connected to the Internet.

The Clinton administration has sided with Internet users, at least for a while, by imposing a three-year moratorium on any new Internet taxes. This moratorium will protect and ensure the continuing development of the Internet and electronic commerce without government interference.

Viruses on the Internet

One of the major concerns on the Internet is the potential for virus attacks. A **virus** is a program that can disrupt or even destroy the normal operations of a computer. A virus can cause a variety of problems, ranging from the appearance of messages on the screen to the actual destruction of files stored on the computer's hard drive, including the computer's operating system.

The nature and structure of the Internet makes it vulnerable to attack. It is free and available to anyone wanting to exchange information, programs, data, and files. The freedom offered on the Internet carries with it a price. One price is the ease with which virus programmers can write virus programs and potentially distribute them to thousands of computers connected to the Internet.

Virus programmers apparently find pleasure in causing damage to computer software and files. Virus programs, like viruses that attack the human body, are numerous and varied in what they do. One virus may simply cause strange images to move about a computer screen, whereas another may result in serious damage to a computer's operating system by erasing important programs. Some do their damage immediately, others are timed to take effect on a specific date.

A virus can infect your computer if you download software or other files from the Internet. One type may corrupt a program or data file causing it to operate strangely. Another type may destroy all the files stored on your computer. Others may cause other kinds of problems.

A typical computer virus hides in a program and remains dormant until the user runs the infected program. When the user runs the infected program, the virus becomes activated. When activated, some viruses will attach themselves to other programs by copying themselves onto them. Currently, several hundred viruses are known. Many are actively traveling the Internet.

In April 1999, two destructive viruses caused serious problems. One virus, named Melissa, appeared in the form of an attachment to e-mail messages. The message informed the recipient that the attachment contained information that the recipient had requested. The virus was automatically activated when the recipient opened the attachment. In addition to disabling the recipient's computer, the virus attached itself and sent e-mail messages to others whose e-mail addresses were stored on the recipient's mailing list. The same contaminated e-mail message was then sent to those addresses. As a result, the virus contaminated hundreds of computers around the world. The other virus, called Chernobyl, was timed to activate on April 26—the anniversary of the Chernobyl nuclear accident that occurred on April 26, 1986, in the former Soviet Union. This virus was also distributed as an attachment to e-mail messages. When activated, this virus erases the first megabyte of data stored on a user's Windows PC hard drive rendering the user's computer inoperable. This virus sometimes affected entire networks. More than 100 cases were reported in Singapore.

Fortunately, **antivirus programs** are available that can detect the presence of viruses and eradicate them. Some effective and popular antivirus programs include Norton Anti-Virus, Virex PC, and WebScan, and VirusScan. Antivirus programs are updated often because new viruses appear frequently. You should install an antivirus program on your computer and should update the program periodically to safeguard against new viruses.

One issue currently being debated is the severity of penalties for distributing a virus over the Internet. Some people feel that harsh penalties should be imposed; others favor milder penalties. However, everyone seems to agree that writing and distributing a virus program is a serious offense and that the author of the virus program deserves to be punished.

Computer viruses themselves are not the only problem. Virus hoaxes (the threat of viruses) can cause serious problems. A **virus hoax** is false information from any source that a computer or computer system has been, or will be, infected by a virus. Imagine the resulting panic at your school if an anonymous caller informed the administration that the school's computer system had been infected by a computer virus. Officials might order an immediate shutdown of the entire computer system as a precaution while computer personnel search for the virus.

As noted earlier, computer viruses are often transmitted as attachments to e-mail messages. Therefore, e-mail users should exercise caution. A user would be wise to avoid opening an e-mail attachment received from an unknown source and should make certain that the e-mail program he or she is using will not open any attachments automatically. According to the results of a recent survey of 300 companies posted on the ZDNet Web site, 32 percent of the respondents blamed their most recent viral run-in on an electronic message attachment.

Copyright Infringement

The nature of the Internet and the World Wide Web is such that anyone having a connection and publishing software can create and publish Web pages on the Web. Such freedom often results in abuses that can occur innocently or deliberately.

One abuse that is not only abusive but also illegal is copyright infringement. **Copyright infringement** refers to the unauthorized use of someone else's material that has been granted copyright protection by the U.S. Copyright Office. A copyright may be granted to cover one's original work, such as a book, article, poem, or music, and grants the copyright holder exclusive rights to the copyrighted material. For example, the publisher of the book you are now using has a copyright to all information contained in the book. Therefore, permission to use any portion of this book must be obtained from the publisher.

Although much of the information and pictures contained on Web pages is not copyrighted, some of it is. Anyone wanting to use materials from other sources, such as other Web pages, to create his or her own Web pages should check to see if the materials are copyrighted before using them. Unauthorized use of copyrighted materials may result in embarrassment and litigation in the courts. In the past, many violators have been sued and fined for copyright violations.

Because use of the Internet and the Web is free, some people believe they should be able to use, and even copy, any materials found on the Web in their own Web pages. Others argue the opposite—that the creators of Web pages should be able to have their pages copyrighted and thereby protected from being copied by others.

This issue has been settled for the time being. Copyright laws do protect one's own creative work. Unless copyright laws are changed, the creator of Web pages should be careful not to violate the laws by copying information and materials from other Web pages without first obtaining written permission.

Consumer Complaints on the Web

Angry consumers and former employees have discovered a new weapon for airing their complaints against companies they feel have mistreated them in some way—the Web. Using chat rooms and launching Web pages, called **rogue Web pages,** disgruntled consumers are targeting companies and pulling off hoaxes that can cost thousands of dollars. These individuals have taken on a number of big-name companies. Some consumer advocates support such actions by irate consumers as a welcomed force for change. However, others are concerned that the uncensored Web fosters misleading information that is available for millions of people to see.

The phenomenon is so new many companies are still considering ways to defend themselves, whereas others are reluctantly tolerant. However, more than 600 companies have hired a private Internet monitoring company, called *eWatch,* to keep track of Web pages critical of the companies.

Some attorneys believe this practice will result in more litigation against angry customers and former employees who post rogue pages on the Web. Before posting a rogue page on the Web, an individual probably should consult with an attorney and have convincing legal evidence of wrongdoing by the company.

Security

Security is a major concern of businesses, organizations, and agencies, many of which have invested millions of dollars to develop programs, files, and data. For example, General Motors Corporation spends millions of dollars designing future automobile models that are stored on their computer systems. Having access to the designs would give competitors an important advantage. General Motors is but one of hundreds of companies that could suffer severe damage if unauthorized users were to gain access to confidential files. Even authors sometimes go to great length to protect the confidentiality of manuscript files.

The adage "if there is a system, someone will figure out a way to beat the system" may be true. Evidence suggests that there are computer users lurking in cyberspace trying to gain access to other computers and files.

Many companies have intranets connected to the Internet, and almost all take extra precautions when any of their computers is connected to the Internet. One precaution is to build firewalls around their systems. The term "firewall" originally referred to a wall built of brick, stone, or other fireproof material that was set between structures to prevent fire from spreading. On the Internet, a **firewall** is hardware or software that restricts information that passes between a private intranet and the Internet. Other measures often taken to ensure security include requiring the use of user IDs and passwords and restricting access to certain parts of the Internet, such as FTP sites and chat groups. Other measures may also be taken to safeguard information.

Information Theft

Information theft is a very serious problem today in our society. Thieves are using the Internet to steal all kinds of information ranging from corporate secrets to individuals' credit card numbers. Thieves can use the Internet and illegally obtained credit card numbers to purchase products and services and charge them to the card owners. Each year, thousands of unsuspecting card owners are billed for millions of dollars in merchandise and services.

America Online recently notified its 8 million subscribers about a growing number of electronic mail messages being received by its members that enable unauthorized persons to use the subscribers' accounts. The messages offer such things as free software or a free pornographic picture. To obtain the gift, the recipient must open a file that is attached to the message. This kind of scheme, in which a secret or concealed file is attached to another message or file, is known as a **Trojan horse**—a term taken from the Greek epic about a large wooden horse filled with marauding soldiers. When the file is opened, a concealed program within the file collects the subscriber's account name and password and returns them to the thief. With access to a subscriber's account, the thief can impersonate the subscriber and purchase products and services online that will be charged to the subscriber. Trojan horse programs have plagued the Internet for many years, and many go undetected by most antivirus programs. The point to remember is to beware of messages offering free gifts.

Crackers and Hackers

The Internet offers exciting challenges to many computer enthusiasts who are willing to devote tireless hours to searching for unique ways of doing things on the Internet. In recent years, two new groups of users have gained widespread attention and caused concern.

One group has been labeled **computer crackers.** These are people who try to gain unauthorized access to computer systems for the purpose of altering, damaging, or stealing information by guessing user IDs and passwords. Sometimes they succeed. Evidence suggests that typical crackers are malicious teenagers who enjoy the thrill of altering or destroying information on a computer system. An example occurred in September 1998 when a group of computer crackers, calling themselves H4CKING FOR G1RL13Z or HFZ, disabled the *New York Times* Web site in what appeared to be an act of revenge against a *Times* reporter. The group peppered certain pages with sexually explicit and threatening messages. The *Times* Web site was taken offline for more than nine hours. The FBI has reported that an average of more than five thousand attempts are made by crackers each day to gain unauthorized access to federal government computer systems.

The other group consists of **computer hackers.** These are individuals who generally have expert knowledge about many computer systems and may test their skills by breaking into computer systems. Although computer hackers do not cause damage or steal information, they may view information stored in computer systems. Hackers tend to be very knowledgeable about computer systems, programming languages, and communications software protocols. After gaining access into a computer system and looking at stored files, a hacker's curiosity is usually satisfied and he or she will move on to the challenge of gaining access to another computer system without altering or destroying computer files.

Both hackers and crackers can cause problems—whether intentional or innocent. Even if no damage is intended, large computer systems monitor attempts to gain access. Information system managers will know if an attempt was made to gain access but may not know whether programs, files, or data were damaged, destroyed, or stolen.

Espionage and Sabotage

On the Internet, **espionage** refers to the act of spying. There are many well-documented cases in which unauthorized persons used the Internet to gain access to government and private computer systems for the purpose of viewing confidential information. Recently, the U.S. government learned that attempts were made by spies of former Soviet Union countries to gain illegal access to U.S. government computer systems and files. Just as there are spies depicted in novels and in the movies, there are spies seeking to penetrate confidential computer files.

Sabotage refers to the willful destruction of property. On the Internet, saboteurs try to gain entry into computer systems to destroy information. The work of saboteurs can be devastating. Imagine the potential consequences if a saboteur broke into the computer system of the Social Security Administration and destroyed the records of millions of citizens. Because of the potential seriousness of acts of sabotage, penalties for these offenses are often severe.

Social Issues, Concerns, and Problems

Some issues, concerns, and problems are social rather than legal. They are considered social because they affect us as a society. Nevertheless, the issues, concerns, and problems discussed in the following sections are controversial and important because of their potential impact on each of us as a user.

Internet Loneliness and Depression

For several years, Internet proponents have held the belief that the Internet affords a positive role as a medium offering easy access by users to distant family members and friends through e-mail and other applications. A two-year study by researchers at Carnegie-Mellon University, however, suggests the opposite may be true. The scientists discovered results that challenge conventional wisdom about cyberspace's impact on society. Researchers had expected to find that the Internet boosted users' sense of well-being and community. Instead, they found that users of chat, e-mail, and electronic bulletin boards devoted more of their time to "shallow online connections" at the expense of time devoted to deeper relationships with family members, friends, and spouses.

More research is needed before firm conclusions are drawn. The study was limited to 169 people in 73 households in the Pittsburgh area. Additional research conducted nationally may reveal different conclusions. If it can be determined that Internet use does, in fact, result in user loneliness and depression, psychologists and psychiatrists may need to provide specialized counseling for affected individuals.

Mailing Lists

Companies and other organizations have used mailing lists for many years to send notices, announcements, and advertisements to those whose names and addresses are on the lists. A **mailing list** is a list of entries (often individuals) in which each entry consists of a name or title, mailing address, telephone number, and other information. One example of a potential mailing list is a local telephone directory. Mailing lists are important to the operations of many companies and organizations, and mailing list use is widespread. In fact, there are thousands of them. Some lists consist of entries that meet specific criteria. For example, one list may contain only names, addresses, and phone numbers of females, whereas another list may be limited to males between the ages of 35 and 50.

Many companies and organizations purchase mailing lists from other sources and may spend considerable amounts for various lists. It is not uncommon for a company or organization to pay $2 or more for each entry on the list. Some companies and organizations specialize in the preparation and sale of mailing lists, which can be lucrative. For example, a mailing list consisting of 10,000 entries at $2 per entry will sell for $20,000.

Some companies and organizations are able to create and store mailing lists for free. Consider a local bank, for example. If the bank has 25,000 customers, there will be 25,000 customer records in its database. Customers were paid nothing for providing this information to the bank, and they probably assume the information will remain confidential. What if the bank puts customer names, addresses, and phone numbers into a mailing list and sells the list to another company or organization? Should customers be concerned? No doubt many would be.

Thousands of companies and organizations purchase, sell, and share mailing lists. Even some colleges and churches have begun the practice. Perhaps without your knowledge, information about you may be stored in databases at several companies and organizations. If you order merchandise from a mail-order business, you may receive several catalogs from other companies shortly thereafter. Obviously, the company with which you placed an order shared or sold your information.

The use of mailing lists by Internet online service companies and service providers has become a controversial issue. Subscribers to a major online service company with several million subscribers recently learned of the company's intention to sell mailing lists containing information about subscribers. News of the service's plan has drawn widespread criticism and threats to sue. As a result, the company has delayed making a final decision.

The central issue concerns ownership of, and the right to use, personal information supplied by subscribers. Once a subscriber provides personal information to an online service or Internet provider, who has legal ownership of the information?

This issue is far from being settled. Mailing lists are the lifeblood for many companies and organizations, and they argue that subscribers supplied the information

E-Commerce International

European Union Bans Sale of Personal Data

The European Union, a group of European countries formed to formulate policies affecting member nations, has enacted a law prohibiting the U.S. style of buying and selling of personal data. The law could affect, and potentially interrupt, electronic commerce with the United States if the two sides fail to resolve deep philosophical and legal differences over protecting privacy. The law is in the form of a directive for member nations. Under European law, each member nation is required to adhere to the directive by enacting its own law. Six member nations have already drafted or enacted such laws.

The European law is intended to prohibit companies from using information about their customers in ways that the customers never intended, such as selling the information to other companies for use in marketing including mailing lists.

The law covers a range of information that companies typically collect about people in the course of daily business operations, from credit card transactions and magazine subscriptions to telephone records and information recorded when users visit Web sites.

In addition to its effect on European Union nations, the directive and laws have the potential to disrupt electronic commerce in the United States. A key provision of the directive would prohibit any company doing business in the European Union from transmitting personal data to any country that does not guarantee comparable privacy protection. The potential impact on the United States is significant because the Clinton administration has adopted a more laissez-faire (hands-off) approach under which data-collection companies would be allowed to police themselves through self-regulating organizations.

At present, there are ongoing diplomatic discussions between the European Union, its member nations, and the United States in an effort to reach a compromise. Without an agreement, the future of electronic commerce between the parties may be in jeopardy.

Source: Winston-Salem (North Carolina) *Journal,* October 27, 1998, pp. 1D–2D.

freely and without reservations and that the company should be allowed to use it in any manner chosen. Others, including subscribers and persons who purchase products and services, argue that the information should not be made available to others without their permission.

As with some other issues, the courts may eventually render a decision. Meanwhile, this issue may become even more controversial and may remain with us for quite some time.

Misinformation

Misinformation may be defined as information that is inaccurate, incomplete, misleading, deceptive, or confusing. Unfortunately, there is nothing to prevent misinformation from being placed on the Internet and, particularly, being inserted into Web pages intended to promote the sale of products and services.

Misinformation can occur for several reasons. It can appear on the Internet as a result of Web site and Web page developers' failure to verify information prior to posting it on the Internet. It can occur simply because those posting the information just assumed it to be accurate. In an effort to conserve space, time, and expense, developers sometimes post a condensed version of the information, thereby rendering the information vague or misleading. However, misinformation can be deliberately posted. A concern is that large amounts of misinformation may cause Internet and Web users to question or perhaps doubt the validity of other information they see online.

An individual or company posting information on the Internet should be careful to verify that the information is factual. Preparing information for posting on the Internet in such a way as to sensationalize the information to make it more appealing to viewers is called **puffing.** Puffing occurs often in electronic commerce advertising when words and terms such as *fastest, longest-lasting, easiest-to-use,* and *simplest* are used to describe products being promoted. Puffing should always be avoided. Information should be presented factually and in an unbiased manner so viewers can accurately determine its value. The accuracy of information is an important concern of Internet users and online customers. Obviously, inaccurate information is useless.

A related concern involves the fact that the amount of information currently available on the Internet and the Web is growing at a phenomenal pace. Some users believe there is already too much information available on the Internet, yet in the months and years ahead, the amount of information will continue to increase—not decrease.

At present, there are more than 100 million pages available on the Web. Many of these pages contain the same or similar information. Some users consider the redundancy of so much of the information to be a problem. For example, some teachers believe that student assignments could be completed faster if some of the redundant information was removed.

All users, including online marketers, should make certain that any information they post is accurate and useful.

Internet Gambling

Internet (online) **gambling** is rampant on the Internet with an estimated 300 gambling sites currently available on the Web (Figure 8.5). Some studies have predicted that, if left alone, revenues from Internet gambling would increase from $650 million in 1998 to $3.1 billion in 2001. This controversial issue has captured the attention of both parents and government officials because Internet gambling involves children as well as adults.

FIGURE 8.5

The Grand Online Casino Home Page

Users can choose from among a variety of betting games. This is but one of hundreds of gambling sites on the Internet.

Previous attempts to legally ban Internet gambling have had little success. New efforts are now being made. In 1998 U.S. Senator Jon Kyl (R-Arizona) sponsored a bill called the Internet Gambling Prohibition Act of 1999 that if passed will ban Internet gambling. The act would extend to the Internet a 1961 law that made sports gambling conducted by telephone or wire illegal. The act would cover all forms of gambling. The U.S. Senate has already approved the legislation, but the House of Representatives has not yet acted. The proposed legislation denies individual states the right to allow Internet gambling within state borders and stipulates that Internet service providers would have to shut down or block access to any Internet gambling site anywhere in the world once told to do so by court order. Also, the bill would levy fines of $20,000 and a four-year prison sentence against site operators. Patrons (persons participating in gambling activities) would pay fines of up to $2,500 and be subjected to sentences of up to six months in jail.

The act will likely face challenges by groups including the American Civil Liberties Union, America Online Inc., the Interactive Services Association, and the United States Internet Council. These groups argue that the bill would require Internet service providers to become surrogate police forces and result in a confusing maze of state regulations and police interventions on the Internet.

Proponents argue that because casino gambling is never legal by telephone or other wired communications medium, it shouldn't be legal over the Internet. Further, they argue that children can access gambling sites and participate in gambling activities without being aware of the potential consequences.

Approval of the proposed bill by the House was expected in 1999. Even so, debate over this issue will likely continue for some time. The full text of the act can be seen at http://thomas.loc.gov. Search for bill number S.692.IS.

Overburdened Internet

Some users express concern that the Internet and the Web, despite their enormous potential, are already overburdened and unable to handle the millions of users who regularly travel through cyberspace.

Evidence suggests that the Internet and Web are not overburdened as a whole, but that some parts of them are. Consider the problems encountered in 1997 when America Online (AOL) changed its fee structure. For a fixed monthly fee, subscribers were allowed unlimited access to AOL's services. Thousands of AOL's 8 million subscribers immediately began taking advantage of their new unlimited access. In fact, many would remain online for hours at a time, thereby tying up AOL servers and preventing others from gaining access. Some users admitted to remaining online 24 hours a day. The problem was that the America Online servers were unable to accommodate all users wanting access. To keep from losing subscribers, America Online began frantically to install a larger number of more powerful servers. Within a short time, the problem was solved. However, many AOL subscribers filed a class-action suit against the company. The company finally reached an out-of-court settlement with subscribers. Other online services and intranets have experienced similar overload problems and have dealt with their problems effectively, as did AOL.

Successful online services and Internet service providers will likely experience overburdens from time to time as more people begin using the Internet. Adjustments will be made to accommodate the increase. Moreover, some popular Web sites periodically experience heavy usage. An example occurred when NASA's *Pathfinder* began sending pictures of the planet Mars back to earth. The demand for access to the NASA Web site by persons wanting to view pictures of Mars far exceeded the ability of NASA's servers. To accommodate public interest, NASA established mirror sites at which viewers were able to see the pictures.

The explosive growth in electronic commerce may present a problem in which some company servers may be unable to accommodate all customers. A slight problem occurred when Apple Computer Corporation introduced its newest Macintosh computer, called the iMac. Immediately following the announcement of the iMac, customers placed thousands of new orders for the machine causing delays in shipments of the product. This problem also was soon corrected. As more companies become involved in electronic commerce applications, more problems and delays can be expected to occur.

Improvements, changes, and adjustments are continually being made to the Internet and the World Wide Web. As users, we will probably encounter access problems in the future. Although delays may be inconvenient, they will probably be minor problems that, in time, will likely be corrected.

Privacy and Cryptology

You need to be aware that it is easy for other people to intercept and read messages sent across the Internet. This is especially true for electronic mail (e-mail) messages and other information such as that supplied when ordering products and services.

One of the major issues regarding electronic mail and online purchases is centered on the issue of **privacy**—that is, whether an employer has a right to intercept and read messages sent by employees. Some employers regularly monitor employee e-mail.

Some employers argue they have a legal right to read employee e-mail because the company or organization owns the e-mail resources, such as computers and software, used for sending and receiving it. Also, employers argue that employees are being paid for the time they spend using e-mail and therefore are using company time. Employees, on the other hand, argue they have a right to privacy and that an e-mail message should therefore be considered the private property of the individual.

A study done by Louis Harris, a respected research firm, showed that about 75 million American adults use a PC at home or work but don't access the

Internet and aren't likely to in the next year. This study identified five factors, shown in Figure 8.6, that would most likely influence them to start using the Internet. Privacy of personal data and communications is identified as the most important factor.

Legal opinions vary on this issue. Some courts have already ruled in favor of employers, and other cases are pending in the courts. The legal trend appears to be rulings based on the merits of individual situations and evidence.

This issue will likely remain controversial for the foreseeable future. Meanwhile, employees should probably refrain from using company resources for personal communications. If they use company resources, they should remember that messages can be intercepted and read, so they should be careful not to include statements that may jeopardize their position with the organization.

The issue of privacy is not limited to e-mail. The Internet is also used for transmitting other highly confidential information, such as business data and credit card numbers. The Internet will never be a safe place to conduct business unless there is some way to protect confidential data.

FIGURE 8.6

Five Factors Influencing Internet Use

According to a study by Louis Harris and Associates, about 75 million American adults use a PC at home or work but don't access the Internet and are not likely to in the next year. Of the adults surveyed, 44 percent cited privacy of personal data and communications as the factor that would most influence them to start using it.

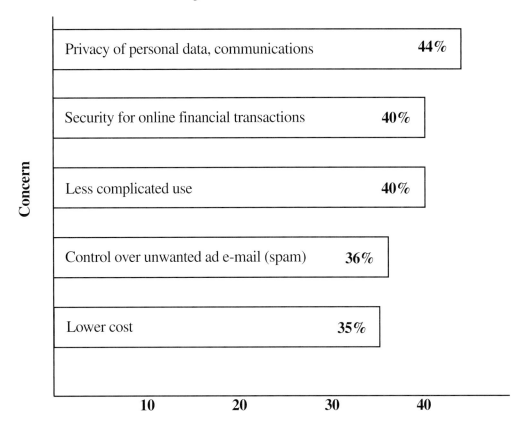

Source: USA Today, September 14, 1996, p. 1A.

The TRUSTe Program

Whether simply surfing or conducting business via the Web, privacy of information is paramount for most users. In recent months, much has been said and written about this important issue. Some users believe the government should enact legislation assuring the confidentiality of personal information supplied over the Internet and guarantee users that the information will not be used for purposes other than that agreed to by individuals who provide the information. For example, many users disapprove of companies and organizations sharing personal information, such as including the information in mailing lists that are shared with or sold to others.

Several surveys have shown that most Internet users prefer that the Internet be self-regulating. Many seem to fear that legislation will be too restrictive and burdensome for both individual users and for private companies and organizations. They argue that legislation would be difficult to enact, difficult to enforce, and overly burdensome for everyone.

An independent, nonprofit organization called TRUSTe has been formed to promote trust and confidence in the Internet and, in doing so, accelerate growth of the Internet industry. TRUSTe has earned a reputation as a leader in promoting privacy policy disclosure, informed user consent, and consumer education. The organization's mission is to accelerate global electronic commerce by educating users about electronic privacy and providing a positive means for companies to build informed consent and trust into their online business models. Since its formation, many well-known companies have joined the TRUSTe program, including IBM, America Online, Compaq, Netscape, The Microsoft Network, Yahoo!, Lands' End, and Disney.

According to information provided by the organization, the cornerstone of the TRUSTe privacy program is the organization's branded online seal, or "trustmark," that is awarded to Web sites that adhere to established privacy principles and agree to comply with the organization's oversight and consumer resolution process. TRUSTe states that when you see the organization's trustmark, you can be assured that the Web site will disclose the following:

- *What* information is being gathered about you
- *How* the information will be used
- *Who* the information will be shared with, if anyone
- *Choices* available to you regarding how collected information will be used
- *Safeguards* in place to protect your information from loss, misuse, or alteration
- *How* you can update or correct inaccuracies in your information

In short, a displayed trustmark signifies to online users that the Web site will openly share, at a minimum, what personal information is being gathered, how it will be used, with whom it will be shared, and whether the user has an option to control its dissemination. Based on such disclosure, users can make informed decisions about whether or not to release their personal identifiable information, such as credit card numbers, to the Web site.

The organization requires all Web sites that display the trustmark to agree with the TRUSTe oversight and complaint resolution procedures. TRUSTe monitors licensees for compliance with program principles and posted privacy standards through a variety of measures, including the following:

- Initial and periodic reviews of the Web site by TRUSTe
- "Seeding," whereby TRUSTe submits personal user information online to verify that a Web site is following its stated privacy policies
- Compliance reviews by a CPA firm
- Feedback and complaints from the online community

The TRUSTe organization solicits user vigilance. Users are encouraged to contact TRUSTe directly to report violations of posted privacy policies, misuse of the trademark, or specific privacy concerns pertaining to a member Web site. The TRUSTe home page contains a link to its Watchdog page where a user can submit a complaint. The URL for the TRUSTe Web site is http://www.truste.org.

Software engineers and programmers have developed a technology that allows data to be secured during transmission. This technology, called **encryption,** allows data to be translated into a secret code. Encryption is the safest way to achieve data security. Once data have been encrypted, they can be transmitted with little concern that they can be intercepted and read by another person. The receiver of encrypted data must have access to a secret key or password to **decrypt** (decode) and thus read the data.

The Year 2000 Dilemma

Computers built between 1950 and 1970 were designed to process large business, engineering, and scientific programs that sometimes contained millions of lines of program code. Memory was both expensive and limited at that time, so millions of software programs were written so that only two digits, rather than four, could be entered for a particular year. The number *64,* for example, would be entered for the year *1964.* To the computer the number *64* meant the year *1964.* During these early years, no one foresaw the potential danger that lay ahead.

As the year 2000 approached, we faced a problem of immense proportions. In spite of years of code correction and system upgrades, some computers still read the year 2000 as the year 1900. The year 2001 will be read as 1901, and so on.

The worldwide dependence on computers means that the potential effects of this problem could be devastating. Suppose, for example, that you owned a bank certificate of deposit that matured on January 1, 2000. On that day, would you have been able to collect your money?

Programmers changed the millions of lines of code in an international attempt to solve the problem, and the task is still not complete. Many large companies, organizations, and government agencies use thousands of computer programs containing millions of lines of code. The cost of making the necessary changes is expected to reach $600 million or more.

Much has been written and posted on the Internet about the year 2000 problem. One source on the Internet where you can learn more is at the address: http://www.year2000.com. You can find other sources by searching the Web.

Useless Web Sites

The quality of information available at various Web sites differs significantly. You probably know already that some sites are interesting and informative whereas others offer little, if anything, of value to the user.

Although the Internet and the World Wide Web are free to anyone wanting to put a site on the Web, including individuals and companies offering products and services for sale over the Internet, some people believe the Web is rapidly becoming cluttered with useless Web sites. Conversely, others feel that anyone has a right to have their own Web page regardless of how others feel about their value or usefulness. This applies to individuals and companies engaged in electronic commerce the same as it applies to private citizens.

As long as the Internet and the Web are free to all users, the views expressed by users are merely academic. No efforts are currently under way to prohibit anyone from placing pages on the Web—nor should there be. The authors of this book believe—like many other people—that to deny this privilege to anyone would be like denying a reader an opportunity to write, and have printed, a letter to the editor of a newspaper.

Online Games

There is growing concern about some of the online games available to young users. Some people, including parents, law enforcement officials, and psychologists, question the potential effects on young users of online games depicting violence. Some people believe that these games have a negative impact on young users and may even influence violent behavior. The April 1999 massacre at Columbine High School in Littleton, Colorado, has focused greater public attention on violent online games. The actual impact of violent online games on young users has not been determined.

User Identification

Recently it become known that the Intel Pentium III microprocessors contain instructions that allow others to obtain the addresses of online users. Hidden within the microprocessor are instructions that transmit a user's computer identification number, called PIN (for personal identification number), to e-mail recipients and to companies and organizations whose Web sites the user visits. There is concern that some businesses and organizations use this information to contact users about products and services or for other purposes.

Although Intel Corporation will provide a user with instructions for disabling this component, some users consider this capability to be an infringement to their privacy. Some users view this microprocessor capability as a violation of trust between the manufacturer and themselves.

Issues and User Responsibilities

Because the Internet, the World Wide Web, and electronic commerce are relatively new and growing at a phenomenal pace, many new and controversial issues and concerns have emerged. Over time, some issues and concerns will be resolved, and new ones will emerge. Some will likely be ignored, and the courts will decide others.

Some issues will remain controversial due to lack of worldwide consensus. Social standards and customs vary among the nations of the world. Individual opinions among citizens are influenced by many factors, including religion, social and political persuasions, and personal and family values. These and many other factors influence human attitudes and beliefs.

As Internet users, we are all responsible for our opinions, actions, and attitudes. To preserve a free and worldwide Internet, each of us has a responsibility to respect the opinions of other users. Only then will each of us be able to enjoy the full benefits of the Internet and the World Wide Web.

SUMMARY

The emergence of the Internet and the World Wide Web has brought new and controversial issues into public awareness. The issue of *who,* if anyone, should control the Internet and Web is extremely controversial.

Etiquette on the Internet is referred to as netiquette (an abbreviation for "Net etiquette"). On the Internet, everyone should be a Netizen, a term that refers to being a good citizen when using the Internet.

Using the Internet and the World Wide Web for advertising is becoming big business. Some believe that much of the advertising on the Internet is misleading or inaccurate. Others believe that advertising informs the public about new products and services and that most ads placed on the Internet are generally accurate and helpful.

Fraud may be defined as "a false representation of a material fact, made with knowledge of its falsity and with the intent to mislead or defraud, that is justifiably relied on by the one to whom it is made and which results in injury to him (or her) because of his (or her) reliance."

A spam is an unwanted, unsolicited e-mail advertising message. A scam is the deliberate attempt to cheat or defraud the public by false or misleading claims about products or services being offered.

The presence of pornographic and obscene materials available on the Internet, including text, pictures, and language, is another issue that concerns many people. To combat this problem, some businesses have installed software on their network servers to block the reception of these materials.

Government taxation of Internet users is a controversial issue. To encourage the continuing growth and development of the Internet and the Web, the federal government has imposed a moratorium on Internet taxes.

A virus is a program that can disrupt or even destroy the normal operations of a computer. Antivirus programs are available that can detect the presence of viruses and eradicate them.

Copyright infringement refers to the unauthorized use of someone else's material that has been granted copyright protection by the U.S. Copyright Office. Copyright laws do protect one's own creative work. Unless copyright laws are changed, the creator of Web pages should be careful not to violate the laws by copying information and materials from other Web pages without first obtaining written permission.

Rogue Web pages are pages posted on the Web by angry consumers and former employees. They are becoming a serious problem for many companies.

Security is a major concern of businesses, organizations, and agencies, many of which have invested millions of dollars to develop programs, files, and data. One method of maintaining security is to build firewalls. On the Internet, a firewall is hardware or software that restricts information that passes between a private intranet and the Internet.

Information theft is a very serious problem today in our society. Thieves use the Internet to steal all kinds of information, ranging from corporate secrets to individuals' credit card numbers.

A computer cracker is a derogatory term that most often refers to a person who tries to gain (and sometimes succeeds in gaining) unauthorized access to computer systems for the purpose of altering, damaging, or stealing information. Computer hackers are individuals who may test their computer skills by breaking into computer systems.

On the Internet, espionage refers to the act of spying. Sabotage refers to the willful destruction of property. On the Internet, saboteurs try to gain entry into computer systems to destroy information.

The use of mailing lists by Internet online service companies and service providers is one currently controversial issue. A mailing list is a list of entries (often of individuals) in which each entry consists of a name or title, mailing address, telephone number, and other information. The central issue concerns ownership of, and the right to use, personal information supplied by subscribers.

Misinformation may be defined as information that is inaccurate, incomplete, misleading, deceptive, or confusing. Unfortunately, there is nothing to prevent misinformation from being placed on the Internet and inserted into Web pages.

Internet gambling is a serious concern of many people. Steps are being taken to enact legislation to ban this practice.

Some users express concern that the Net and the Web are already overburdened and unable to handle the millions of users who regularly travel through cyberspace. Evidence suggests that the Internet and the Web are not overburdened, but that some parts of them are.

One of the major issues regarding electronic mail is centered on *privacy*—that is, whether an employer has a right to intercept and read messages sent by employees. The issue of privacy is not limited to electronic mail messages. The Internet is also used for transmitting other highly confidential information, such as business data and credit card numbers. A technology called encryption allows data to be translated into a secret code. The receiver of encrypted data must have access to a secret key or password to decrypt (decode) and thus read the data.

Although the Internet and the World Wide Web are free to anyone wanting to put a site on the Web, some people believe the Web is rapidly becoming cluttered with useless Web sites and information.

KEY TERMS

antivirus program (230)	firewall (232)	rogue Web pages (231)
computer cracker (233)	fraud (226)	sabotage (233)
computer hacker (233)	information theft (232)	scam (227)
copyright infringement (231)	Internet gambling (236)	spam (227)
	mailing list (234)	spam-scam (227)
decrypt (244)	misinformation (236)	Trojan horse (232)
encryption (244)	netiquette (223)	virus (230)
espionage (233)	Netizen (224)	virus hoax (231)
ethics (223)	privacy (238)	
etiquette (223)	puffing (236)	

END-OF-CHAPTER ACTIVITIES

Matching

Match each term with its description.

a. netiquette **e.** computer cracker **h.** sabotage
b. misinformation **f.** encryption **i.** privacy
c. copyright infringement **g.** firewall **j.** virus
d. mailing list

_____ **1.** Allows data to be translated into a secret code.

_____ **2.** An issue concerning whether or not an employer has a right to intercept and read employee messages.

_____ **3.** A program that can disrupt or destroy the normal operations of a computer.

_____ **4.** Rules for acceptable behavior on the Internet.

_____ **5.** The willful destruction of another's property.

_____ **6.** The unauthorized use of someone else's material that has been granted a copyright by the U.S. Copyright Office.

_____ **7.** Hardware or software that restricts information that passes between a private intranet and the Internet.

_____ **8.** Information that is inaccurate, incomplete, misleading, deceptive, or confusing.

_____ **9.** Usually refers to a person who tries to gain unauthorized access to computer systems for the purpose of altering, damaging, or stealing information.

_____ **10.** A list of entries (often individuals) in which each entry consists of a name, mailing address, telephone number, and other information.

Review Questions

1. In the chapter, a list of Ten Commandments for computer ethics was presented. Without referring to the list, recite as many of the commandments as you can remember.

2. Some guidelines for electronic communications were presented. Without referring to the chapter, state as many guidelines as you can remember.

3. Many companies and organizations use mailing lists to contact prospective customers and inform them about products and services. Should online service companies and Internet service providers be allowed to sell subscriber information to others? Explain and give reasons for your answer or opinion.

4. Internet fraud has become a serious problem. What does the word *fraud* mean? Are there ways in which fraud can be minimized or eliminated from the Internet?

5. One of the most controversial issues today is the presence of pornography on the Internet. In your opinion, is it possible for pornography to be banned from the Internet? Why or why not?

6. Two groups of Internet users are called computer hackers and computer crackers. What is the main difference between the actions of these groups of users?

7. Define each of the following terms that were explained in the chapter.

   (a) fraud
   (b) computer hacker
   (c) spamming
   (d) Netizen
   (e) cryptology
   (f) virus
   (g) firewall
   (h) misinformation

Activities

1. Using your browser, go to the Web site http://www.fau.edu/rinaldi/ten.html. A list of articles will be displayed. Click on the article "The Net: User Guidelines and Netiquette" by Arlene Rinaldi and read this article. This informative site contains pages explaining proper Internet ethics and behavior. If you are unable to access this site, do a search using the word *Netiquette* and read the information available.

2. Using a search engine, locate five documents containing information about the issue of privacy. Select and print the article you believe best explains this issue.

3. Using a search engine, locate several documents containing information about different viruses. For each virus, prepare a brief written summary describing the harm to a computer system that may be caused by the virus.

4. Using a browser, visit 10 different Web sites. Compare the information available at each site. In your opinion, is the information at any site visited useless?

5. Several issues, concerns, and problems were explained in the chapter. Choose one specific issue, such as spamming or mailing lists, and do a thorough search for more information about the issue. After studying the information you find, prepare a written summary of the information you located and studied.

6. This is a group activity. Your instructor will divide the class into groups of four or five students. Each student in a group will use the Internet to locate information concerning a specific Internet issue, such as privacy, fraud, or pornography. After accessing the information, members of each group will prepare a written report summarizing the group's findings.

Present and Emerging Trends and the Future

AFTER COMPLETING THIS CHAPTER, YOU WILL:

1. Explain the meaning of the term *trend,* and give five examples of trends that are now occurring in our society.
2. Briefly explain the difference between a *standard* and a *de facto standard.*
3. Identify some trends in computer hardware and software since computers were first introduced.
4. Identify how computer hardware has improved as a result of miniaturization.
5. Briefly explain the meaning of the term *connectivity* and tell why good connectivity is important in the computer field.

6. Briefly identify some of the changes we can expect in data communications and in human resources.

7. Briefly explain how the future roles of businesses and institutions will change.

8. Briefly identify some of the expected changes in computer hardware and software.

9. In the chapter, a prediction is made that communication bandwidths will increase. Briefly explain the importance of broader bandwidths to the Internet.

10. Identify and briefly explain changes expected to occur in the area of electronic commerce.

Authors of computer-related books and articles seem to enjoy speculating about the future. On almost any topic, individuals have opinions. Authors are no exception. Years ago, Charles McCabe of the *San Francisco Chronicle* stated that "any clod can have the facts, but having an opinion is an art."

Making accurate predictions is, at best, risky. However, many authors have dared to take such risks. Some have had limited success, whereas others have failed miserably.

Interestingly, most failures have resulted from the authors' inability to predict *when* technological advancements would be made, rather than from their ability to predict *what* advancements would be made. Actually, many earlier predictions came true sooner than predicted. Based on these predictions, it may be said that we are already living in the future. Today, we are surrounded by amazing new technologies that, according to some earlier predictions, should not have been available for another several years.

Throughout this chapter, we will identify several present trends and speculate about future developments that will likely affect computer hardware and software, the Internet, the World Wide Web, and electronic commerce. Each prediction is based on recent research findings and on research currently under way. Thus, the predictions that follow are reasonable, and most, if not all, should eventually prove to be accurate. But then again, time alone will tell. The chapter represents an interesting and reasonable gaze into a crystal ball to catch a glimpse of what we may expect in the future. Some of what we will see may change the way we live our lives and conduct our daily activities. It will be a fascinating journey into the future. Let's get started!

Present and Emerging Trends

The word **trend** refers to a movement or progression in a general direction. We often hear this word in everyday conversation to describe a pattern of change, such as warmer weather or higher food prices. For example, saying "the temperature is getting warmer" indicates to a listener that the trend (or direction) of daily climates is toward warmer temperatures. However, this does not mean that the temperature will rise each and every day. It simply means that over a period of time, temperatures are becoming warmer.

Trends may, and often do, change over a period of time. One example is that of women's clothing. Over a period of a few years, the trend may be toward dresses that are shorter in length, followed by another period of years during which the trend may be toward dresses that are longer.

In the computing field, we often experience changing trends. Some trends continue for several years, whereas others are short lived. For example, the present trend is toward computers that are smaller, faster, and more powerful. The trend in printers is toward models that are capable of printing text and images that are sharper and more detailed. The trend in modems is toward faster machines.

In the following sections, we examine some current trends that are having an impact on computer hardware and software, data communications, the Internet, the Web, and electronic commerce. Current trends impact all these areas because they are interrelated. Trends affecting computer hardware and software also affect the Internet, the World Wide Web, and electronic commerce because all are interrelated. For example, communications media such as telephone lines and satellite systems used for Internet communications are also used with the Web and with electronic commerce systems. Trends related to the Internet affect not only the Internet but also the Web and electronic commerce.

Standardization

A **standard** is a definition or a format that has been approved by a recognized standards organization or is accepted as a de facto standard by the industry. A **de facto standard** is a format, language, or protocol that has become a standard not because it has been approved by a standards organization but because it is widely used and recognized by the industry as being standard. Examples of de facto standards include the Hayes command set for controlling modems, the Hewlett-Packard Printer Control Language (PCL) for laser printers, and the Postscript page description language for laser printers.

In recent years, controversy has surrounded several Internet standards. For example, Sun Microsystems has charged Microsoft Corporation with altering Sun's Java programming language, claiming the altered version as its own, and using the altered version in some of Microsoft's software. Issues such as this one are usually either resolved by the parties or decided by the courts.

The absence of universally accepted standards can be a problem for Internet and Web users. Users may experience problems downloading information from the Internet. The absence of universally accepted financial payment standards hinders the development of financial payment systems that could facilitate the transfer of electronic payments and funds among banks and other financial institutions. Standards play a key role in electronic commerce applications.

In the future, the trend will continue shifting away from de facto standards and toward the establishment and acceptance of standards approved by recognized and accepted standards organizations. This trend will streamline electronic commerce applications and open the way for the development of new Internet and electronic commerce technologies, including transmissions protocols that will promote future growth and development in these dynamic areas.

Computer Hardware and Software

Early computers were huge and heavy devices costing millions of dollars. One of the earliest computers, called the **UNIVAC 1,** tipped the scales at 16,000 pounds. It contained more than 5,000 vacuum tubes and was capable of performing the then-remarkable feat of 1,000 mathematical calculations per minute. Even its developers were amazed at its incredible capability.

These early computing monsters are now viewed as dinosaurs and most are now housed in museums. Though they were marvels in their time, no one would even consider buying one of them today.

Ever since computers began appearing in the late 1940s and early 1950s, the obvious trends have been toward the development and manufacture of computers that are smaller, faster, more powerful, more versatile, and with expanded capabilities and storage capacities. A comparison of the UNIVAC 1 and a modern state-of-the-art notebook is shown in Figure 9.1.

Today, users are demanding computers that are smaller, faster, and more powerful, and manufacturers are meeting their demand. This trend will likely continue as mobile users need computers they can carry with them in their work and travels.

Another hardware trend is toward improvements in computer components and peripheral devices, including monitors, modems, printers, and graphics and sound cards. Higher-resolution monitors, faster modems, high-resolution printers, and improved graphics and sound cards are being introduced almost daily.

The trend in software is toward software that allows users to be more productive and toward integrated **software suites** that contain useful programs that function smoothly together so that data can be moved from one application to another. As more and more users take advantage of opportunities available with the Internet, the Web, and electronic commerce, improvements are being made to browsers and search engines, and new browsers and search engines are being introduced periodically. Businesses are pressuring communications companies and hardware and software developers to design and produce equipment and software to facilitate electronic commerce applications.

The quality of software is increasing rapidly while, at the same time, software prices are declining. Software programs are becoming more functional, allowing users to accomplish tasks that, until recently, were impossible.

Miniaturization

Modern computers are extremely fast and have enormous capabilities made possible, at least in part, from **miniaturization**—that is, the technology that has made it possible to densely pack more and more tiny electronic circuits together on all kinds of computers and components. Miniaturization has also resulted in

FIGURE 9.1

UNIVAC 1 and IBM ThinkPad 570

(a) This view of the UNIVAC 1 shows the console and some of the 10 tape drive units in the background. The computer's memory was housed in a 10-foot-by-6-foot walk-in box that contained the computer components and wiring. Total memory was 1,000 words.

Source: Lawrence Livermore Web site, www.llnl.gov/vem/picthist.html.

(b) Miniaturization has enabled the production of small notebook computers. The computer shown here is much cheaper, but smaller, faster, and more powerful than the earlier large computers. Actually, this computer is hundreds of times more powerful than its early predecessors.

Source: IBM Web site, www.ibm.com.

(a)   (b)

smaller computers and components without sacrificing the devices' capabilities or speeds.

Improvements in manufacturing technologies are resulting in even greater miniaturization, called **microminiaturization,** in which electronic circuits are invisible to human eyes. More and more, manufacturing plants are being equipped with computer-controlled robots used to produce tiny computer microprocessors, computer chips, circuit boards, and other components. Operating under the control of complex computer programs, these amazing robots can quickly place microscopic electronic circuits and connections at precise locations on chips, boards, and other electronic devices.

Many small computer devices have been introduced as a result of miniaturization and many others will appear in the future. The earliest electronic calculators were fairly large devices, but newer ones are much smaller and offer greater capabilities. The current trend toward all kinds of smaller, faster, and more powerful computing devices will likely continue indefinitely.

Internet and Web Appliances

A trend continues toward the development of useful devices that facilitate the access to, and use of, the Internet and the Web. Several manufacturers have introduced devices that, when connected to a standard TV set, allow users to access the Internet and view Web pages through their TV screens. Figure 9.2 shows one example of this type of device.

Several companies now offer Internet and Web appliances, and other new and improved devices are being developed—a trend that will likely continue as more users are eager to have Internet access wherever they are and at any time.

Connectivity

Connectivity is a term used by computer professionals that refers to a program or device's ability to link with other programs and devices. For example, a desktop computer that can import (receive) data from a variety of other devices and can export (send) data in many different formats to other devices is said to have *good connectivity.* On the other hand, a computer that has trouble linking into a computer network is said to have *poor connectivity.* For example, some

FIGURE 9.2

Sony WebTV Appliance

By connecting Sony Corporation's WebTV appliance to your television set, you can use it to access the Internet and view Web pages on your screen. Several companies currently manufacture similar devices.

Source: Sony Corporation.

E-Commerce Technology

Motorola Makes Net Push with Mobile Phones

In a move to regain some of its market share lost to Nokia and Ericsson, Motorola announced that all of its mobile phones will include browsing capabilities next year. The telecommunications equipment maker said its phones will be compliant with the Wireless Application Protocol (WAP)—Internet mobile phone technology—as soon as interoperability standards are approved at the close of 1999. A Motorola executive said that although Internet phones will have only minor market share by 2000—in time they'll make up 100 percent of the mobile phone market.

Bob Growney, Motorola's chief operating officer, stated that "This means that consumers can expect to see the first Internet browsing capabilities appearing on a Motorola GSM phone by the end of 1999, and across Motorola's entire phone range in the year 2000." Motorola believes this new technology will help the company to win back some of the consumers it lost last year to competitors.

According to company officials, the WAP technology that will become available this year will give handset phones Internet access. However, next year's availability of a new operating system, called EPOC, will enhance the functions of Internet phones from Motorola and other mobile phone manufacturers. The EPOC operating system represents a joint venture of the top three mobile phone manufacturers—Motorola, Nokia, and Ericsson, along with Palmtop computer manufacturer Psion.

Although Internet phones will account for only a minor market share in 1999, Growney believes that, in time, Internet phones will make up 100 percent of the mobile phone market.

Imagine commuting to work along a busy thoroughfare and seeing the motorist alongside you weaving through the traffic while browsing the Web on a mobile phone. Perhaps an unsettling thought!

notebook computers have this problem. The concept of connectivity is illustrated in Figure 9.3.

Poor connectivity is a continuing problem in the computer industry. Perhaps the main reason is the absence of acceptable standards. Some manufacturers insist that others accept and use protocols and standards they have established for their products. This leads to multiple protocols and standards, which results in the inability of some devices to connect to other devices.

The trend is toward greater connectivity. Hardware and software manufacturers now realize that a hodgepodge of different protocols and standards harms both their own company and the entire computer industry. Also, the federal government has established a task force to work with manufacturers, communications companies, and private groups and individuals to set industrywide protocols and standards. A main government goal is to promote further development and use of the Internet and the Web as vehicles to foster the expansion of electronic commerce.

Data Communications

Good connectivity is vital to effective data communications. The term **data communications** refers to the transmission of data from one computer to another or

FIGURE 9.3

Connectivity

Good connectivity implies that various devices and media work together to use the Internet effectively. Without effective connectivity, accessing and using the Internet would be more difficult.

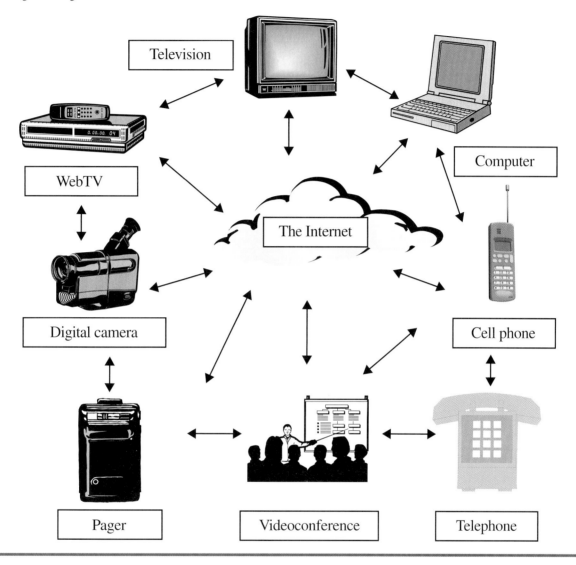

from one device to another. A **communications device** is any device that assists in data transmission. Examples of communications devices include modems, cables, and ports.

A **communications company** is one that enables communications between users from dispersed locations. For example, a telephone company provides a link between computers at remote locations, such as one computer located in Atlanta, Georgia, and another in Los Angeles, California.

The current trend is toward the improvement of communications devices and capabilities. For example, recent improvements in modem speeds and capabilities have been made. Within the past few years, modem speeds have increased from 18 kilobytes per second to 56 kilobytes per second. By the time you read this, modem speeds will likely have increased even more.

Human Resource Trends

Thousands of businesses, organizations, and government agencies are engaged in electronic commerce, and others are entering this dynamic new arena each day. Those already engaged in electronic commerce and others joining their ranks are actively recruiting trained and experienced computer professionals in an effort to be competitive.

The demand for skilled technical personnel has skyrocketed during recent months. Newspaper and magazine notices appear daily for specialized positions. Companies are actively recruiting Web developers, network managers, Webmasters, communications specialists, and other employees to fill vacancies in technical areas. Even colleges and universities are scurrying to recruit trained and experienced individuals who can assist the institution in getting online.

Several academic institutions have and are continuing to establish online courses and programs. Some are beginning to offer complete degree programs over the Internet. Trained Internet specialists are needed to accomplish this and make the programs successful.

During recent years and months, hundreds of individuals have become trained in specialized areas such as Web developers, network managers, Webmasters, and communications specialists, and hundreds more are seeking education, training, and experience in these areas. The most aggressive recruiters of potential employees with these skills are private businesses and government departments and agencies. Hundreds of companies now view their presence on the Internet as essential in order to be competitive. In recent weeks, newspaper articles have identified a few company officials who lost their jobs because of their failure to take advantage of opportunities available on the Internet.

Many companies now recognize the advantages available in electronic commerce. Using the Internet for the procurement of supplies and the monitoring of shipments represents a significant cost savings for many companies. Of equal importance is the potential for sales afforded to them by using the Internet to market goods and services and to respond quickly to customers and suppliers.

Significant changes in human resources are evident in many businesses, organizations, and agencies. A major trend now exists in which students and others are becoming educated and trained in specialized areas that will unlock the door for future employment opportunities. The demand for well-trained specialists will likely outpace the supply during the foreseeable future.

Changing Roles of Businesses and Institutions

Many businesses and institutions, including colleges and universities, are undergoing significant organizational and operational changes resulting from the development and rapid growth of the Internet and the Web. The Internet and the Web have opened up amazing opportunities that, until a few years ago, could not have been imagined.

The Internet and the Web have played a major role in the way many businesses now conduct their operations. Thousands of established retailers have embraced this new technology as a means of marketing their products and services and communicating with customers and suppliers. Other retailers are eagerly following their lead. Many recognize the potential of the Internet as an efficient and cost-effective vehicle for reaching new and large customer markets. Dell Computer Corporation has achieved success by using the Internet to sell computers it manufactures. Amazon.com has achieved amazing online success. The Internet has enabled startup retailers with minimal financial resources to get started in business and to compete with larger and more established firms. Each day, new retailer sites appear on the Web as more and more companies are entering this new marketing arena.

Not all business electronic commerce applications are between businesses and customers. In fact, most electronic commerce applications are business-to-business applications. A significant trend is that of businesses using the Internet to communicate with employees, suppliers, government agencies (such as taxing agencies), and the public. Hundreds of businesses now post procurement bid announcements on the Internet. Interested suppliers can respond by offering their bids for the supplies and materials identified on electronic bid forms. Some companies now transfer tax collections to the taxing agencies electronically via the Internet. Using the Internet, employees are able to submit suggestions or grievances to management via e-mail. Personnel officers can post employment notices and electronic application forms at their Web sites, and applicants can apply for employment by completing the forms and submitting their employment resumes.

Colleges, universities, and textbook publishing companies have discovered the Internet as a useful vehicle for offering online courses of study and programs to prospective students around the world—a phenomenon called distance learning. **Distance learning** may be defined as the electronic transfer of information from a college or publisher's host computer system to a student's computer at a remote site and the transmission of required responses from the student's computer to the host computer system. A course presented in this manner is called an **online course.** Several institutions and some publishers are actively involved in distance learning, and there is little doubt that others will follow. Millions of interested students are unable to attend classes on a regular schedule for a variety of reasons. For them, distance learning offers an opportunity to pursue or continue their education. Some people have described this new learning method as the classroom of the future.

FIGURE 9.4

University of Phoenix Home Page

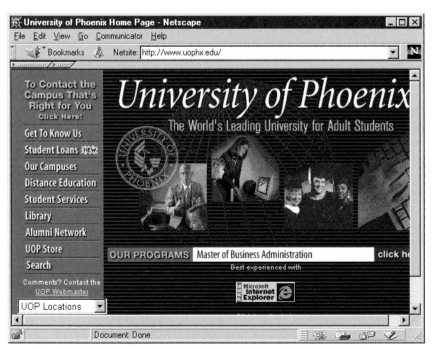

FIGURE 9.5

Dryden Online Web Site

The University of Phoenix offers a variety of online courses and programs. You can learn more about the university's offerings at www.uophx.edu. The university's home page is shown in Figure 9.4.

In an effort to reach more students and to make learning more versatile and flexible, some publishers have become involved in distance learning by offering a variety of online courses. The Dryden Press, a leading publisher of college textbooks, offers a variety of online courses for academic classes and for individuals (Figure 9.5). You can visit the company's Web site at www.drydenonline.com.

In the preceding sections, we learned about several trends that are now occurring. Because the Internet, the World Web, and electronic commerce are still relatively new phenomena, many of these trends will continue into the foreseeable future, whereas others may diminish and become less important. Still other trends will surely emerge, as trends are always occurring in our society.

In the following sections, we will peek briefly into the future. Much of what we see will seem reasonable and sane, but some may be viewed as less realistic. As we begin our journey into the future, be careful not to scoff aloud. More than 20 years ago and prior to personal computers, the author of this book speculated to his class that students would someday be able to take their own small computers with them to their classes. Immediately, laughter echoed throughout the classroom. The echoes have long since fallen silent.

The Future: Computer Hardware and Software

Technical articles appear frequently containing speculations and predictions about computer hardware. Fewer articles, however, predict advances in computer software. Historically, advances in software have tended to lag behind advances in hardware. The reason is that computers and other hardware devices typically are designed and produced before software is developed for these devices. The lag time may be brief or may last for a considerable period. Next, we will look at potential future developments in computer hardware followed by a glimpse at possible advances in software.

Hardware

Manufacturers of computer equipment know that if they are to remain competitive they must continually improve their existing products and develop new ones. The result is that new and improved products are introduced almost daily.

The development of hardware products may require years of careful research and planning. Successful hardware manufacturers often establish timetables showing the planning, design, development, testing, and introduction schedules of new products years ahead of their actual release. For various reasons, some products are never produced. However, thousands of new and improved products are finally produced and introduced to the public.

There is little doubt about the future for many hardware products. As new and improved microprocessors are developed, computers of all types and sizes will become faster, smaller, and more powerful. Within a few years, personal computer speeds will reach one gigahertz and perhaps even faster.

Computer monitors with amazingly high resolution will be introduced. Flat-panel color displays requiring less desk space will become more common as the cost of these devices declines.

Improvements in production technologies will allow manufacturers to produce internal storage chips and boards containing greater storage capacities. Internal storage costs will continue to decline making computers less expensive.

Various types of new and improved auxiliary storage devices and media will appear. During the past few years, we have seen hard disk capacities increase from 10 megabytes to more than 25 gigabytes. It is conceivable that hard disk capacities may reach 100 gigabytes within a few years. Floppy disk capacities will also increase. The disks themselves will likely become smaller yet contain far greater storage capacities. New auxiliary storage devices and media will emerge. One possibility is that of a small optical disk about the size of the familiar 3½-inch floppy disk and capable of holding the equivalent of five full-length movies. Another possible and perhaps imaginary step toward increased storage and faster speed lies in the possible development of biologically grown and produced chips called biochips. Theoretically, a **biochip** would consist of organically grown molecules assembled into tiny circuits. Should these molecular biochips actually be developed, their closeness and density would result in computers that contain much more storage and are several times faster. Although biochips exist only in theory, remember that theory can, and sometimes does, become reality.

Modern graphics boards are already available that provide for the access and display of clear and detailed images and pictures. However, users are starting to demand graphics boards capable of capturing and displaying clearer images and pictures with greater detail. Internet and electronic commerce users want to be able to view Web pages in the highest possible resolution and clarity. Manufacturers will surely respond to user needs in a positive manner by making these components available.

In the future, changes are likely to occur in personal computers themselves. With the dramatic increase in the number of Internet users, we may eventually see keyboards with a special key that, when pressed, provides for immediate Internet access without the user having to enter a series of instructions, passwords, and user identification numbers. All the necessary information will be entered and stored only one time. Afterward, a user will need only to press a single Internet-access key.

Computers are now available that allow the user to install a tiny video camera and software that allow the user to transmit and receive video images to and from other computers similarly equipped (Figure 9.6). In the future, many personal computers will come already equipped with this kind of technology, and the technology itself will be much improved and offer greater clarity. These improved video technologies will enable a user to communicate verbally with another user by pressing one or a few keys that will automatically activate the system. Imagine yourself being able to converse with a friend or family member via your computer simply by pressing one or a few keys on your computer keyboard.

Voice and video technologies will be improved in the future and new and better technologies will emerge. Before long, users will communicate with each other regularly using these technologies.

Software

In the near future and during the years ahead, we can expect remarkable improvements in software, especially in Internet, Web, and electronic commerce software. Advances will occur in software suites. Recall that a *software suite* is a group of applications programs, bundled and sold as a single package, that are designed to work well together. Available software suites include Microsoft's Office Professional, Corel's Office Suite, and the Lotus SmartSuite, as well as several others. We can expect to see improvements in suite programs introduced on a regular basis. Some of the less popular programs in software suites will be discarded and replaced by new and different programs.

Entirely new operating systems and application programs will be introduced. New programs will appear that will allow users to perform innovative and exciting

FIGURE 9.6

Intel's Show and Share Video System

computing tasks. Software will allow users to monitor and regulate household and office systems, such as electricity and water usage, heating and air-conditioning, lighting, telephone and messaging, and to monitor and even block the receipt of unwanted television and Internet content. Software will eventually become available that will allow users to perform virtually any imaginable computer application or task.

Significant improvements will be made to browsers and search engines, both of which will become faster and offer more features. As new upgrades are introduced, we can anticipate improved interfaces, faster access, and greater versatility.

Over time, new Web languages will be introduced. These languages will allow Web page developers to design pages that include images in virtual reality form.

Improvements will occur in Web page design programs, such as Microsoft's FrontPage, and new programs will be introduced. Learning to use these programs will become easier for first-time users, and the programs will offer an even greater number of design tools and features.

The most notable improvements will occur in electronic commerce software. IBM, a leader in electronic commerce software, frequently announces new and improved software products that allow companies to streamline their electronic commerce applications (Figure 9.7). The market for electronic commerce software is expanding rapidly. Many producers of electronic commerce software programs are taking advantage of the opportunities they foresee in the future.

The Future: Data Communications

Some of the most impressive and useful advances will occur in voice and data communications. Without a doubt, data transmission bandwidths will expand. Recall that the term *bandwidth* refers to the amount of data that can be transmitted via a given communications channel such as a computer network or a telephone line. Utilities companies, such as AT&T, MCI, and Sprint, are currently spending millions of dollars to develop fiber-optic cables, transmitters, and other communications devices and media with much broader bandwidths (capacities) than those currently available.

FIGURE 9.7

IBM E-Commerce

IBM Ties Gains to Internet; Shares Soar

International Business Machines Corp. shares rose $20.50 to $246 Thursday after Chief Executive Louis Gerstner said the world's No. 1 computer maker is gaining sales from its electronic-commerce strategy. IBM helped propel the Dow Jones industrial average to a record 11,107.19, up 106.82.

Gerstner told a meeting of financial experts Wednesday that IBM is getting $20 billion, or a quarter of its annual sales, from products and services that incorporated Internet technology into customers' computer networks. He also forecast pent-up demand next year for the services, software, and computers that help companies conduct online business.

"He showed tangible evidence that the Internet is benefiting IBM," said Steve Milunovich, an analyst at Merrill Lynch, who rates the stock a "buy."

Source: *Charlotte* (N.C.) *Observer,* May 14, 1999, page D1.

Telephone companies and their subsidiaries are currently spending millions of dollars to research new technologies that will allow faster voice and data communications. Lucent Technologies, a world leader in communications technologies and research, recently issued a press release indicating the company's plans for a major research center at Raleigh, North Carolina. It will build a lab at North Carolina State University to research ways to cram more waves of data carrying light onto fiber-optic cables (Figure 9.8). According to a recent announcement, Lucent plans to invest $25 million and employ 500 people at an average salary of $75,000 a year and plans to occupy the new facility by spring of 2000.

Lucent Technologies is also a leader in Dense Wave Division Multiplexing (DWDM) technology. **Dense Wave Division Multiplexing (DWDM)** is a technology that allows communications providers to transmit different wavelengths, or colors, of light on the same fiber strand, thereby increasing the fiber's bandwidth (capacity). Lucent has the largest market share (30 percent) of the $1.6 billion U.S. DWDM equipment market. Lucent was the first company to market an 80-channel DWDM system, called the WaveStar OLS 400G, which can transmit 400 gigabytes per strand of fiber.

Like Lucent Technologies, other companies also are researching new technologies that will allow faster and more efficient voice and data communications—a trend likely to continue indefinitely. The rapid growth of the Internet and electronic commerce requires improved communications technologies and capabilities. Without these improvements, the Internet will likely become stagnant and its potential will not be realized.

Other companies that produce devices for data communications are also seeking to improve existing devices and to develop new ones with wider bandwidths. Each week thousands of new Internet users are going online, and hundreds of additional companies, organizations, and agencies are establishing their presence on the Internet in order to be competitive. This is placing an increasingly heavy burden on existing communications technologies. To meet this continually increasing demand

FIGURE 9.8

Fiber-Optic Cable Showing Individual Strands

for access and usage, communications companies are eagerly developing new technologies that provide faster access and can accommodate user needs.

Manufacturers of communications devices, such as modems, are also improving their products and developing new ones. Companies, like 3COMM Corporation that produce computer modems, are developing faster and more efficient devices. To remain competitive, these companies must, and will, continue to explore new and improved technologies that will allow for faster transmission of data communications among computers around the world.

Cables that now link computers in a network will gradually be replaced by improved infrared technologies that render network links virtually invisible. Apple Computer Corporation, for example, is now working to develop notebook computers that can operate without cables as part of a network. If and when developed, users of these mobile computers should be able to access and transmit electronic mail, and these computers should be able to function similarly to network computers we now use.

One thing is certain. In the future data communications channels, devices, media, and technologies will to be improved. Recall that until fairly recently cellular phones were unavailable. Today, cellular devices and technologies are common. Perhaps someday cellular computers will become as common as today's cellular phones. Surely, the future holds tremendous promise for the rapid development of better data communications technologies.

The Future: The Internet and the World Wide Web

There can be little doubt that the continuing growth and expansion of the Internet and the World Wide Web will occur, not only in this country but around the world. In almost every country, including both developed and undeveloped ones, the Internet and the Web will become an integral part of society.

Some countries are embracing Internet and Web technologies faster than others, as evidenced by the rapidly increasing numbers of individuals, businesses, and organizations going online. Even in some countries where the political establishment and cultural bias has resisted these technologies, there is evidence that resistance to the Internet and the Web is weakening.

The Internet

The Internet will experience a surge in the number of Internet service providers and online service companies. Some well-known companies have already announced plans to begin providing subscribers with Internet access. America Online (AOL) has announced that it will offer interactive services to DirectTV's seven million customers beginning in the year 2000. This will bring together this nation's largest online service and its biggest television satellite broadcaster. Other companies are developing similar plans.

The marriage of online services and satellite broadcasters may well alter what we now know as home entertainment centers consisting of television sets, VCRs, stereo systems, and videodisk players. In the future, such home entertainment centers are likely to also include Internet access that allows the viewing of Web pages through a TV. With high-definition television available, users should be able to view Web pages that are much clearer and have greater detail.

We can look forward to significant improvements in Internet technologies. Newspapers, magazines, and other forms of news media frequently offer announcements of new and improved Internet technologies. New and improved processors are making Internet access and use faster and more convenient. Internet and Web servers are becoming faster and more dependable. Faster and more reliable modems are being introduced. Communication channel bandwidths are being broadened that provide for more data and faster transmission. The Internet of the future will offer faster access and transmission and expanded opportunities for all users.

The Internet is growing and changing at an extraordinary pace. In the future, new ways will be found for accessing the Internet and different types of information will be available. New portable Internet appliances will provide access to the Internet from remote locations.

Most people who use the Internet from home use a modem for access. Actually, modems are a slow way to transfer information. Eventually, most users will have much faster access, allowing them to watch movies or listen to CD-quality sound over the Internet.

Electronic mail messages now must be typed before they can be sent to friends and colleagues. Eventually, video e-mail will become available. A **video e-mail** system will allow you to record a video and send it over the Internet. When the recipient checks the e-mail, the recipient will be able to view the video you sent.

Virtual reality, a computer-generated three-dimensional world, allows users to view pictures and images that appear more like they can be seen with the human eye. In the future, much of what we will see on Web pages will appear in virtual reality form. We will be able to visually walk through electronic shopping malls and visit other planets and see images in more realistic detail. We will be able to envision precisely how clothing will look on us and closely inspect the components of products, such as automobiles and lawn mowers, before making a purchase.

The World Wide Web

There will be a tremendous increase in the number of Web sites appearing on the World Wide Web. In fact, we are now beginning to run out of top-level domain names—that is, the last part of a domain name that identifies the geographical location or type of organization. To solve this problem, new top-level domains have been proposed and are likely to be approved soon. Figure 9.9 shows a list of original top-level domain names and the proposed top-level domain names.

Anyone wanting to do so can establish a presence on the World Wide Web. Each day more and more individuals are doing just that. Among the newcomers

FIGURE 9.9

Original and Proposed Domain Names

ORIGINAL	TYPE OF ORGANIZATION
.com	Commercial business
.org	Nonprofit organization
.edu	Educational institution
.gov	Governmental entity
.net	Internet service provider
.us	United States
.mil	Military

PROPOSED	TYPE OF ORGANIZATION
.firm	Business
.web	Web-related organization
.rec	Entertainment-related organization
.nom	Individual
.info	Organization providing general information
.arts	Arts-related organization
.store	Online merchant and seller

FIGURE 9.10
Grant Hill Web Site

are professional superstars, like NBA star Grant Hill, who are using the Web to promote their careers (Figure 9.10). Others, including professional sports agents are going online both to promote their careers and to solicit business arrangements with future professional athletes. In the future, we can expect thousands of new Web sites to appear. Some sites will simply offer information to interested users.

The Future: Electronic Commerce

Electronic commerce has proven to be a worldwide phenomenon, the explosive growth of which has, and continues to be, almost mind-boggling. Within a few years, electronic commerce, in its various forms and applications, has grown from a theoretical concept to a multibillion dollar reality. Few people could have imagined the impact that electronic commerce would have on the world economy, especially on the economies of the United States and on other technologically advanced countries.

Most of the experts and research organizations that keep track of developments in this dynamic field agree that the future of electronic commerce holds tremendous promise for individuals, businesses, organizations, and governments. In addition to state and local governments, the federal government views the potential for electronic commerce with keen optimism. Support for electronic commerce by the federal government is evidenced by the establishment of a special task force charged with the responsibility of overseeing electronic commerce developments and coordinating its continued expansion among various groups.

During the months and years ahead, the number of individuals, businesses, organizations, and agencies involved in electronic commerce applications will increase drastically. Some will become involved simply to provide information to the general public.

Clinton Administration Backs Web Commerce

Washington—President Clinton, touting electronic commerce as an engine for global economic growth, said Monday [November 30, 1998] his administration is taking steps to promote buying and selling on the Internet. They include pushing for better consumer protection against cyber-fraud.

"We must give consumers the same protection in our virtual mall they now get at the shopping mall," Clinton said at a White House ceremony attended by executives from major "e-commerce" companies.

The president also said his administration would work with the Federal Communications Commission and U.S. trading partners to promote the development of faster Internet connections. "For many people, connections are so slow that shopping at the virtual mall is filled with frustration," he said.

Clinton cited projections that this year more than 40 percent of Americans with home computers will shop for holiday gifts online compared with 10 percent during last year's holiday season.

"If the virtual mall is to grow, we must help small businesses and families gain access to the same services at the same speed that big business enjoys," Clinton said. More needs to be done, he said, to build confidence among consumers that they can shop online with safeguards against being cheated.

"People should get what they pay for online; it should be easy to get redress if they don't," he said, adding that his administration wants the online industry—not the government—to provide the protections.

In response to Clinton's remarks, the National Fraud Center, a private fraud-prevention company, applauded the administration for steering away from imposing government anti-fraud regulations.

"Self-regulation is the most practicable way to protect legitimate privacy concerns because it recognizes that in the real world, there can be no one single solution to govern every situation," said Norman Willox Jr., president of the National Fraud Center.

Clinton also announced that the U.S. and Australian governments had agreed on a common approach to promoting electronic commerce. It includes supporting the indefinite extension of a May 1998 World Trade Organization declaration not to impose customs duties on electronic transactions.

At Clinton's White House event, Vice President Al Gore said "e-commerce" is a boon not just for the wealthiest countries. He cited the example of a Ugandan woman, Helen Mutono, who uses the Internet to sell Ugandan baskets and gives the proceeds to children orphaned by AIDS. And he said a village near Chincehros, Peru, had gained a five-fold increase in its income by using an online partnership with an international export company to ship its vegetables to buyers in New York.

"In this emerging digital marketplace nearly anyone with a good idea and a little software can set up shop and then become the corner store for an entire planet," Gore said.

Gore said there are 27 million purchases made every day on the Internet, and that total electronic commerce is projected to grow to $300 billion annually in a few years.

"Any desktop can be a doorway to a global mall" that is open 24 hours a day, 365 days a year, Gore said.

The president also directed the Commerce Department and the U.S. trade representative to work with the Federal Communications Commission to push for increased private investment in high-speed networks so consumers and businesses are not saddled with Internet slowdowns. "The information superhighway becomes a dirt path before it reaches America's homes," the White House statement said.

Source: This article was released to the public via the White House Web site at www.whitehouse.gov.

Online Merchants and Retailers

In the future, many new businesses will emerge that will use the Internet to sell their products and services. As competition intensifies, some online merchants will be successful but others will disappear. In the future, those online merchants and retailers that survive will be the ones that implement and practice innovative advertising and marketing techniques.

Many established businesses that, until now, were satisfied selling their products and services in more traditional ways will establish Web sites to advertise and market products and services online. Just as some large businesses are presently doing, many others will begin allocating larger and larger online marketing budgets. Web portals, including such well-known portals as America Online, Netscape, Yahoo!, and Lycos will aggressively compete for advertising sales and revenues. In short, billions of dollars will be spent for advertising on the Internet, and improvements will be made in advertising methods and techniques.

The Internet Advertising Bureau announced that Internet advertising revenues reached $1.92 billion for 1998, easily surpassing the estimated $1.58 billion in revenues from the more traditional billboard advertising. The 1998 figure surpassed the $906.5 million figure for 1997. And the Internet as an advertising medium is barely four years old.

Electronic Payment Systems

In the near future, technological improvements will be made in electronic payment systems. Although the use of smart cards is a widely accepted practice in some European countries, their use has not gained widespread acceptance in the United States. A **smart card** is a small credit-card-sized plastic card that contains a microprocessor and memory circuits used for identifying and authenticating the card's owner. When used for making online purchases, the card is inserted into an electronic device that captures and transmits information from the card to the merchant. Funds are then transferred from the purchaser's bank account to the merchant's account.

In the future, the use of smart cards will become more widely accepted and their use will increase as improvements are made in smart card technologies. Some manufacturers are now researching various smart card technologies. Future computers may even come with components, such as embedded slots, that will facilitate online purchases using smart cards for making online payments.

We can expect other forms of electronic payment systems to appear. Manufacturers and online merchants alike are eager to develop new systems that will simplify online payments for purchases of products and services.

Supply-Chain Management

Without adequate inventories, retailers like Wal-Mart and Sears would soon be out of products to sell. The uninterrupted and timely flow of inventories from manufacturers to retailers is critical for both the manufacturers and sellers. Electronic commerce technologies, including hardware and software, provide a means whereby the timely and continuing flow of inventories from manufacturer to seller occurs smoothly and efficiently.

The same is true for product manufacturers. The timely and efficient flow of raw materials and other supplies from suppliers to manufacturers is essential. Interruptions or delays in the delivery of raw materials and supplies often result in interruptions and delays in production schedules that can prove costly to suppliers and manufacturers alike.

More and more manufacturers, retailers, and suppliers are embracing electronic commerce technologies in their efforts to better manage inventories and to streamline other business operations. In the future, more business of all kinds will install and implement network systems that will allow them to capitalize on the opportunities made available with electronic commerce.

Career Opportunities

The Internet, the Web, and electronic commerce have opened new and interesting career opportunities, several of which can command selective employment options and high salaries. In the following sections, we examine a few new and potentially rewarding careers.

Web Page Designer

One of the fastest-growing and most interesting career opportunities today is that of Web page designer. Many businesses and organizations are recruiting individuals who can design attractive and informative Web pages that contain information and graphics on topics such as company products and services, college and university programs, and organizational services. Many businesses and organizations employ their own Web page designers who create such pages and update existing ones as needed. Others have turned to private companies that employ a staff of Web page designers who can design, construct, and maintain Web pages for their clients.

Many colleges and universities now offer programs and courses in this field. In addition to courses in computer concepts and the Internet, students typically complete courses in word processing, computer graphics, multimedia applications, and in Internet programming languages, such as Java and HyperText Markup Language. There are also other ways to obtain the training needed to become a Web page designer. Training facilities around the country and computer retailers offer intensive training courses that a student can complete in a few days. A Web page designer should possess excellent typing skills, be creative, and should be self-motivated. Professional Web page designers often work independently of others and with minimum supervision. Many are self-employed professionals who contract with businesses and other organizations to design Web pages according to the specifications and requirements determined by the customer.

Because of the relative scarcity of well-trained and experienced Web page designers and the high demand for their services, these professionals can earn lucrative salaries and enjoy a variety of employment opportunities.

Data Communications Specialist

You probably know already that data communications systems allow the transfer of data between locations. The responsibility for these systems falls to data communications specialists. A **data communications specialist** is responsible for developing, implementing, and maintaining the communications networks and the communications software that control the flow of data among devices in the network.

Several colleges are now offering majors with an emphasis in the area of data communications. In addition to basic computer courses, students usually must complete courses in database fundamentals and structures, query languages, and data communications.

Employers typically require new employees to obtain experience in data communications prior to being promoted to the position of data communications specialist. This is usually obtained by working in the area of data communications under the supervision of an experienced senior professional.

The rapid growth and expansion of the Internet and the Web have created a high demand for data communications specialists, which has boosted salaries to impressive levels. Employment opportunities are available with businesses, nonprofit organizations, and federal, state, and local governments.

Internet Service Representative

A relatively new career opportunity is that of Internet service representative, sometimes referred to as an ISR. An **Internet service representative** answers telephone and electronic inquiries from customers who encounter problems while installing communications or related software on their computer or who experience difficulties when trying to access the Internet.

Employment opportunities are available with Internet service providers and online service companies. With the rapidly growing popularity of the Internet and World Wide Web, ISPs and online services are adding millions of new subscribers each year, many of whom are inexperienced computer users. Experienced users are sometimes unfamiliar with the software they will use to access the Internet and the Web. Internet service providers and online service companies provide subscribers with phone numbers they can use to speak to Internet service representatives to obtain help in solving any problem they may encounter.

To qualify for employment, an applicant should possess basic computer skills, should have good verbal communications skills, and should enjoy helping customers solve problems. The employer trains new employees in the installation and use of software, including browsers and search engines. Before being left alone to respond to customer inquiries and problems, employees are typically required to demonstrate the knowledge and expertise acquired during training.

Some companies offer both full-time and part-time employment. Many part-time employees are high school or college students. Successful employees may advance to higher-level supervisory or management positions within the organization.

Teleconferencing Specialist

A **teleconferencing specialist** is a trained and skilled individual who can design, install, and operate teleconferencing systems that are needed by businesses, organizations, and others. Teleconferencing systems consist of audio-visual equipment, including cameras and electronic presentation devices, that when connected via computers allow participants to immediately communicate orally and visually. For example, a camera can capture a speaker's image and words at one location and transmit the image and words to viewers and listeners.

Other potential career opportunities will emerge in the future. Keep in mind that electronic commerce is a barely four years old. As we move forward into the next century, many changes will take place in this exciting field. Even experienced professionals cannot foresee all of the changes and events that may occur over the next few years. One thing we can be certain of is that the next decade will bring forth changes that will have a significant impact on our lives.

SUMMARY

Several trends are now occurring in the computer field and with the Internet, the World Wide Web, and electronic commerce. In the future, the trend will continue to shift away from de facto standards and toward the establishment and acceptance standards approved by recognized and accepted standards organizations.

Today, the trend is toward computers that are smaller, faster, and more powerful and toward improvements in computer components and peripheral devices, including higher resolution monitors, faster modems, high-resolution printers, and improved graphics and sound cards. There is also a trend toward devices that facilitate access to the Internet and the Web. Other trends include improvements in connectivity and data communications.

The trend in software is toward programs that allows users to be more productive including integrated software suites, new Web page languages, and new Web creation software programs.

The future will also bring continuing improvements in data communications devices and media.

The Internet, the World Wide Web, and electronic commerce are fairly recent developments in the world economy. We will experience rapid advances and changes in existing Internet, Web, and e-commerce technologies, as well as new developments and discoveries. We should anticipate a significant increase in the number of online merchants. Advances will be made in electronic payment systems, and new technologies will enable businesses to streamline and better manage company supply chains.

New career opportunities will emerge in the future. A few examples of new and potentially rewarding careers include Web page designer, data communications specialist, Internet service representative, and teleconferencing specialist. Many other career opportunities will become available as Internet, Web, and electronic commerce acceptance and use increases, as they surely will.

KEY TERMS

biochip (257)
communications
  company (253)
communications device
  (253)
connectivity (251)
data communications
  (252)
data communications
  specialist (266)

de facto standard (249)
Dense Wave Division
  Multiplexing
  (DWDM) (260)
distance learning (255)
Internet service
  representative (267)
microminiaturization
  (251)
miniaturization (250)

online course (255)
smart card (265)
software suite (250)
standard (249)
teleconferencing
  specialist (267)
trend (248)
UNIVAC 1 (249)
video e-mail (262)
virtual reality (262)

END-OF-CHAPTER ACTIVITIES

Matching

Match each term with its description.

a. miniaturization	**e.** software suite	**i.** connectivity
b. standard	**f.** video e-mail	**j.** distance learning
c. communications	**g.** trend	**k.** communications device
d. UNIVAC 1	**h.** virtual reality	**l.** de facto standard

_____ **1.** A movement or progression in a general direction.

_____ **2.** A definition or a format that has been approved by a recognized organization or accepted as de facto by the industry.

_____ **3.** The transmission of data from one computer to another or from one device to another.

_____ **4.** Any device that assists in data transmission.

_____ **5.** Technology that has made it possible to densely pack more circuits together on all kinds of computers and components.

_____ **6.** A group of applications programs, bundled and sold as a single package, that are designed to work well together.

_____ **7.** A format, language, or protocol that is not an official standard but is accepted as a standard by the industry.

_____ **8.** A future technology that will allow you to record a video and send it over the Internet.

_____ **9.** A program or device's ability to link with other programs and devices.

_____ **10.** One of the earliest computers.

_____ **11.** A computer-generated three-dimensional world.

_____ **12.** The electronic transmission of information from a college or publisher's host computer system to a student's computer at a remote site and the transmission of required responses from the student's computer to the host computer system.

Review Questions

1. Briefly explain the meaning of the term *trend,* and give an example.

2. Briefly distinguish between a standard and a de facto standard.

3. Explain the meaning of the term *connectivity.* Give one example of good connectivity and one example of poor connectivity.

4. Briefly explain the nature of distance learning.

5. Briefly describe the main responsibility of a data communications specialist.

Activities

1. In recent weeks, several newspapers have carried articles identifying new computer hardware and software technologies. Visit the library at your school and browse through recent editions of several newspapers. Find three articles in which the writer identifies and explains new or improved computer hardware or software technologies. Prepare a brief written summary of each article.

2. For this activity, visit a business in your area that is involved in electronic commerce. Ask to speak with the person in charge of electronic commerce applications. During your conversation with this person, inquire about what he or she believes will be some future developments or improvements in electronic commerce. Prepare a list of suggestions offered by the person with whom you spoke.

3. Distance learning is becoming a popular method for studying specific courses online. One company that offers online computer courses is The Dryden Press. Visit The Dryden Press Web site at www.drydenonline.com. During your visit, prepare a written list of online courses offered by the company.

4. This is a team project. Your instructor will divide the class into groups (teams) with four or five students on each team. Several computer magazines contain articles with predictions of future developments in electronic commerce. The following table lists the Internet addresses of a few popular magazines. Each team member will visit one of these sites and find two articles containing a minimum of one prediction about future developments in electronic commerce. After reading two articles, each student will prepare a brief written summary of each article. Next, members of the group will combine all summaries into a group report and turn the report in to the instructor.

MAGAZINE NAME	WEB ADDRESS
PCMagazine	http://www.pcmagazine.com
Infoworld	http://www.infoworld.com
PCWeek	http://www.pcweek.com
Datamation	http://www.datamation.com
Computer World	http://www.computerworld.com
PCWorld	http://www.pcworld.com

A P P E N D I X   A

Getting Started on the Internet and Web

More than 43 million homes now have access to the Internet and the World Wide Web and thousands more are going online each week. People with varying backgrounds, ages, and skill levels are moving quickly to take advantage of the numerous opportunities the Internet offers. You too can quickly and easily join millions of other users who are taking advantage of this new and exciting technology. In this appendix, you will learn how you can get started with the Internet and the Web.

The information contained in an appendix can be learned at any time—even before learning material in earlier chapters of the book. For this reason, the first sections of this appendix are an overview of some basic information presented in the chapters. Following the overview, we proceed with the objective of learning how to get started using the Internet and the World Wide Web.

The Internet and the World Wide Web

Today, we are experiencing and enjoying an evolution in technology that is changing the world. It is called the **Internet.** You've learned already that the Internet is a worldwide collection of networks connecting millions of users in hundreds of countries. For users around the world, the Internet affects the way we live, work, learn, play, and communicate. It is shaping our world, our future, and our lives with the opportunities it offers. Never before in the history of the world have so many had access to such a valuable resource. No one knows its actual size, and no single individual, group, or organization owns or controls it. Yet, in a sense, we are all owners of this self-regulated technology that is expanding so rapidly it is virtually impossible to keep track of the number of networks, information services, databases, hardware and software packages, and information being made available to users.

The Internet offers tremendous opportunities for learning, for communicating, for visiting interesting and exciting places, and for establishing one's own online presence. As a user, you can visit new and different places, view rare art exhibits, and even play hundreds of different and challenging online games. You can make new friends and participate with groups sharing interests similar to yours. The Internet opens up a world of reality and a world of fantasy for everyone.

The **World Wide Web** (also called the **Web, WWW,** or **W3**) is a global system of linked computer networks that allows users to jump from one place on the Web to another place on the Web. It is a retrieval system based on technologies that organize information into Web pages.

Access to some networks may be restricted to authorized users and some information stored on networks is restricted to authorized users with passwords. Thus, not all sites on the Internet are available to everyone. Sites that are accessible to anyone are called **Web sites** and are a part of the World Wide Web. Although the Web is smaller, it is the fastest growing part of the Internet.

The amount and kinds of available information varies among Web sites and is in the form of Web pages. A **Web page** is a hypermedia file stored at a particular Web site. A **hypermedia file** is a file containing any combination of text, graphics, sound, and video. Web pages may also contain one or more hyperlinks to other Web sites and to other pages available at the same site or at a different Web site. A **hyperlink** (or simply **link**) is typically displayed as boldfaced text, underlined text, or as an icon that, when clicked on using a mouse, takes you to another Web site or Web page.

Internet and Web Applications

The Internet and the Web provide users with access to information sources, databases, libraries, multimedia, and much more. Perhaps equally important, they provide an efficient way for companies and organizations to conduct business operations within the organization, with suppliers and customers, and with others. Using electronic commerce technologies, the Internet and the Web make it possible for individuals and businesses to market products and services and to conduct other business activities.

Internet and Web use is not limited to private individuals and businesses. Medical expertise in the finest research hospitals is immediately available for consultation by other doctors working in remote regions of Africa, India, or South America. Students can correspond with professors at their school and with other individuals throughout the world. Online shopping on the Internet has exploded in recent years and will become even more common in the future. As shown in Figure A.1, the Internet and the Web offer a variety of applications. The following sections identify some popular ones.

FIGURE A.1

Internet and Web Activities

Computers in homes serve a variety of functions. These are the 10 most popular Internet activities.

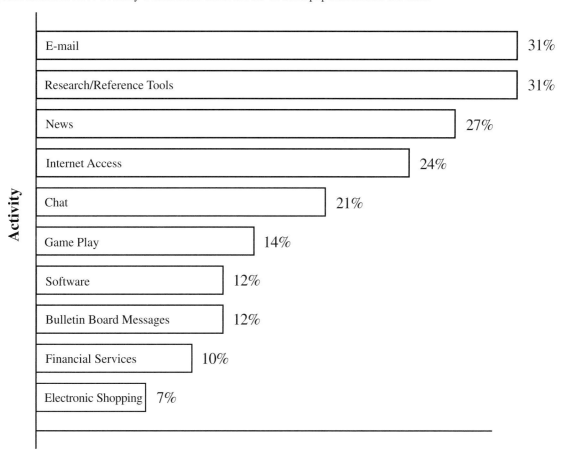

Percentage of Households

Electronic Mail

An **electronic mail system** allows you to send and receive messages electronically through, and between, networks from one computer to another computer (Figure A.2). Each sender and recipient has a unique e-mail address. An e-mail address usually consists of the person's user name, followed by the @ symbol and their computer's domain name (such as jadams@worthington.com). An e-mail address uniquely identifies a person on the Internet, similar to the way a person's name, street address, city, state, and ZIP code identify the person's mailing address.

Finding Information

A vast storehouse of information awaits you on the Web. Easy-to-use search engines provide you with a way to search for, locate, and view information. A **search engine** is a software program that facilitates queries by allowing a user to enter search criteria to locate specific information on the Web. A **query** is a word or phrase entered in a search engine program that specifies the type of information you want to view. In short, a search engine allows a user to search for, locate, and retrieve information on the World Wide Web.

Information Retrieval

Universities, libraries, and government agencies have large databases filled with information available to Web users. By simply knowing and accessing the database containing the desired information, a user can retrieve information on thousands of topics.

FIGURE A.2

Electronic Mail

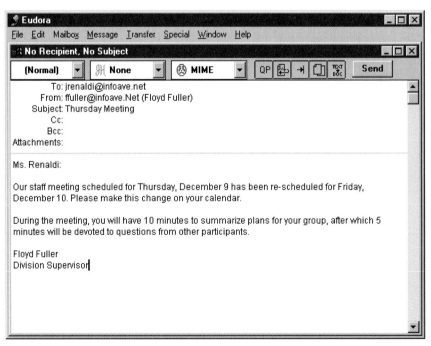

Source: Eudora version 1.4.4

Chat Groups (Chat Rooms)

Special software applications, called **chat programs,** allow individuals to use the Web to communicate with other people having similar interests. Many people join groups, called **chat groups** or **chat rooms,** to discuss topics of mutual interest, such as current events, politics, or the environment. Comments and opinions, often frank and uncensored, can be exchanged freely and anonymously with other group participants.

Entertainment

The Web can be used for playing online games. Many games are stored at various Web sites and can be accessed by users wanting to play a game. Chess, checkers, monopoly, bridge, and a variety of other games are available. Some users have even tried gambling on the Internet, although this is not widespread for various reasons—one being that it's hard to collect your winnings.

Home Shopping

Thousands of products and services can be purchased via the Web. Each year consumers purchase millions of products and services ranging from airline tickets to automobiles. Computer manufacturers, including Compaq Computer Corporation, IBM, Dell Computer Corporation, and Gateway (Figure A.3), have Web sites that allow customers to purchase computer products directly from the manufacturer. Thousands of companies are beginning to use the Web as an efficient and cost-effective way to market their products and services.

Internet and Web Access

For students, access to the Internet and the World Wide Web is often provided by the school. You can gain access by using one of the computers located in a computer

FIGURE A.3
Gateway Home Page

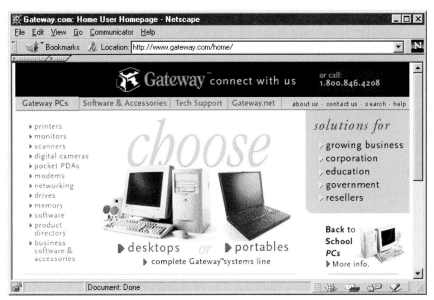

lab. Many college dormitory rooms are equipped with a cable students can use to connect their personal computers to the school's local area network. Many colleges allow students living off campus to access the school's local area network by using a modem to connect a computer via a telephone line.

Not everyone is fortunate enough to have free and unlimited access to the Internet. After you graduate, or if you are not a student, you might still want to have access to the Internet from your home or office. Although some employers provide access for employees, others may not. Individuals without Internet access can obtain access from commercial companies. However, purchasing access is similar to purchasing other important goods and services in the market. Knowing what you want and how to go about obtaining it will enable you to make a better decision. In the next section, we examine some things you should know and do before you commit to a company to provide you with access to the Internet.

Getting Started—The Preliminaries

Getting access to the Internet can be frustrating and time-consuming. If you will be purchasing access, there are some things you should do before making a commitment.

Establish Your Objectives

To access the Internet and perform other activities, such as word processing, you need a computer capable of performing these and other applications. Before making a purchase, you need to decide what you will use your computer for and how efficient you want to become as a user. You also should decide what you might use it for in the future. For example, your immediate objective may be word processing, but later you might want to become involved in desktop publishing activities. Both immediate and long-range objectives are important because desktop publishing programs tend to be larger and more complex than word processing programs. For desktop publishing applications, you may need a faster computer with more internal storage. A good idea is to prepare a list of potential uses for a computer system before making a purchase. The list you prepare can be a valuable reference as you determine your specific needs.

Determine Your Needs

After compiling your list of objectives, you need to determine your needs. For example, if one of your objectives is to use the Internet, you will need a modem. To download pictures and sound from the Internet, you will also need a sound card and a graphics card. In short, you will need specific equipment to accomplish specific objectives.

Gather Information

Before making a purchase, gather information that can help you make good decisions. The process of gathering information includes comparative shopping. Before making a purchase, compare several brands as well as sellers. Talk with other users that you trust. Ask how they use their computers. If you plan to use the Internet, talk with individuals who already have access. Learn how they obtained access and whether they are satisfied with their arrangement. Some brands offer more attractive warranties. Some companies offer unlimited online technical assistance when you need help. The more informed you are, the better decisions you are likely to make.

Compare Costs and Services

Always compare costs and services. The most expensive products or services are not always the best. The best advice is to shop carefully by asking questions, comparing benefits and costs, talking with other customers, talking with vendors, and requesting printed information you can use to become knowledgeable about the obligations, warranties, and services available from potential suppliers. For example, costs and services offered by an Internet service provider often depend on the kind of service you want.

Make Your Decision

Only after you have established your objectives, determined your needs, and compared costs and services can you make good decisions. A good rule is to make your decisions only after becoming well informed. Know what you need and want, whether your purchase satisfies your needs, and whether you can justify your commitment.

If you decide you want to have access to the Internet, you will need some specific computer hardware and software. In the following sections, we examine specific hardware and software that can help you become a proficient Internet user.

Hardware You Need

To access the Internet, you need specific computer hardware. You should be mindful that the Internet is continually changing. As changes occur, hardware requirements may also change. Be prepared to upgrade or modify your system when necessary.

Computer

A basic computer typically includes a system unit, a keyboard, a monitor, and a mouse. However, many newer computers may contain additional components. Before purchasing a computer, find out what is included with the computer you are considering. For relatively easy and simple applications, such as word processing, almost any computer will likely be satisfactory. However, for Internet use a fast computer with a high-resolution color monitor is preferable. Both computer speed and monitor resolution are important. If you are thinking of buying an older computer, computer professionals recommend a computer with a minimum microprocessor speed of 133 megahertz (MHz). If you will be buying a new computer, most new computers operate at speeds of 333 megahertz or faster, making them suitable for Internet use. Speeds in the range of 333 megahertz to 600 megahertz allow you to move about the Internet and the Web and to retrieve information quickly. Using a slower computer will likely result in your waiting longer while jumping from one location to another location or retrieving information from a specific Web site.

Random-access memory (RAM) (also called **primary storage**) refers to temporary storage capacity inside your computer. Any information entered into or received by your computer is temporarily stored in RAM. For example, any information you retrieve using the Internet is first brought into and stored temporarily in RAM inside your computer and then displayed on your computer screen. Your computer should contain enough RAM to hold your programs and information you receive using the Internet. At present, the RAM capacity of your computer should be a minimum of 16 megabytes (MB). A capacity of 32 megabytes, or more, is better. If you are considering buying a computer with 16 megabytes, make certain the computer contains expansion slots that will allow you to add more RAM capacity now or later.

Secondary storage allows for the permanent storage of programs, data, and information. Examples include floppy disks and hard disks. Most modern PCs come equipped with both types. When using the Internet, either can be used to store retrieved information.

A high-resolution color monitor allows you to take advantage of impressive graphics available at many Web sites. Most Web pages contain graphical images and pictures in vivid color and you want to be able to capture and display these images on your screen. For the Internet, a minimum resolution of 640 pixels by 480 pixels is barely acceptable, whereas a resolution of 1,600 by 1,200 offers impressive color and clarity.

Modem

To access the Internet from your home, you need a modem. A **modem** is an electronic device that enables a computer to transmit (send and receive) data over telephone lines. Your modem should be a relatively fast one. Most vendors offer newer and faster modems that operate at speeds up to 56 kilobits per second. A slower modem requires more time to send and receive information across the Internet and the Web.

You cannot receive data faster than they are being sent. For example, if the speed of your modem is 56 kilobits and data are being sent to your computer at 28.8 kilobits per second, you will receive them at the same speed they are sent regardless of the speed of your modem.

Add-ons and Plug-ins

An **add-on board,** also called an **expansion board,** is an electronic circuit board (or card) that can be installed inside a computer to provide additional capabilities. Add-on boards can be particularly useful when accessing Web sites, viewing Web pages, and retrieving and storing information.

An add-on is designed to complement other products. Several add-on boards are available that you can install in your personal computer to give it additional capabilities. An example of an add-on board is a sound board. A **sound board** is an electronic board installed inside a personal computer that allows you to hear sounds available at some Web sites, as well as music on CD-ROM disks.

Another useful add-on board is a graphics board (also called graphics card). A **graphics board** is an electronic board installed inside a personal computer that speeds up graphics-intensive programs such as games and enables you to capture and display vivid pictures and images (Figure A.4).

Many newer personal computers are **multimedia computers,** which means they come with add-on boards already installed. If your computer does not already have needed add-ons, they can be purchased at computer stores or from the manufacturer. Before purchasing an add-on board for your computer, you should request a demonstration.

A **plug-in** is a software program that, when loaded into a computer, improves performance. Some application programs, including Netscape's Navigator browser, contain plug-ins that are automatically loaded into the computer when the browser is activated. All new browsers have plug-ins that are automatically loaded into your computer when the browser is activated.

Numerous plug-ins are available. Some are free and others must be purchased. An example of a useful free plug-in is Adobe Systems' Acrobat Reader, which enables a user to access, retrieve, and print forms, such as job application forms.

FIGURE A.4
Add-on Graphics Board

Upgrades

A new version of a hardware or software product designed to replace an older version of the same product is called an **upgrade.** Software companies frequently sell upgrades at discount prices to prevent customers from switching to other products. To install an upgrade on your computer, you must have an earlier version already installed.

Upgrades of Internet products are offered at regular intervals. Some software companies allow a user to download a newer version of a particular product. When you *download* a program, you receive the new program via your modem and store the program on your computer. For example, when Netscape Communications Corporation introduces a new version of its popular browser program, a user of an earlier version can simply download the new version. Netscape makes the downloading process easy. Usually, a user can download the new version just by clicking on the name of the new version shown on the Netscape home page and then following the instructions that appear on the screen.

Because the Internet is continually changing, you will occasionally find a need to upgrade your software and your hardware. Upgrades will enable you to take advantage of new features and applications available on the Internet.

Software You Need

A typical personal computer comes with some software already installed, including an operating system. The operating system should include a **graphical user interface (GUI),** which takes advantage of the computer's graphics capabilities (Figure A.5). Various graphical user interfaces, such as Microsoft's Windows 98, offer special features including pointers, icons, windows, and menus—all of which make a personal computer easier to use. More recently, some computer manufacturers and sellers have begun selling computers with a modem, modem communications software, and Internet software already installed. Unless this software is already installed on your computer, you will need to install it before you can access the Internet.

FIGURE A.5

A Graphical User Interface

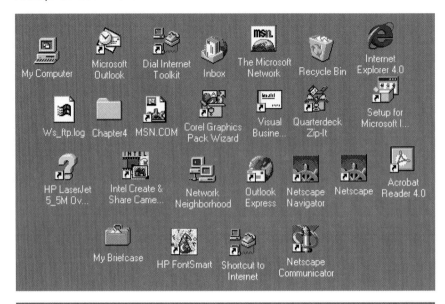

Communications Software

Communications software is an application that allows you to send and receive information over telephone lines through a modem. Without communications software, you cannot connect your computer to another computer, such as a Web server.

Communications software is produced by several manufacturers and is usually included with your modem. It is also available from Internet service providers and online service companies, both of which are explained later in this chapter. Unless you are an experienced Internet user, you might benefit by obtaining a communications software program from one of these. If you will be using an Internet service provider or subscribing to an online service, either will provide the software you need and assist you in its installation. After making arrangements with the company, the company will send the software, detailed printed information for installing it on your computer, and a telephone number for technical assistance you can use to contact a company technician. If you are unable to install the software properly, you can use the telephone number to contact a technician for assistance. While on the telephone, the technician can provide step-by-step instructions for installing the software.

Communications software includes several basic programs. One of the programs contains instructions for data transfer speed. This program should allow for a data transfer speed at least as fast as the maximum speed of the modem you will be using.

Another program allows for automatic queuing and redialing. This can be a useful feature if you use your modem to access a service that is frequently busy, such as an electronic *bulletin board service* (BBS). By entering the telephone number in a queue, the communications software will continue redialing the number until you are connected to the bulletin board.

Some communications software contains other useful programs and features. For example, *file transfer protocols (FTPs)* enable you to transmit binary files or ASCII files over a telephone line (Figure A.6). A **binary file** is a machine-readable-only file in which data are in the form of only two numbers (0s and 1s). Executable files and numeric files are typically in binary format. An **ASCII file** is

FIGURE A.6
An FTP Screen

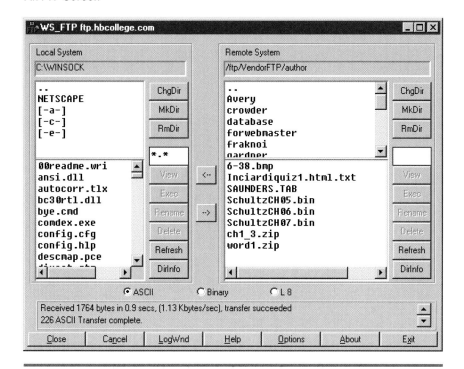

a human-readable file in which the data are in the form of text. The more protocols the package supports, the better.

Many files and programs are available on the Internet that are not part of the
World Wide Web. You can access these files and programs using file transfer protocol. **File transfer protocol (FTP)** is a popular Internet application that allows
you to retrieve files from another computer on the Internet and place them onto
your computer—a process called **downloading.** You can download many types of
files, including text files, files that you can run on your computer, graphics files,
and audio files. FTP can also be used to transfer files from your computer to another computer—a process called **uploading.**

An FTP site is a computer on the Internet where files are stored. Many colleges
and universities, government agencies, companies, organizations, and individuals
maintain FTP sites. Some FTP sites allow for **anonymous access,** which means
that you can access files at these sites without entering a user ID or password.
Some anonymous FTP sites allow you to view files without having to enter anything at all. Others allow you to access files by entering the word *anonymous*
when prompted to enter your user ID or password. Some FTP sites are private, allowing only users with account numbers and passwords to access files. To access
files at these sites, you must use an authorized user ID and/or password.

A user can send or receive large files, such as lengthy reports, over the Internet
by using FTP. FTP programs allow you to choose whether a file is to be sent in
ASCII format or binary format. Files containing text are usually sent as ASCII
files, whereas graphics files (such as pictures or drawings) are sent as binary files.
Upon arrival at its destination, the files can be converted into readable form by
using a word processor or other program.

The more features available with your communications software package, the
better. When discussing communications with a potential supplier, inquire about
the features available with the communications software.

Web Browsers

To use the Internet, you need a browser. A **browser** is a software tool (program) that makes it easy for the user to access and display Web pages by removing the complexity of having to remember the syntax of commands to find and display the pages. In short, a browser allows a user to navigate the Web easily and quickly. Some popular browsers, including Netscape's Navigator and Microsoft's Internet Explorer, are free and can be downloaded from the company. Several software products have one or more built-in browsers allowing a user to switch back and forth between a browser and other applications.

If you subscribe to an Internet service provider or to a commercial online service company, such as the Microsoft Network or America Online, the company will include at least one browser with the software you receive to install on your computer. Before subscribing to an Internet service provider, inquire about the programs and the features available with the programs included in the software package.

Before acquiring a browser for your own use, consider the features you want. Some basic features you should consider include the browser's functions, ease of use, speed, framing capability, multimedia support, publishing capability, and security.

- *Functions.* Newer browsers offer users several useful functions, including e-mail, bulletin board access, and chat groups. Some functions may be important, whereas others may not. For example, e-mail capability is important if you will be sending and receiving messages. On the other hand, Telnet may not be important unless you plan to access a remote host computer, such as the main computer on a university campus. Although you might not need a particular function now, you might later discover a need for it.

- *Ease of use.* Most browsers are easy to learn and use. Most offer tools, including a menu bar, tool bars, and special buttons, that allow you to locate, retrieve, save, and print Web pages, along with other tasks.

- *Speed.* When moving between Web sites and pages, you will discover that some Web pages take considerable time to retrieve and display. Some browsers are faster than others in the manner in which they handle complex graphical images, such as pictures and illustrations. A capability, called **progressive graphics capability,** allows a low-resolution version of images to be displayed quickly while more data needed to sharpen the images are being downloaded to your computer. This allows you to get an idea of what the final image will look like while you're waiting for the remainder of the data to be downloaded. If you're not impressed with what you are seeing, you can switch to another Web page. Browsers designed to run under a graphical user interface, such as Microsoft's Windows 98, support a feature called **multitasking** that allows you to perform multiple operations in parallel. For example, with multitasking you can be conducting a library search while a file is being downloaded to your computer from an FTP site.

- *Multimedia support.* Multimedia capability has become essential for many computer applications, including Internet and Web applications. Multimedia capability allows you to display text and graphics, to hear sounds like voice and music, and to enjoy animation effects on your screen. Most browsers now have multimedia capability. To enjoy the full benefits of multimedia, your computer must also have multimedia capability, including a graphics board, sound board, and high-quality speakers.

■ *Publishing capability.* Like thousands of other individuals, eventually you might want to publish your own Web page. Many browsers and other programs have built-in Web-publishing capabilities. For example, the latest version of Microsoft Word, a popular word processing program, makes Web-publishing simple. Using Word, you need only type information you want on a page and instruct Word to save what you've typed in HTML format.

■ *Security.* The security of information is a serious concern for many users. Personal information is not always as secure as one might prefer. In an age when information travels freely through cyberspace, the information can be intercepted and used in potentially harmful ways. For example, suppose you use your computer to order a product advertised on the Internet and enter your credit card account number to complete the order. There have been cases where the information was intercepted and the account number used fraudulently by another person. You can protect yourself by refusing to supply important personal information, such as credit card numbers and your address, over the Internet.

Newer browsers offer better security. Although it may still be possible for information you supply to be intercepted by others, newer browser versions offer greater security by encrypting the information you supply.

Search Engines

A **search engine** is a program that allows a user to search for, locate, and retrieve information on the World Wide Web. Unlike a browser, in which an address is entered to access a specific Web site, a search engine allows a user to locate specific information and automatically retrieve Web pages by entering search criteria. For example, assume you want to find information about the Battle of Gettysburg for a report you are writing for a history class. You can use a search engine to retrieve a list of articles on this topic simply by typing your search criteria—in this case *Battle of Gettysburg*—into the search box and clicking on the search button. A list of articles will appear on your screen. Then you can read a listed article just by clicking on it.

Many excellent search engines are available. Some of the more popular names include Yahoo!, InfoSeek, Excite, Lycos, and AltaVista, to name just a few. Also, some browsers contain a Search button. By clicking on the Search button, a list of search engines appears from which you can make a selection (Figure A.7).

Some search engines do a better job of searching that do others. AltaVista, for example, searches more databases than some others do.

Connecting Your Computer to the Internet

Connecting to the Internet normally requires two steps, selecting a service provider and installing the software supplied by the service provider to get your computer set up and operating properly. Both steps are important because you will want to be able to take full advantage of the many benefits the Internet has to offer.

Service Providers

Although there are several ways to connect to the Internet, the two most common are through commercial online services and Internet service providers (ISPs). When choosing an online service or a service provider, you should inquire about

FIGURE A.7
Yahoo! Home Page

the speed of the modem used by the service or provider. This speed should be at least as fast as the speed of your own modem. If it is slower, you will be unable to take advantage of the speed of your modem.

COMMERCIAL ONLINE SERVICES

Several commercial online services are available. A **commercial online service** provides a wide range of information and services to subscribers for a subscription fee. In addition to providing access to the Internet, commercial online services typically provide special kinds of information, such as timely news items, information arranged into groupings, newsgroups, e-mail, and business information. By providing links to various kinds of information, subscribers can easily locate information they are seeking (Figure A.8).

Commercial online services offer the same basic information available to anyone on the Internet. However, the way in which the service organizes and presents the information makes it easier for subscribers to access the information and move from one location to another location on the Internet. Most commercial online services offer such features as e-mail attachments, chat groups, Telnet, and FTP. If you plan to subscribe to a commercial online service and one or more of these features are important for you, make sure the features you want are available.

The way in which information is organized and presented by most commercial online services makes using the Internet easier for subscribers. In addition, these services typically provide subscribers with browsers and with online help when needed.

The combined services offered by commercial online services are attractive to many potential subscribers who are usually willing to pay the subscription fees charged for their services. If you need only access to the Internet without the extra services available from a commercial online service, you might want to consider obtaining access by subscribing to an Internet service provider (ISP) or to an Internet access provider (IAP).

FIGURE A.8

America Online (AOL) Home Page

INTERNET SERVICE PROVIDERS

Private commercial companies that provide basic Internet services are called **Internet service providers (ISPs).** Services provided typically include access to the Internet, electronic mail, links to browsers and search engines, and the opportunity to communicate with other individuals and groups. Many are local companies listed in the phone book, although some are national companies. Some large telecommunications companies, including AT&T and MCI, have begun offering Internet access to their customers.

INTERNET ACCESS PROVIDERS

Some providers, called **Internet access providers (IAPs),** offer only access to the Internet. If you subscribe to an IAP, you will be able to connect to the Internet, but you may not have access to electronic mail or other services. Internet access providers are typically small independent companies that offer access only to area residents.

Some Internet providers have their own network system, called **backbone,** to handle their Internet operations. Smaller providers are sometimes resellers that purchase or lease connectivity from larger companies and sell connection service to subscribers.

Choosing a Service Provider

Choosing a service provider varies among individuals because some criteria are more important than others are. Criteria you should consider prior to making a final decision include cost, speed, support and service, and ease of use.

COST

Many commercial online services and service providers offer various plans. Each plan offers a different level of service and accompanying fee. For example, a provider may provide 15 hours per month of online time for a fee of $9.95 per month with each additional hour at $2.00 per hour. The same provider may offer unlimited online time, called **connect time,** for $19.95 per month. Another provider may offer the first 20 hours for $15.95 with an additional charge of $3.00 per hour.

In choosing a provider, consider telephone cost. Long-distance service can be expensive. If you subscribe to a commercial online service that does not offer a local telephone access, you should expect to pay long-distance charges each time you access the Internet.

SPEED

The speed at which the service works should be an important consideration. If you have a modem with a speed of 56 kbps but the service moves data to you at a speed of 38.8 kbps, you will be able to receive information only at the rate of 38.8 kbps. If the service uses an ISDN line or a T1 line, you will be able to send and receive data faster, because both are high-speed transmission lines. An **ISDN** line (short for **Integrated Services Digital Network**) is a special digital telephone line that allows you to connect to the Internet at very high speeds. To use an ISDN line you need a special ISDN modem and an Internet provider that offers ISDN access. A **T1 line** is a leased telephone line that can carry data at speeds of 1.544 megabits of data per second or faster. Like ISDN, to use a T1 line you need a special modem and a provider that offers T1 access. If you need even faster access, faster T lines are available.

When large volumes of information are to be sent or received, an individual, business, or organization might lease one of these lines. Leasing an ISDN or T1 line is expensive. The expense can be justified only when there is a definite need.

SUPPORT AND SERVICE

Most service providers allow you to call them when you need assistance. If you're like most users, you will occasionally encounter problems for which you will need technical assistance. Before signing up with a provider, request a telephone number where you can contact a technician and call the number—several times if necessary—until you reach an operator. If you have trouble reaching a technician, or if you experience long delays, you might consider a different service.

You should also inquire about the number of users assigned to each of the service's modems or numbers. If the number exceeds 15, you may experience delays in getting connected.

Eventually, you may decide you want to create and display your own Web page at the service's site. Find out whether this service is available and whether there is an extra charge for this service. Some services provide free Web-authoring software and authoring assistance to subscribers.

EASE OF USE

Another criterion is the relative ease with which you can use the software provided by an Internet service provider. Are the interfaces, menus, and buttons easy to identify and use? Are the installation software, the browser, and other features easy to use so you won't find it necessary to spend lots of time obtaining technical assistance?

Before selecting a service provider, you should talk with companies that provide service in your area. Be sure you get satisfactory answers to any questions you ask. Figure A.9 is a list of questions that are typically asked. You may have additional questions you want the provider to answer.

FIGURE A.9

Questions to Ask of Service Providers

1. Can I use a telephone access number in my local calling area?

2. Do you offer toll-free telephone access in case I am on the road? Will I be charged extra for this service, and if so, how much?

3. Do you offer a fixed monthly price for unlimited use? If so, how much is it?

4. Which browser and e-mail services do you provide?

5. Can I use another browser and e-mail reader of my own choosing?

6. Do you offer more than one e-mail account per subscription? If so, how many?

7. Do you offer 56-kbps modem access? If so, do you charge extra for this faster access?

8. If you offer 56-kbps access, will the standard you use work with my 56-kbps modem?

9. Do you offer free Web-page postings? If so, how many megabytes of server space will I get?

10. Do you offer wizards or other software to help me set up a home page?

Setting Up Your Computer

Whether you will be using an online service company or a service provider, you have to set up your computer before you can access the Internet. The service you select will likely provide you with a **setup package** that contains an instruction manual together with a diskette or CD-ROM containing installation software. Typically, all you need to do to install the software is follow the instructions contained on the diskette or CD-ROM. For example, if you are using Microsoft's Windows 95 operating system, the setup package includes a CD-ROM; you first insert the CD-ROM into the designated drive, such as drive E. You then click on the Start button, then click on RUN. When the dialog box appears, click on OK. Then just follow the instructions that appear on your screen. Figure A.10 shows the first screen you will see when installing the setup disk for America Online (AOL). The installation procedure is similar for most online services. During installation, you will be asked to provide specific information, such as your name, the kind of service you want, your method of payment, the telephone number to which your computer is connected, and your modem type and speed.

Setting up your computer for a service provider is usually a little more involved. For example, you may also be required to enter a code number for your modem and specify your maximum modem speed. If you need assistance, you can contact the company's technical assistance department for help.

After completing the setup procedure, an access icon may be placed on your screen. If so, immediate access will be yours by clicking on the icon. By clicking on the icon and logging on to the service, you can begin accessing the Internet and the Web and using the features available to you, such as e-mail and chat. Then you will be ready to begin your journey through cyberspace to a universe of information that awaits your visit.

FIGURE A.10

America Online Initial Setup Screen

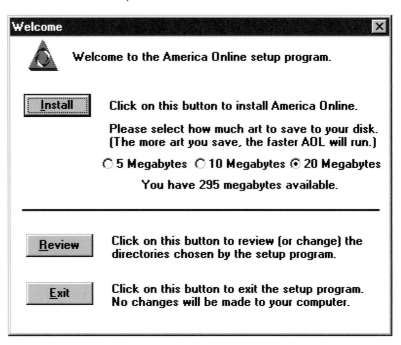

KEY TERMS

add-on board (278)
anonymous access (281)
ASCII file (280)
backbone (285)
binary file (280)
browser (282)
chat groups (chat rooms) (275)
chat programs (275)
commercial online service (284)
communications software (280)
connect time (286)
downloading (281)
electronic mail system (274)
expansion board (278)
file transfer protocol (FTP) (281)

graphical user interface (GUI) (279)
graphics board (278)
hyperlink (link) (272)
hypermedia file (272)
Integrated Services Digital Network (ISDN) (286)
Internet (272)
Internet access provider (IAP) (285)
Internet service provider (ISP) (285)
modem (278)
multimedia computers (278)
multitasking (282)
plug-in (278)
progressive graphics capability (282)
query (274)

random-access memory (RAM; also called primary storage) (277)
search engine (274)
secondary storage (278)
setup package (287)
sound board (278)
T1 line (286)
upgrade (279)
uploading (281)
Web page (272)
Web sites (272)
World Wide Web (the Web, WWW, W3) (272)

APPENDIX B

Getting Started with Browsers and Search Engines

Since the introduction of the Internet and the World Wide Web, interest and use have grown at a phenomenal rate. In a single day, millions of users access the Internet to visit thousands of Web sites. Each location on the Web, called a **Web site,** contains useful information that, until recently, was unavailable online. The Web allows a user to move about, from one Web site to another.

Browsing (Surfing) the Web

Once you're connected to the Internet you can begin browsing through cyberspace to visit thousands of interesting and even fascinating sites. The term **browsing** (also called **surfing**) means "to move about," just as you may browse through a bookstore or shopping mall. Like shoppers in a mall, Internet users often browse from one Web site to another to see what is available. When people refer to "browsing or surfing the Net," they usually are talking about using the World Wide Web. Browsing the Web is an art that can be mastered quickly after learning a few basics and gaining a little experience. Browsing is not only fun, but it is also educational.

The Internet offers much more than interesting Web sites. You can use the Internet to send and receive electronic mail messages, purchase products and services, chat with other people whose interests are similar to yours, and much more. In essence, the Internet and the Web open up virtually unlimited opportunities to explore our world.

Web Browsers

A **browser** is a software program that makes it easy to find and display Web pages. Using a browser, you can surf the Web easily and quickly.

Browsers are designed to work with a graphical user interface, such as Microsoft's Windows 95 or the Macintosh operating system. Just as a graphical user interface makes using your computer easier by allowing you to just point and click to make selections, browsers make using the Internet and World Wide Web easier. In most cases an icon representing the browser is placed on the computer desktop when a browser program is installed.

Internet Addresses (URLs)

Web browsers typically contain a place where you type an address for the Internet or Web site you want to visit or for a specific Web page you want to retrieve. An easy way to understand a Web site address is to first think of an address you might place on the envelope of a letter to another person. A typical address would include the recipient's name, address, city, state, and ZIP code. A hypothetical address is shown in Figure B.1.

The postal service understands the address and will use it to deliver the letter to the correct recipient. The letter is first sent to a postal distribution center in Columbia, South Carolina, where all incoming mail is sorted by city location. In this case, Ms. Adam's letter will be placed into a group of letters for delivery to homes located on Maple Drive. A mail carrier will deliver the letter to 318 Maple Drive to be retrieved from the mailbox by Ms. Adams.

Internet addresses (URLs) achieve the same purpose. On the Internet and the World Wide Web, you can specify the exact location of the site you want to visit or document you want to retrieve.

FIGURE B.1
Hypothetical Postal Address

A postal address and an Internet address serve the same purpose. A postal address makes it possible for the postal service to locate the specified recipient. An Internet address makes it possible for a user to locate the specified Web site or page.

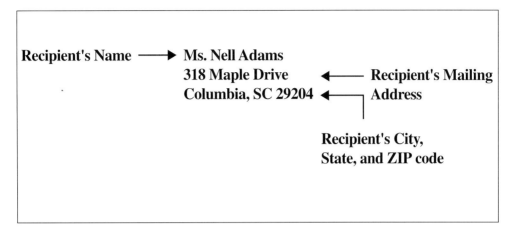

The technical name for an Internet or Web address is **Uniform Resource Locator** (or URL and pronounced "earl"). If you know the URL (address) for a specific Web site, you can access the site quickly by typing the site's URL in the browser's designated location. An URL must always be typed correctly.

After typing the URL for the site or page you want and pressing the Enter key, your request is sent to the Internet, where Internet routers examine it to determine the specific Web server to which your request is to be sent. The Web server receives your request and uses the HTTP protocol to determine which page, file, or object is being requested. On finding the requested home page, file, or object, the server sends it back to your computer, where it is displayed on your computer screen.

Protocols are required for transferring data between computers. Most Web pages use a protocol called **HTTP,** which stands for **HyperText Transfer Protocol,** for transferring data from a host computer to your computer. In most cases, you often must specify the specific protocol at the beginning of the address you type. Thus, the first part of an address indicates the protocol being used, such as the http protocol.

Internet addresses are typed in lowercase. Most addresses begin with the letters *http,* followed by a colon, two slashes, the letters *www* (for World Wide Web), and a period (Figure B.2). However, not all Web addresses require that the letters "www" be typed as a part of the address. For example, the address for Netscape's home page is "http://home.netscape.com." There are also other formats for Internet addresses.

Most Internet-capable computers have a text-based address, called a domain name. A **domain name** identifies the computer's address—that is, the location of the computer. The domain can include the name of the computer, along with other address information such as a college, department, geographical location, or type of organization. The last part of a domain name identifies the type of site. Figure B.3 shows examples of top-level domains that identify the type of site.

The third part of the address, which is optional, is the file specification. The *file specification* is the name of a particular file or file folder. At some Web sites, a vast amount of information is available for retrieval and viewing. At these sites,

An Internet Address (URL)

Typing the correct address, or URL, in the specified location of your browser will enable you to retrieve the Web page you want to view.

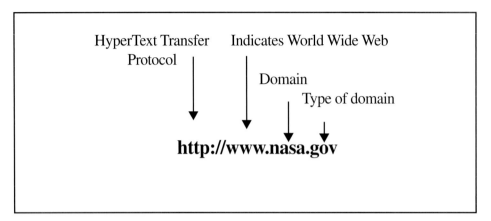

Top-Level Domains

Top-level domains are included in Internet addresses to identify the type of site. For example, ".gov" typed as part of the domain indicates the site is a government site.

DOMAIN	DESCRIPTION	EXAMPLE
.gov	Federal, state, and local governmental entities	NASA, the U.S. Department of the Interior
.edu	Educational institutions	A college or university
.com	Commercial entities	The Dryden Press, Microsoft Corp., Dell Computer Corp.
.net	Network service providers	BestWeb Service Provider
.org	Nonprofit organizations	Public Broadcasting System
.mil	Military services	U.S. Army, U.S. Navy

information is often arranged and stored in folders, just as you might store information in a file cabinet. If you know the name of the particular file you are seeking, or the name of the folder containing the information, accessing the information is easier and faster.

How a Browser Works

A Web browser is a client software program your computer uses to access and display Web pages. Browsers are available for almost any kind of computer. Your browser displays information on your screen by interpreting the HyperText Markup Language (HTML)—that is, the language used to create most Web pages. A displayed home page, as well as other pages at a particular Web site, typically contains links to other pages, files, and resources.

Codes in HTML files determine how your browser displays the text, graphics, links, and multimedia files on a home page. The codes contain references to the text, graphics, and files you want to retrieve. Your browser uses the codes to find the files on the Web server and to then retrieve and display them on your computer screen.

If a page contains links to other Web sites, files, or resources, you can click on a link to have your browser retrieve the specified information. If a link specifies a file to be downloaded, clicking on it will instruct your browser to copy it to your computer.

Starting a Browser

Starting your browser is a relatively simple and easy task. Before you can start your browser, the desktop screen must be displayed. On most personal computers, the program you are using, such as Microsoft Windows, is activated when the computer is turned on. Once the desktop screen is displayed, you can start your browser by simply double-clicking on the browser icon—that is, by positioning the pointer on the browser icon and pressing a mouse button twice (Figure B.4). Another icon, perhaps resembling an hourglass, will appear. This indicates that the browser is being loaded into your computer. In a few seconds, the browser's window (home page) will appear on your screen.

Two Popular Web Browsers

Currently, the two most popular and widely used browsers are Netscape Communications Corporation's Navigator and Microsoft Corporation's Internet Explorer. Usage of these two browsers is fairly evenly split among users. Collectively, they are used by more than 95 percent of all browser users. Both work similarly and offer similar features.

In the following sections we examine each browser. As we examine these two, you likely will notice their similarities.

Netscape Navigator

Netscape's Navigator is a popular Web browser. You can activate Navigator by double-clicking on the Navigator icon displayed on your desktop screen after starting your computer.

FIGURE B.4

Navigator and Internet Explorer Icons

The Windows 95 Desktop screen contains icons, such as the Netscape Navigator and Internet Explorer icons, representing applications or groups of applications. The user can select an application by moving the mouse to point to and click on an application (icon). Once a selection is made, the desktop screen disappears and is replaced by the selected application.

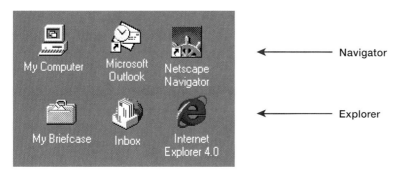

After activating the browser, the browser window (home page) will appear on your screen (Figure B.5). Navigator's window contains a variety of information categories. The categories include autos, business, computing & Internet, and several others. Within each category are links to specific topics. For example, in the Netscape category there is a link to Y2K. Clicking on the Y2K link accesses another page containing information about the potential Y2K problem and links to other Y2K information sources.

The top bar of the Navigator window is the title bar where the name of the current Web site or the title of a specific Web page is displayed. Navigator's home page, for example, displays the message "Welcome to Netscape."

Immediately below the title page is the menu bar. The menu bar includes available options, each with pull-down menus, and works like the menu bars in word processing and spreadsheet programs.

Below the menu bar is the navigation toolbar, which allows you to perform tasks by clicking on one of the buttons. This is usually a faster method than using the menu bar. Printed on each button is a word or icon that identifies the button's function. For example, selecting the Print button causes the displayed page to be printed.

The Search button allows you to begin a search for information on the Internet. The Guide button directs you to some interesting places on the Internet. Clicking the Security button displays security data about information being accessed.

Below the navigation toolbar is the location box for entering the address of the desired Web site or page. To go to the desired site, you must type the Uniform Resource Locator (URL) in the box labeled "Location:" and then either press the Enter key or click on the Open button on the toolbar. The URL is updated automatically as the user goes from one Web site to another or from one Web page to another page.

FIGURE B.5

Netscape Navigator Window

Netscape's window, or home page, contains menus, tools, and buttons useful for browsing the Internet and the Web. An understanding of the home page helps a user to become more efficient.

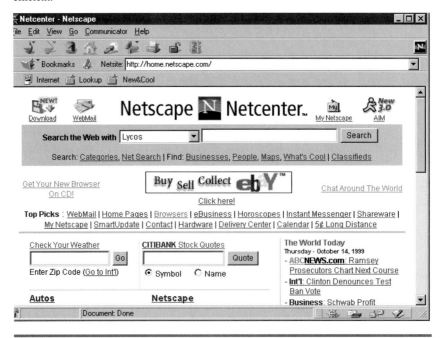

Below the location box is the personal toolbar containing a group of directory buttons that access the user to new and interesting pages. Selecting the New&Cool button causes Navigator to display a two-item menu. The What's New item contains links to some of the newer Web pages. Selecting the What's Cool item causes Navigator to display links to some unique and interesting Web pages. Both the What's New and the What's Cool pages are updated frequently by Netscape Communications Corporation as more pages become available. Some pages that are available on a given day may not be available a day or two later.

The large area below the directory buttons is the display area. When Navigator is first activated, the Netscape home page is displayed in this area. The home page contains current information from Netscape Communications Corporation and a list of categories of information with links to other pages. As new Netscape products and upgrades become available, they are identified on Netscape's home page and can be downloaded by selecting a designated link and following the instructions displayed on the screen. When other sites are visited, pages from these sites are displayed.

Below the display area at the right is a group of buttons that allow you to quickly access other applications. The first button, which resembles a ship's steering wheel, is the button you can click to access Netscape Navigator. The next button to the right, which resembles a small envelope, allows you easy access to your mailbox so you can read your electronic mail messages. The next button provides access to any discussion groups to which you may belong. The last button in this group allows you to compose a document. In the lower left corner is a button that resembles a lock. An open lock indicates that the information you want to access is unlocked and is therefore available to you. A closed lock indicates that the information is unavailable.

Netscape Navigator is a powerful and full-featured browser. Here, only a few features were explained. There are many sources that provide a more detailed explanation of Navigator's features, including the *User's Manual* and numerous books devoted to a thorough explanation of the browser.

Internet Explorer

The Navigator window and the Internet Explorer window have several similarities. For example, both typically contain links to other Web sites, pages, and resources.

Explorer's top bar also displays the title of a Web site or Web page currently being displayed on your screen. If you switch to another Web site or page, the title of the site or page is displayed.

Immediately below the title of the page is the menu bar. The menu bar includes available options, each with pull-down menus, and works like other program menu bars.

Below the menu bar is the toolbar, which allows you to perform tasks quickly by simply clicking on one of the buttons. For example, clicking on the Print button causes the displayed page to be printed. Clicking on the History button displays a list of Web pages previously accessed. Printed on each button is a word and an icon that identify the button's function.

Below the toolbar is the Address box for entering the address of the desired location. To go to the desired site, you need to type the Uniform Resource Locator (URL) in the box and then press the Enter key. The URL is updated automatically as the user moves from one Web site to another site or from one Web page to another page.

Below the Address box is the Links bar, which includes preselected links to preselected pages. Included are links to Best of the Web pages, The Microsoft Network, and Product News about Microsoft products. Internet Explorer allows you to add links of your own to the Links bar.

The large area below the Address box is the display area. When Explorer is first activated, the home page of your online service or service provider is displayed in this area. The home page contains current information from the service or provider as well as possible links to other pages. As new products and upgrades become available, they may be identified on the service's or provider's home page and can be downloaded by selecting a designated link and following the instructions displayed on the screen. When other sites are visited, pages from these sites are displayed.

Like Navigator, Internet Explorer is a powerful and full-featured browser. Here, only a few basic features were explained. There are many sources that provide a more detailed explanation of Explorer's features, including the *User's Manual* and numerous books devoted to a thorough explanation of the browser.

Other Internet and Web Activities

The Internet and the World Wide Web offer users a variety of ways to communicate with other individuals and groups and to find and retrieve information. As you become familiar with the Internet and the Web, you will likely want to explore these features and opportunities. Using the Internet, you can send and receive messages electronically, participate in chat groups, and find information on almost any subject. These are just a few of the opportunities available on the Internet.

Electronic Mail

Electronic mail, or **e-mail,** is probably the most popular Internet feature. With it, a user can type a message and send it immediately to another person on the Internet who has e-mail capability. Most Web browsers can be used to send and receive messages across the Internet. Millions of e-mail messages are sent each day, and they can be saved, printed, and even forwarded to others.

E-mail users can communicate with groups of other people by subscribing to a mailing list. A mailing list is a database comprised of the addresses of every individual in a group. When a message is sent to the group as a whole, each individual within the group will receive it. You can subscribe to, or withdraw from, a mailing list by sending an e-mail message to the group's mailing list administrator.

To send an e-mail message to another person, you must know the recipient's correct e-mail address. Users of electronic mail typically use abbreviations of their name. However, some use a name that is different than their own. For example, John Smith might prefer to use an alias or nickname, such as "Cyberjohn" or "Smitty." This is perfectly acceptable for e-mail usage. Consider the following hypothetical e-mail address of Richard Jones, a professor of business at Central State University:

rjones@centralstate.edu

Reading from left to right, a string of characters identifies the recipient's user name (a set of unique characters that Central State University's mail server assigns to this person's mailbox), followed by the @ symbol, followed by the mail server's domain name. The @ symbol represents the word *at* and separates the user name from the host computer. The domain name identifies the computer where the mail server is located. In the example, the domain shown identifies the network computer at Central State University. The far right portion of the address identifies Central State University as an educational institution. The computer at

Central State University will receive an e-mail message sent to Richard Jones and will place the message in Richard Jones's mailbox from which Jones can retrieve the message.

Internet Relay Chat (IRC)

An interesting way to communicate over the Internet is by using Internet Relay Chat (IRC), which allows Internet users all over the world to communicate (chat) with each other by typing messages on their keyboards. The typed words are immediately relayed to people's computers throughout the world and displayed on their screens for them to see and read. Because IRC works in "real time" (meaning immediately), one can read the words as they are being typed.

Like browsers, IRC works on a client-server model. To use IRC, the user needs client software on the computer. IRC clients are available for IBM-compatibles, Macintoshes, UNIX, and other kinds of computers. The servers are called IRC servers and use server software.

When you want to use IRC, you first make a connection to the Internet and then start your client software. You will need to log into an IRC server on the Internet. IRC servers located throughout the world are connected in a network so they can send messages to one another.

When a user connects to a server, a specific "channel" is joined, and a username is selected to identify the user at a chat session. A variety of channels cover various topics.

After joining a channel, a user is able to see the conversations as they occur. The user can join the conversation by typing a message on the keyboard. The message is transmitted from the client software on the user's PC to the IRC server to which the user is connected. The message is forwarded from the user's IRC server to other IRC servers where other people on the user's channel are logged in. Each IRC server sends the message to the client software of the people connected to the channel at each server. People at their computers can read the message and respond if they choose to do so.

Information Search

Millions of documents covering thousands of different topics are available on the Web. You can retrieve and read documents containing information on almost any topic you can imagine. Searching for, and finding, needed information is an important and useful activity for many people, particularly for students needing information in their studies.

In cyberspace, an unlimited reservoir of information awaits you. Searching is an important activity that allows users to locate and retrieve information useful in their educational pursuits, research, and work. In the following sections, you will learn how special programs called search engines allow you to quickly and easily search for and find the information you want.

Searching the Web

Until recent years, searching for information was frequently a tedious, time-consuming, and sometimes frustrating experience. Occasionally a searcher using a library would be unable to find the desired information or learn that another person had already checked out the book or document containing the needed information.

In recent years, many libraries have modernized by computerizing their card catalogs. A computer or terminal is used to search for the desired information by entering specific search criteria such as a topic, title, name, or event. After initiating a search, the computer accesses and searches a database using the search criteria entered by the user. Often, a list of references and the exact location of each reference will be displayed on the computer or terminal screen. Using this information, the user can go to a location and find the desired information.

Fortunately, you can use a computer to seek and find information on the Web. The computer must have access to the Internet and have special software, such as a search engine, installed in the computer. Simply defined, a **search engine** is a program that allows you to locate and retrieve information on the World Wide Web (WWW). Browser home pages usually include a Search button. Clicking on the Search button displays a list of search engines from which you can choose. When you begin using a search engine, usually the first page you see is the search engine's home page with a place for you to enter your search criteria. You can begin your search by entering search criteria and then clicking the Search button.

What You Can Find and Do on the Web

The World Wide Web consists of hundreds of thousands of computers. It continues to grow as thousands of new users come online every month. The result is an ever-increasing number of Web sites, with each site offering its own information to the public. This information is readily available to anyone having the capability to find it.

The Web contains millions of documents with information about thousands of people, places, events, and other topics. You can do research; find people; read your horoscope; get stock quotations; shop for merchandise and services; apply for a loan; make airline and hotel reservations; display weather maps; retrieve and view pictures, movies, and sound clips; and even enjoy visual tours of foreign countries. The amount and kinds of information available is virtually unlimited, and more information is being added and updated each day.

Reasons for Searching

There can be many reasons for a user to search the Web. Although the number of reasons can be extensive, some of the more common reasons are curiosity, need, research, work, and business.

Curiosity

Curiosity is a valid reason for conducting a search. You might simply want to know if information on a specific topic is available. For example, you might be interested in knowing if information is available about Lake Tahoe, Nevada. Using a computer with Internet access and search capability, you can perform a search for information about Lake Tahoe.

A search for information can result in several thousand documents being found. In such cases, a user may find it confusing and even impossible to read all the documents. A user can avoid this kind of problem by performing a more restrictive (advanced) search; for example, by searching for Lake Tahoe hotels.

Need

A user might have a need for specific information. Suppose, for example, that you are interested in a vacation to the Caribbean island of Aruba and that you want to learn about the island. You can find numerous documents on the Web about Aruba just by searching.

Research

Conducting research is an important reason for searching the Web. There are occasions when nearly every user engages in research. Students who are assigned research topics can save time and find more information sources by searching the Web.

Lawyers sometimes find the Web to be an indispensable resource, and many lawyers regularly search the Web to find legal precedents. For example, a privately owned database called WestLaw contains court transcripts of every case tried in the United States during this century. Using key search words such as *Smith vs. Jones,* an attorney can retrieve the transcript of this trial to learn how the case was tried and what the verdict was. Scientists use the Web for research into their area of interest. For example, a geologist can search the Web for information about rock formations and composition. A chemist can use the Web to find information about a specific chemical element or compound. Using the Web, a physician can search for information about a particular illness and treatment. Even a consumer can find information about a particular product or service.

Work

Many people find the Web useful in their work. Authors often use it to find up-to-date information on topics for a book being written. For example, an author preparing the manuscript for a new book about computers can search the Web for information about new computers, storage devices, printers, and software.

Recently, a real estate developer searched the Web to learn about the availability of land on the Caribbean island of St. Thomas. The developer was able to locate information about specific parcels of available land, prices, and real estate taxes. After finding a suitable parcel, the developer purchased the property on which a new hotel will be constructed.

Business

Many companies use the Web to conduct normal business activities. Manufacturers use it to discover new raw material sources, to locate suppliers, and to attract potential employees. Retailers are able to find new markets for their products and services and to check on competitors. Mail-order businesses can obtain information about shippers and other means for distributing their products and services.

When you enter a keyword or a phrase, called a **query,** a search engine systematically searches the World Wide Web for documents on that specific topic. The search engine scans its database to determine which documents contain the keyword(s) you entered. The titles of documents found (if any), together with a hyperlink to each document, will be listed on your screen.

Some Popular Search Engines

Several popular search engines are available that allow you to search the Web for information, but it is not necessary for you to learn all of them because they work similarly. However, you need to be aware that there are differences in the way each searches for information. Just as a library card catalog cannot possibly contain a card for every book or publication in the world, it is impossible for a search engine to catalog every page on the World Wide Web. On the Web, different search engines perform different types of searches. In the following sections, we will look at some of the more popular search engines and the technique each uses to search the World Wide Web.

AltaVista

AltaVista (www.altavista.com), originally launched by Digital Equipment Corporation in 1995 and later acquired by Compaq Computer Corporation, is one of the newer search engines with searching capabilities for several different Web resources. AltaVista is one of the largest and most popular search engines on the Web, with more than 30 million entries.

The AltaVista search engine maintains an index of all pages found on the Web (Figure B.6). It uses a special program called Scooter to find new and updated pages on the Web. When a new or updated page is found, Scooter copies all the text from the Web page and stores it in the index.

When using AltaVista for a search, you type keywords or phrases to identify the information you want to find. The program searches its index for Web pages containing the word or phrase you typed and displays a list of the pages it found. From the list you can select the pages you want to view.

AltaVista allows you to do a simple search or an advanced search. A simple search is executed by typing words separated by a space, or a phrase surrounded by quotation marks. AltaVista will search for documents and pages that contain the exact combination of words surrounded by the quotation marks. An advanced search provides you with more control over your search by displaying only Web pages containing the word or phrase you specify. For example, if you type *bicycles* AND NOT *motorcycles,* AltaVista will display pages containing the word

FIGURE B.6

AltaVista Home Page

AltaVista is one of the newer and most powerful search engines. Notice the rectangular box used to type keyword(s) representing the topic being searched. After typing the keyword(s) and clicking the Search button, a search is executed.

Examples of Advanced Searches Using AltaVista

With AltaVista, you can perform advanced searches to find the information you want.

KEYWORDS AND PHRASES	WHAT ALTAVISTA DISPLAYS
baseball AND football	Web pages containing the words *baseball* and *football*
baseball OR football	Web pages containing the word *baseball* or the word *football*
baseball NEAR football	Web pages containing the words *baseball* and *football* within 10 words of each other

bicycles but will not display pages containing the word *motorcycles.* Figure B.7 shows other examples of advanced searches.

As you can see, AltaVista is a powerful and versatile search engine. It provides you with a high degree of flexibility concerning how you can execute a search of the World Wide Web.

Excite

One of the most comprehensive search engines available on the Web is Excite (www.excite.com), which offers a reference section and online maps for locations across the United States and around the world. The Excite database contains more than 50 million Web pages. When you type keywords or phrases representing information you want to find, Excite searches all the Web pages in its database. When pages are located that contain the information you requested, Excite displays a list of those pages.

Like other search engines, the Excite home page includes a Search box in which you type keywords or phrases for the information you want to find. It also contains several broad information categories from which you can choose. Each category is linked to other Web pages with updated information. Figure B.8 shows the Excite home page with a list of categories from which you can make a selection.

If you select a channel from the list on Excite's home page, such as Business and Investing, another page will be displayed containing additional lists. One list offers links to other Web sites, another offers links to news items, and a third list provides links to stock market quotations.

When a search is executed, Excite displays 10 results at a time. Beside each item on the list is a rating that indicates the success of the search. Excite allows you to search for a specific group of words. To find a Web page containing the exact keyword(s) you typed, you need to type quotation marks around the word(s) you want to find. Your search can be made more precise by typing a symbol in front of a word without leaving any spaces between the symbol and the word. For example, if you type + bicycles – motorcycles, Excite will locate Web pages containing the word *bicycles* but not the word *motorcycles.*

Excite's main database contains more than 60 million Web pages, but not all pages are available to the public. The staff at Excite reviews and makes available more than 65,000 Web pages through which you can search. The reviewed pages are judged on the basis of how well they are organized and developed. The pages the staff deems acceptable are made available for you to access.

When you perform a search, Excite displays a list of pages. Beside each page title is a rating that indicates the success of your search. For example, a rating of

Excite Home Page

The Excite home page contains a list of channels that serve as links to information about a particular topic. For example, if you click on the Business channel, another page containing additional links will be displayed.

100 percent indicates that the page definitely contains the word(s) or phrase that you entered when you began your search. A rating of 50 percent indicates that there is only a 50–50 chance that the word or phrase that you entered is contained in the page. The rating helps you decide which pages you want to view. Excite can be accessed by using the Net Search button of Netscape browsers.

Lycos

Another search engine, Lycos (www.lycos.com), searches both titles and Web pages for keywords entered by a user. The Lycos search form contains several options for controlling a search on the Web.

With its database of more than 70 million Web pages, Lycos allows you to find a wealth of interesting information on the Web. In addition, you can use Lycos to search for images and sounds. When Lycos enters Web pages into its database, it also indexes all accompanying images, sounds, and animation files it finds in the pages.

When you enter search criteria (keywords or phrases) for the information you are seeking, Lycos searches its database for Web pages containing the words you entered and displays a list of pages. Each item on the list contains a hyperlink to the corresponding Web page.

Like other search engines, Lycos allows you to restrict your search by entering special symbols with the words you type. Figure B.9 shows some ways to make your search more precise.

The Lycos home (search) page contains useful links to other information. You can display road maps, city guides, pictures, sounds, and more. For example, you can access information about a city, such as Charlotte, North Carolina, by selecting City Guide and then following the instructions on your screen.

FIGURE B.9

Examples of Advanced Searches Using Lycos

Lycos allows advanced searches to find the information you want. Shown are examples of using specific words to restrict your search to the information you want.

SEARCH REQUEST	SEARCH RESULT
island	Web pages containing the word *island* and not pages containing the words *islands* or *islander*
show$	Web pages containing the word *show,* even when it is part of larger words such as *shower* or *showboat*
dolphins – Miami	Web pages containing the word *dolphins* but not the word *Miami*

Lycos is a versatile and popular search engine. It can be accessed with Netscape browser's Net Search button or can be accessed directly through its Internet address.

Infoseek

Infoseek (www.infoseek.go.com) is a highly rated search engine from Infoseek Corporation. Using Infoseek, you can search a database containing a large number of magazines and more than 19 million Web pages.

When you undertake a search, Infoseek uses the keyword(s) or phrase you typed in the Seek box on the home page to find titles containing the word(s) you entered. The titles found (if any) are displayed on your screen as a list with hyperlinks to the documents identified in the list. The first 10 titles located are listed initially, along with a brief summary of the document's contents. Clicking on the "Next 10" link displays the next 10 titles, and so on. By clicking on a title on the list, Infoseek retrieves the document and displays it on your screen.

Like some other search engines, Infoseek provides tips for searching the Web. One tip, for example, is that you can conduct a search by typing a specific question, by enclosing a phrase in quotes, or by capitalizing a typed name.

NetFind

AOL's new search engine, NetFind (www.aol.com/netfind), offers a user an easy and comprehensive way to find information on the World Wide Web. With NetFind, you can find people, businesses, organizations, phone numbers, e-mail addresses, a variety of newsgroups, and even Web sites for children. There's almost no limit to the various kinds of information you can retrieve using this powerful search engine (Figure B.10).

NetFind searches the Web for names and addresses of people, businesses, and organizations and stores them in a directory. Whether you are an individual, a business, or an organization, NetFind contains a form that allows you to add your name and address to the directory. Once added, this information becomes available for anyone to access.

NetFind's capabilities are certainly not limited to finding persons, businesses, and organizations. Using this search engine, you can search for, and probably find, information on virtually any topic. In the Search text box, you can type any combination of words, topics, or phrases and then just click the Find button. A list of findings will be displayed on the screen, along with links to the information sources.

America Online subscribers can access NetFind by clicking on the NetFind button. For other users, NetFind can be accessed directly through its Internet address.

NetFind Home Page

America Online's NetFind is a powerful and versatile search engine. NetFind is available to America Online subscribers and to other users. A user who is not an AOL subscriber can access NetFind by using a browser and typing "www.aol.com/netfind" in the address box. Once NetFind is accessed, a search is initiated by entering words or topics in the Search box and clicking on the Find button.

Yahoo!

The final search engine we will present is Yahoo! (www.yahoo.com), one of the most popular and widely used search engines available. Yahoo! was created at Stanford University by two students who wanted to keep a list of Web sites they liked and might want to revisit. Later they decided to share their list with others in the Internet community. Within a brief time, their list became increasingly popular, which encouraged them to add more sites and to provide users with the opportunity to submit their sites to the list. Yahoo! is now a public company.

The Yahoo! home page is simple and easy to use. It contains a list of information categories and a Search box for typing search criteria (words or phrases). The Yahoo! home page is shown in Figure B.11.

The staff at Yahoo! reviews and catalogs every Web site in the Yahoo! directory. Each category contains Web sites with similar information. Yahoo! allows you to browse through the categories and subcategories until you find pages containing information you want to see.

Among the special features available with Yahoo! are News Headlines, Special Categories, and Personal Information. Clicking on News Headlines allows you to read news stories from around the world. The stories are updated each hour. By clicking on Special Categories, you can view a list of unique sites. Clicking on Personal Information allows you to choose topics of special interest to you and enables you to have Yahoo! create a custom page for you that causes only the information you request to be displayed.

The search engines presented are just some of the ones available, and you can expect others to be created and made available in the future. Those that have been

FIGURE B.11
Yahoo! Home Page

The Yahoo! home page is easy to use and is self-explanatory. To begin a search, all the user needs to do is to type keyword(s) or a phrase, type a number for the number of titles to be displayed, and then click on the Search button. Notice the information categories listed on the page. By selecting a category, Yahoo! will display a list of related titles representing links to documents available on the World Wide Web.

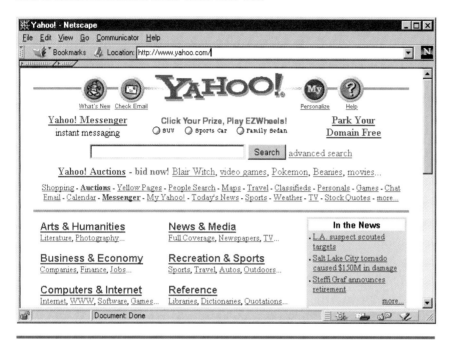

explained here are among the more popular ones. They are improved and updated periodically and, equally important, they are free. All you need to do to access the one of your choice is to type its URL. User needs vary. Before deciding which search engine best suits your needs, try each one. After trying all of the search engines, you can better determine which one is best for you. Yahoo! can be accessed with Netscape browsers' Net Search button and other browser programs.

Using Keywords and Symbols to Search

Search engines allow you to type words or phrases to find titles of Web pages that contain the words or phrases you type. Typing a single word will likely result in a long list of titles being found and displayed. In such cases, it may be impossible for you to read all the titles listed, because the list may include several thousand. One way to avoid this dilemma is to narrow your search by typing several words that define it more precisely. For example, if you type the word *apples* in the Search box, the search engine you are using will probably find many more titles than if you type the words *Red Delicious apples*. Remember that you can achieve a more precise search if you type a more detailed query in the search box.

Most search engines allow the use of words and special symbols, called **operators,** to limit a search to specific information. These include a plus sign (+), a minus sign (−), and the words AND, OR, and NOT. For example, if you type *apples AND oranges* you may expect the list of titles displayed to include titles containing both words. However, if you type *apples NOT oranges,* you may expect a list of titles containing only the word *apples* to be displayed.

Most search engine pages include a Help button or Tips button. Clicking on this button will display helpful tips or hints for searching and will help you perform more effective searches.

Search Programs

Search engines represent the most popular way to search the Internet and the World Wide Web, but searches can also be made using search programs. A search program runs on your own computer and is similar to other application programs. Search programs are useful for those who perform frequent Web searches and are available for purchase from computer stores and by downloading from the manufacturer.

Search programs are an efficient way to search for information on the Web. Many allow you to perform searches while you are involved with other tasks. You can schedule a search to be performed at any time, even while you are away or during the night.

Some search programs submit your requests for information to several search engines on the Web. Perhaps without your being aware of it, the program will be using several search engines at once to find the information you request.

Several excellent search programs are available. Examples include Teleport Pro, WebFerret, and WebSeeker.

KEY TERMS

browser (290)
browsing (surfing) (290)
domain name (291)
electronic mail (e-mail) (296)

HyperText Transfer Protocol (HTTP) (291)
operators (305)
query (299)
search engine (298)

Uniform Resource Locator (URL) (291)
Web site (290)

Add-on board (expansion board). An electronic circuit board (or card) that can be installed inside a computer to provide additional capabilities. (278)

Analog data. Data represented as patterns of waves. (45)

Anonymous access. The ability to access files at an FTP site without having to enter a user ID or password. (82, 281)

Antivirus program. A computer program that can detect the presence of viruses and eradicate them. (17, 230)

ASCII file. A file in which the data is in the form of human-readable text. (39, 280)

Automated clearinghouse. An automated entity established for the purpose of transferring funds electronically from one account to another account. (151)

Automotive Network eXchange (ANX). A joint venture by Daimler-Chrysler, General Motors, and Ford to build a system that links them with their suppliers through a virtual private network. The goal is to save billions of dollars in inventory costs. Deliveries of materials are coordinated and shipped to assembly plants as they are needed. (152)

Bandwidth. The amount of data or information that can travel across a communications channel (such as a telephone line, coaxial cable, or satellite channel) during a specified period of time. (211)

Banner. A rectangular graphic displayed in marquee fashion on a Web page. (16, 215)

Batch processing. A processing method in which a batch (collection) of transactions are collected, stored, and processed at one time. (90)

Baud rate. A measure of modem speed measured as the number of bits (0s and 1s) that can be transmitted per second. (33)

Bid. An attempt by a person or business to acquire, win, or obtain something of value, such as a contract to sell products and/or services to another entity. (165)

Binary file. A machine-readable-only file in which data is in the form of only two numbers (0s and 1s). (39, 280)

Biochip. A theoretical computer chip that would consist of organically grown molecules assembled into tiny circuits. (257)

Bridge. Hardware and software that allows two *similar* networks to communicate. (4, 38)

Browser. A software tool (program) that makes it easy to find and display Web pages. (6, 72, 282, 290)

Browsing (surfing). Moving about from one location to another location on the World Wide Web. (6, 72, 290)

Bus network. A type of network in which all computers are linked by a single line of cable, called a *bus*. (5, 53)

Business. A profit-seeking enterprise that engages in numerous activities to provide products and services to consumers in an economic system. (132)

Capital.   A factor of production that can be in the form of money, physical facilities, information, technology, and/or equipment. (134)

Cellular modem.   A type of modem often contained in a laptop or notebook computer that does not require wires. (33)

Chat group (chat room).   A technology that allows users and participants to discuss topics of mutual interest. (8, 83, 275)

Chat program.   A special computer program that allows a user to communicate with others. (8, 275)

Client/server model.   A network model in which a person uses a personal computer (called the client) to send requests to another computer (called the server) that relays the information back to the client. (2, 50)

Clip art.   Stored figures, cartoons, and images that can be inserted into Web pages. (15, 209)

Coaxial cable.   A copper wire surrounded by a thick band of insulation, wire mesh, and rubber or plastic. (40)

Commercial online service.   A commercial service that provides a wide range of information and services to subscribers for a subscription fee. (284)

Communication.   A meaningful exchange of information. (138)

Communications (data communications).   The transmission (sending and/or receiving) of data and information between two or more computers over communications media, such as standard telephone lines. (31)

Communications company.   A company, such as a telephone company, that provides communications services between remotely dispersed locations. (253)

Communications device.   Any device that assists in data transmission. Examples of communications devices include modems, cables, and ports. (253)

Company site.   A Web site created and posted by a private company to sell products and services to customers and to attract new customers. (195)

Communications medium.   A physical linkage that allows a computer in one location to be connected to a computer in another location for the purpose of transmitting and receiving data and information. (4, 39)

Communications software.   Software that allows you to connect your computer to another computer on which programs and data are stored, and to access the stored programs and data. (4, 38, 280)

Communications specialist.   An individual responsible for developing, implementing, and maintaining the communications networks and the communications software that control the flow of data among devices in a network. (23)

Computer cracker.   An individual who tries to gain unauthorized access to computer systems to alter, damage, or steal information by guessing user IDs and passwords. (19, 233)

Computer hacker.   An individual who generally has expert knowledge about computer systems and tests his/her skills by breaking into computer systems. (19, 233)

Connect time.   The amount of time a user is actually connected online to the Internet. (286)

Connectivity.   A term that refers to a program or device's ability to link with other programs and devices. The trend is toward greater connectivity. (21, 251)

Content convergence.   The translation of all types of content information into digital form, including text, sound, graphics, movies, music, videos, and business documents and advertisements. (85)

Controlling. The management function of monitoring employee performance and activities, keeping the organization on track toward its goals, and making corrections and adjustments as needed. (136)

Copyright infringement. The unauthorized use of material that has been granted copyright protection by the U.S. Copyright Office. (231)

Credit account. A promise by the customer to pay for online purchases upon receipt of a periodic statement from the seller. (107)

Credit card. A small plastic card issued by a financial institution and containing essential information that allows the customer to make credit purchases that are charged to the customer's account with the financial institution. (108)

Data communications (communications). The transmission (sending and/or receiving) of data and information between two or more computers over communications media, such as telephone lines. (2, 30, 252)

Data communications specialist. A person that develops, implements, and maintains communications networks and software that control the flow of data among devices in the network. (266)

De facto standard. A format, language, or protocol that has become a standard not because it has been approved by a standards organization but because it is widely used and recognized by the industry. (20, 249)

DefenseLINK. The starting point for finding military procurement information online. (172)

Dense Wave Division Multiplexing (DWDM). A technology that allows communications providers to transmit different wavelengths, or colors, of light on the same fiber strand, thereby increasing the fiber's bandwidth (capacity). (260)

Device convergence. The development and introduction of various computers, televisions, and other devices that facilitate the transfer of information from one location to another location. (85)

Digital bill-paying. Using a computer and software to pay bills online over the Internet. (124)

Digital camera. A special type of camera that captures a picture (photograph) and stores it in digital format on a storage medium, such as a disk. (15, 209)

Digital data. Data represented as groups of 0s and 1s. (44)

Digitized picture. A picture (photograph) taken with a digital camera. (15, 209)

Directory. A storage method for storing files at FTP sites, similar to storing files in a metal file cabinet. (82)

Distance learning. The electronic transfer of information from a college or publisher's host computer system to a student's computer at a remote site and the transmission of required responses from the student's computer to the host computer system. (255)

Domain name. A name used to identify a specific computer on the Internet. A domain can include the name of the computer, along with other address information such as a college, department, geographical location, and/or type of organization. (291)

Downloading. The process of transferring files from a host computer to a client computer. (81, 281)

E-book. A small, hand-held wireless device to which books can be downloaded. (123)

Efficiency. The allocation of resources required to achieve specific organizational goals in a cost-effective manner. (142)

Electronic bulletin board system (BBS). A computer system that maintains an electronic list of messages where anyone with access to the bulletin board can post messages, read existing messages, or delete messages. (4, 48)

Electronic commerce. A modern business methodology in which information, products, services, and payments are exchanged via computer networks within a global society. (85, 100, 146)

Electronic data interchange (EDI) system. A system in which computers are used to automatically transfer inventory, delivery, and billing information between organizations, replacing the flow of paper documents with electronic data. (12, 90, 149)

Electronic funds transfer (EFT) system. A computerized system that enables payments to be made electronically. (90)

Electronic mail (e-mail). A fast and inexpensive way of sending, receiving, storing, and forwarding messages electronically. (4, 296)

Electronic mail system (e-mail). A system that allows users to send and receive messages electronically through, and between, networks from one computer to another computer. (8, 47, 79, 274)

Electronic shopper (e-shopper). A person who uses the Internet to shop for products and/or services. (9, 101)

Electronic shopping mall. An online mall with many electronic stores offering a variety of products and services, such as computers, clothing, and sporting goods. (9, 103)

Electronic ticket. A ticket purchased online using a computer that can be picked up at the business from which the purchase was made. (118)

Encryption. A method for ensuring security in which data is converted into a coded form before transmission and decoded upon receipt. (83, 244)

Espionage. The act of spying. (19, 233)

Ethics. A term that refers to personal standards involving one's behavior. (17, 223)

eXtensible Markup Language (XML). A newer computer language used to create Web pages. (6, 73, 203)

External communication. The exchange of useful information between an organization and its audiences. (141)

External environment. An environment that includes entities outside the organization including individuals and groups, suppliers, competitors, agencies, and technologies. (146)

External modem. A self-contained modem that plugs into a computer in the same way you would plug in a keyboard. (33)

Extranet. A private computer network set up by a company that allows certain users, such as outside employees and authorized customers and suppliers, to access the company's internal computerized applications and data via the Internet. (60)

Facsimile (fax) machine. An electronic device that makes it possible to transmit documents and drawings over telephone lines from one location to another in a manner that is faster and often cheaper than sending the document overnight or through the mail. (4, 48)

Factors of production. Elements (inputs) combined to produce products and services. (133)

Fax/modem. An add-in board that enables users to send and receive faxes using their computers. (49)

Fiber-optic cable. A cable that consists of tiny threads of insulated glass or plastic capable of transferring billions of bits of data per second. (43)

File server. A special type of computer that allows other computers to share its resources. (4, 52)

File Transfer Protocol (FTP). A program that allows a user to send and receive files over the Internet. (81, 281)

Financial EDI. A technology that provides for the electronic transmission of payments and associated remittance information between a payer and payee, and their respective banks. (12, 150)

Firewall. Hardware and/or software that restricts information passing between a private network and the Internet. (18, 58, 232)

Fraud. A false representation of a material fact, made with knowledge of its falsity and with the intent to mislead or defraud, that is justifiably relied on by the one to whom it is made and which results in injury to him (or her) because of his reliance. (226)

Free market system. A type of economy in which private individuals and companies can produce and sell products and services with minimal government involvement. (132)

FTP client software. Software installed on a client computer that enables a user to use FTP. (82)

FTP daemon. A program on an FTP server that enables you to transfer (upload or download) files. (82)

Gateway. Hardware and software that allows communication between *dissimilar* networks. (3, 37)

Gopher. A program released in 1991 that was the first point-and-click way of navigating the files on the Internet. (68)

Government site. A Web site created and maintained by a unit of government—federal, state, or local. (196)

Graphical user interface (GUI). An operating system component, such as Microsoft's Windows 98, that offers special features including pointers, icons, windows, and menus—all of which make a personal computer easier to use. (279)

Graphics board. An electronic board installed inside a personal computer that enables the user to capture and display vivid pictures and images. (278)

Home page. The first page displayed on a particular Web site. (6, 73, 192)

Host computer. A more powerful minicomputer or mainframe computer to which other smaller computers are connected. (52)

HTML editor. A part of the HTML language that allows a user to insert HTML tags in pages. (202)

HTML tag. A code embedded within the text on a Web page to identify how text, links, and images are to be displayed on the pages. (202)

Human resources. Resources that all people provide to produce products and services. (133)

Hyperlink (link). Boldfaced text, underlined text, or an icon that, when clicked on using a mouse, takes you to another Web site or Web page. (5, 71, 272)

Hypermedia file. A file containing any combination of text, graphics, sound, and video. (5, 71, 272)

Hypertext document. A Web document that contains highlighted text that connects to other Web pages and Web sites. (202)

HyperText Markup Language (HTML). A computer language used to create Web pages. (6, 73, 202)

HyperText Transfer Protocol (HTTP). A communications protocol for transferring data from a host computer to a user's computer. (76, 291)

Icon. A small picture or symbol on a computer screen that represents an object, a program, or an activity. (72)

Information. Data that has been processed so as to make it useful for a specific purpose, such as making a decision. To be useful, information must be accurate, complete, and timely. (138)

Information Superhighway (I-Way). A term coined by Vice President Al Gore to describe the administration's plan to deregulate communication services and widen the scope of the Internet by opening carriers, such as television cable, to data communication. (68)

Information system. A set of interrelated components working together to collect, retrieve, process, store, and distribute information needed for the successful planning, control, coordination, analysis, and decision making in a business or other organization. (146)

Information theft. A problem in which a thief uses the Internet to steal all kinds of information ranging from corporate secrets to credit card numbers. (18, 232)

Integrated Services Digital Network (ISDN). A technology that makes it possible for users to transmit information in digital form along traditional copper-based telephone lines. (45, 286)

Intelligent shopping agent. A computer program that can aid shoppers seeking bargain prices or additional product information. (9, 105)

Interest. Payments for the use of capital. (134)

Internal communications. Communications that occur *within* an organization. Examples include memos, departmental meetings, training sessions, and phone conversations. (140)

Internal modem. A type of modem contained on a circuit board that is inserted into a slot inside a computer. (33)

International environment. A business environment in which a company must comply with international laws, restrictions, customs, and changes. (146)

Internet (Net). A global network of computers linked together via communications software and media for the purpose of sharing information. (5, 66, 272)

Internet access provider. A private commercial company that only offers access to the Internet. (285)

Internet Explorer. A popular Web browser. (6, 72)

Internet Protocol (IP) address. A unique number assigned to a computer. (70)

Internet service provider. A private commercial company that provides basic Internet services, such as access to the Internet, electronic mail, links to browsers and search engines, and the opportunity to communicate with other individuals and groups. (285)

Internet service representative. A person that answers telephone and electronic inquiries from customers who encounter problems while installing communications or related software on their computer or who experience difficulties when trying to access the Internet. (23, 267)

Intranet. A network that is normally restricted to users *within* a company or organization. (56)

Intranet suite. A collection of software applications contained in one package. (57)

ISDN line. A special digital telephone line that allows connection to the Internet at very high speeds. Use of an ISDN line requires a special ISDN modem and an Internet provider that offers ISDN access. (45, 286)

Java. An Internet language developed by Sun Microsystems that radically alters the way applications and information can be retrieved, displayed, and used over the Internet. (68)

Just-in-time production system (JIT). A computer-based system that eliminates the need to maintain large inventories by providing materials for production at the exact time they are needed. (148)

Leading. A management function that involves the use of influence to motivate employees to achieve an organization's goals. (136)

Local area network (LAN). A private communications network that serves the needs of companies located in the same building with two or more computers or in nearby buildings, such as a college campus. (4, 52)

Local environment. A business environment that encompasses local customers, suppliers, competitors, stockholders, and local regulators with which the business must interact on a local basis. (145)

Local online shopping. Online shopping limited to specific Web sites located in close proximity to the customer. (101)

Mail server. A type of server on which e-mail messages are stored and routed to their destination. (57)

Mailing list. A list of entries (often individuals) in which each entry consists of a name or title, mailing address, telephone number, and other information. (19, 234)

Management. The attainment of organizational goals in an effective and efficient manner through planning, organizing, leading, and controlling organizational resources. (136)

Metropolitan Area Network (MAN). A computer network that is limited to a geographical area, such as a city or town. (51)

Microminiaturization. Manufacturing technologies that make it possible for manufacturers to produce electronic circuitry so small that it is invisible to the human eye. (251)

Microwave system. A communications system in which data is transmitted through the atmosphere in the form of high-frequency signals similar to radio waves. (40)

Miniaturization. Manufacturing technologies that have made it possible to densely pack more and more tiny electronic circuits together on all kinds of computers and components. Miniaturization has resulted in smaller computers and components without sacrificing the devices' capabilities or speeds. (250)

Misinformation. Information that is inaccurate, incomplete, misleading, deceptive, or confusing. (236)

Modem. An electronic device that enables a computer to send and receive data over telephone lines by converting the data into a form that can be carried along a standard telephone line. (3, 33, 278)

Mosaic. The first graphics-based Web browser that became available in 1993. (68)

Multimedia. A combination of sound, images, graphics, and text. (15, 209)

Multimedia computer. A computer capable of retrieving, displaying, and producing multimedia effects including text, graphical images, and sound. (278)

Multiplexer. An electronic device that increases the efficiency of a network system by allowing 8, 16, 32, or more low-speed devices, such as PCs, to share simultaneously a single high-speed communications medium, such as a telephone line. (34)

Multitasking. The capability of a computer to perform multiple operations concurrently. (282)

National Acquisition Internet Service (NAIS). A service that allows NASA and commercial companies to conduct business transactions online. (174)

National environment. A business environment in which a company must interact with national suppliers, federal agencies, competitors, and national regulators. (145)

National Science Foundation Network (NSFNET). A network developed and implemented in 1989 by the National Science Foundation that connected various supercomputers located throughout the United States, thereby providing users with enormous computing power. (68)

Natural resources. Inputs that are used in their natural states, including land, forests, and mineral deposits, such as oil. (133)

Netiquette. A term that refers to the rules for acceptable behavior on the Internet. (17, 223)

Netizen. A term that refers to being a good citizen when using the Internet. (224)

Netscape Navigator. A popular Web browser. (6, 72)

Network. A computer configuration that consists of two or more computers connected by means of communications media. (2, 50)

Network Interface Card (NIC). An electronic circuit card installed in one of the computer's internal expansion slots that connects to the cable or wireless technology used to connect computers and other devices to the network. The card contains circuits that coordinate the transmission and receipt of information. (3, 34)

Network topology. The method in which computers and peripherals are configured to form networks. (52)

Not-for-profit organization. An organization that is formed and exists for purposes other than to earn profits. Not-for-profit organizations exist in both the public and private sectors of our economy, and they play important roles in our society. (134)

Online auction. A Web site that allows you to place a bid for a specific item. (125)

Online banking. Traditional banking services available over the Internet between the bank and a customer. (124)

Online catalog. A computerized version of a printed catalog. (9)

Online course. A course of study made available via the Internet by a college, university, or textbook publisher. (255)

Online education. The study of a particular subject or course by using a computer and modem to access course information and materials available from publishers' Web sites. (122)

Online information and news. Current news provided by news organizations to users having access to the Internet. (122)

Online investing. Using a computer and Internet access to purchase and/or sell stocks, bonds, commodities, insurance, or other financial assets including mutual funds and annuities. (124)

Online shopping (electronic shopping or e-shopping). The process of using a computer, modem, and Internet access to locate, examine, purchase, sell, and pay for products over the Internet. (9, 101)

Open Systems Interconnection (ISO) model. A communications model established by the *International Standards Organization* for communications equipment manufacturers to adopt and follow. (46)

Operator. The use of words and special symbols that limit a search to specific information when using a search engine. (305)

Organization site. A site on the Web typically sponsored by a not-for-profit organization that promotes the organization's purposes and activities. (196)

Organizing. The management function of assigning tasks, delegating authority to individuals who perform the tasks, and allocating resources needed to perform the tasks. (136)

Outsourcing. A business strategy or decision whereby one business hires another business to perform tasks or functions previously handled by the company's internal staff and systems. (212)

Packet. A fixed-length block of data. (3, 70)

Password. A secret series of characters that enable a user to access a computer, file, or program. (5, 55)

People-to-People System (PPS). A communications system that directly connects individuals or groups to communicate and collaborate on common problems or specific issues. (88)

People-to-System-to-People System (PSPS). A communications system in which a computer is added to a network to supply support, storage, or coordination for all users. The central computer allows participants to connect and work with one another, concurrently or at different times. (89)

Personal site. A Web site created by an individual and posted on the Web. (194)

Planning. The management function of identifying and defining future organizational goals and deciding on the tasks and resources needed to complete the tasks and achieve the organizational goals. (136)

Print server. An electronic device that allows multiple users to use the same printer. (52)

Privacy. A controversial Internet issue over whether an employer has a right to intercept and read messages sent by employees. (19, 238)

Procurement. The act of acquiring or obtaining products and services. (12, 165)

Productivity. A measure of the relationship between (ratio of) the value of products and services produced and the cost incurred in producing them. (144)

Professional Web site developer. An individual or group that specializes in developing Web sites and pages for customers who pay a fee for the service. (213)

Profit. The reward for businesspeople, called **entrepreneurs**, who take risks by combining capital (including money, machinery, and equipment), employees, materials, and other resources to produce the products and services wanted and needed by other members of society, including individuals, households, government, and other businesses. (133)

Profitability. A firm's ability to earn profits, which represent the difference between the revenues derived from the sale of products and services and the costs of producing the products and services. (144)

Progressive graphics capability.   The capability of a computer to display a low-resolution version of images quickly while more data needed to sharpen the images is being downloaded to the computer. (282)

Protocol.   A set of rules and procedures for exchanging information between computers. A protocol determines the format for how computers interact, or communicate, with each other and how errors are detected. (4, 45)

Pub file.   A file stored at an FTP site that is available to anyone. (82)

Public access network.   A network maintained by telephone companies—called common carriers—such as the Bell network, MCI, US Sprint, and AT&T, that provides voice and data communications channels across long distances to anyone who can pay the fee. (52)

Puffing.   Preparing information for posting on the Internet in such a way as to sensationalize the information to make it more appealing to viewers. (236)

Quality.   The value (or perceived value) of a firm's products and services. (142)

Query.   A word or phrase entered in a search engine program that specifies the type of information you want to view. (80, 274, 299)

Random Access Memory (RAM) (also called **primary storage**).   Temporary storage capacity inside a computer. (277)

Rent.   Payments for the use of natural resources. (133)

Ring network.   A type of network in which each computer is connected to two other computers. (5, 53)

Rogue Web page.   A Web page created and posted by a disgruntled consumer that targets a company by spreading a hoax about the company. (231)

Router.   An electronic device that directs the flow of blocks of information, called packets, between networks and across the Internet. (3, 34)

Sabotage.   The willful destruction of property. (19, 233)

Satellite.   A solar-powered electronic device in orbit around the earth that contains a number of small, specialized radios called *transponders*. The transponders receive signals from transmission stations on the ground called *earth stations*, amplify the signals, and transmit them to the appropriate locations. (42)

Satellite system.   A communications system in which data transmission is achieved by using communications satellites that are positioned 22,300 miles above the equator and orbit the earth at exactly the same speed as the earth's rotation. (42)

Scam.   The deliberate attempt to cheat or defraud the public by false or misleading claims. (17, 227)

Scanner.   A device that scans and captures all or part of a printed page, photograph, or image in a format that can be interpreted by a computer. (15, 209)

Schematic.   A drawing that shows a procedure or relationships. (209)

Search engine.   A computer program that allows a user to search for, locate, and retrieve, information on the World Wide Web. (8, 80, 274, 298)

Secondary storage.   A storage device, such as a disk drive, that enables computer programs, data, and information to be permanently stored (saved) on a storage medium, such as a floppy disk or hard disk. (278)

Security server.   A type of server used to prevent unauthorized access to programs and files stored on an intranet. (57)

Server.   Software installed on a computer network that allows users to share files, applications software, and hardware devices. (3, 34)

Service.   The intangible tasks of satisfying consumer or business needs. (13, 142, 167)

Set-up package. A software package that contains an instruction manual together with a diskette or CD-ROM containing installation software. (287)

Smart card. A small, credit card-sized plastic card that contains a microprocessor and memory circuits used for identifying and authenticating the card's owner. (265)

Software suite. A software package that contains useful programs that function smoothly together so that data can be moved from one application to another. (20, 250)

Sound. Multimedia in the form of words, music, or special sound effects, such as those made by an automobile engine or a waterfall. (16, 209)

Sound board. An electronic board installed inside a personal computer that allows you to hear sounds available at some Web sites, as well as sounds available on many CD-ROM disks. (278)

Spam. An unwanted, unsolicited e-mail advertising message. (17, 227)

Standard. A definition or a format that has been approved by a recognized standards organization or that is accepted as a de facto standard by the industry. (20, 249)

Star network. A network in which multiple computers and peripheral devices are linked to a central, or host, computer in a point-to-point configuration. (5, 52)

System-to-System System (SSS). A network-to-network linkage that provides for the flow of information into an organization, between involved departments needing access to the information, to and from suppliers, and to and from customers. (90)

Telecommunications. The combined use of computers, networks, and communications media that enables information to be transmitted and received among computers throughout the world. (31, 139)

Telecommuting. The process of working at home and communicating with the office via a computer and modem. (49)

Teleconferencing. An "electronic" (instead of face-to-face) meeting conducted between people at distant locations. (48)

Teleconferencing specialist. A trained and skilled individual who can design, install, and operate teleconferencing systems that are needed by businesses, organizations, and others. (267)

Teleprocessing. The use of a computer and communications equipment to access stored files on computers in other locations. (31)

Text. Any combination of words, phrases, and paragraphs. (15, 209)

Token ring network. A type of network in which a pattern of bits, called a *token*, is passed from one computer to another sequentially around the ring. Only when a computer has the token may the computer transmit a communication. (5, 55)

Topology. A method for classifying computer networks. (5)

Transaction Processing System (TPS). An information system that uses standard procedures to collect and process the routine, day-to-day transactions that flow through an organization. (8, 90)

Transmission Control Protocol/Internet Protocol (TCP/IP). A protocol that governs the flow of data across the Internet by specifying the rules for creating, addressing, and transmitting information—a process known as *packet switching*. (70)

Transmission convergence. The compression and storage of information in digitized form so that it can travel efficiently over various types of communications media. (85)

Trend. A movement or progression in a general direction. (20, 248)

Turnkey system. A system that a provider designs, develops, installs, maintains, and guarantees. (211)

Twisted pairs cable. One of the older communications media consisting of insulated wires twisted together. One of the wires in each pair is for sending, the other for receiving. (39)

T1 line. A leased telephone line that can carry data at speeds of 1.544 megabits of data per second, or faster. To be able to use a T1 line a user needs a special modem and a provider that offers T1 access. (286)

Underemployment. A term that refers to resources that are not employed in their most efficient uses. (142)

Unemployment. A lack of resources necessary for the successful completion of a project. (142)

Uniform Resource Locator (URL). The address of a specific Web site or Web page. (6, 73, 192, 291)

Upgrade. A new version of a hardware or software product designed to replace an older version of the same product. (279)

Uploading. The process of transferring files from a client computer to a host computer. (82, 281)

Username. A name or word used to gain access to a computer system. (5, 55)

Uuencode. A program that contains instructions for both encoding and decoding files. (82)

Value added network. A company that uses the facilities of common carriers to offer the public additional communications services for a subscription fee. (52)

Value chain. A concept in which a business firm is viewed as a series of basic, or chain, activities, each of which adds value to the firm's products or services. (11, 147)

Video conferencing. The use of computers and television cameras to transmit video images and the sound of the participants to a remote location that has compatible equipment. (4, 48)

Video conferencing specialist. A trained and skilled individual who can design, install, and operate video conferencing systems that are needed by businesses, organizations, and others. (23)

Video e-mail. A potential future e-mail system that allows a user to record a video and send it over the Internet. (22, 262)

Virtual reality. A computer-generated, three-dimensional world that allows a user to view pictures and images that appear to be realistic and lifelike. (262)

Virtual Reality Modeling Language (VRML). A Web language that allows a user to create three-dimensional objects and environments, called *VRML worlds*. (14, 203)

Virtual storefront. A computerized storefront (entryway) through which potential customers can enter to view, and possibly purchase, a company's products and services. (9, 103)

Virus. A program that can disrupt or even destroy the normal operations of a computer. (17, 230)

Virus hoax. False information from any source that a computer or computer system has been, or will be, infected by a virus. (231)

Voice mail. A computer's version of an answering machine service. (4, 47)

Wages. The payments made for the use of human resources (labor). (133)

Web author. An individual who creates or produces Web pages. (14, 193)

Web document. An electronic document stored on a Web server. (192)

Web host. A Web server connected to the World Wide Web. (211)

Web page. A hypermedia file stored at a particular Web site. (5, 71, 192, 272)

Web page designer. An individual skilled in designing attractive and informative Web pages. (192)

Web portal. A Web site that functions as a doorway to information available on the Web and to various Web sites. (22)

Web publishing. A term that refers to the placing of Web pages on a Web server. (14, 193)

Web server. A network device on which Web pages are stored. (14, 192)

Web server program. A computer program that allows users outside the organization to access the stored information. (192)

Web site. A site available on the World Wide Web. (5, 71, 193, 272, 290)

Webmaster. A trained individual responsible for managing a Web site. (14, 193)

Wide Area Network (WAN). A communications network that covers a large geographical area. An example is a long-distance telephone network. (51)

Workstation (node). A term that refers to a computer linked to a network. (52)

Worldwide online shopping. A type of shopping in which a customer goes online to find the best buys regardless of the location of the seller. (101)

World Wide Web (Web, WWW, or W3). A global system of linked computer networks that allows users to jump from place to place on the Web. (5, 71, 272)

WS_FTP. A file transfer protocol used in a Windows environment to access files from computers around the world. (83)